Mastering Azure Machine Learning

Perform large-scale end-to-end advanced machine learning in the cloud with Microsoft Azure Machine Learning

Christoph Körner and Kaijisse Waaijer

Mastering Azure Machine Learning

Copyright © 2020 Packt Publishing

All rights reserved. No part of this book may be reproduced, stored in a retrieval system, or transmitted in any form or by any means, without the prior written permission of the publisher, except in the case of brief quotations embedded in critical articles or reviews.

Every effort has been made in the preparation of this book to ensure the accuracy of the information presented. However, the information contained in this book is sold without warranty, either express or implied. Neither the authors, nor Packt Publishing, and its dealers and distributors will be held liable for any damages caused or alleged to be caused directly or indirectly by this book.

Packt Publishing has endeavored to provide trademark information about all of the companies and products mentioned in this book by the appropriate use of capitals. However, Packt Publishing cannot guarantee the accuracy of this information.

Authors: Christoph Körner and Kaijisse Waaijer

Technical Reviewers: Alexey Bokov and Marek Chmel

Managing Editors: Utkarsha Kadam and Athikho Sapuni Rishana

Acquisitions Editor: Poornima Kumari

Production Editor: Deepak Chavan

Editorial Board: Ayaan Hoda

First Published: April 2020

Production Reference: 1150720

ISBN: 978-1-78980-755-4

Published by Packt Publishing Ltd.

Livery Place, 35 Livery Street

Birmingham B3 2PB, UK

Table of Contents

Preface i

Section 1: Azure Machine Learning 1

Chapter 1: Building an end-to-end machine learning pipeline in Azure 3

Performing descriptive data exploration 4
    Moving data to the cloud 6
    Understanding missing values 7
    Visualizing data distributions 8
    Finding correlated dimensions 10
    Measuring feature and target dependencies for regression 12
    Visualizing feature and label dependency for classification 14

Exploring common techniques for data preparation 16
    Labeling the training data 17
    Normalization and transformation in machine learning 19
    Encoding categorical variables 20
    A feature engineering example using time-series data 21
    Using NLP to extract complex features from text 22

Choosing the right ML model to train data 22
    Choosing an error metric 24
    The training and testing split 25
    Achieving great performance using tree-based ensemble models 25
    Modeling large and complex data using deep learning techniques 26

Optimization techniques 26
    Hyperparameter optimization 27
    Model stacking 28
    Azure Automated Machine Learning 29
Deploying and operating models 29
    Batch scoring using pipelines 30
    Real-time scoring using a container-based web service 31
    Tracking model performance, telemetry, and data skew 32
Summary 32

Chapter 2: Choosing a machine learning service in Azure   35

Demystifying the different Azure services for ML 36
    Choosing an Azure service for ML 38
    Choosing a compute target for Azure Machine Learning 41
Azure Cognitive Services and Custom Vision 44
    Azure Cognitive Services 45
    Custom Vision—customizing the Cognitive Services API 49
Azure Machine Learning with GUIs 53
    Azure Machine Learning designer 53
    Azure Automated Machine Learning 57
    Microsoft Power BI 59
Azure Machine Learning workspace 60
    Organizing experiments and models in Azure Machine Learning 62
    Deployments through Azure Machine Learning 66
Summary 67

Section 2: Experimentation and Data Preparation   69

Chapter 3: Data experimentation and visualization using Azure   71

Preparing your Azure Machine Learning workspace 72
    Setting up the ML Service workspace 73
    Running a simple experiment with Azure Machine Learning 78
    Logging metrics and tracking results 85
    Scheduling and running scripts 88
    Adding cloud compute to the workspace 91

Visualizing high-dimensional data 97
    Tracking figures in experiments in Azure Machine Learning 97
    Unsupervised dimensionality reduction with PCA 100
    Using LDA for supervised projections 103
    Non-linear dimension reduction with t-SNE 105
    Generalizing t-SNE with UMAP 107

Summary 109

Chapter 4: ETL, data preparation, and feature extraction   111

Managing data and datasets in the cloud 112
    Getting data into the cloud 112
    Managing data in Azure Machine Learning 116
    Exploring data registered in Azure Machine Learning 121

Preprocessing and feature engineering with Azure Machine Learning DataPrep 125
    Parsing different data formats 126
    Building a data transformation pipeline in Azure Machine Learning 129

Summary 140

Chapter 5: Azure Machine Learning pipelines — 143

Benefits of pipelines for ML workflows — 144
- Why build pipelines? — 145
- What are Azure Machine Learning pipelines? — 146

Building and publishing an ML pipeline — 147
- Creating a simple pipeline — 148
- Connecting data inputs and outputs between steps — 151
- Publishing, triggering, and scheduling a pipeline — 156
- Parallelizing steps to speed up large pipelines — 161
- Reusing pipeline steps through modularization — 165

Integrating pipelines with other Azure services — 168
- Building pipelines with the Azure Machine Learning designer — 168
- Azure Machine Learning pipelines in Azure Data Factory — 170
- Azure Pipelines for CI/CD — 171

Summary — 173

Chapter 6: Advanced feature extraction with NLP — 175

Understanding categorical data — 176
- Comparing textual, categorical, and ordinal data — 177
- Transforming categories into numeric values — 178
- Categories versus text — 185

Building a simple bag-of-words model — 186
- A naive bag-of-words model using counting — 186
- Tokenization – turning a string into a list of words — 188
- Stemming – rule-based removal of affixes — 190
- Lemmatization – dictionary-based word normalization — 191
- A bag-of-words model in scikit-learn — 193

Leveraging term importance and semantics 195
Generalizing words using n-grams and skip- grams 195
Reducing word dictionary size using SVD 197
Measuring the importance of words using tf-idf 198
Extracting semantics using word embeddings 200
Implementing end-to-end language models 203
End-to-end learning of token sequences 204
State-of-the-art sequence-to-sequence models 205
Text analytics using Azure Cognitive Services 205
Summary 208

Section 3: Training Machine Learning Models   211

Chapter 7: Building ML models using Azure Machine Learning   213
Working with tree-based ensemble classifiers 214
Understanding a simple decision tree 215
Combining classifiers with bagging 219
Optimizing classifiers with boosting rounds 221
Training an ensemble classifier model using LightGBM 222
LightGBM in a nutshell 223
Preparing the data 225
Setting up the compute cluster and execution environment 229
Building a LightGBM classifier 232
Scheduling the training script on the Azure Machine Learning cluster 236
Summary 240

Chapter 8: Training deep neural networks on Azure — 243

Introduction to deep learning — 244
Why DL? — 244
From neural networks to DL — 246
Comparing classical ML and DL — 250

Training a CNN for image classification — 253
Training a CNN from scratch in your notebook — 254
Generating more input data using augmentation — 258
Moving training to a GPU cluster using Azure Machine Learning compute — 260
Improving your performance through transfer learning — 265

Summary — 268

Chapter 9: Hyperparameter tuning and Automated Machine Learning — 271

Hyperparameter tuning to find the optimal parameters — 272
Sampling all possible parameter combinations using grid search — 274
Trying random combinations using random search — 279
Converging faster using early termination — 281
Optimizing parameter choices using Bayesian optimization — 285

Finding the optimal model with Azure Automated Machine Learning — 288
Advantages and benefits of Azure Automated Machine Learning — 289
A classification example — 292

Summary — 297

Chapter 10: Distributed machine learning on Azure — 301

Exploring methods for distributed ML — 302
- Training independent models on small data in parallel — 303
- Training a model ensemble on large datasets in parallel — 305
- Fundamental building blocks for distributed ML — 308
- Speeding up DL with data-parallel training — 310
- Training large models with model-parallel training — 312

Using distributed ML in Azure — 314
- Horovod—a distributed DL training framework — 315
- Implementing the HorovodRunner API for a Spark job — 317
- Running Horovod on Azure Machine Learning compute — 318

Summary — 320

Chapter 11: Building a recommendation engine in Azure — 323

Introduction to recommender engines — 324

Content-based recommendations — 326
- Measuring similarity between items — 329
- Feature engineering for content-based recommenders — 331
- Content-based recommendations using gradient boosted trees — 332

Collaborative filtering—a rating-based recommendation engine — 333
- What is a rating? Explicit feedback as opposed to implicit feedback — 334
- Predicting the missing ratings to make a recommendation — 336
- Scalable recommendations using ALS factorization — 338

Combining content and ratings in hybrid recommendation engines 339
    Building a state-of-the-art recommender using the Matchbox Recommender 340
Automatic optimization through reinforcement learning 341
    An example using Azure Personalizer in Python 342
Summary 345

Section 4: Optimization and Deployment of Machine Learning Models

Chapter 12: Deploying and operating machine learning models

Deploying ML models in Azure 351
    Understanding the components of an ML model 352
    Registering your models in a model registry 354
    Customizing your deployment environment 356
    Choosing a deployment target in Azure 358

Building a real-time scoring service 359

Implementing a batch scoring pipeline 362

Inference optimizations and alternative deployment targets 365
    Profiling models for optimal resource configuration 365
    Portable scoring through the ONNX runtime 366
    Fast inference using FPGAs in Azure 368
    Alternative deployment targets 369

Monitoring Azure Machine Learning deployments 371
    Collecting logs and infrastructure metrics 372
    Tracking telemetry and application metrics 374

Summary 374

Chapter 13: MLOps—DevOps for machine learning   377

Ensuring reproducible builds and deployments 378
Version-controlling your code 380
Registering snapshots of your data 381
Tracking your model metadata and artifacts 383
Scripting your environments and deployments 385

Validating your code, data, and models 387
Rethinking unit testing for data quality 387
Integration testing for ML 390
End-to-end testing using Azure Machine Learning 391
Continuous profiling of your model 392

Summary 392

Chapter 14: What's next?   395

Understanding the importance of data 397
The future of ML is automated 399
Change is the only constant – preparing for change 400
Focusing first on infrastructure and monitoring 402
Controlled rollouts and A/B testing 403
Summary 405

Index   409

Preface

About

This section briefly introduces the authors, the reviewers, the coverage of this book, the technical skills, and the prerequisites that you'll need to get started.

About Mastering Azure Machine Learning

The increase being seen in data volume today requires distributed systems, powerful algorithms, and scalable cloud infrastructure to compute insights and train and deploy **machine learning** (ML) models. This book will help you improve your knowledge of building ML models using Azure and end-to-end ML pipelines on the cloud.

The book starts with an overview of an end-to-end ML project and a guide on how to choose the right Azure service for different ML tasks. It then focuses on Azure Machine Learning and takes you through the process of data experimentation, data preparation, and feature engineering using Azure Machine Learning and Python. You'll learn advanced feature extraction techniques using **natural language processing** (NLP), classical ML techniques, and the secrets of both a great recommendation engine and a performant computer vision model using deep learning methods. You'll also explore how to train, optimize, and tune models using Azure Automated Machine Learning and HyperDrive, and perform distributed training on Azure. Then, you'll learn different deployment and monitoring techniques using Azure Kubernetes Services with Azure Machine Learning, along with the basics of MLOps—DevOps for ML to automate your ML process as CI/CD pipeline.

By the end of this book, you'll have mastered Azure Machine Learning and be able to confidently design, build and operate scalable ML pipelines in Azure.

About the authors

Christoph Körner recently worked as a cloud solution architect for Microsoft, specialising in Azure-based big data and machine learning solutions, where he was responsible to design end-to-end machine learning and data science platforms. For the last few months, he has been working as a senior software engineer at HubSpot, building a large-scale analytics platform. Before Microsoft, Christoph was the technical lead for big data at T-Mobile, where his team designed, implemented, and operated large-scale data analytics and prediction pipelines on Hadoop. He has also authored three books: *Deep Learning in the Browser* (for *Bleeding Edge Press*), *Learning Responsive Data Visualization*, and *Data Visualization with D3 and AngularJS* (both for *Packt*).

Kaijisse Waaijer is an experienced technologist specializing in data platforms, machine learning, and the Internet of Things. Kaijisse currently works for Microsoft EMEA as a data platform consultant specializing in data science, machine learning, and big data. She works constantly with customers across multiple industries as their trusted tech advisor, helping them optimize their organizational data to create better outcomes and business insights that drive value using Microsoft technologies. Her true passion lies within the trading systems automation and applying deep learning and neural networks to achieve advanced levels of prediction and automation.

About the reviewers

Alexey Bokov is an experienced Azure architect and Microsoft technical evangelist since 2011. He works closely with Microsoft's top-tier customers all around the world to develop applications based on the Azure cloud platform. Building cloud-based applications for challenging scenarios is his passion, along with helping the development community to upskill and learn new things through hands-on exercises and hacking. He's a long-time contributor to, and coauthor and reviewer of, many Azure books, and, from time to time, is a speaker at Kubernetes events.

Marek Chmel is a Sr. Cloud Solutions Architect at Microsoft for Data & Artificial Intelligence , speaker and trainer with more than 15 years' experience. He's a frequent conference speaker, focusing on SQL Server, Azure and security topics. He has been a Data Platform MVP since 2012 for 8 years. He has earned numerous certifications, including MCSE: Data Management and Analytics, Azure Architect, Data Engineer and Data Scientist Associate, EC Council Certified Ethical Hacker, and several eLearnSecurity certifications.

Marek earned his MSc degree in business and informatics from Nottingham Trent University. He started his career as a trainer for Microsoft Server courses and later worked as Principal SharePoint and Principal Database Administrator.

Learning objectives

By the end of this book, you will be able to:

- Setup your Azure Machine Learning workspace for data experimentation and visualization
- Perform ETL, data preparation, and feature extraction using Azure best practices
- Implement advanced feature extraction using NLP and word embeddings
- Train gradient boosted tree-ensembles, recommendation engines and deep neural networks on Azure Machine Learning
- Use hyperparameter tuning and Azure Automated Machine Learning to optimize your ML models
- Employ distributed ML on GPU clusters using Horovod in Azure Machine Learning
- Deploy, operate and manage your ML models at scale
- Automated your end-to-end ML process as CI/CD pipelines for MLOps

Audience

This machine learning book is for data professionals, data analysts, data engineers, data scientists, or machine learning developers who want to master scalable cloud-based machine learning architectures in Azure. This book will help you use advanced Azure services to build intelligent machine learning applications. A basic understanding of Python and working knowledge of machine learning are mandatory.

Approach

This book will cover all required steps for building and operating a large-scale machine learning pipeline on Azure in the same order as an actual machine learning project.

To get the most out of this book

Most code examples in this book require an Azure subscription to execute the code. You can create an Azure account for free and receive USD 200 of credits to use within 30 days using the sign-up page at https://azure.microsoft.com/free.

The easiest way to get started is by creating an Azure Machine Learning Workspace (Basic or Enterprise) and subsequently creating a Compute Instance of VM type `STANDARD_D3_V2` in your workspace. The Compute Instance gives you access to a JupyterLab or Jupyter Notebook environment with all essential libraries pre-installed and works great for the authoring and execution of experiments.

Rather than running all experiments on Azure, you can also run some of the code examples—especially the authoring code—on your local machine. To do so, you need a Python runtime—preferably an interactive runtime such as JupyterLab or Jupyter Notebook—with the Azure Machine Learning SDK installed. We recommend using Python>=3.6.1.

> **Note**
>
> You can find more information about installing the SDK at https://docs.microsoft.com/python/api/overview/azure/ml/install?view=azure-ml-py

We will use the following library versions throughout the book if not stated otherwise. You can as well find a detailed description of all libraries used for each chapter in the Github repository for this book (link available in the *Download resources* section).

Library	Version
azureml-sdk	1.3.0
pandas	0.23.4
numpy	1.16.2
scikit-learn	0.20.3
tensorflow	1.13.2
keras	2.3.1
seaborn	0.10.0
matplotlib	3.2.1

If you are using the digital version of this book, we advise you to type the code yourself or access the code via the GitHub repository (link available in the *Download resources* section). Doing so will help you avoid any potential errors related to the copying and pasting of code.

To get the most out of this book, you should have experience in programming in Python and have a basic understanding of popular ML and data manipulation libraries such as TensorFlow, Keras, Scikit, and Pandas.

Conventions

Code words in the text, database table names, folder names, filenames, file extensions, pathnames, dummy URLs, user input, and Twitter handles are shown as follows:

"The **substring(start, length)** expression can be used to extract a prefix from a column into a new column "

Here's a sample block of code:

```
for url in product_image_urls:

res = cs_vision_analyze(url, key, features=['Description']) caption = res['description']['captions'][0]['text']
```

On many occasions, we have used angled brackets, <>. You need to replace these with the actual parameter, and not use these brackets within the commands.

Download resources

The code bundle for this book is also hosted on GitHub at https://github.com/PacktPublishing/Mastering-Azure-Machine-Learning. You can find the YAML and other files used in this book, which are referred to at relevant instances.

We also have other code bundles from our rich catalog of books and videos available at https://github.com/PacktPublishing. Check them out!

Section 1: Azure Machine Learning

In the first part of the book, the reader will come to understand the steps and requirements of an end-to-end machine learning pipeline and will be introduced to the different Azure Machine Learning. The reader will learn how to choose a machine learning service for a specific machine learning task.

This section comprises the following chapters:

- *Chapter 1, Building an end-to-end machine learning pipeline in Azure*
- *Chapter 2, Choosing a machine learning service in Azure*

Building an end-to-end machine learning pipeline in Azure

This first chapter covers all the required components for running a custom end-to-end **machine learning** (**ML**) pipeline in Azure. Some sections might be a recap of your existing knowledge with useful practical tips, step-by-step guidelines, and pointers to using Azure services to perform ML at scale. You can see it as an overview of the book, where we will dive into each section in great detail with many practical examples and a lot of code during the remaining chapters of the book.

First, we will look at data experimentation techniques as a step-by-step process for analyzing common insights, such as missing values, data distribution, feature importance, and two-dimensional embedding techniques to estimate the expected model performance of a classification task. In the second section, we will use these insights about the data to perform data preprocessing and feature engineering, such as normalization, the encoding of categorical and temporal variables, and transforming text columns into meaningful features using **Natural Language Processing** (**NLP**).

In the subsequent sections, we will recap the analytical process of training an ML model by selecting a model, an error metric, and a train-testing split, and performing cross-validation. Then, we will learn about techniques that help to improve the prediction performance of a single model through hyperparameter tuning, model stacking, and **automated machine learning**. Finally, we will cover the most common techniques for model deployments, such as online real-time scoring and batch scoring.

The following topics will be covered in this chapter:

- Performing descriptive data exploration
- Common techniques for data preparation
- Choosing the right ML model to train data
- Optimization techniques
- Deploying and operating models

Performing descriptive data exploration

Descriptive data exploration is, without a doubt, one of the most important steps in an ML project. If you want to clean data and build derived features or select an ML algorithm to predict a target variable in your dataset, then you need to understand your data first. Your data will define many of the necessary cleaning and preprocessing steps; it will define which algorithms you can choose and it will ultimately define the performance of your predictive model.

Hence, data exploration should be considered an important analytical step to understanding whether your data is informative to build an ML model in the first place. By analytical step, we mean that the exploration should be done as a structured analytical process rather than a set of experimental tasks. Therefore, we will go through a checklist of data exploration tasks that you can perform as an initial step in every ML project—before starting any data cleaning, preprocessing, feature engineering, or model selection.

Once the data is provided, we will work through the following data exploration checklist and try to get as many insights as possible about the data and its relation to the target variable:

1. Analyze the data distribution and check for the following:
   - Data types (continuous, ordinal, nominal, or text)
   - Mean, median, and percentiles
   - Data skew
   - Outliers and minimum and maximum values
   - Null and missing values
   - Most common values
   - The number of unique values (in categorical features)
   - Correlations (in continuous features)

2. Analyze how the target variable is influenced by the features and check for the following:
   - The regression coefficient (in regression)
   - Feature importance (in classification)
   - Categorical values with high error rates (in binary classification)

3. Analyze the difficulty of your prediction task.

By applying these steps, you will be able to understand the data and gain knowledge about the required preprocessing tasks for your data—features and target variables. Along with that, it will give you a good estimate of what difficulties you can expect in your prediction task, which is essential for judging required algorithms and validation strategies. You will also gain an insight into what possible feature engineering methods could apply to your dataset and have a better understanding of how to select a good error metric.

> **Note**
>
> You can use a representative subset of the data and extrapolate your hypothesis and insights to the whole dataset

Moving data to the cloud

Before we can start exploring the data, we need to make it available in our cloud environment. While this seems like a trivial task, efficiently accessing data from a new environment inside a corporate environment is not always easy. Also, uploading, copying, and distributing the same data to many **Virtual Machines (VMs)** and data science environments is not sustainable and doesn't scale well. For data exploration, we only need a significant subset of the data that can easily be connected to all other environments—rather than live access to a production database or data warehouse.

There is no wrong practice of uploading **Comma-Separated Values (CSV)** or **Tab-Separated Values (TSV)** files to your experimentation environment or accessing data via **Java Database Connectivity (JDBC)** from the source system. However, there are a few easy tricks to optimize your workflow.

First, we will choose a data format optimized for data exploration. In the exploration phase, we need to glance at the source data multiple times and explore the values, feature dimensions, and target variables. Hence, using a human-readable text format is usually very practical. In order to parse it efficiently, a delimiter-separated file, such as CSV, is strongly recommended. CSV can be parsed efficiently and you can open and browse it using any text editor.

Another small tweak that will bring you a significant performance improvement is compressing the file using Gzip before uploading it to the cloud. This will make uploads, loading, and downloads of this file much faster, while the compute resources spent on decompression are minimal. Thanks to the nature of the tabular data, the compression ratio will be very high. Most analytical frameworks for data processing, such as pandas and Spark, can read and parse Gzipped files natively, which requires minimal-to-no code changes. In addition, this only adds a small extra step for reading and analyzing the file manually with an editor.

Once your training data is compressed, it's recommended to upload the Gzipped CSV file to an Azure Storage container; a good choice would be Azure Blob storage. When the data is stored in Blob storage, it can be conveniently accessed from any other services within Azure, as well as from your local machine. This means if you scale your experimentation environment from an Azure notebook to a compute cluster, your code for accessing and reading the data will stay the same.

A fantastic cross-platform GUI tool to interact with many different Azure Storage services is **Azure Storage Explorer**. Using this tool, it is very easy to efficiently upload small and large files to Blob storage. It also allows you to generate direct links to your files with an embedded access key. This technique is simple yet also super effective when uploading hundreds of **terabytes (TBs)** from your local machine to the cloud. We will discuss this in much more detail in *Chapter 4, ETL, data preparation, and feature extraction*.

Understanding missing values

Once the data is uploaded to the cloud—for example, using Azure Storage Explorer and Azure Blob storage for your files—we can bring up a Notebook environment and start exploring the data. The goal is to thoroughly explore your data in an analytical process to understand the distribution of *each* dimension of your data. This is essential for choosing any appropriate data preprocessing feature engineering and ML algorithms for your use case.

> **Note**
>
> Please keep in mind that not only the feature dimensions but also the target variable needs to be preprocessed and thoroughly analyzed.

Analyzing each dimension of a dataset with more than 100 feature dimensions is an extremely time-consuming task. However, instead of randomly exploring feature dimensions, you can analyze the dimensions ordered by feature importance and hence significantly reduce your time working through the data. Like many other areas of computer science, it is good to use an 80/20 principle for the initial data exploration and so only use 20% of the features to achieve 80% of the performance. This sets you up for a great start and you can always come back later to add more dimensions if needed.

The first thing to look for in a new dataset is **missing values** for each feature dimension. This will help you to gain a deeper understanding of the dataset and what actions could be taken to resolve those. It's not uncommon to remove missing values or impute them with zeros at the beginning of a project—however, this approach bears the risk of not properly analyzing missing values in the first place.

> **Note**
>
> Missing values can be disguised as *valid* numeric or categorical values. Typical examples are minimum or maximum values, -1, 0, or NaN. Hence, if you find the values 32,767 (= $2^{15}-1$) or 65,535 (= $2^{16}-1$) appearing multiple times in an integer data column, they might well be missing values disguised as the maximum signed or unsigned 16-bit integer representation. Always assume that your data contains missing values and outliers in different shapes and representations. Your task is to uncover, find, and clean them.

Any prior knowledge about the data or domain will give you a competitive advantage when working with the data. The reason for this is that you will be able to understand **missing values**, **outliers**, and **extremes** in relation to the data and domain—which will help you to perform better imputation, cleansing, or transformation. As the next step, you should look for these outliers in your data, specifically for the following values:

- The absolute number (or percentage) of the null values (look for Null, "Null", "", NaN, and so on)
- The absolute number (or percentage) of minimum and maximum values The absolute number (or percentage) of the **most common value (MODE)** The absolute number (or percentage) of value 0
- The absolute number (or percentage) of unique values

Once you have identified these values, we can use different preprocessing techniques to impute missing values and normalize or exclude dimensions with outliers. You will find many of these techniques, such as group mean imputation, in action in *Chapter 4, ETL, data preparation, and feature extraction*.

Visualizing data distributions

Knowing the outliers, you can finally approach exploring the **value distribution** of your dataset. This will help you understand which transformation and normalization techniques should be applied during data preparation. Common distribution statistics to look for in a continuous variable are the following:

- The mean or median value
- The minimum and maximum value
- The 25th, 50th (median), and 75th percentiles
- The data skew

Common techniques for visualizing these distributions are boxplots, density plots, or histograms. *Figure 1.1* shows these different visualization techniques plotted per target class for a multi-class recognition dataset. Each of those methods has advantages and disadvantages—boxplots show all relevant metrics, while being a bit harder to read; density plots show very smooth shapes, while hiding some of the outliers; and histograms don't let you spot the median and percentiles easily, while giving you a good estimate for the data skew:

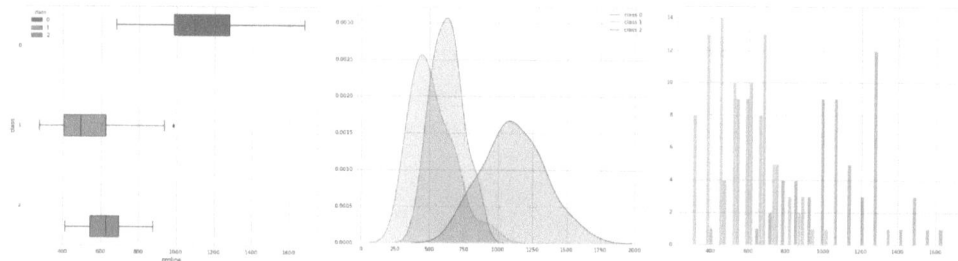

Figure 1.1: Common techniques for visualizing data distributions—namely, boxplots, density plots, and histograms

From the preceding visualization techniques, only histograms work well for categorical data (both nominal and ordinal)—however, you could look at the number of values per category. Another nice way to display the value distribution versus the target rate is in a binary classification task. *Figure 1.2* shows the *version number* of Windows Defender against the malware *detection rate* (for non-touch devices) from the Microsoft malware detection dataset:

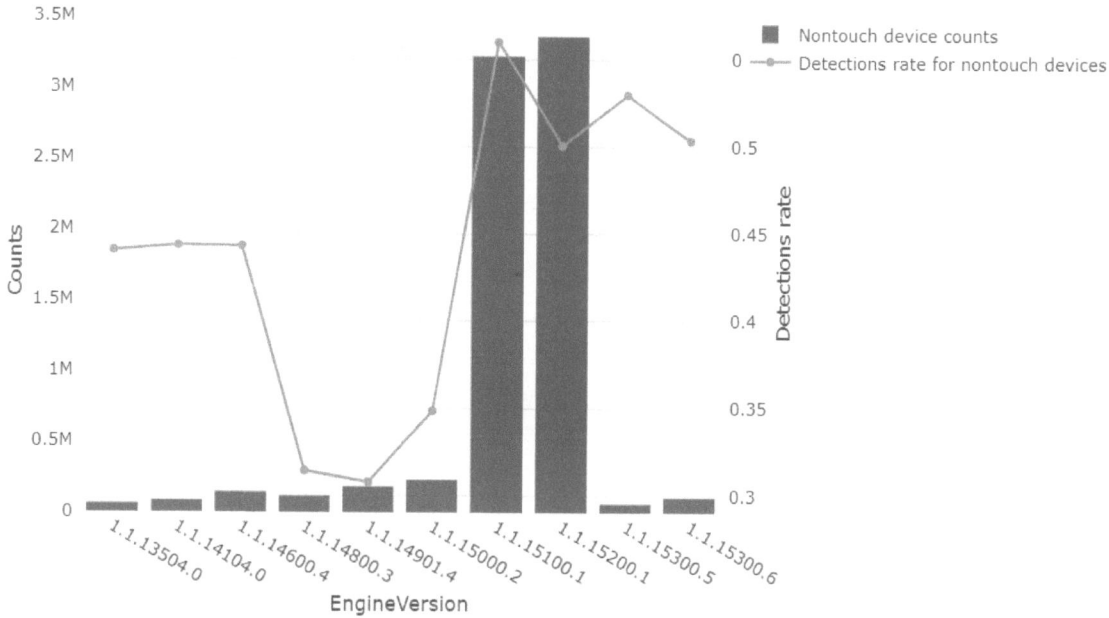

Figure 1.2: The version number of Windows Defender against the malware detection rate (for non-touch devices)

Many statistical ML algorithms require that the data is normally distributed and hence needs to be normalized or standardized. Knowing the data distribution helps you to choose which transformations need to be applied during data preparation. In practice, it is often the case that data needs to be transformed, scaled, or normalized.

Finding correlated dimensions

Another common task in data exploration is looking for correlations in the dataset. This will help you dismiss feature dimensions that are highly correlated and therefore might influence your ML model. In linear regression models, for example, two highly correlated independent variables will lead to large coefficients with opposite signs that ultimately cancel each other out. A much more stable regression model can be found by removing one of the correlated dimensions.

The **Pearson correlation coefficient**, for example, is a popular technique used to measure the linear relationship between two variables on a scale from -1 (strongly negatively correlated) to 1 (strongly positively correlated). 0 indicates no linear relation between the two variables in the Pearson correlation coefficient.

Figure 1.3 shows an example of a correlation matrix of the Boston housing price dataset, consisting of only continuous variables. The correlations range from -1 to 1 and are colored accordingly. The last row shows us the linear correlation between each feature dimension and the target variable. We can immediately tell that the **median value (MEDV)** of owner-occupied homes and the **lower status (LSTAT)** percentage of the population are negatively correlated:

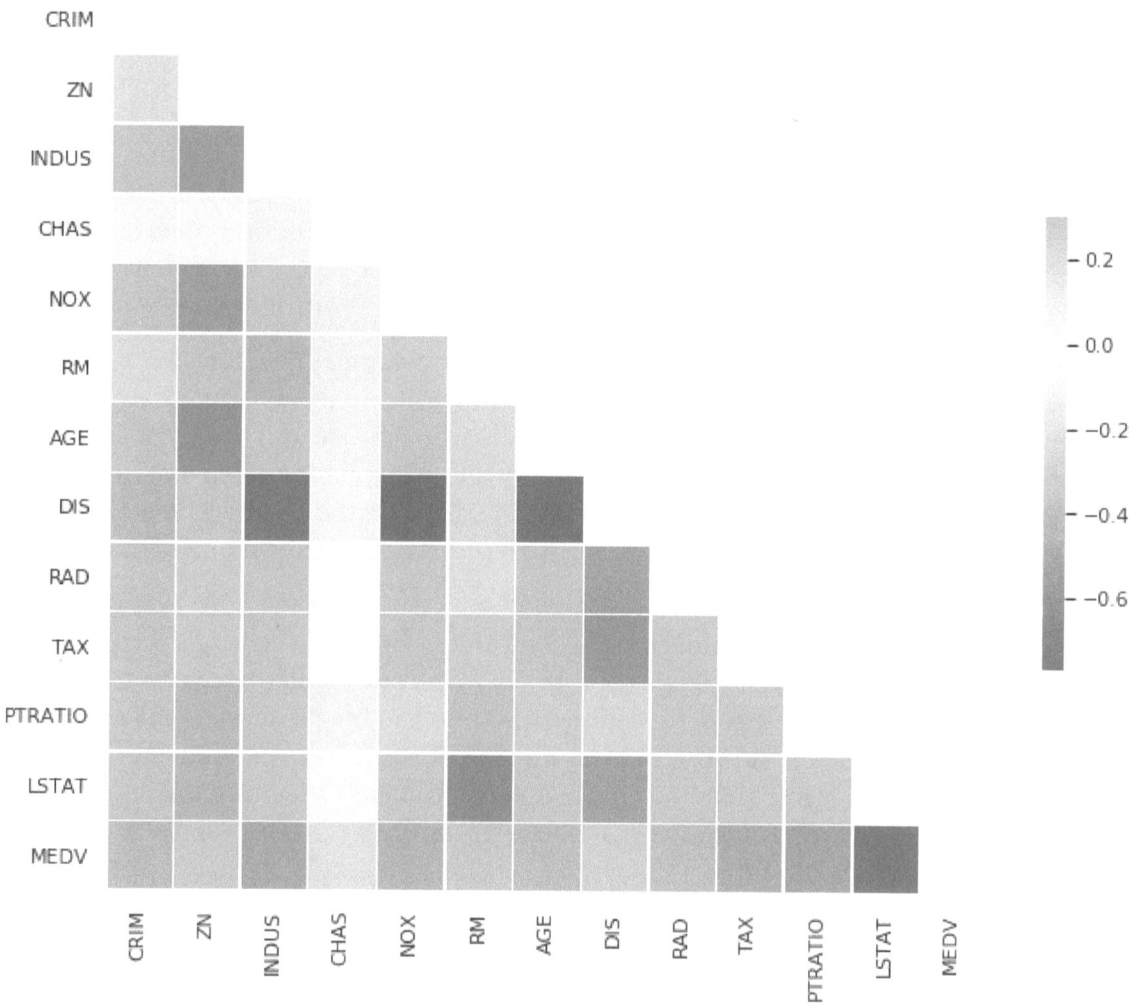

Figure 1.3: An example of a correlation matrix of the Boston housing price dataset, consisting continuous variables

It is worth mentioning that many correlation coefficients can only be between numerical values. Ordinal variables can be encoded, for example, using integer encoding and can also compute a meaningful correlation coefficient. For nominal data, you need to fall back on different methods, such as Cramér's V to compute correlation. It is worth noting that the input data doesn't need to be normalized (linearly scaled) before computing the correlation coefficient.

Measuring feature and target dependencies for regression

Once we have analyzed missing values, data distribution, and correlations, we can start analyzing the relationship between the features and the target variable. This will give us a good indication of the difficulty of the prediction problem and hence, the expected baseline performance– which is essential for prioritizing feature engineering efforts and choosing an appropriate ML model. Another great benefit of measuring this dependency is ranking the feature dimensions by the impact on the target variable, which you can use as a priority list for data exploration and preprocessing.

In a regression task, the target variable is numerical or ordinal. Therefore, we can compute the correlation coefficient between the individual features and the target variable to compute the linear dependency between the feature and the target. High correlation, and so a high absolute correlation coefficient, indicates a strong linear relationship exists. This gives us a great place to start for further exploration. However, in many practical problems, it is rare to see a high (linear) correlation between the feature and target variables.

One can also visualize this dependency between the feature and the target variable using a scatter or regression plot. *Figure 1.4* shows a regression plot between the feature *average number of rooms per dwelling* (**RM**) and the target variable *median value of owner-occupied homes* (**MEDV**) from the UCI Boston housing dataset. If the regression line is at 45 degrees, then we have a perfect linear correlation:

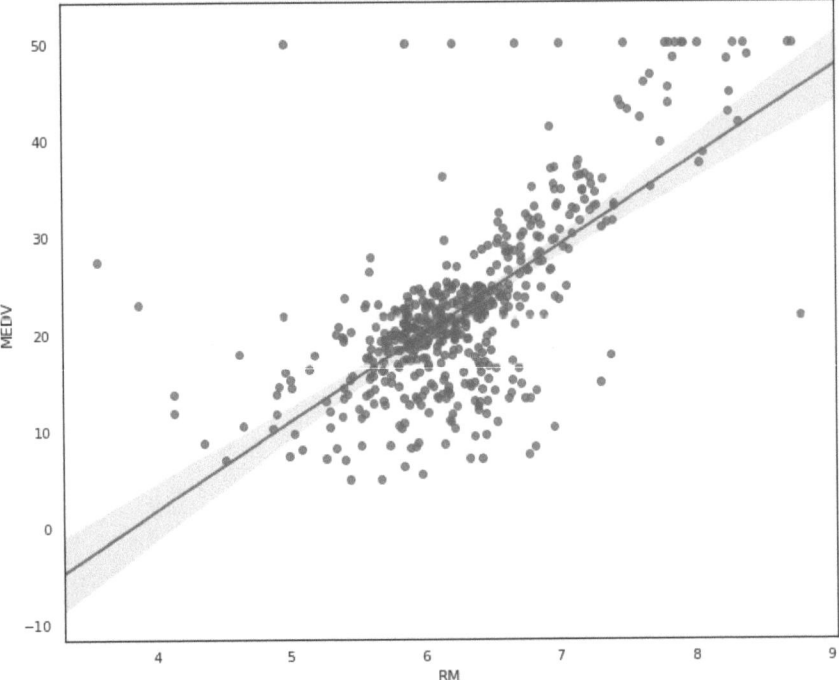

Figure 1.4: A regression plot between the feature, RM, and the target variable, MEDV

Another great approach to determining this dependency is to fit a linear or logistic regression model to the training data. The resulting model coefficients now give a good explanation of the relationship—the higher the coefficient, the larger the linear (for linear regression) or marginal (for logistic regression) dependency on the target variable. Hence, sorting by coefficients results in a list of features ordered by importance. Depending on the regression type, the input data should be normalized or standardized.

Figure 1.5 shows an example of the correlation coefficients (the first column) of a fitted **Ordinary Least Squares (OLS)** regression model:

	coef	std err	t	P>|t|	[0.025	0.975]
CRIM	-0.1214	0.033	-3.678	0.000	-0.186	-0.057
ZN	0.0470	0.014	3.384	0.001	0.020	0.074
INDUS	0.0135	0.062	0.217	0.829	-0.109	0.136
CHAS	2.8400	0.870	3.264	0.001	1.131	4.549
NOX	-18.7580	3.851	-4.870	0.000	-26.325	-11.191
RM	3.6581	0.420	8.705	0.000	2.832	4.484
AGE	0.0036	0.013	0.271	0.787	-0.023	0.030
DIS	-1.4908	0.202	-7.394	0.000	-1.887	-1.095
RAD	0.2894	0.067	4.325	0.000	0.158	0.421
TAX	-0.0127	0.004	-3.337	0.001	-0.020	-0.005
PTRATIO	-0.9375	0.132	-7.091	0.000	-1.197	-0.678
LSTAT	-0.5520	0.051	-10.897	0.000	-0.652	-0.452
intercept	41.6173	4.936	8.431	0.000	31.919	51.316

Omnibus:	171.096	Durbin-Watson:	1.077
Prob(Omnibus):	0.000	Jarque-Bera (JB):	709.937
Skew:	1.477	Prob(JB):	6.90e-155
Kurtosis:	7.995	Cond. No.	1.17e+04

Figure 1.5: The correlation coefficients of the OLS regression model

While the resulting R-squared metric (not shown) might not be good enough for a baseline model, the ordering of the coefficients can help us to prioritize further data exploration, preprocessing, and feature engineering.

Visualizing feature and label dependency for classification

In a classification task with a multi-class nominal target variable, we can't use the regression coefficients without further preprocessing the data. Another popular method that works well out of the box is fitting a simple tree-based classifier to the training data. Depending on the size of the training data, we could use a decision tree or a tree-based ensemble classifier, such as **random forest** or **gradient-boosted** trees. Doing so results in a feature importance ranking of the feature dimensions according to the chosen split criterion. In the case of splitting by entropy, the features would be sorted by *information gain* and hence, indicate which variables carry the most information about the target.

Figure 1.6 shows the feature importance fitted by a tree-based ensemble classifier using the entropy criterion from the UCI wine recognition dataset:

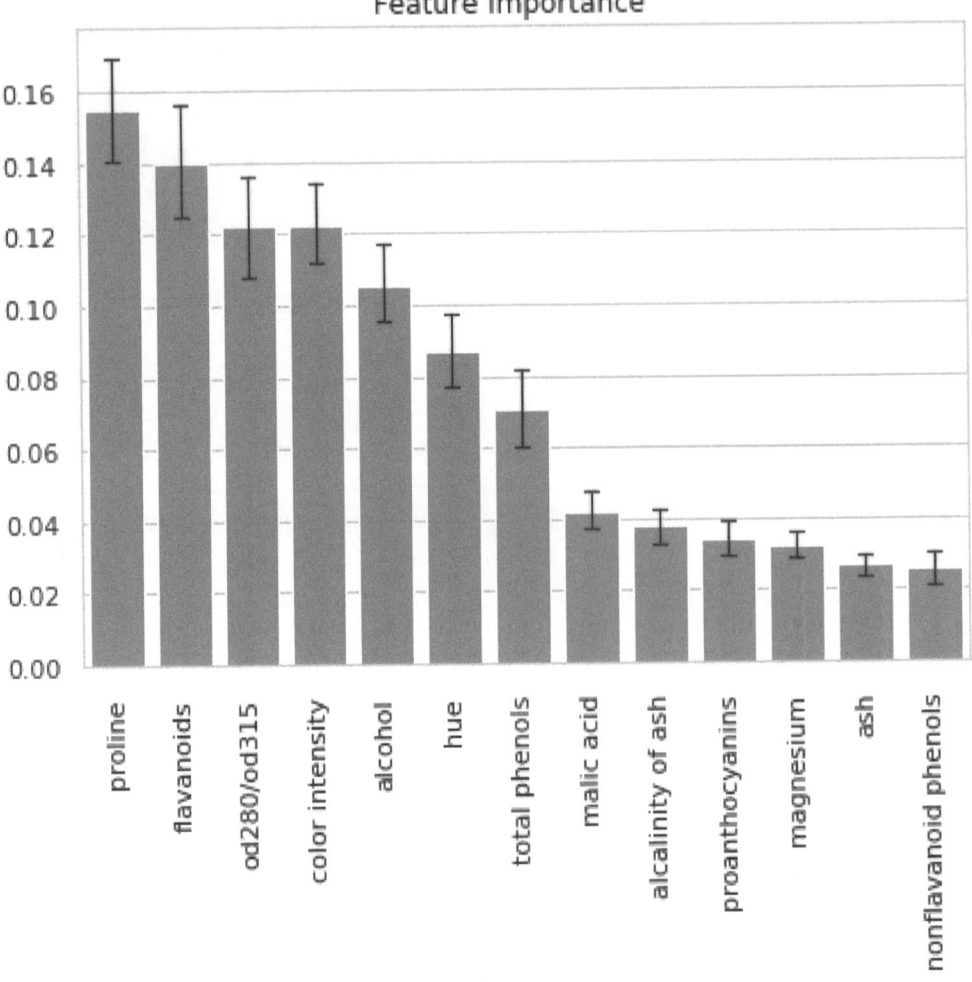

Figure 1.6: A tree-based ensemble classifier using the entropy criterion

The lines represent variations in the information gain of features between individual trees. This output is a great first step to further data analysis and exploration in order of feature importance.

Here is another popular approach to discovering the separability of your dataset. *Figure 1.7* shows two graphs–one that is linearly separable (left) and one that is not separable (right)–show a dataset with three classes:

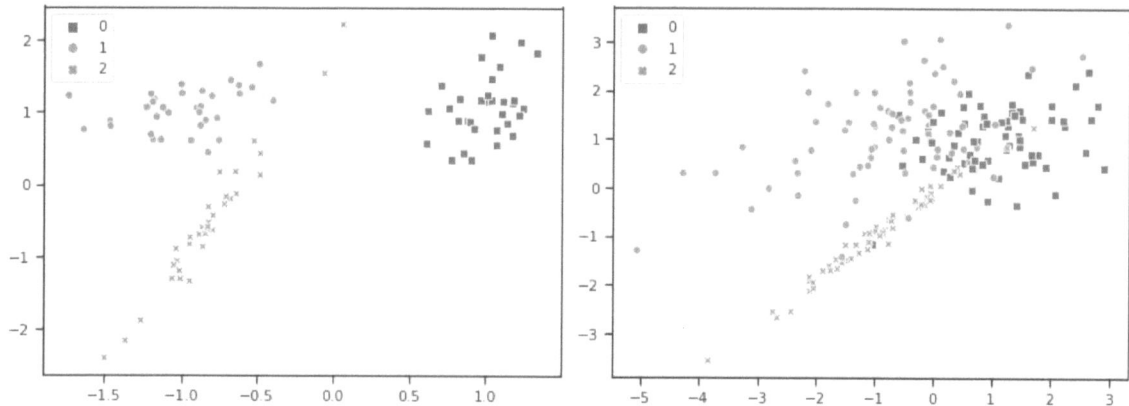

Figure 1.7: The graphs showing the separability of the dataset

You can see this when looking at the three clusters and the overlaps between these clusters. Having clearly separated clusters means that a trained classification model will perform very well on this dataset. On the other hand, when we know that the data is not linearly separable, we know that this task will require advanced feature engineering and modeling to produce good results.

The preceding figure showed two datasets in two dimensions; we actually used the first two feature dimensions for visualization. However, high-dimensional most data cannot be easily and accurately visualized in two dimensions. To achieve this, we need a projection or embedding technique to embed the feature space in two dimensions. Many linear and non- linear embedding techniques to produce two-dimensional projections of data exist; here are the most common ones:

- **Principal Component Analysis (PCA)**
- **Linear Discriminant Analysis (LDA)**
- **t-Distributed Stochastic Neighbor Embedding (t-SNE)**
- **Uniform Manifold Approximation and Projection (UMAP)**

Figure 1.8 shows, the LDA (left) and t-SNE (right) embeddings for the 13-dimensional UCI wine recognition dataset (https://archive.ics.uci.edu/ml/datasets/wine). In the LDA embedding, we can see that all the classes should be linearly separable. That's a lot we have learned from using two lines of code to plot the embedding before we even start with model selection or training:

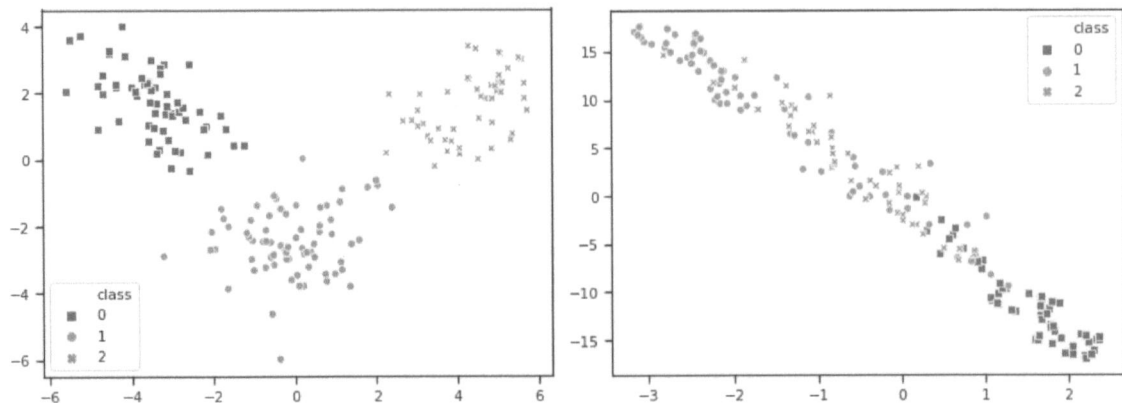

Figure 1.8: LDA (left) and t-SNE (right) embeddings for the 13-dimensional UCI wine recognition dataset

Both the LDA and t-SNE embeddings are extremely helpful for judging the separability of the individual classes and hence the difficulty of your classification task. It's always good to assess how well a particular model will perform on your data before you start selecting and training a specific algorithm. You will learn more about these techniques in *Chapter 3, Data experimentation and visualization using Azure*.

Exploring common techniques for data preparation

After the data experimentation phase, you should have gathered enough knowledge to start preprocessing the data. This process is also often referred to as **feature engineering**. When coming from multiple sources, such as applications, databases, or warehouses, as well as external sources, your data cannot be analyzed or interpreted immediately.

It is, therefore, of imminent importance to preprocess data before you choose a model to interpret your problem. In addition to this, there are different steps involved in data preparation, which depend on the data that is available to you, such as the problem you want to solve, and with that, the ML algorithms that could be used for it.

You might ask yourself why data preparation is so important. The answer is that the preparation of your data might lead to improvements in model accuracy when done properly. This could be due to the relationships within your data that have been simplified due to the preparation. By experimenting with data preparation, you would also be able to boost the model's accuracy later on. Usually, data scientists spend a significant amount of their time on data preparation, feature engineering, and understanding their data. In addition to this, data preparation is important for generating insights.

Data preparation means collecting data, cleaning it up, transforming the data, and consolidating it. By doing this, you can enrich your data, transform it, and as mentioned previously, improve the accuracy of your model. In fact, in many cases, an ML model's performance can be improved significantly through better feature engineering.

The challenges that come along with data preparation are, for example, the different file formats, the data types, inconsistency in data, limited or too much access to data, and sometimes even insufficient infrastructure around data integration. Another difficult problem is converting text, such as nominal or ordinal categories or free text, into a numeric value.

The way people currently view data preparation and perform this step of the process is through the extract, transform, and load tools. It is of utmost importance that data within organizations is aligned and transformed using various data standards. Effective integration of various data sources should be done by aligning the data, transforming it, and then promoting the development and adoption of data standards. All this effectively helps in managing the volume, variety, veracity, and velocity of the data.

In the following subparagraphs, some of the key techniques in data preparation, such as labeling, storing, encoding, and normalizing data, as well as feature extraction, will be shown in more depth.

Labeling the training data

Let's start with a bummer; the first step in the data preparation journey is labeling, also called **annotation**. It is a bummer because it is the least exciting part of an ML project, yet one of the most important tasks in the whole process. *Garbage in, garbage out*—it's that simple. The ultimate goal is to feed high-quality training data into the ML algorithms, which is why labeling training data is so important.

While proper labels greatly help to improve prediction performance, the labeling process will also help you to study the dataset in greater detail. However, let me clarify that labeling data requires deep insight and understanding of the context of the dataset and the prediction process. If we were aiming to predict breast cancer using CT scans, we would also need to understand how breast cancer can be detected in CT images in order to label the data.

Mislabeling the training data has a couple of consequences, such as **label noise**, which you want to avoid as it will the performance of every downstream process in the ML pipeline, such as feature selection, feature ranking and ultimately model performance. Learning relies crucially on the accuracy of labels in the training dataset. However, we should always take label noise into account when aiming for a specific target metric because it's highly unlikely that all the provided labels will be absolutely precise and accurate.

In some cases, your labeling methodology is dependent on the chosen ML approach for a prediction problem. A good example is the difference between object detection and segmentation, both of which require completely differently labeled data. As labeling for segmentation is much more time-consuming than labeling for object detection or even classification, it is also an important trade-off to make before starting an ML project.

There are some techniques you can use to speed up the labeling process, which are hopefully provided by your labeling system:

- **Supervised learning**: Through supervised learning, an ML model could recommend the correct labels for your data at labeling time. You can then decide whether you use the predicted label or choose a different or modified label. This works very well with object detection and image data.

- **Active learning**: Another technique to accelerate the labeling process is to allow a semi-supervised learning process to learn and predict based on a few manually labeled samples. Using those labeled samples, the model automatically proposes new labels that can either be accepted or changed and modified. Each label will fine-tune the model to predict better labels.

- **Unsupervised learning**: Through clustering similar data samples together, the labeling environment can prioritize which data points should be labeled next. Using these insights, the labeling environment can always try to propose loads of greatly varying samples in the training data for manual labeling.

Labeling is a necessary, long, and cost-intensive step in an ML process. There are techniques to facilitate labeling; however, they always require the domain knowledge to be carried out properly. If there is any chance that you can collect labeled data through your application directly, you are very lucky and should start collecting this data. A good example is collecting training data for a click-through rate of search results based on the actual results and clicks of real users.

Normalization and transformation in machine learning

Normalization is a common data preprocessing technique where the data is scaled to a different value range through a (linear) transformation. For many statistical ML models, the training data needs to follow a certain distribution and so it needs to first be normalized along all its dimensions. The following are some of the most commonly used methods to normalize data:

- Scaling to unit length, or standard scaling
- Minimum/maximum scaling
- Mean normalization
- Quantile normalization

In addition to these, you can also monitor normalization by ensuring the values fall between 0 and 1 in the case of probability density functions, which are used in fields such as chemistry. For exponential distribution and Poisson distribution, you could use the coefficient of variation because it deals well with positive distributions.

> **Note**
>
> In ML algorithms such as **Support Vector Machines** (**SVM**), logistic regression, and neural networks, a very common normalization technique is standardization, which standardizes features by giving them a 0 mean and unit variance. This is often referred to as a standard scaler.

Besides linear transformations, it's also quite common to apply non-linear transformations to your data for the same reason as for normalization, which is to pass the assumption for a specifically required distribution. If your data is skewed, you can use power or log transformations to normalize the distributions. This is very important, for example, for linear models where the normality assumption is a required conditional to the predictor's vector. For highly skewed data, you can also apply these transformations multiple times. For data ranges containing 0, it's also common to apply log plus 1 transformations to avoid numerical instability.

Encoding categorical variables

With a real-world dataset, you will quickly reach the limits of normalization and transformation as the data for these transformations needs to be continuous. The same is true for many statistical ML algorithms, such as linear regression, SVM, or neural networks; the input data needs to be numerical. Hence, in order to work with categorical data, we need to look at different numerical encoding techniques.

We differentiate between three different types of categorical data: ordinal, nominal, and textual (for example, free text). We make this distinction between nominal and textual data as textual data is often used to extract semantic meaning whereas nominal categorical data is often just encoded.

There are various types of numerical encoding techniques you could use. They are listed here:

- **Label encoding**: This is where each category is mapped to a number or label. The labels for the categories are not related to each other; therefore, categories that are related will lose this information after encoding.

- **One-hot encoding**: Another popular approach is dummy coding, also called one-hot encoding. Each category is replaced with an orthogonal feature vector, where the dimension of the feature vector is dependent on the number of distinct values. This approach is not efficient with high cardinality features.

- **Bin encoding**: Even though bin encoding is quite similar to one-hot encoding, it differs from storing categories as binary bitstrings. The goal of bin encoding is to hash the cardinalities into binary values and each binary digit gets one column. This will result in some information loss; however, you can deal with fewer dimensions. It also creates fewer columns and so the speed of learning is higher and more memory efficient.

- **Count encoding**: In count encoding, we replace the categorical values with the relative or absolute count of the value over the whole training set. This is a common technique for encoding large amounts of unique labels.

- **Target encoding**: In this encoding methodology, we replace the categorical value with the mean value of the target variable of this category. This is also effective with high-cardinality features.

- **Hashing encoding**: This is used when there are a lot of large-scale categorical features. The hash function maps a lot of values into a small, finite set of values. Different values could create the same hash, which is called a **collision**.

We will take a closer look at some of these encoding techniques in *Chapter 6, Advanced feature extraction with NLP*.

A feature engineering example using time-series data

Feature engineering is strongly dependent on the domain of your dataset. When dealing with demographics or geographics, you can model personas and demographic metrics or join geographic attributes, such as proximity to a large city, or to the border, GDP, and others. Let's look at an example of time-series data, which is extremely common in real- world examples.

Many real-world datasets have a temporal dependency and so they store the date and time in at least one of the dimensions of the training data. This date-time field can be treated either as an encoded or an ordinal categorical variable, depending on the distribution of the date-time variable.

Depending on the distribution and patterns in the date-time data, you want to transform the date-time field into different values that encode a specific property of the current date or time. The following are a few features that can be extracted from date-time variables:

- The absolute time
- The hour of the day
- The day of the week
- The day of the month
- The day of the year
- The month of the year

If you see a periodic relationship between a dimension over time, you can also encode the cycle features of the time dimension. This can be achieved by computing the absolute hour of the day to compute the sine and cosine components of the normalized hour of the day. Using this technique, the resulting values will contain a cyclic dependency on the encoded date-time dimension.

Another great way of improving your model's performance is to include additional data in your training data. This works really well on the date-time dimension as you can, for example, join public holidays, public events, or other types of events by date. This lets you create features such as the following:

- The number of days until or since the next or last campaign
- The number of days until or since the next or last holiday
- Mark a date as a public holiday
- Mark a date as a major sporting event

As you can see, there are many ways to transform and encode date-time variables. It is encouraged to dive into the raw data and look for visual patterns in the data that should be interpreted by the ML model. Whenever you deal with a date-time dimension, there is room for creative feature engineering.

Using NLP to extract complex features from text

Using NLP to extract features from text is very useful as an input for ML models. NLP is used to apply ML algorithms to text and speech and is often used to preprocess raw text data and categorical embeddings. We often distinguish between occurrence-based embeddings, such as bag-of-words, and semantic embeddings, such as Word2Vec. NLP is extremely useful for any time that you are dealing with textual data.

Similar to categorical embeddings, NLP techniques transform text into numerical values. These values are often high-dimensional and need to be simplified–commonly done through **Singular Value Decomposition (SVD)**–or aggregated. Some popular techniques that are used in NLP to extract features from text are as follows:

- Lemmatization, stemming, and stop-word removal n-grams
- tf-idf
- Embeddings, such as Word2vec
- Fully trained models, such as sequence-to-sequence models

If we aim to convert text to numerical values, we can practically implement encodings using bag-of-words predictors, Word2Vec embeddings, or sequence-to-sequence models. The same idea can be extended to documents where instead of learning feature representations for words, you learn them for documents.

We will take a closer look at feature extraction through NLP and all the previously mentioned techniques in *Chapter 6, Advanced feature extraction with NLP*.

Choosing the right ML model to train data

Similar to data experimentation and preprocessing, training ML model is an analytical, step-by-step process. Each step involves a thought process that evaluates the pros and cons of each algorithm according to the results of the experimentation phase. Like in every other scientific process, it is recommended that you come up with a hypothesis first and verify whether this hypothesis is true afterward.

Let's look at the steps that define the process of training an ML model:

- **Define your ML task**: First, we need to define the ML task we are facing, which most of the time is defined by the business decision behind your use case. Depending on the amount of labeled data, you can choose between non-supervised, semi-supervised, and supervised learning, as well as many other subcategories.

- **Pick a suitable model to perform this task**: Pick a suitable model for the chosen ML task. This includes logistic regression, a gradient-boosted tree ensemble, and a deep neural network, just to name a few popular ML model choices. The choice is mainly dependent on the training (or production) infrastructure (such as Python, R, Julia, C, and so on) and on the shape of the data. It is recommended that you favor simple traditional ensemble techniques, such as gradient-boosted tree ensembles, when training data is limited. These models perform well on a broad set of input values (ordinal, nominal, and numeric) as well as training efficiently and they are understandable. When strong generalization and expressiveness is required, and given a reasonable amount of training data, you should go with deep learning models. When limited data is available to build a highly complicated model (for example, for object detection), it is recommended you use pre-trained models as feature extractors and only train the classifiers on top. However, whenever possible, it is recommended you build on top of pre- trained models when deep learning techniques are used.

- **Pick a train-validation split**: Splitting your data into a training and validation set gives you additional insights in the performance of your training and optimization process. This includes a group shuffle split, temporal split, stratified split, and so on.

- **Pick or implement an error metric**: During the data experimentation phase, you should have already come up with a strategy on how to test your model's performance. Hence, you should have picked a validation split and error metric already. If you have not done so, I recommend you evaluate what you want to measure and optimize (such as absolute errors, relative errors, percentages, true positive rates, true negative rates, and so on). This includes F1-score, MSE, ROC, weighted Cohen's kappa, and so on.

- **Train a simple model using cross-validation**: Finally, when all the preceding choices are made, you can go ahead and train your ML model. Optimally, this is done as cross-validation on a training and validation set, without leaking training data into validation. After training a baseline model, it's time to interpret the error metric of the validation runs. Does it make sense? Is it as high or low as expected? Is it (hopefully) better than random and better than always predicting the most popular target? What's the influence of the random seed on this result?

Once the answers to these questions are gathered, you can go back to the fun part: improving the model performance—by data analysis, feature engineering and data preprocessing.

Choosing an error metric

After looking at the relationship between the feature and target dimensions, as well as the separability of the data, you should continue to evaluate which error metric will be used to train the ML model later on. There are many metric choices that measure absolute, squared, and percentage errors for regression, as well as the accuracy, true positive rate, true negative rate for classification, and weighted distance metrics for ordinal categories—just to name a few.

> **Note**
>
> Defining an appropriate error metric for an optimization problem is not straightforward as it depends on multiple circumstances. In a classification problem, for example, we are confronted with the precision- recall dilemma, you can either optimize for maximal precision (and hence minimize false positives) or for maximal recall (and hence maximize true positives). Either decision will result in a different model with opposite strengths and weaknesses.

Many machine learning practitioners don't value the importance of a proper error metric highly enough but instead go with the default metric for their use case (for example, accuracy, mean squared error, and so on). If you find yourself in this trap, remember the importance of the right error metric. The choice of error metric is absolutely critical and might even result in your ML use case succeeding or failing.

Before diving into model training and optimization—which includes tasks such as model selection and parameter tuning—it is useful to understand the baseline performance and the model's robustness to noise. The first can be achieved by computing the error metric using only the target variable with the highest occurrence as a prediction—this will be your baseline performance. The second can be done by modifying the random seed of your ML model (for example, the tree-based model used for feature importance) and observing the changes to the error metric. This will show you what decimal place you can trust the error metric to.

The training and testing split

Once you have selected an ML approach and an error metric, you need to think about splitting your dataset for training. Optimally, the data should be split into three disjointed sets: a training, a validation, and a testing set. We use multiple sets to ensure that the model generalizes well on unseen data and that the reported error metric can be trusted. Hence, you can see that dividing the data into representative sets is a task that should be performed as an analytical process.

You need to avoid training data leaking into the validation or testing set, hence overfitting the training data and skewing the validation and testing results, at all costs. To ensure this, you need to always create disjointed datasets and use the validation set for cross-validation and parameter tuning and the testing set only for reporting your final model performance.

There are many different techniques available, such as stratified splitting (sampling based on class distributions), temporal splitting, and group-based splitting. We will take a look at these in *Chapter 7, Building ML models using Azure Machine Learning*.

Achieving great performance using tree-based ensemble models

Many amazing traditional ML approaches exist, such as naive Bayes SVM, and linear regression. However, there is one technique that, due to its flexibility, gets you started quickly while delivering great prediction performance without a ton of tuning and data preparation. While most decision tree-based ensemble estimators fit this description, we want to look at one in particular: gradient-boosted trees.

In the previous section, we mentioned that building a baseline model for estimating the baseline performance is a good start to every ML project. Indeed, we will see in many chapters that building a baseline model helps you focus on all the important aspects of your project, such as the data, infrastructure, and automation.

Decision trees are extremely versatile. They can be used with numerical and categorical data as input and can predict both continuous and categorical values. Tree-based ensemble models combine many weak learners into a single predictor based on decision trees. This greatly reduces the problem of the overfitting and instability of single decision trees. When boosting, we use an iterative approach to optimize the model performance by weighting misclassified training samples after each training iteration. The output after a few iterations using the default parameter usually delivers great baseline results for many different applications.

In *Chapter 7, Building ML models using Azure Machine Learning*, we have dedicated a complete section to training a gradient-boosted tree-ensemble classifier using LightGBM, a popular tree-ensemble library from Microsoft.

Modeling large and complex data using deep learning techniques

To capture the meaning of large amounts of complex training data, we need large parametric models. However, training parametric models with many hundreds of millions of parameters is no easy task, due to exploding and vanishing gradient, loss propagation through such a complex model, numerical instability, and normalization. In recent years, a branch of such high parametric models achieved extremely good results through many complex tasks—namely, deep learning.

Deep neural networks work extremely well on complex prediction tasks with large amounts of complex input data. Most models combine both the feature extractor and classification/regression parts and are trained in a fully end-to-end approach. Fully connected neural networks—also called **Artificial Neural Networks (ANNs)**—work very similar to logistic regression models, with a different loss function and the stacking of multiple layers. **Convolutional Neural Networks (CNNs)** use local constraint connections with shared weights to remove the number of required parameters while taking advantage of data locality. They work extremely well with image data where the convolution and pooling layers correspond to classical computer vision filters and operators.

Recurrent Neural Networks (RNNs) and **Long Short-Term Memory (LSTM)** layers help to model time dependency by keeping a state over time. Most model architectures can take advantage of parallel computing through **General Programming Graphical Processing Units (GPGPU)**, or even virtualized or dedicated deep learning hardware.

Chapter 8, Training deep neural networks on Azure, and *Chapter 10, Distributed machine learning on Azure*, are dedicated to training large, complex deep learning models on a single machine and distributed GPU clusters.

Optimization techniques

If we have trained a simple ensemble model that performs reasonably better than the baseline model and achieves acceptable performance according to the expected performance estimated during data preparation, we can progress with optimization. This is a point we really want to emphasize. It's strongly discouraged to begin model optimization and stacking when a simple ensemble technique fails to deliver useful results. If this is the case, it would be much better to take a step back and dive deeper into data analysis and feature engineering.

Common ML optimization techniques, such as hyperparameter optimization, model stacking, and even automated machine learning, help you get the last 10% of performance boost out of your model while the remaining 90% is achieved by a single ensemble model. If you decide to use any of those optimization techniques, it is advised to perform them in parallel and fully automated on a distributed cluster.

After seeing too many ML practitioners manually parametrizing, tuning, and stacking models together, we want to raise the important message that training and optimizing ML models is boring. It should rarely be done manually as it is much faster to perform it automatically as an end-to-end optimization process. Most of your time and effort should go into experimentation, data preparation, and feature engineering—that is, everything that cannot be easily automated and optimized using raw compute power. Prior knowledge about the data and an understanding of the ML use case and the business insights are the best places to dig deeper into when investing time in improving the model performance.

Hyperparameter optimization

Once you have achieved reasonable performance using a simple single model with default parameterization, you can move on to optimizing the hyperparameters of the model. Due to the combination and complexity of multiple parameters, it doesn't make a lot of sense to waste time on tuning the parameters by hand. Instead, this tuning should always be performed in an optimal automated way, which will always lead to a better cross- validation performance.

First, you need to define the parameter search space and sampling distribution for each trainable hyperparameter. This definition is either a continuous or categorical region with different sampling distributions; for example, uniform, logarithmic, or normal distributed sampling. This can usually be done by generating a parameter configuration using a hyperparameter optimization library.

The next thing you need to decide is the sampling technique of parameters in the search space. The three most common sampling and optimization techniques are the following:

- Grid sampling
- Random sampling
- Bayesian optimization

While the first two algorithms sample either in a grid or at random in the search space, the third algorithm performs a more intelligent search through Bayesian optimization. In practice, random and Bayesian sampling are used most often.

> **Note**
>
> To avoid any unnecessary compute time spent on wrong parameter configurations, it is recommended to define early stopping criteria when using hyperparameter optimization.

Training many combinations of different parameter sets is a computationally complex task. Hence, it is strongly recommended to parallelize this task on multiple machines and track all parameter combinations and model cross-validation performance at a central location. This is a particularly beneficial task for a highly scalable cloud computing environment where these tasks are performed automatically. In Azure Machine Learning, you can use the HyperDrive functionality to do exactly this. We will look at this in great detail in Chapter 9, *Hyperparameter tuning and Automated Machine Learning*.

Model stacking

Model stacking is a very common technique used to improve prediction performance by putting a combination of multiple models into a single stacked model. Hence, the output of each model is fed into a meta-model, which itself is trained through cross-validation and hyperparameter tuning. By combining significantly different models into a single stacked model, you can always outperform a single model.

Figure 1.9 shows a stacked model consisting of different supervised models in level 1 that feed their output into another meta-model. This is a common architecture that further boosts prediction performance once all the feature engineering and model tuning options are fully exploited:

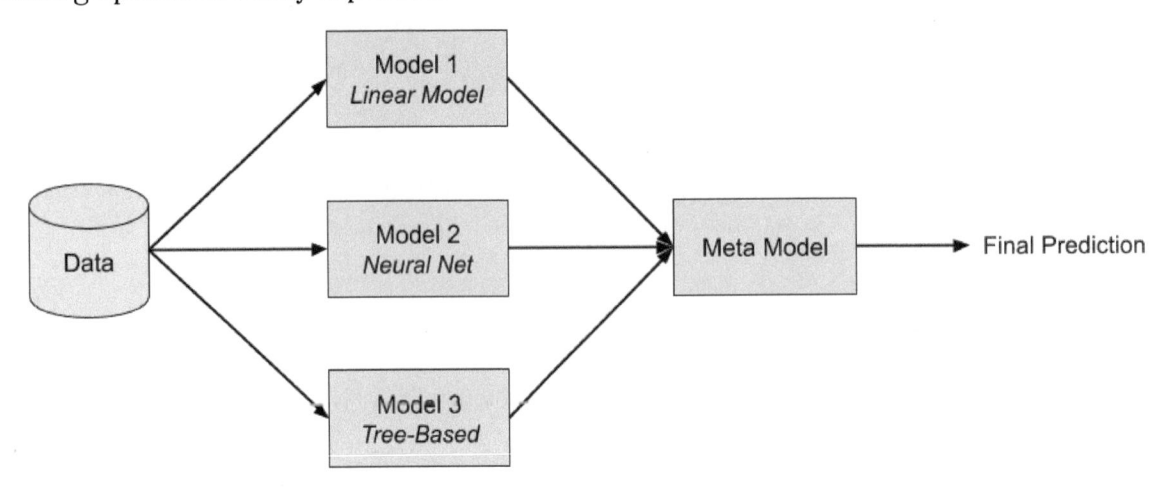

Figure 1.9: Model stacking

Model stacking adds a lot of complexity to your ML process while almost always leading to better performance. This technique will get out the last 1% performance gain of your algorithm. To efficiently stack models into a meta ensemble, it is recommended that you do it fully automated; for example, through techniques such as Azure Automated Machine Learning. One thing to be aware of, however, is that you can easily overfit the training data or create stacked models that are magnitudes larger in size than single models.

Azure Automated Machine Learning

As we have shown, constructing ML models is a complex step-by-step process that requires a lot of different skills, such as domain knowledge (prior knowledge that allows you to get insight into data), mathematical expertise, and computer science skills. During this process, there is still human error and bias involved, which might not only affect the model's performance and accuracy, but also the insights that you want to gain out of it.

Azure Automated Machine Learning could be used to combine and automated all of this by reducing the time to value. For several industries, automated machine learning can leverage ML and AI technology by automating manual modeling tasks, such that the data scientists can focus on more complex issues. Particularly when using repetitive ML tasks, such as data preprocessing, feature engineering, model selection, parameter tuning and model stacking, it could be useful to use Azure Automated Machine Learning.

We will go into much more detail and see real-world examples in *Chapter 9, Hyperparameter tuning and Automated Machine Learning*.

Deploying and operating models

Once you have trained and optimized an ML model, it is ready for deployment. Many data science teams, in practice, stop here and move the model to production as a Docker image, often embedded in a REST API using Flask or similar frameworks. However, as you can imagine, this is not always the best solution depending on your use case requirements. An ML or data engineer's responsibility doesn't stop here.

The deployment and operation of an ML pipeline can be best seen when testing the model on live data in production. A test is done to collect insights and data to continuously improve the model. Hence, collecting model performance over time is an essential step to guaranteeing and improving the performance of the model.

In general, we differentiate two architectures for ML-scoring pipelines, which we will briefly discuss in this section:

- Batch scoring using pipelines
- Real-time scoring using a container-based web service

These architectures are discussed in increasing order of operational complexity, with offline scoring being the least complex and asynchronous scoring being the more complex system. The complexity arises from the number of components involved in operating such a pipeline at scale.

Finally, we will investigate an efficient way of collecting runtimes, latency, and other operational metrics, as well as model performance. It's also good practice to log all scored requests in order to analyze and improve an ML model over time.

Both architectures, as well as the monitoring solutions, will be discussed in more detail and implemented in *Chapter 12, Deploying and operating machine learning models*.

Batch scoring using pipelines

With **offline scoring**, or **batch scoring**, we are talking about an offline process where you evaluate an ML model against a batch of data. The result of this scoring technique is usually not time-critical and the data to be scored is usually larger than the model. This process is usually used when an ML model is scored within another batch process, such as a daily, hourly, or weekly task.

Here is what we expect as input and output data:

- **Input**: A location to find the input data
- **Output**: A response with all the scores

While the input and output format is quite intuitive, we still want to give a list of examples of when such an architecture is used. The reason for this is that you can decide the proper architecture for your use case when dealing with a similar ML task. Here are some practical examples:

- A recommendation engine of a streaming service generates new recommendations every week for the upcoming week.
- A classification algorithm of a mobile telecommunication operator computes a churn score for every customer once a month.

If the model was trained on a distributed system, it is very common to perform batch scoring on the same system that was used for training as the scoring task is identical to computing the score for the test set.

Real-time scoring using a container-based web service

The term **online synchronous scoring**, or **real-time scoring**, refers to a technique where we score an ML model and instantly need the resulting score. This is very common in stream processing, where single events are scored in real time. It's obvious that this task is highly time-critical and the execution is blocked until the resulting score is computed.

Here is what we expect as input and output data:

- **Input**: One or multiple observations
- **Output**: A response with a single score

The input and output configuration is also quite intuitive. Here are some practical examples of typical real-time scoring use cases:

- An object detection algorithm in a self-driving vehicle detects obstacles so it can control and steer the vehicle safely around the objects.
- An object detection algorithm detects faces in a camera image and focuses the camera.
- A classification algorithm decides whether the current product on the conveyor meets the quality standards.

Models for online synchronous scoring services are often deployed to the cloud as parallelized services in a distributed cluster with a load balancer in front of them. This way, the scoring cluster can be easily scaled up or down when higher throughput is required. If the latency requirements are restricted, these models are also deployed to edge devices, such as mobile phones or industrial computers, in order to avoid a round trip of the data to the nearest cloud region.

Tracking model performance, telemetry, and data skew

Tracking the proper metrics of a deployed ML model is essential. While popular metrics about include consumed CPU time, RAM, GPU memory, as well as latency, we also want to focus on the model's scoring performance. As we have already seen, most real-world data has a dependency on time and so many habits change over time. Operating an ML model in production means also continuously guaranteeing the quality and performance of the model.

In order to track the model's performance, you can use a standard application monitoring tool, such as Azure Application Insights or any other highly scalable key-value database. This is important to understand how your users are using your model and what your model is predicting in production.

Another important insight is tracking the data used for scoring the model. If we keep this data, we can compare it to the training data used for the deployed model and compute the data skew between the training data and the scoring data. By defining a threshold for maximum model skew, we can use this as a trigger to re-train the model once the skew is too big. We will see this in action in *Chapter 12, Deploying and operating machine learning models*.

Summary

In this chapter, we saw an overview of all the steps involved in making a custom ML pipeline. You might have seen familiar concepts for data preprocessing or analytics and learned an important lesson. Data experimentation is a step-by-step approach rather than an experimental process. Look for missing values, data distribution, and relationships between features and targets. This analysis will greatly help you to understand which preprocessing steps to perform and what model performance to expect.

You now know that data preprocessing, or feature engineering, is the most important part of the whole ML process. The more prior knowledge you have about the data, the better you can encode categorical and temporal variables or transform text to numerical space using NLP techniques. You learned that choosing the proper ML task, model, error metric, and train-test split is mostly defined by business decisions (for example, object detection against segmentation) or a performance trade-off (for example, stacking).

Using your newly acquired skills, you should now be able to draft an end-to-end ML process and understand each step from experimentation to deployment. In the next chapter, we will look at an overview of which specific Azure services can be used to efficiently train ML models in the cloud.

2
Choosing a machine learning service in Azure

In the previous chapter, we learned what an end-to-end **Machine Learning** (**ML**) process looks like. We went through the different steps, from data exploration to data pre-processing, training, optimization, deployment, and operation. In this chapter, we want to find out how to best navigate through all available ML services in Azure and how to select the right one for your goal. Finally, we will explain why the **Azure Machine Learning** is the best choice for building custom ML models. This is the service that we will use throughout the book to implement an end-to-end ML pipeline.

First, we will take a look at the different Azure services for ML and **Artificial Intelligence** (**AI**), and discuss their differences and similarities. Some of the services will be completely managed with little flexibility, whereas other services will give you great flexibility but not everything will be managed. We will also take a look into the different execution runtimes and compute targets.

In the next section, we jump right into Azure Cognitive Services, a pre-trained ML endpoint for many domains and prediction tasks. We will then cover customized Cognitive Services, which is a way to fine-tune a Cognitive Service for a specific task or domain. The Custom Vision tool is a great example of a customizable computer vision service.

Next, we will cover ML tools with **Graphical User Interfaces** (**GUIs**) in Azure. The best tool for building ML workflows in Azure is Azure Machine Learning designer, the successor of the popular service Azure ML Studio (classic). It is easy to use and has tight integration into the Azure Machine Learning workspace. We will also take a look at Azure Automated Machine Learning (especially the visual interface) and its advantages over Azure Machine Learning designer.

Finally, in the last section, we will cover the basics of Azure Machine Learning, the tool that we will use throughout this book to build a fully automated end-to-end ML pipeline in Azure. Besides the main terminology and functionality, we will also propose how to gradually move an existing ML project to Azure Machine Learning. This will give you the same benefits as starting a completely new project in Azure Machine Learning, ranging from model tracking to automated deployments and auto-scaling training clusters.

The following topics will be covered in this chapter:

- Demystifying the different Azure services for ML
- Azure Cognitive Services and Custom Vision
- Azure Machine Learning with GUIs
- Azure Machine Learning workspace

Let's jump right in and start demystifying the different Azure services for AI and ML!

Demystifying the different Azure services for ML

Azure offers many services that can be used to perform ML – you can use a simple **Virtual Machine** (**VM**), a pre-configured VM for ML (also called **Data Science Virtual Machine** (**DSVM**)), Azure Notebooks using a shared free kernel, or any other service that gives you compute resources and data storage. Due to this flexibility, it is often very difficult to navigate through these services and pick the correct service for implementing an ML pipeline. In this section, we will provide clear guidance about how to choose the optimal ML and compute services in Azure.

First, it is important to discuss the difference between a simple compute resource, an ML infrastructure service, and an ML modeling service. This distinction will help you to better understand the following sections about how to choose these services for a specific use case:

- A **compute resource** can be any service in Azure that provides you with computing power, such as VMs, managed clusters of VMs (Azure Batch, Azure Databricks, and so on), container execution engines (Azure Kubernetes Services, Azure Container Instance, Azure Functions, Azure IoT Edge, and so on), or hybrid compute services such as App Service. This service is usually used for experimentation or is managed from an ML infrastructure service.

- An **ML infrastructure** service helps you implement, orchestrate, automate, and optimize your ML training, pipelines, and deployments. Using such a service, you would usually implement your own preprocessing and ML algorithms using your own frameworks. However, the service would support you with infrastructure for the training, optimization and deployment process. Azure Machine Learning is a service in Azure that falls into this category and will be the service that we use throughout this book.

- Finally, an **ML modeling service** is a service that helps you to create or use ML models without writing your own code. Services such as Cognitive Services, **Azure Automated Machine Learning**, Azure Machine Learning designer, and Custom Vision can be found in this category. While this division into three different categories might seem intuitive, there are many overlaps between the services, such as the graphical model designer in Azure Machine Learning, and others.

The following pipeline is a typical choice of Azure Machine Learning and compute services in a real-world example for a predictive quality model that can be deployed on an on-premise edge device for stream processing:

- Track experiments, pipelines, trained models, and containers using Azure Machine Learning
- Run experiments in Azure Notebook using a DSVM
- Preprocess a large dataset using Azure Databricks
- Label the dataset using Custom Vision
- Create an object detection mode without code using Custom Vision
- Deploy the model to Azure IoT Edge

As you can see, there are many ways to combine services to build a pipeline. There are many different aspects to consider when choosing the best ML and compute services for an ML use case, which depend greatly on the problem statement, domain, team, skills, preferences, budget, and so on. Evaluating the trade-offs for every use case is an essential task when comparing the different services.

Choosing an Azure service for ML

Let's start with choosing a service for ML and hence, a service to implement, orchestrate, and augment your ML pipeline. The trade-offs are similar when evaluating a managed **Platform-as-a-Service (PaaS)** offering versus the more flexible **Infrastructure-as-a-Service (IaaS)** software. In general, the Azure Machine Learning can be ordered by increasing flexibility and operational effort. Here is a list in sorted order of its flexibility and operational effort:

- A fully managed service with pre-trained models for scoring only.
- A managed service with pre-trained models and customization through transfer learning.
- A managed service with GUI to experiment, build, train, and deploy models.
- A managed service to orchestrate compute resources and facilitate ML processes.
- Individual compute services to experiment, train, and deploy models.

Before we look into a decision tree that helps you to decide which service to use, you should think about the trade-off between flexibility and operational complexity.

Consuming an object detection algorithm through an API is many magnitudes easier, faster, and cheaper than training and deploying your own object detection model.

However, if you need the flexibility of choosing a specific model or algorithm that is not supported as a service (for example, segmentation), then you don't have a choice but to implement it on your own.

A good rule of thumb is to always prefer a managed and trained ML service when possible. If this is not possible, you should evaluate whether the ML algorithm can be consumed as a service and fine-tuned for your domain or if it has to be built from scratch. If the model has to be built, then the next step to consider is whether it should be done from within a GUI or programmatically. Ultimately, if the model is trained programmatically, you need to choose the underlying data storage and compute infrastructure. Our advice is to choose or build on top of pre-trained APIs and models whenever possible.

Figure 2.1 shows the guideline toward choosing the correct ML service according to the logic that we've just discussed:

```
Choosing an Azure
Machine Learning service
            │
            ▼
    Task and domain
    available in Cognitive Service? ──── Task available in Custom
            │                             Cognitive Service?
            │ no                                  │
            │                                     │           GUI tool?
         yes│                                     │ no ──────────┐
            │                                  yes│              │            Modeling knowledge?
            ▼                                     ▼              │ no ──────────┐
         Azure                               Customize         yes│              │
     Cognitive Service                    Cognitive Services     │              │ ─── yes ───┐
                                                                 ▼             no│            │
                                                               Azure            │            │
                                                          Machine Learning      ▼            │
                                                             designer      Azure Automated   │
                                                                           Machine Learning  ▼
                                                                                           Azure
                                                                                      Machine Learning
```

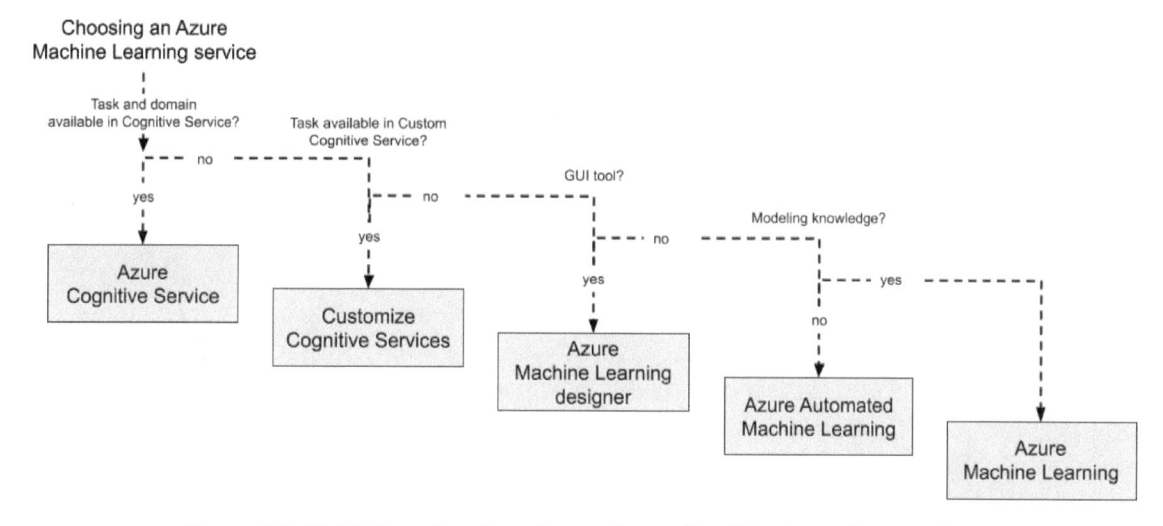

Figure 2.1: Guidelines for choosing an Azure Machine Learning service

According to the previous diagram, we are asking the following question: *Can you consume a pre-trained model or do you have to build a custom model on your own?*

This is the first and most important question to ask yourself. Does the ML problem you are trying to solve already exist, and did someone already solve it? If, for example, you want to detect faces in images, you could use an existing pre-trained model from the Cognitive Services API rather than building, training, and deploying this functionality on your own. As a rule of thumb, if you are working with vision, language (audio), or text, the chance is high that such a model already exists.

If you are building on top of an existing algorithm but for a specialized domain, you can use custom Cognitive Services to fine-tune a pre-trained model for your domain. If you want to detect faulty products on a production line using camera images, you can use Custom Vision for fine-tuning the Vision Cognitive Service API for the domain of your products. The same rule of thumb is true for custom Cognitive Services: if you are working with vision, language (audio), or text, the chance is high that such a model already exists and can be fine-tuned.

In both of the previous cases, you don't have to implement a full end-to-end ML pipeline on your own but rather can consume the service as a fully managed API or service. Likewise, when you are developing a completely new model, you have to manage your ML pipeline on your own. As a rule of thumb, if you are working with **Internet-of-Things (IoT)** sensor data (and you're doing more than statistical anomaly detection), you most likely need to build the prediction model on your own.

In Azure, you have various choices to build your end-to-end ML pipelines for training, optimizing, and deploying custom ML models:

- Build your own tools
- Use open source tools, such as Azure Databricks with ML Flow
- Use a GUI tool, such as Azure Machine Learning designer
- Use Azure Machine Learning

While we completely understand that it sounds like a lot of fun to build your custom solution on top of open source tools, or that it sounds easy to start with a GUI tool, we strongly advise you to first look into Azure Machine Learning. It is a really fantastic service that provides you with a common workspace for all your ML experiments, pipelines, compute resources, datasets, Conda environments, Docker images, and trained models, and a comprehensive SDK to interact with these resources. Hence, it is an excellent choice as your ML infrastructure service.

In Azure Machine Learning, you can decide between code-first usage through the Python SDK or a GUI tool Azure Machine Learning designer which is replacing the deprecated Azure ML Studio (classic) service. It's worth mentioning that the SDK is absolutely brilliant and offers more functionality than the GUI or the service accessed via the Azure portal. It also helps you a lot to automate and orchestrate your infrastructure. Hence, we strongly recommend you to build your ML infrastructure through the Azure Machine Learning SDK.

> **Note**
>
> If you are not a Python user, the Azure Machine Learning SDK is also available for the R language.

If you are still not convinced, let me give you a teaser of what you can do from within a Python script or Notebook with a few lines of code:

1. Create and start an auto-scaling training cluster using GPUs.
2. Submit multiple training experiments to the cluster and track their results.
3. Store the best models in the model registry.
4. Create an Azure Kubernetes cluster.

5. Deploy the best model from your experiments to the Kubernetes cluster.
6. Shut down and remove the GPU cluster.
7. Implement a **Continuous Integration/Continuous Deployment (CI/CD)** pipeline that does all the preceding points.

If this sounds intriguing, we strongly recommend you to read the book and follow all discussed code examples in the following chapters, as we will perform everything mentioned in the preceding steps.

Choosing a compute target for Azure Machine Learning

In a typical ML project, you easily move between exploring data, labeling data, preprocessing data, exploring models, training models, optimizing models, and deploying a scoring service. Hence it probably means that you need different compute services for the different stages in your ML pipeline, for example, training a deep learning image recognition model has different requirements than preprocessing image data and scoring the model for single images.

Before we jump into compute targets, we want to clarify two important terms that we will use frequently in this book. When using the Azure Machine Learning SDK, we usually deal with two different compute targets which both run a Python interpreter:

- The authoring runtime
- The execution runtime

The authoring runtime is a lightweight Python runtime used to call the Azure Machine Learning SDK and orchestrate your infrastructure. You usually use the authoring environment to create compute resources, trigger training runs, build environments, and deploy models. No real compute is done in this environment, and hence lightweight Python interpreters such as Visual Studio Code running Python locally, an Azure Notebook, or a single Azure Machine Learning compute instance are commonly used.

The execution environment, on the other hand, is used to execute your ML training or scoring code. The Python interpreter does the real work; you likely need a beefy machine if you want to train a deep learning model. You will often use Azure Machine Learning training cluster (also called **AML Compute**), **Azure Kubernetes Service (AKS)**, or **Azure Container Instance (ACI)** as execution environments.

In a typical workflow, you use an authoring environment to create a compute cluster (the execution environment) through the Azure Machine Learning SDK, and then submit the training script to this cluster again using the Azure Machine Learning SDK. Here is a tiny example:

1. First, we create a cluster and deploy an ML training script to that cluster. This is the code we would run in the authoring environment:

    ```
    from azureml.core.compute import ComputeTarget, AmlCompute
    from azureml.core.compute_target import ComputeTargetException
    from azureml.train.estimator import Estimator

    # Create the cluster
    config = AmlCompute.provisioning_configuration(
        vm_size='STANDARD_D2_V2', max_nodes=4)
    cluster = ComputeTarget.create(ws, "cluster", config)
    cluster.wait_for_completion(show_output=True)

    # Submit the training script to the cluster
    estimator = Estimator(
        compute_target=cluster, entry_script='train.py',
        conda_packages=['tensorflow'])
    run = experiment.submit(estimator)
    run.wait_for_completion(show_output=True)
    ```

    As you can see in the preceding code, we create **AmlCompute** cluster with 4 nodes. Then we submit an experiment to this cluster, which is an abstraction of an environment and a training script, **train.py**. Under the hood, Azure Machine Learning will do all the work for us to create the cluster, schedule the script and return the results.

2. On the execution environment, the Python interpreter will now run the **train.py** script. This is how the script would look and what work would be done in the execution environment. First, we pre-process the training data and convert labels to one-hot encoded feature vectors:

    ```
    import keras

    # Normalize training data
    x_train = x_train.astype('float32')
    x_test = x_test.astype('float32')
    x_train /= 255
    x_test /= 255
    ```

```
# Convert class vectors to binary class matrices.
y_train = keras.utils.to_categorical(y_train, num_classes)
y_test = keras.utils.to_categorical(y_test, num_classes)
```

3. Next, we build a simple **Convolutional Neural Network (CNN)** architecture, using a two-dimensional convolution with pooling, a fully connected hidden layer, and softmax output (we will discuss similar architectures in more detail in Chapter 8, *Training deep neural networks on Azure*:

```
from keras.models import Sequential
from keras.layers import Dense, Dropout, Activation, Flatten
from keras.layers import Conv2D, MaxPooling2D

model = Sequential()
model.add(Conv2D(32, (3, 3), input_shape=x_train.shape[1:]))
model.add(Activation('relu'))
model.add(MaxPooling2D(pool_size=(2, 2)))
model.add(Flatten())
model.add(Dense(128))
model.add(Activation('relu'))
model.add(Dense(num_classes))
model.add(Activation('softmax'))
```

4. Next, we define an optimizer and a learning rate, and compile the Keras model:

```
# initiate RMSprop optimizer
opt = keras.optimizers.rmsprop(lr=0.0001, decay=1e-6)
model.compile(loss='categorical_crossentropy',
  optimizer=opt,
metrics=['accuracy'])
```

5. Finally, we can train and evaluate the model:

```
model.fit(x_train, y_train, batch_size=batch_size, epochs=epochs,
validation_data=(x_test, y_test), shuffle=True)

# Score trained model
scores = model.evaluate(x_test, y_test) print('Test loss:', scores[0])
```

In the preceding code, we build a simple Keras CNN and fit it using the RMSProp optimizer. Here is where all the work is done regarding the training of the ML model – in the execution environment.

> **Note**
> It's worth noting that you can train your models on your own (such as by using PySpark in Azure Databricks) in the authoring runtime and use the Azure Machine Learning only to track experiments and models.

If you are working in Azure, popular choices for compute are the following:

- **Authoring runtime**:
  - **Experimentation**: Azure Notebooks (example, with DSVM or shared compute)
  - **Training**: An Azure Machine Learning compute instance
- **Execution runtime**:
  - **Training and optimization**: An Azure Machine Learning training cluster
  - **Deployment**: Azure Kubernetes Service

As you can see, picking the right compute service is not that simple because it depends on the current task you are performing. You should always try to find the right trade-off between flexibility and costs. This overview should help you to pick the correct service for either running your authoring or execution environment for training custom ML model using Azure Machine Learning as your infrastructure service. In the next section, we will take a look into how we can leverage pre-trained models as a service without worrying about any infrastructure or compute target.

Azure Cognitive Services and Custom Vision

If you are dealing with a well-defined general ML problem, such as classification, object or face detection in computer vision, **Optical Character Recognition** (**OCR**) and handwriting recognition, speech-to-text and text-to-speech, translation, spell-checking, key word and entity extraction, or sentiment analysis, the chances are high that these services have already been implemented and battle-tested in Azure. In a lot of cases, it greatly saves you time, resources, and effort by reusing these services instead of training similar models from scratch.

If your problem space is very general—such as detecting and matching faces from a camera image to an ID image—or detecting adult content in user-uploaded media, then you can look into Cognitive Services. The Cognitive Services website features demos for almost all the APIs and you can go and try them out for your use case.

If your domain is very specific but uses one of the previously discussed algorithms, it is very likely that you can use a custom Cognitive Service, that is, a pre-trained Cognitive Service model fine-tuned for your customized domain. This works very well in general for image classification and object detection, for example, for detecting manufacturing errors and automated quality control. Using such a customized model is a good trade-off between costs, resources, and effort. Due to fine-tuning, these models usually result in a fairly good performance with a low number of training samples, which is optimal for a small **Proof of Concept (PoC)**.

Azure Cognitive Services

Cognitive Services is a collection of APIs for pre-trained ML models divided into six categories: Vision, Speech, Knowledge, Search, Language, and Anomaly Detection. They implement well-defined common problems in these categories, such as image classification, speech-to-text, anomaly detection, and many more. Cognitive Service models can be consumed using a REST API from any programming language.

In general, it is a best practice to not reinvent the wheel and hence to reuse functionality that is already available. It will most likely be more efficient to use the Face Detection API from the Azure Cognitive Services than to build a complete and continuous end-to-end ML pipeline and train the same model from scratch. While it is a lot easier to use the Cognitive Services API instead, your application requires an internet connection to reach the API.

The following is a simple example for calling the Cognitive Services API for computer vision. We will use the Analyze Image API to extract categories, tags, and description from the image:

```python
import requests

def cs_vision_analyze(img_url, key, features=['Tags'], ...):
    endpoint = 'https://%s.api.cognitive.microsoft.com' % region
    baseurl = '%s/vision/v1.0/analyze' % endpoint
    headers = {'Content-Type': 'application/json',
        'Ocp-Apim-Subscription-Key': key}
    params = {'visualFeatures': ','.join(features), 'language': lang}
    payload = {'url': img_url}

    r = requests.post(baseurl, json=payload, params=params, headers=headers)
    return r.json()


url = 'https://..Tour_Eiffel_Wikimedia_Commons.jpg'
key = '<insert subscription key>'
features = ['Categories', 'Tags', 'Description']
res = cs_vision_analyze(url, key, features=features)
print(res)
```

As you can see in the preceding code example, using Cognitive Services boils down to sending an HTTP request. In Python, this is straightforward using the fantastic **requests** library. The response body contains standard JSON and encodes the results of the Cognitive Service API. The resulting JSON output from the API will have the following structure:

```
{
    "categories": [...],
    "tags": [...],
    "description"" {...},
    "requestId": "...",
    "metadata":
    {
```

```
        "width": 288,
        "height": 480,
        "format": "Jpeg"
    }
}
```

The **categories** key contains object categories and derived classifications, such as a landmark detection result including a confidence score:

```
"categories":
[
    {
        "name": "building_",
        "score": 0.9453125,
        "detail":
          {
            "landmarks":
              [
                {
                    "name": "Eiffel Tower",
                    "confidence": 0.99992179870605469
                }
              ]
          }
    }
]
```

The **tags** key shows you multiple tags for the image with a confidence score that is relevant for the whole image:

```
"tags": [
    {
        "name": "outdoor",
        "confidence": 0.99838995933532715
    },
    {
        "name": "tower",
        "confidence": 0.63238395233132431
    }, ...
]
```

Finally, the **description** tag gives you more tags and an auto-generated image caption—isn't that amazing?

```
"description":
{
  "tags":
  [
      "outdoor", "building", "tower", ...
  ],
  "captions":
  [
      {
          "text": "a large clock tower in the background with Eiffel Tower in the background",
          "confidence": 0.74846089195278742
      }
  ]
}
```

The result of the Cognitive Services computer vision API is just one example of how this service can be used. We requested the image features of **categories**, **tags**, and **description** from the API, which are returned as keys of the JSON object. Each of the category and tag predictions returns the top results in combination with a confidence value. Some categories might trigger other detection models, such as faces, handwritten text recognition, and OCR. From the preceding example, you can see that it would be straightforward to automatically add image captions to your product images in a retail application using the following code:

```
for url in product_image_urls:
    res = cs_vision_analyze(url, key, features=['Description'])
    caption = res['description']['captions'][0]['text']
    print (caption)
```

You can see that this is the fastest way to implement/use a scalable deep learning-based image analysis service, such as creating a caption for an image. It takes you literally no more than five minutes to integrate this functionality into your own application. However, you also see that you can only use the functionalities (for example, labels in classification) that are provided by Microsoft. A good example is object detection or instance segmentation in medical images. There doesn't exist any out-of-the-box model for these use cases in the computer vision API of Cognitive Services. In this case, you can still benefit from Cognitive Services by customizing the model for your specific domain – this is exactly what Custom Vision does for common computer vision tasks.

Custom Vision—customizing the Cognitive Services API

Many developers find Cognitive Services pretty useful but limited in terms of the application domain. Here are two common examples showing this limitation:

- For a plastics manufacturer, the class labels offered by the object detection API doesn't cover all of their product categories.

- For a service dealing with transcribing medical records, many of the medical terms are not recognized or are transcribed incorrectly.

You can customize an increasing amount of ML services in Azure. The following customizable Cognitive Services are available at the time of writing this book:

- Custom Vision (classification and object detection)
- Customizable speech recognition and transcription
- Customizable voices for text-to-speech
- Customizable translation
- Custom intent and entity recognition in text

In these situations, you can still benefit from the ease of use, technology and service infrastructure behind Cognitive Services. Custom Cognitive Services let you train your models on top of existing Cognitive Service models by using transfer learning. For computer vision services, you are offered a nice UI to classify your images and tag your objects, and subsequently train the model using a state-of-the-art model and error metrics. *Figure 2.2* shows what the training looks like in the Custom Vision service for object detection:

Figure 2.2: A custom Vision service for object detection

You can see in *Figure 2.2* that training is as easy as clicking the Train button in the top right. You don't have to write any code or select an error metric to be optimized, it's all managed for you. In the screenshot you see the result of training, with three metrics that are automatically computed on a validation set. By moving the classification probability threshold on the top left, you can even shift the weight toward higher precision or higher recall depending on whether you want to avoid false positives or maximize true positives.

Once the model is trained and published, it can be consumed using a REST API like we did with Cognitive Services. The following code block is a sample snippet for Python using the **requests** library:

```python
import requests


def cs_custom_vision(img_url, key, project_id, iteration_name, ...):
    endpoint = 'https://%s.api.cognitive.microsoft.com' % region
    url = '%s/customvision/v3.0/Prediction/%s/detect/iterations/%s/url' \
% (endpoint, project_id, iteration_name)
    headers = {'Content-Type': 'application/json', 'Prediction-Key': key}
    payload = {'url': img_url}
    r = requests.post(url, json=payload, headers=headers)
    return r.json()
```

In the preceding code, we implement a function that looks very similar to the one we used with Cognitive Services. In fact, only the endpoints and **requests** parameter have changed. We can now call the function as before:

```python
url = 'https://..Wood_Plate.jpg'
key = '<insert custom vision key>'
project_id = '00ae2d88-a767-4ff6-ba5f-33cdf4817c44'
iteration_name = 'Iteration2'
res = cs_custom_vision(url, key, project_id, iteration_name)
print(res)
```

The response is also a JSON object and now looks like the following:

```
{
    "Id":"7796df8e-acbc-45fc-90b4-1b0c81b73639",
    "Project":"00ae2d88-a767-4ff6-ba5f-33cdf4817c44",
    "Iteration":"59ec199d-f3fb-443a-b708-4bca79e1b7f7",
    "Created":"2019-03-20T16:47:31.322Z",
    "Predictions":
    [
        {
            "TagId":"d9cb3fa5-1ff3-4e98-8d47-2ef42d7fb373",
            "TagName":"defect",
            "Probability":1.0
        },
        {
            "TagId":"9a8d63fb-b6ed-4462-bcff-77ff72084d99",
            "TagName":"defect",
            "Probability":0.1087869
        }
    ]
}
```

The preceding response now contains a **Predictions** key with all the predictions and confidence values from Custom Vision. As you can see, the example looks very similar to the Cognitive Services example. However, we need to pass arguments to specify the project and published iteration of the trained model. Using this built-in serving API we save ourselves a lot of effort in implementing and operating a deployment infrastructure. However, if we want to use the trained model somewhere else (for example, in an iPhone or Android application, or in a Kubernetes cluster), we can export the model in many different formats (including Tensorflow, CoreML, ONNX, and so on).

Custom Cognitive Services are a fantastic way to efficiently test or showcase an ML model for a custom application domain when dealing with a well-defined ML problem. You can use either the GUI or API to interact with these services and consume the models through a managed API or export them to any device platform. Another benefit is that you don't need deep ML expertise to apply the transfer learning algorithm, and can simply use the predefined models and error metrics.

If you require full customization of the algorithms, models, and error metrics, you need to implement the model and ML pipeline on your own. In the following sections, we will discuss how this can be done using either GUI or code-first tools.

Azure Machine Learning with GUIs

Azure provides a few great tools with GUIs that can be used to directly train and deploy a data pipeline and ML model or reuse this functionality from a different service.

We will look into three different services: Azure Machine Learning designer, Azure Automated Machine Learning, and Power BI. From these three services, only Azure Machine Learning designer is a traditional GUI-based service with which you can customize data pipelines, transformations, feature extraction, and ML model validations in an interactive block-based environment.

The other two services are both based on the power of the Automated Machine Learning engine, which we can access either through the Automated Machine Learning GUI, through an SDK, or through Power Query transformations in Power BI. Automated Machine Learning provides fantastic capabilities to create powerful ML models using zero code. Let's take a look at the individual services, how they are used, and how they compare to each other.

Azure Machine Learning designer

Azure Machine Learning designer is replacing the deprecated yet widely adopted Azure ML Studio (classic) service to build, train, optimize, and deploy ML models using a GUI. It provides a robust and large amount of features, algorithms, and extensions through R and Python support. It's a fantastic no-code environment in which to build complex ML models for clustering, regression, classification, anomaly detection, and recommendation models as well as data, statistical, and text analysis.

The main interface in Azure Machine Learning designer lets you build ML models by connecting functional blocks to the graph of operations. *Figure 2.3* shows an overview of the interface. It's easy to get started, pull in functional blocks from the left to read in data, preprocess data, perform feature selection, or use an ML algorithm for model training:

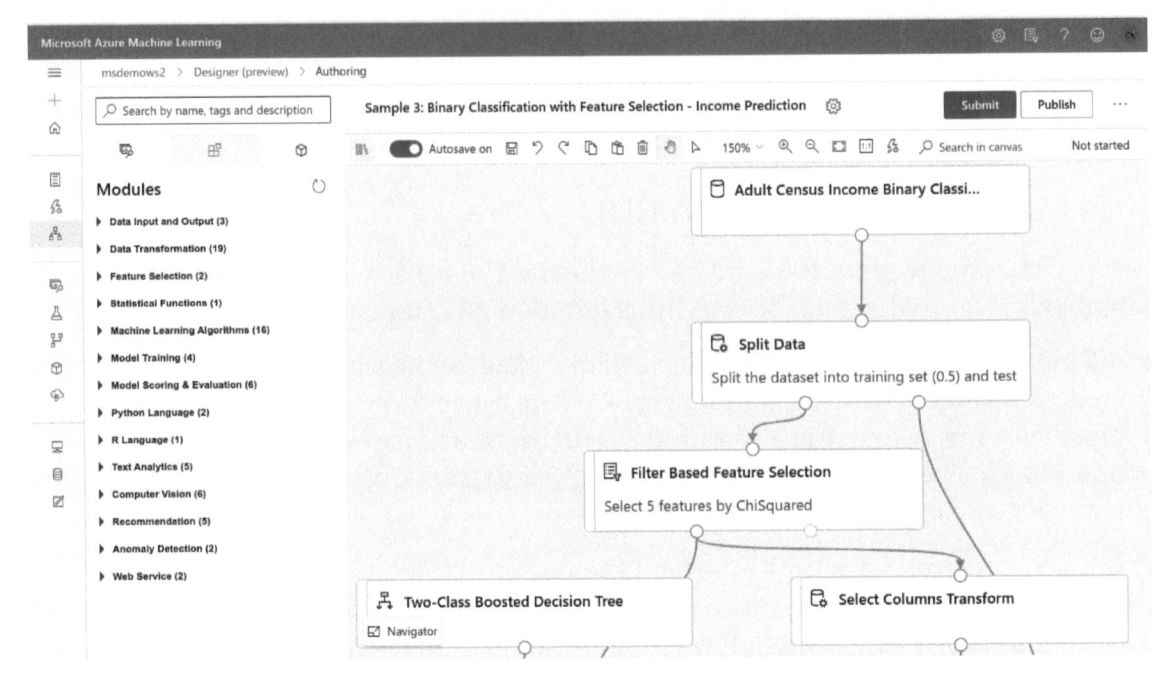

Figure 2.3: An overview of the main interface in Azure Machine Learning designer

In *Figure 2.3*, we can see the default view when opening a project. Once we put all blocks in place and connect them using the block connections, we can press **SUBMIT** to evaluate the graph of operations. This will spin compute resources for you and train the model for you – you only have to specify your compute instances.

Azure Machine Learning designer lets you easily import data from many different sources, and many from within Azure. Loading a CSV file from Blob Storage is just a click away. It also provides many powerful conversions for data formats and data types, normalization, and cleaning blocks.

As more and more functional block modules get added to your workspace, you can create complex data preprocessing, model training, and validation pipelines. *Figure 2.4* shows a typical pipeline for a regression model using a Linear Regression block. First we read the data, clean it, and split it into training and testing sets. We use the training set to train the regression model and the testing data score and evaluate it.

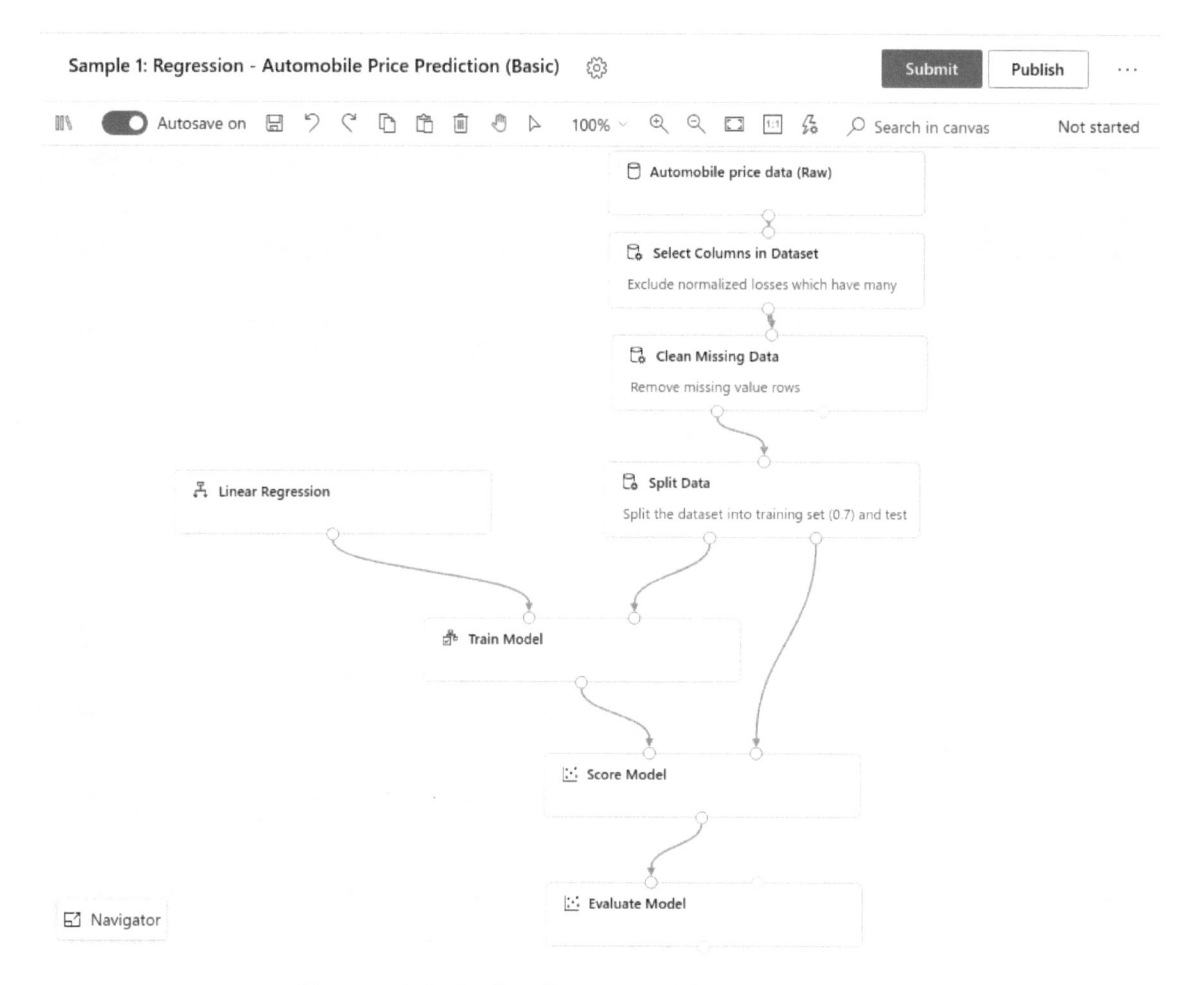

Figure 2.4: A pipeline for Automobile Price Prediction

As you can see in Figure 2.4, while it is nice to structure your data flow in functional blocks, the whole workspace can get quite convoluted and hard to reason with. You can also extend the functionality of Azure Machine Learning designer by using custom code blocks for Python or R. We actually used two Rscript blocks in the preceding data flow. This is very convenient as we can now build reusable blocks of abstracted functionality.

In each Python code block, we define a function that takes up to two Pandas DataFrames as inputs and can output the transformed dataset. This is the skeleton of the Python code block function where we need to define the transformation code:

```python
# imports up here can be used to
import pandas as pd


# The entry point function can contain up to two input arguments:
# Param<dataframe1>: a pandas.DataFrame
# Param<dataframe2>: a pandas.DataFrame
def azureml_main(df_1 = None, df_2 = None):

    # Return value must be of a sequence of pandas.DataFrame
    return df_1,
```

One of the reasons why Azure Machine Learning designer is very popular lies in its deployment capabilities. If you have created a data pipeline and trained a model, you can save the trained model within your Azure Machine Learning workspace. Now, within a few clicks you can create a web service using this model to either retrain the model with new data or deploy a scoring service. The user input is defined through the very same data import block that we used previously for the training data. We then connect the user input with the trained model, score the model, and return the output to the web service. With another click you can deploy the pipeline to production using a web service plan. It's literally 5 minutes of work and a couple of clicks to deploy a trained model, which is absolutely convenient.

Azure Machine Learning designer is a great tool if you want to get started quickly building complex workflows and preconfigured ML models in a GUI environment and deploy them as services to production. Despite being used by many companies, I don't think it is the best tool to implement ML models in Azure for complex end-to-end workflows. The models and blocks are too difficult to use properly for people with no coding or ML experience, and not flexible enough for those people with experience. Therefore, it sits in a difficult spot and is often misused by users who don't know exactly what they are doing.

However, not knowing about ML shouldn't stop users from training ML models using the right tools. I just think there are better tools that fit this audience – and one of those is definitely Automated Machine Learning, which provides a better level of abstraction to non-experienced users. Let's take a look!

Azure Automated Machine Learning

Users that have no experience with training ML models should not have to choose, parameterize, or configure algorithms for training. At the same time, everyone should be given the possibility to create a prediction model for a conforming dataset. In the democratization of AI we aim to give every user that can use a spreadsheet application the possibility to train ML models on a specified region of data in the spreadsheet. But how should this be done if a user has no or limited knowledge about ML?

Azure Automated Machine Learning to the rescue! Azure Automated Machine Learning is a no-code tool that lets you specify a dataset, a target column, and ML tasks to train an ML model for you. That's what we think is a great abstraction for a user who just wants to fit training data to a target variable. *Figure* 2.5 shows the last step in the Automated Machine Learning interface, where the user needs to choose the ML task to be solved for the specified data:

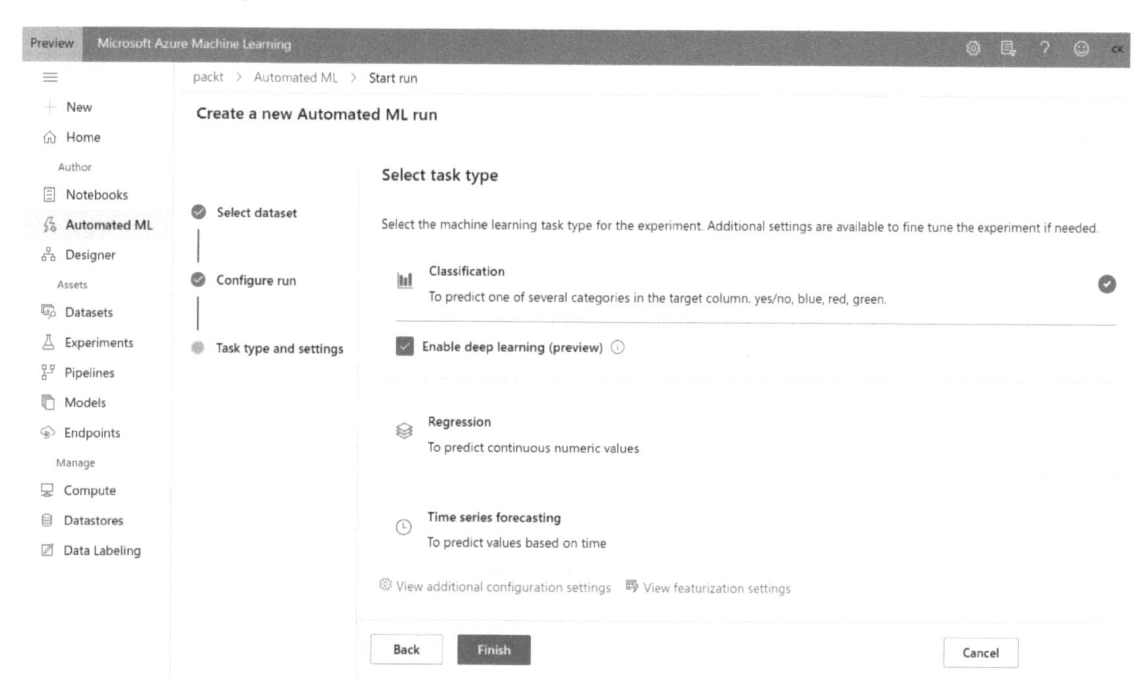

Figure 2.5: Creating an Automated Machine Learning run

As we see in *Figure* 2.5, Automated Machine Learning currently supports classification, regression, and time series forecasting tasks. Together with the informative explanations for each task, this is something we can put into the hands of ordinary Excel users or help ML engineers to quickly build and deploy a great baseline model. We will see this in much more detail in *Chapter 10, Distributed machine learning on Azure*.

58 | Choosing a machine learning service in Azure

However, to get you excited already, you can see in *Figure 2.6*, some additional output that you get in Automated Machine Learning for each tested and optimized model. Automated Machine Learning gives you access to all training runs, all trained models and their performances, and useful metrics and insights, such as the ROC curve, the gain curve, and a confusion matrix (the latter in the case of a classification task):

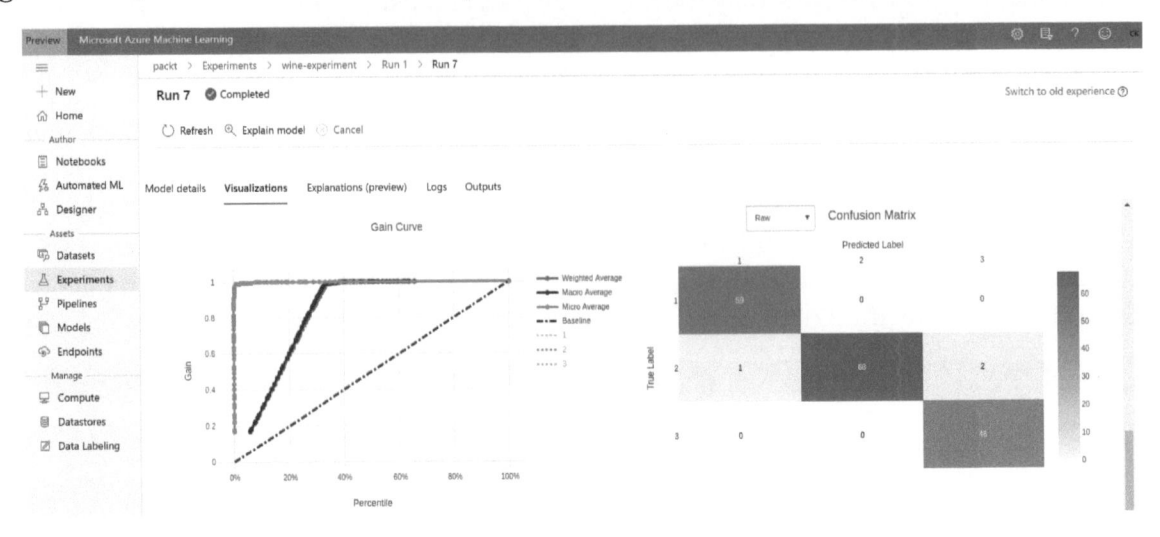

Figure 2.6: Additional output for each tested and optimized model using Automated Machine Learning

> **Note**
>
> Automated Machine Learning is also provided through the Azure Machine Learning SDK in Python. There you have the same functionality available directly from your authoring environment.

Automated Machine Learning is a fantastic milestone in providing a true ML-as-a-Service platform with a great abstraction for non-experienced and highly skilled users. This service will power the AI capabilities in tomorrow's products. What if automated training of ML models would be available as a single button in Excel, such as a single button to transform a given data range using Automated Machine Learning? While this sounds really cool, it is already reality in the Power Query transformation view of Power BI – the same thing that also powers Excel's data transformation capabilities. We will see what this looks like in action in the following section.

Microsoft Power BI

Microsoft Power BI is a fantastic self-service **Business Intelligence (BI)** tool that can connect to multiple data sources, load, transform, and join data there, and create custom visualization and insights. It looks and feels just like another Microsoft Office tool, similar to using Excel or PowerPoint. This makes it a self-service BI tool as it is very easy to use, fast, and extremely flexible.

Power BI or actually the Power Query editor of Power BI Service premium—the Power BI online service—has a very similar Automated Machine Learning interface built in as we just saw in the previous section. In fact, they are based on the same Automated Machine Learning engine that can be now configured through multiple services and the Automated Machine Learning package of the Azure Machine Learning SDK. This gives us access to all of the capabilities of Automated Machine Learning directly within Power BI for data transformations based on classification or regression tasks.

Figure 2.7 shows an overview of the Automated Machine Learning view in Power BI after selecting the **Add a machine learning model** action in the entities view. At the time of writing, this feature is only available as a preview in the Power BI premium online service:

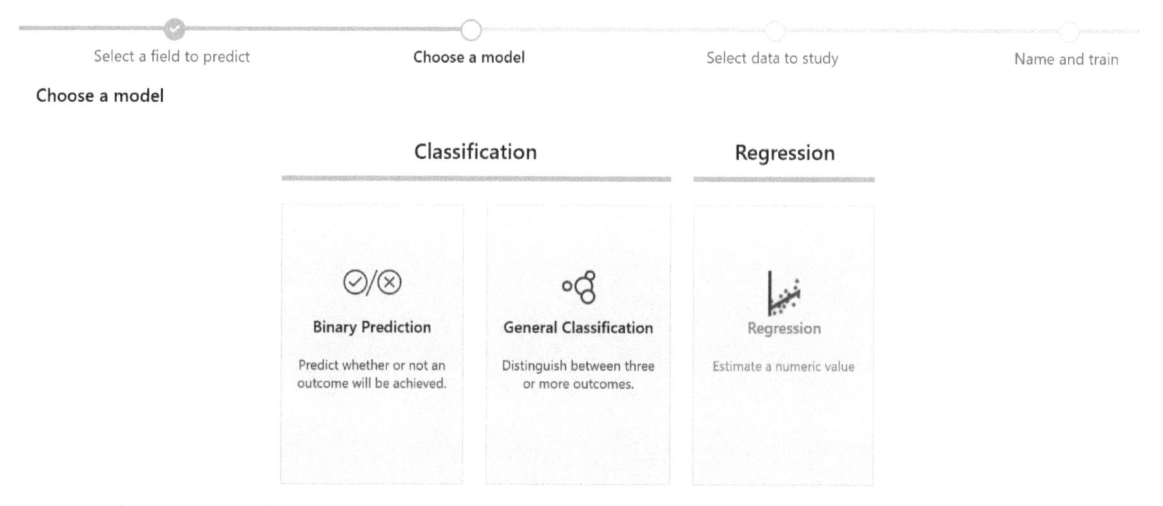

Figure 2.7: Adding a machine learning model using Power BI premium online service

While I understand that you won't start training your models in Power BI using Automated Machine Learning right now, it is important to know what is currently possible and what the trends are for the future. And one thing is for sure: the democratization of AI and ML for ordinary office users is advancing fast.

If you found the GUI tools interesting, but you're aiming to create your custom ML code using your own frameworks and training code, then the best service to support you is Azure Machine Learning.

Azure Machine Learning workspace

Azure Machine Learning is the newest member of the ML service family in Azure. It was initially built as an umbrella to combine all other ML services under a single workspace, and hence is also often referred to as the Azure Machine Learning workspace. Currently, it provides, combines, and abstracts many important ML infrastructure services and functionality such as tracking experiment runs and outputs, a model registry, an environment and container registry based on Conda and Docker, a dataset registry, pipelines, compute and storage infrastructure, and much more.

Besides all of the infrastructure services, it also integrates Azure Automated Machine Learning, Azure Machine Learning designer (, and a data-labeling UI in a single workspace that can share the same infrastructure resources. It is, in fact, the ML service that you are looking for if you want to do something serious. In many cases, it does all you can ask for and more. In this section, we will look primarily at the ML infrastructure functionality.

While Azure Machine Learning provides a great new UI (which unfortunately is called **Machihne Learning Studio and should not be confused with ML Studio classic**), we will mostly use its functionality through the SDK instead. We will use the Python SDK in order to run the orchestration commands in an environment that we are already using for data visualization and exploration in a Jupyter notebook. *Figure 2.8* shows the UI of Azure Machine Learning in the Azure portal:

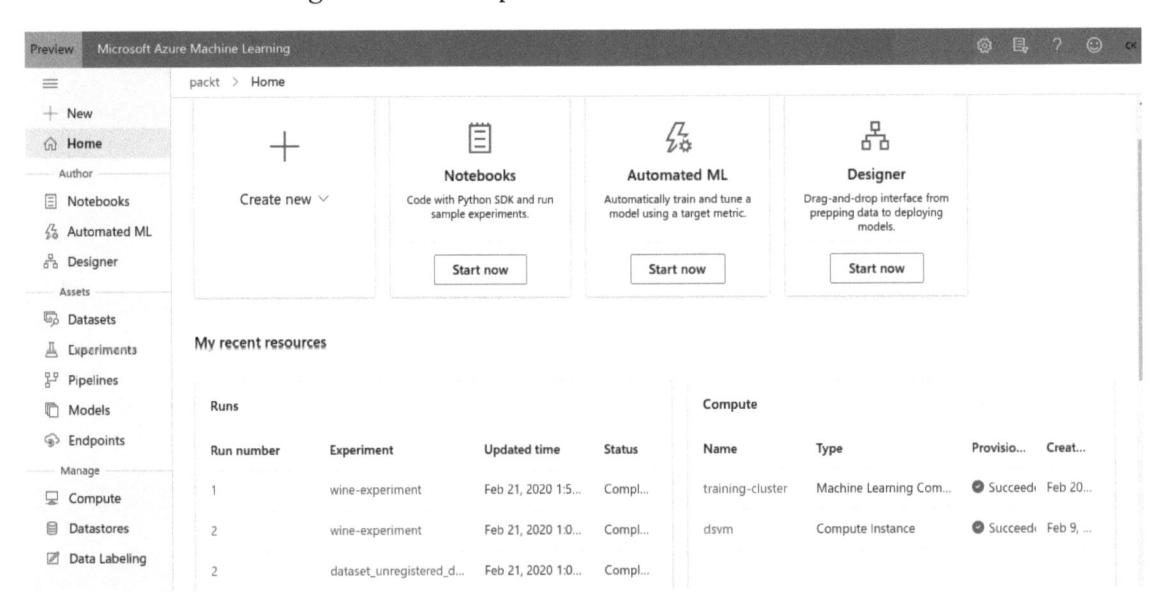

Figure 2.8: The UI of Azure Machine Learning in the Azure portal

In Azure Machine Learning, we can easily manage different compute resources through the UI and SDK. Most of the time, we will use three types of compute resources throughout the different steps in the ML process:

- **A compute instance for the authoring runtime and Jupyter**: This is similar to a DSVM.

- **An auto-scaling training cluster for the ML execution runtime during training**: This is an Azure Machine Learning compute cluster.

- **An inferencing cluster for the execution runtime during scoring**: This is a managed Kubernetes cluster using Azure Kubernetes Service.

It's worth mentioning that each of those services can be created from Python using the SDK in less than 10 lines of code. The same is true for storage resources. We can use the ML SDK to manage Blob Storage containers in the ML workspace. This is very neat as it allows us to efficiently store outputs from training runs, artifacts such as trained models or training scripts, dataset snapshots, and much more.

Besides managing infrastructure, Azure Machine Learning can do a lot more for us. Most importantly, it can track our experiment runs and collect output files, artifacts, logs and custom metrics—such as training loss and more. This is by far the most powerful gateway drug into the Azure Machine Learning world. By simply annotating your existing ML project, you can track all your model scores – even during the training per epoch – stream your log output, collect all your output images, and collect and store the best model for each iteration or run. This is like magic, as with a few simple statements you won't lose a model for a particular training run ever again and you can keep track of training losses per run.

Datasets, environments, and models can be tracked and versioned in Azure Machine Learning using a few lines of code. This gives you the great benefit of being able to keep a predictable history of changes in your workspace. By doing this you can create repeatable experiments that always read the same data snapshot for a training run, use the same specified Conda environment, and update the trained model in the model history and artifact store. This brings you on track toward a CI/CD approach for your training pipeline.

Speaking of pipelines, Azure Machine Learning lets you abstract pieces of authoring code into pipelines. A pipeline could run data preparation jobs in parallel, create and start training clusters, and execute a training script on the cluster. You can see how everything guides you toward a repeatable, versioned, end-to-end pipeline for your training process. The greatest part, however, is that you don't have to go all-in to benefit from Azure Machine Learning.

Instead, you can start little by little, adding more and more useful things into the training process and then gradually move an existing or new ML project to the Azure Machine Learning workspace. We will take a brief look at the deployment capabilities of Azure Machine Learning in *Chapter 12, Deploying and operating machine learning models*.

Let's first explore how you can track experiments in Azure Machine Learning, before seeing how we can train models using our own frameworks and tools.

Organizing experiments and models in Azure Machine Learning

Azure Machine Learning provides you with all necessary infrastructure and service so that you as a user can concentrate on writing implementing your ML code. The easiest way to start using Azure Machine Learning and experience its capabilities is to start organizing your training experiments and runs in Azure Machine Learning. Through a few small changes, you can get real-time training insights, tracking performance per run, exported logs, exported outputs, and tracked and versioned trained models. The best part is that this works on any machine on any Python interpreter.

Figure 2.9 gives you a good reference for what you can expect. Simply getting all your experiment runs tracked and collected at a single place. The view is fully configurable, with metrics on the left, charts on the top, and the table on the bottom can be configured to your liking. And you get all this (and a lot more) by not changing anything to do with your current behavior by simply adding a few lines of code to your training script:

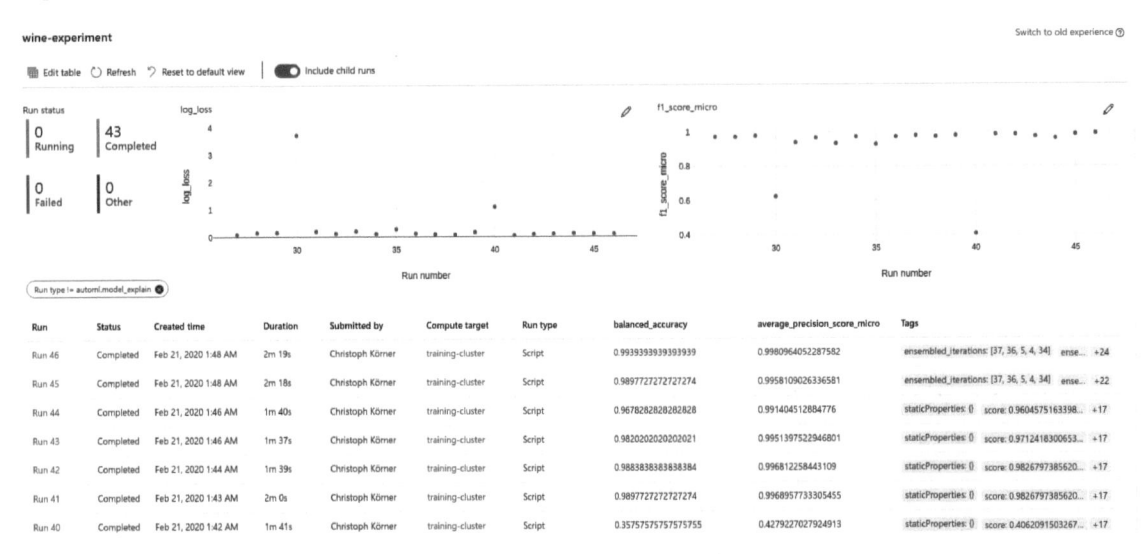

Figure 2.9: Organizing experiments and models in Azure Machine Learning

You can see in *Figure 2.9*, all your ML experiment runs tracked. You see automatic parameters such as training duration, when it started, what's the status, and how the run performed. Besides that, you can send custom metrics, tags, and a lot more. We will hopefully cover all possibilities throughout this book, but it's worth mentioning that you can get from no tracking in your code to the preceding screenshot in 10 minutes.

> **Note**
>
> By start using Azure Machine Learning you don't have to change anything in your current workflow, but simplify your life by using the tracking and logging features for experiment runs, metrics, logs, and models.

In Azure Machine Learning, your ML tasks are organized as experiments. Each experiment now can have multiple runs, and run output and metrics will be aggregated per experiment. Hence, if you are trying to implement a credit score prediction service, you can call your experiment **credit-score-regression**. Here is an example of how to add this information to your Python project using Azure Machine Learning. Please note that all experiments and runs that don't yet exist will automatically be created for you by default:

```
from azureml.core import Workspace, Experiment


# Configure workspace and experiment
ws = Workspace.from_config()
exp = Experiment(workspace=ws, name="credit-score-regression")
```

Next, you experiment with different features, models, and parameters and hence we want to track all these efforts to see which one was the best. This is called a *run* in Azure Machine Learning; to start a run and to track a few epochs of our training we add the following code to the project:

```
run = exp.start_logging()


for i in range(1, n_epochs):
  loss = model.train_epoch(...)
  run.log('loss (train)', loss)
```

The preceding code will now send all loss values per iteration to Azure Machine Learning and make these values available under the run. What is really amazing here is that we can either send the same metric with multiple values (as we just saw) or with a single value (in the next example). When sending multiple values like the training loss per epoch, Azure Machine Learning automatically creates a visualization for you – when sending a single value, it will show as a single value in the UI and use the value for the runs in the overview table and in aggregations. Per the default configuration, Azure Machine Learning will show you (for example) the max accuracy from all of your training runs in the overview if you add accuracy as a single metric in your run. The following snippet shows how to log a single metric:

```
# Save model scores
scores = model.evaluate(X_test, y_test, verbose=1)
run.log('accurcay (test)', scores[1])
```

This section is non-exhaustive; we won't cover everything Azure Machine Learning can track. However, it's essential to mention that you can track any additional outputs of your pipeline similar to how we collect metrics. The following snippet shows you how to track a trained model that has previously been saved to disk:

```
# Upload the best model
run.upload_file(model_name, model_path)
```

The file you want to save doesn't need to be a trained model, it can be anything that you want to save additionally with your run. Please note that the run can be configured to automatically upload your current training script, collect everything from an outputs folder, and stream everything from a logs folder to Azure Machine Learning. However, if the artifact is a model, you can also register this model in the model registry. Again, this is one simple command to track your trained model, which will be automatically connected with the run:

```
# Register the best model
run.register_model(model_name, model_path=model_name,
    model_framework='TfKeras')
```

We don't necessarily need to specify additional information, such as the framework used for training the model. However, if we do so we will get many additional benefits including, model explanations, no-code deployments, and much more. We will see more of this in *Chapter 7, Building ML models using Azure Machine Learning*, and *Chapter 12, Deploying and operating machine learning models*, respectively.

In *Figure 2.10*, you see what you get when uploading and registering a model with your run: a central place where your models are linked with your experiment runs and their metrics. You won't ever lose a trained model again, nor run out of disk space to save trained models, nor have to remember which parameters were used to train this model or what the test performance was like during that run, among many other things:

Run 42 ✓ Completed

↻ Refresh   ⊕ Explain model   ⊘ Cancel

Model details | Visualizations | Explanations (preview) | Logs | Outputs

Properties

Algorithm name
StandardScalerWrapper, LightGBM

Primary metric
Accuracy

Score
0.9826797385620916

Sdk version
1.1.0rc0

Deploy status
No deployment yet

[Deploy model]   [Download model]

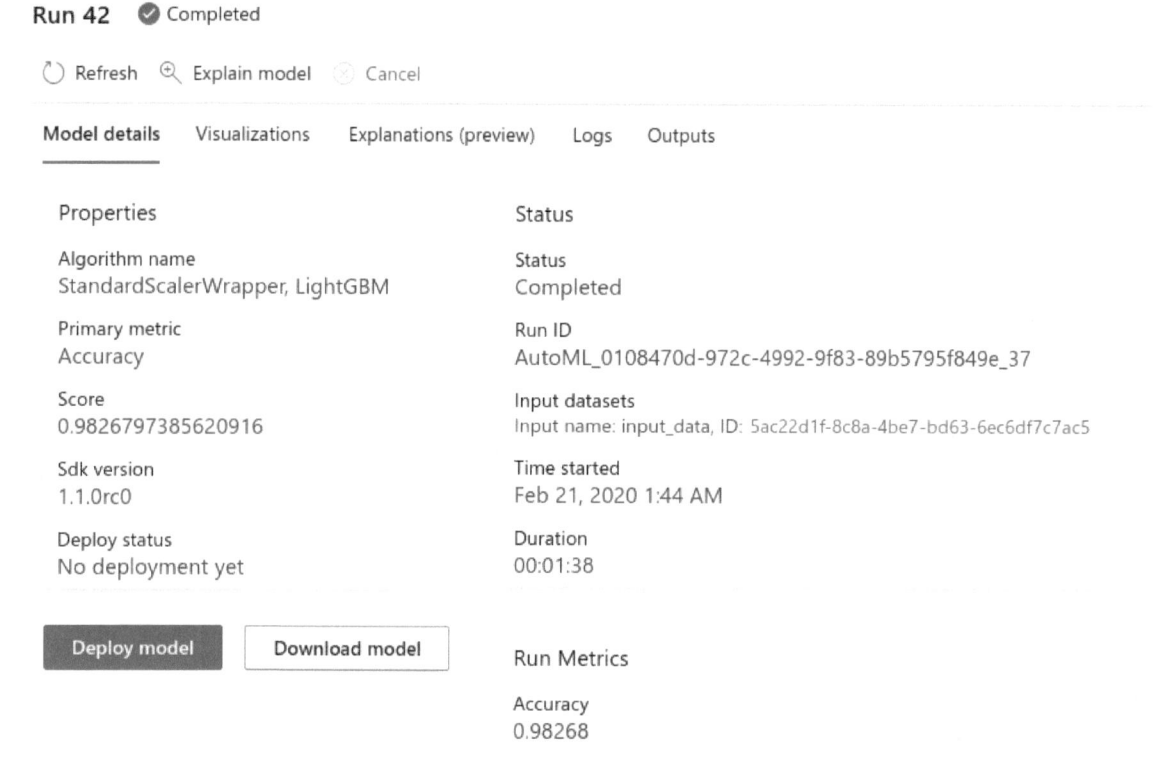

Status

Status
Completed

Run ID
AutoML_0108470d-972c-4992-9f83-89b5795f849e_37

Input datasets
Input name: input_data, ID: 5ac22d1f-8c8a-4be7-bd63-6ec6df7c7ac5

Time started
Feb 21, 2020 1:44 AM

Duration
00:01:38

Run Metrics

Accuracy
0.98268

Figure 2.10: Details of the uploaded and registered model in Azure Machine Learning

In the summary of a run, we can also find a button to directly deploy a model. With a few more clicks or just three lines of code in Python, we can get from a training run to a trained model, and on to a model deployed as a container service in the cloud. It allows you to turn a model into a scoring service in seconds. This is simply impressive and there are so many great benefits from this—imagine serving all your trained models effortlessly in a staging environment, being able to run end-to-end testing on your models, and using fully automated CI/CD pipelines.

Deployments through Azure Machine Learning

We hope you've got a good impression of what is possible with Azure Machine Learning, and we have covered only a tiny part of its functionality. However, the same is true for all other features – Azure Machine Learning solves your infrastructure problems and lets you focus on developing great data pipelines, feature extractors, and predictive models. This becomes extremely obvious when looking at the deployment features of Azure Machine Learning.

In Azure Machine Learning, we broadly differentiate between two types of deployments:

- The first type is deploying trained models as a web service for online scoring. We can automatically deploy models to Azure Kubernetes Services to benefit from containerization, auto-scaling, and blue-green deployments. There are many additional enterprise features, including authentication, multiple endpoints for A/B testing, telemetry collection, and much more.

- The second deployment type is for batch scoring large amounts of data through a service. In Azure Machine Learning, this works through the usage of pipelines. Your scoring script is parameterized and wrapped into an Azure Machine Learning Pipeline, which itself can be deployed as a web service. Calling this web service can now parameterize and trigger any task that you implement in the batch scoring script, such as reading files from Blob storage, scoring them, and writing the results back into a CSV file. Besides that, you can use the same deployment type to trigger the re-training of your models.

Besides standard deployment, you can always pull in the trained models from the model registry into any Python interpreter. This means you can download your model in any Python environment, be it PySpark on Azure Databricks or the Python runtime within Azure Data Explorer. This opens the door for many advanced custom deployment methods, where only the sky is the limit.

If you use standard ML models trained via sklearn and other supported frameworks, you can use no-code deployments to deploy the model directly from the model registry. This will automatically configure your environment, pull in the right Docker base image and Python packages, use a default scoring script, and deploy the model as a web service to an Azure Container Instance. This is a fantastic feature for integration and end-to-end testing, as well as for staging and QA environments. Again, this might be something you could implement yourself given enough time, but it is really convenient to use straight out of the box.

Another great point to mention is that Azure allows you to deploy multiple models to the same endpoint on Azure Kubernetes Service. For each endpoint, you can configure the amount of traffic in percentage that should be automatically routed there. On top of this – as for all deployed services – we get automated telemetry data and monitoring out of the box. The amazing part is that all this works with a couple of lines of Python code through your authoring environment. We will see this in great depth in *Chapter 12, Deploying and operating machine learning models*.

Azure Machine Learning can do a lot more besides tracking experiment metrics and models, and deploying these models to Kubernetes. However, this should simply give you an understanding of what can be done with minimal effort, 30 minutes of your precious time, and an existing training pipeline. You also saw that there was no restriction in any way toward which frameworks, models, or functionalities you used; it will work in a straightforward way if you use Python (or R).

Summary

In this chapter, we learned the differences between multiple ML and AI services in Azure. You can now easily navigate through various Azure services and know which ML task requires which service. If your task and data is available for Cognitive Services, then it is very convenient to simply use the Cognitive Services API for prediction. This is the case for common computer vision tasks, such as object detection of common objects, image captioning and tagging, face detection, handwritten text recognition, landmark detection, and many other text and language tasks.

If you need to build custom models for data from custom domains, you can choose to pick a tool with a GUI such as Azure Machine Learning designer. However, if you don't know how to select and configure a good custom ML model, Automated Machine Learning would be a better choice for you.

Finally, if you want to create your own custom model, your best choice is the Azure Machine Learning. It is a great tool that enables you to build fully automated end-to-end ML pipelines and deployments using your own frameworks and environments. You learned that orchestrating all infrastructure automation is done through the authoring environment, which will automatically schedule your training runs on the execution runtime – this could, for example, be an auto-scaling GPU cluster.

Azure Machine Learning is also the service that we use throughout this book to help you implement such a pipeline. In the next chapter, we will take a look at how to set up and prepare your Azure Machine Learning workspace and master data exploration in Azure using embeddings and data visualizations.

Section 2: Experimentation and Data Preparation

In the second part of the book, the reader will learn how to load a dataset into Azure, visualize the data using two-dimensional embeddings, experiment with the data and models in a notebook environment, and preprocess the data for subsequent training.

This section comprises the following chapters:

- *Chapter 3, Data experimentation and visualization using Azure*
- *Chapter 4, ETL, data preparation, and feature extraction*
- *Chapter 5, Azure Machine Learning pipelines*
- *Chapter 6, Advanced feature extraction with NLP*

3
Data experimentation and visualization using Azure

In the previous chapter, we learned how to navigate different Azure services for implementing ML solutions in the cloud. We realized that the best service for training custom ML models programmatically and automating infrastructure and deployments is Azure Machine Learning. In this chapter, we will set up the Azure Machine Learning workspace, create a training cluster, and perform data experimentation while collecting all artifacts in Azure.

First, you will learn how to prepare and interact with your ML workspace. Once set up, you will be able to perform and track experiments in Azure, as well as trained models, plots, metrics, and snapshots of your code. This can all be done from your authoring Python environment; for example, Jupyter using Azure Machine Learning compute instances—similar to **Data Science VMs (DSVMs)** or any Python interpreter running in PyCharm, VS Code, and so on. We will first run experimentation code locally in the authoring environment and gradually move to an auto-scaling training cluster.

In the second part of this chapter, we will apply the knowledge learned and perform dimensionality reduction to visualize high-dimensional datasets. We will also track these visualizations together with the key metrics in Azure Machine Learning. First, we will compare two linear projections: **Principal Component Analysis (PCA)** and **Linear Discriminant Analysis (LDA)** as an example of unsupervised and supervised embedding. Then we will look at two popular unsupervised non-linear techniques: **t-Distributed Stochastic Neighbor Embedding (t-SNE)** and **Uniform Manifold Approximation and Projection (UMAP)**. This will help you to experiment with any dataset quickly and save your experiments in Azure Machine Learning.

Let's dive right in to set up your Azure Machine Learning workspace. We recommend you follow along with us in your Azure account, using Azure Cloud Shell, Azure Machine Learning, and an Azure Machine Learning compute instance. Don't worry if some of this still sounds unfamiliar; we will tackle the setup and experimentation one step at a time.

The following are the topics that will be covered in this chapter:

- Preparing your Azure Machine Learning workspace
- Visualizing high-dimensional data

Preparing your Azure Machine Learning workspace

In the first section, we will set up the ML workspace in Azure using the Azure command line. This will help you to create development, staging, and production environments repeatedly. You can do parts from your local machine, for example, running Azure command-line scripts or a simple Python authoring environment, or do it in the cloud using Azure Cloud Shell. Using the preconfigured shell in Azure is the quickest method, as all required extensions and aliases are already preinstalled and configured for you.

We will then run simple experiments from your authoring and experimentation environment (for example, your local development machine or a small mcompute instance in Azure Machine Learning) and then smoothly transition to an Azure Machine Learning training cluster—a highly scalable execution environment on Azure. The great thing about this setup is that from then on you will be able to decide whether you want to run code on your local development machine (and still benefit from many of the features of Azure Machine Learning) or you want to run it on a pre-configured VM or auto-scalable training cluster.

A great approach to discover Azure Machine Learning is to take a current ML project and start adding bits and pieces from Azure Machine Learning to enhance the project. We will start tracking the working directory, the output artifacts (for example, a trained model), as well as all relevant metrics for each run of your experiment. Later, we can register models and switch between execution environments, or tune the parameters. This should give you a very smooth transition from your current workflow and a great onboarding experience for Azure Machine Learning—using only a few lines of code at a time.

Setting up the ML Service workspace

Throughout this book, we will try to automate as many manual steps as possible, to give you a way to reproduce all environments and experiments. There are many different methods to set up resources in Azure programmatically: ARM templates, the Azure CLI, Azure SDKs, Terraform, and many more tools are available. In general, we will use the Azure CLI to setup and configure the Azure Machine Learning workspace, and later exclusively use the Azure Machine Learning SDK for Python to set up and configure training clusters and other resources.

> **Note**
>
> Using this approach will greatly facilitate the reproducibility and automation of all the tasks performed in Azure. If you are new to the Azure CLI, you should go ahead and install it now through the information provided in the Azure documentation: https://docs.microsoft.com/cli/azure/install-azure-cli-windows. If you already have the Azure CLI installed, please make sure you have the latest available version, which is required for many of the new ML features.

Let's set up the Azure Machine Learning workspace following these steps:

1. First, we need to install the Azure Machine Learning extension for the Azure CLI. This will allow you to interact with Azure Machine Learning through the command line. Let's install the ML extension using the following command:

   ```
   $ az extension add -n azure-cli-ml
   ```

2. Once installed, you will be able to use the extension using the **az ml** command. Make sure that, before you continue, you run the following command to explore the actions provided by the Azure CLI ML extension:

   ```
   $ az ml -h
   Group
     az ml : Access Machine Learning commands.

   Subgroups:
     computetarget : Access compute context related commands.
     datastore : Manage and use datastores.
     experiment : Manage experiments in the AzureML Workspace.
     folder : Access folder related commands.
     model : Manage machine learning models.
     pipeline : Access and manage machine learning pipelines.
     run : Manage and submit AzureML runs.
     service : Manage operationalized services.
     workspace : Access workspace related commands.
   ```

3. Next, create a new resource group, **mldemo**, in the **westus2** region and an Azure Machine Learning workspace, **mldemows**. This will create not only the workspace but also all other required resources for our ML project, such as **StorageAccount**, **ServicePrincipal**, **AppInsights**, and the **KeyVault** container. These services are all part of your Azure Machine Learning workspace:

   ```
   $ az group create -n mldemo -l westus2
   { ... }
   $ az ml workspace create -w mldemows -g mldemo
   Deploying StorageAccount with name mldemowsstorage01509a813. Deploying AppInsights with name mldemowsinsightsd847e989.
   Deployed AppInsights with name mldemowsinsightsd847e989. Deploying KeyVault with name mldemowskeyvaultba9841b6.
   Deployed KeyVault with name mldemowskeyvaultba9841b6. Deployed StorageAccount with name mldemowsstorage01509a813. Deploying Workspace with name mldemows.
   Deployed Workspace with name mldemows.
   { ... }
   ```

As you can see, the preceding command created multiple resources, together with the Azure Machine Learning workspace, that are required for running ML experiments. `KeyVault` will be used to automatically manage your secrets and keys under the hood; `StorageAccount` will be used to store artifacts such as source files, trained models, and data; `AppInsights` will be used to track your experiment metrics and telemetry data of deployments.

4. In the next step, we change to a working directory in your shell and export the Azure Machine Learning workspace configuration to disk. This will help us to load the configuration from this file rather than keeping track of your subscription ID and ML workspace name in your scripts:

```
$ az ml folder attach -w mldemows -g mldemo -e mldemos
{
  "Experiment name": "mldemos",
  "Project path": "~/ch03-data-experimentation",
  "Resource group": "mldemo",
  "Subscription id": "***",
  "Workspace name": "mldemows"
}
```

The preceding command creates an `.azureml/` folder in the current working directory that contains your workspace configuration. It also creates an `.amlignore` file, which defines all file patterns for files and folders that should be ignored by Azure Machine Learning. These files won't be uploaded during a snapshot in an experiment run – similar to a `.gitignore` file in your version control system.

5. In the subsequent step, we can install the Python extensions to interact with Azure Machine Learning from within Python. The extension is really powerful, and let's you not only interact with Azure Machine Learning but also create training clusters, deployment clusters, and much more.

> **Note**
>
> Please note that this only has to be done if you run your experiments on your own machine—and not in the pre-configured Azure Machine Learning compute or **Data Science Virtual Machine** (**DSVM**) in Azure.

If you are running locally, you need to install the Python SDK for Azure and Azure Machine Learning. Here is a snippet of how to achieve this using pip and Python 3:

```
python3 -m pip install azure-cli azureml-sdk
```

If you want to run your authoring environment in the cloud, you can simply navigate to your Machine Learning workspace in Azure and open the Azure Machine Learning interface to use the Notebook viewer provided there. *Figure 3.1* shows the Azure Machine Learning interface. You can see the **Notebooks** tab in the left menu. Selecting this tab gives you a fully-fledged Notebook environment directly in your workspace:

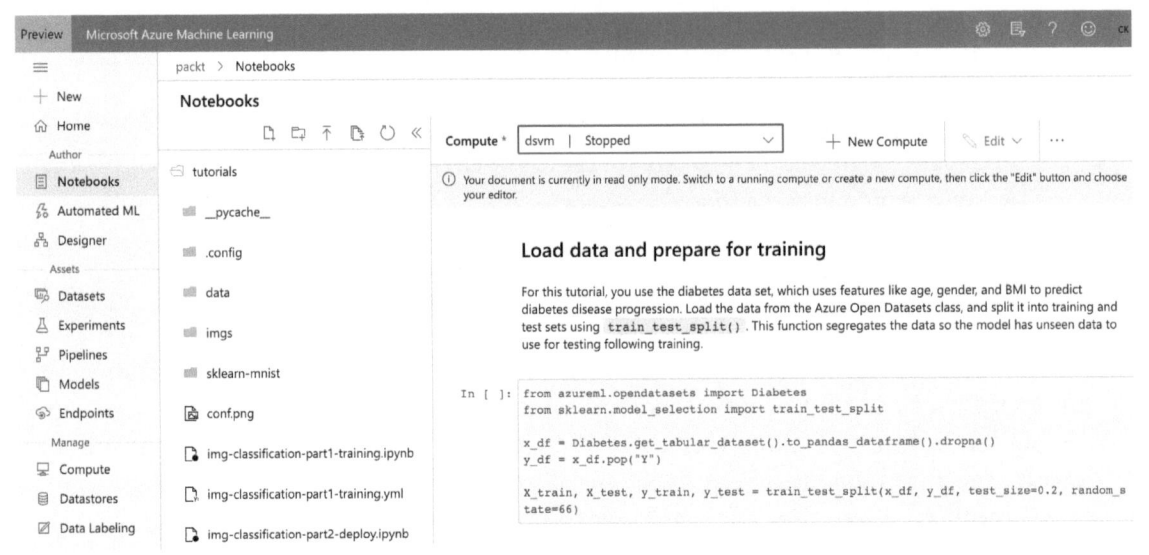

Figure 3.1: The notebooks viewer in Azure Machine Learning

To run code in this environment, click on **Compute** and create a compute instance for your notebook. Once finished, you will also see an option to start a separate Jupyter notebook or JupyterLab session if you prefer those environments.

However, you can also continue by running the following code locally with the Azure and Azure Machine Learning Python SDKs installed. *Figure 3.2* shows how this looks in the Azure Machine Learning interface. You can click on **JupyterLab** to open a JupyterLab session on this compute instance:

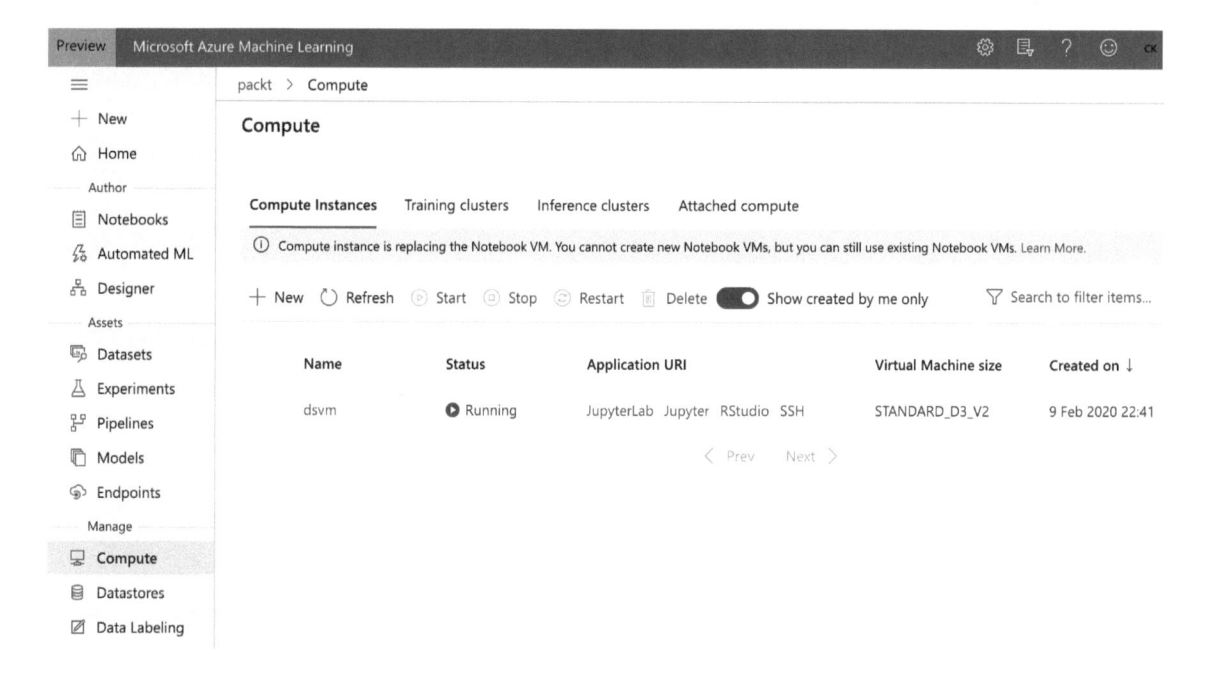

Figure 3.2: A compute instance preview showing the status of the running code in Azure Machine Learning

Figure 3.2 shows you how to quickly set up a full-fledged authoring and experimentation environment in the Azure Machine Learning workspace by simply deploying a compute instance. If you prefer a more integrated experience, you can also switch back to the **Notebooks** tab in the left menu and execute notebooks using this compute.

> **Note**
>
> Compute instances were previously called Notebook VMs and are similar to pre-configured DSVMs.

6. Next, we can load the workspace configuration from this file without explicitly specifying the workspace and subscription in every experiment. In an interactive Python notebook environment or any Python interpreter you have handy, you can run the following code to load your workspace in the current context:

```
from azureml.core import Workspace

ws = Workspace.from_config()
```

The preceding code will load your configuration from the configuration directory we created earlier using the Azure CLI. Whenever you run code in an Azure Machine Learning compute instance, you get these settings pre-configured with your workspace.

> **Note**
>
> Loading the workspace in Python will prompt you to log in into your Azure account to allow the communication between your current compute environment and your Azure Machine Learning workspace.

Running the previous code block will output an interactive link to sign into your Azure account using a device code. Please follow the link and use the provided code for the sign in to grant your current execution environment access to your Azure Machine Learning workspace. If you run a non-interactive Python script rather than a notebook environment, you can provide the Azure CLI credentials to sign into your Azure account as follows:

```
from azureml.core import Workspace
from azureml.core.authentication import import AzureCliAuthentication cli_auth = AzureCliAuthentication()
ws = Workspace.from_config(auth=cli_auth)
```

Once you have successfully loaded the workspace into the ws object, you can continue adding tracking capabilities to your ML experiments. We will use this object to create experiments, runs, log metrics, and register models.

Running a simple experiment with Azure Machine Learning

One great use case for starting with Azure Machine Learning is to add advanced logging, tracking, and monitoring capabilities to your existing ML pipeline. Imagine you have a central place to track your ML experiments from all your data scientists, monitor your training and validation metrics, collect your trained models and other output files, as well saving a snapshot of the current environment. We can achieve this by simply adding a few lines of code to your training scripts.

In the Azure Machine Learning workspace, an experiment groups a set of runs. A run is a single execution of your experiment (your training script) with different settings, models, code, data, and so on but with the same comparable metric. You use runs to test multiple hypotheses for a given experiment and track all results within the same experiments. A run is then used for tracking and collecting information. We will now create an experiment and, subsequently, a run:

1. First, load and create an experiment. The following line of code will create a new experiment or load an existing experiment in the ML workspace with the provided name:

   ```
   # Load or create an experiment
   exp = Experiment(workspace=ws, name="cifar10_cnn_local")
   ```

   The preceding code creates an experiment with the name **cifar10_cnn_local** once a new run is tracked, and nothing more. If an experiment with the same name already exists, the invocation returns the existing experiments. All runs in this experiment are now grouped together and can be displayed and analyzed on a single dashboard.

2. Once we have loaded an experiment, we can create a **run** object and start the logging of this run for the current Python script or notebook:

   ```
   # Create and start an interactive run
   run = exp.start_logging(snapshot_directory='examples')
   ```

   The preceding code actually not only creates and initializes a new run; it also takes a snapshot of the current environment—defined through the **snapshot** directory—and uploads it to the Azure Machine Learning workspace. To disable this feature, you need to explicitly pass **snapshot_directory=None** to the **start_logging()** function. You might be wondering why we are specifying a separate directory instead of referring to the current directory. The reason for this that we only want to track the **examples** directory here as it contains all our code samples. However, feel free to set this to the current directory.

   In addition, also using the **.amlignore** file, we can specify which part of the current working directory should not be tracked in the workspace. By using only two lines of code, you can track a snapshot for each execution of your experimentation runs automatically—and hence never lose code or configurations and always come back to the specific code, parameters, or models used for one of your ML runs. This is not very impressive yet, but we are just getting started.

   Figure 3.3 shows the tracked files for a specific experiment run in Azure Machine Learning:

packt > Experiments > cifar10_cnn_local > Run 2

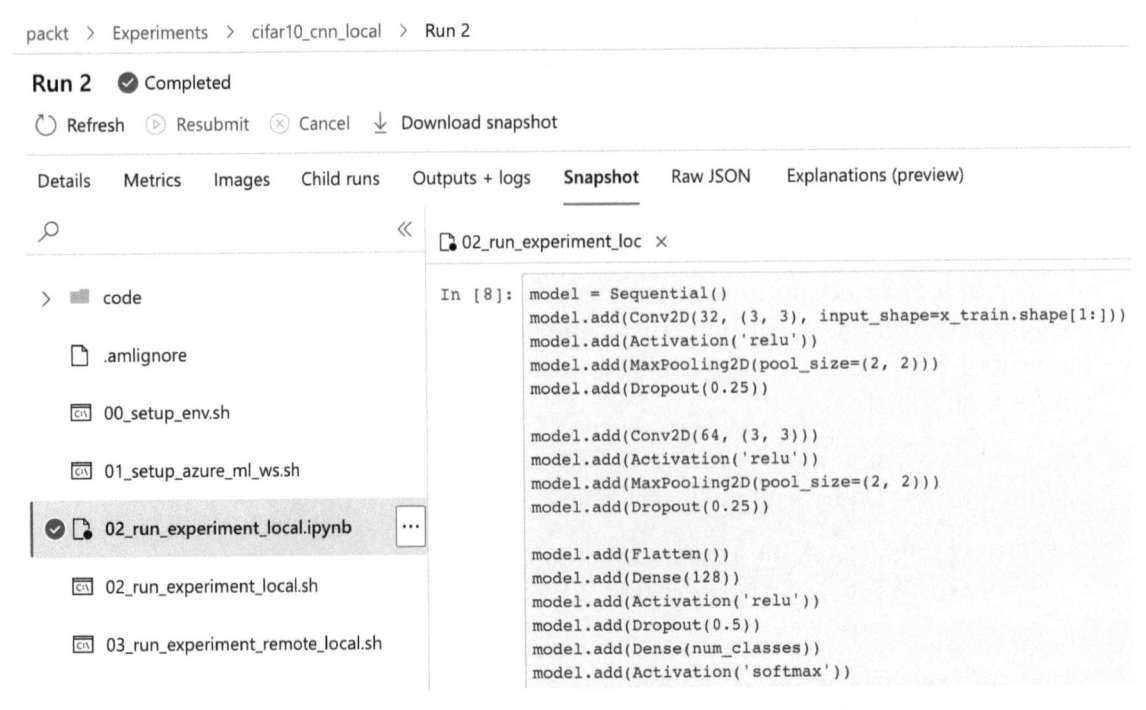

Run 2 ✓ Completed

↻ Refresh ▷ Resubmit ⊗ Cancel ↓ Download snapshot

Details | Metrics | Images | Child runs | Outputs + logs | **Snapshot** | Raw JSON | Explanations (preview)

```
02_run_experiment_loc  ×

In [8]:  model = Sequential()
         model.add(Conv2D(32, (3, 3), input_shape=x_train.shape[1:]))
         model.add(Activation('relu'))
         model.add(MaxPooling2D(pool_size=(2, 2)))
         model.add(Dropout(0.25))

         model.add(Conv2D(64, (3, 3)))
         model.add(Activation('relu'))
         model.add(MaxPooling2D(pool_size=(2, 2)))
         model.add(Dropout(0.25))

         model.add(Flatten())
         model.add(Dense(128))
         model.add(Activation('relu'))
         model.add(Dropout(0.5))
         model.add(Dense(num_classes))
         model.add(Activation('softmax'))
```

Files panel:
- code
  - .amlignore
  - 00_setup_env.sh
  - 01_setup_azure_ml_ws.sh
  - ✓ 02_run_experiment_local.ipynb
  - 02_run_experiment_local.sh
  - 03_run_experiment_remote_local.sh

Figure 3.3: Tracking code execution using tracked files

3. If you run your code in a script rather than in a notebook, it is good practice to wrap your training code in a **try** - **except** block in order to propagate the status of your run to Azure. If the training run fails, then the run will be reported as a failed run in Azure. You can achieve this by using the following code snippet:

```
run = exp.start_logging()
try:
  # train your model here
  run.complete()
except:
  run.cancel()
  raise
```

We included the **raise** statement in order to fail the script when an error occurs. This would normally not happen as all exceptions are caught. You can simplify the preceding code by using **with** statement. This will yield the same result and is much easier to read:

```
with exp.start_logging() as run:
    # train your model here
    pass
```

4. Besides the **snapshot** directory, which is uploaded before the run starts, the **outputs** and **logs** directories are special in a run. Once a run is completed using **run.complete()**, all content of the **outputs** directory is automatically uploaded into the Azure Machine Learning workspace. In a simple example using Keras, we could checkpoint the best model per epoch to the **outputs** directory and hence automatically version and track the trained model for each experiment:

```
import os
from keras.calbacks import ModelCheckpoint

outputs_dir = os.path.join(os.getcwd(), 'outputs')
model_name = 'keras_cifar10_trained_model.h5'
model_path = os.path.join(outputs_dir, model_name)

# define a checkpoint callback
checkpoint_cb = ModelCheckpoint(model_path,
  monitor='val_loss',
  save_best_only=True)

# train the model
model.fit(x_train, y_train,
  batch_size=batch_size,
  epochs=epochs,
  validation_data=(x_test, y_test),
  callbacks=[checkpoint_cb])
```

In the preceding code, we train a Keras model and write the best model to the defined output folder each iteration. Hence, whenever we run the training with the previous experiment tracking, the model gets uploaded automatically once the run is completed.

We can see (in *Figure 3.4*) that the best model was uploaded to the Azure Machine Learning workspace. This is also very convenient as you won't lose track of your trained models anymore. On top of that, all artifacts are stored in Blob storage, which is highly scalable and inexpensive:

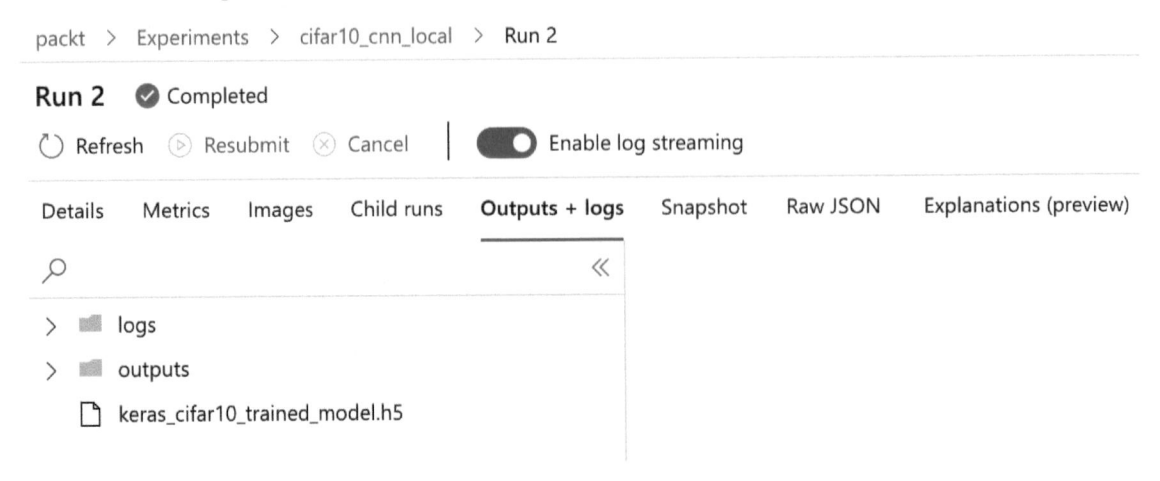

Figure 3.4: The Outputs + logs tab in the Azure Machine Learning workspace

The **Logs** directory will be streamed if the training script is invoked through `ScriptRunConfig` rather than executing directly—we will see this in action in the next section. This means your logs will appear and get updated when they occur and not only at the end of each run.

Another great utility to add is registering the trained model in the model artifact store of Azure Machine Learning. To do so, you only need to invoke the `run.register_model()` method, as in the following code snippet:

```
# Upload the best model
run.upload_file(model_name, model_path)


# Register the best model
run.register_model(model_name, model_path=model_name,
    model_framework='TfKeras')
```

In the preceding code, we first force the upload of the model. This is needed because all output resources are only uploaded when the run is completed, and not immediately. Hence, after uploading the model, we can simply register it in the model store. The model is versioned and made available in the model store, as seen in *Figure 3.5*:

packt > Models > keras_cifar10_trained_model.h5:1

keras_cifar10_trained_model.h5:1

◯ Refresh   + Deploy   ↓ Download

Details   Artifacts   Endpoints   Explanations (preview)   Datasets

Attributes

Version
1

ID
keras_cifar10_trained_model.h5:1

Date registered
19/04/2020, 19:54:41

Description
--

Framework
TfKeras

Framework version
--

Experiment name
cifar10_cnn_local

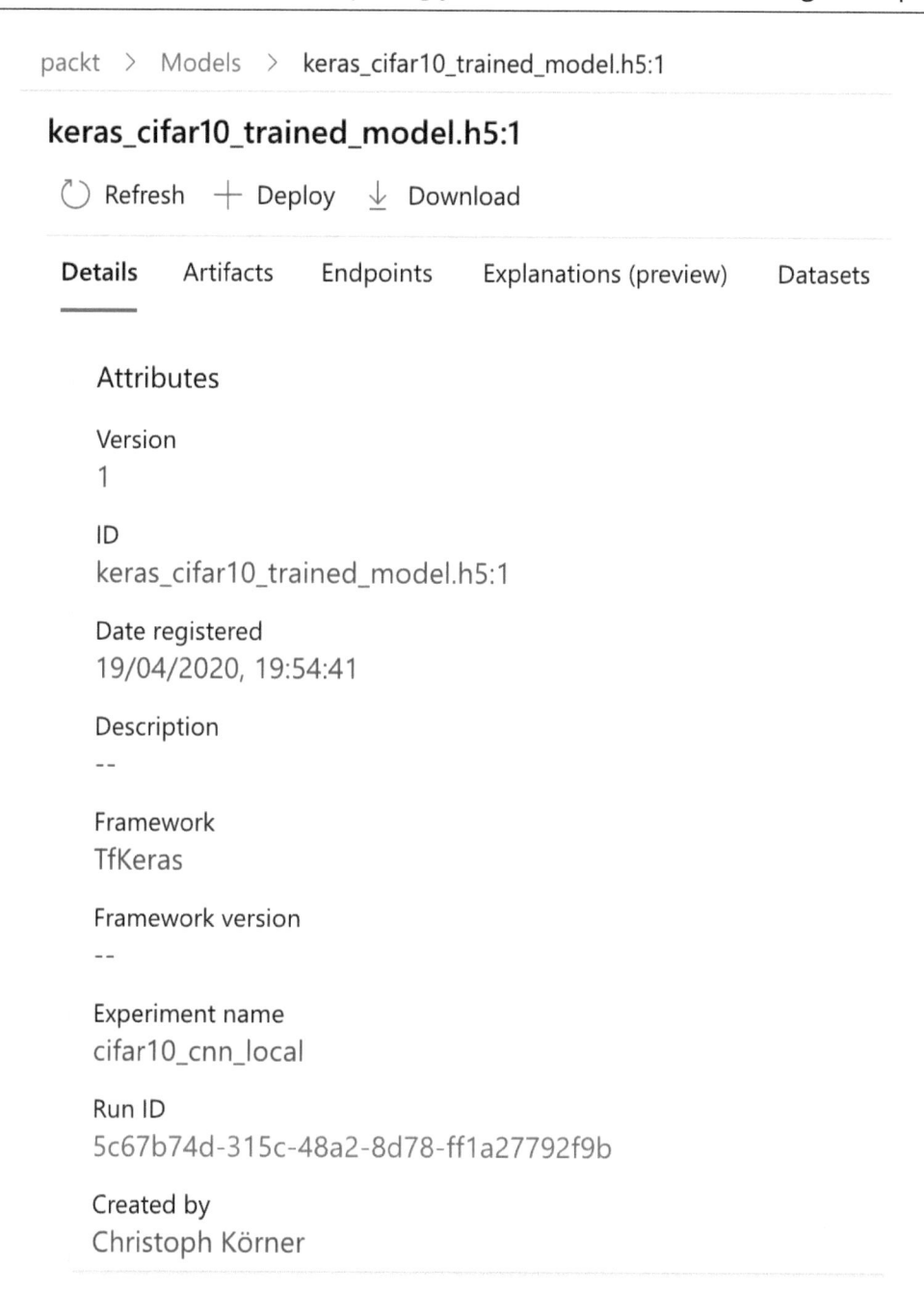

Run ID
5c67b74d-315c-48a2-8d78-ff1a27792f9b

Created by
Christoph Körner

Figure 3.5: Details of the registered model in Azure Machine Learning

The model can then be used for automatic deployments from Azure Machine Learning. We will look at this in a lot more detail in *Chapter 12, Deploying and operating machine learning models*.

Using the previous code, we would always update the model with a new version as soon as a new model is available. However, this doesn't automatically mean that the new model has a better training or validation performance. Therefore, a common approach is to register the new model only if the specified metric is better than the highest previously stored metric for the experiment. Let's implement this. We can return a generator of metrics from a defined experiment using the following function:

```
from azureml.core import Run


def get_metrics_from_exp(experiment, metric, status='Completed'):
    for run in Run.list(exp, status=status):
        yield run.get_metrics().get(metric)
```

The preceding generator function yields the specified tracked metric for each run that is completed. Now, we can use this function to return the best metric from all previous experiment runs. We use the best metric to compare the evaluated score from the current model and decide whether we should register a new version of the model. We should do this only if the current model performs better than the previous recorded model. The code for this functionality looks like this; we expect the model to track a metric called **Test accuracy**. We will learn how to log this metric in the next section:

```
# Get the highest test accuracy
best_test_acc = max(get_metrics_from_exp(exp, 'Test accuracy'))


# Evaluate the current model
scores = model.evaluate(x_test, y_test, verbose=1)


# Upload the model
run.upload_file(model_name, model_path)


if scores[0] > best_test_acc:
    # Register the best model as a new version
    run.register_model(model_name, model_path=model_name)
```

In the preceding code, we now register the model only if the score of the new model is higher than the previously stored best score. Nevertheless, we upload and track the model binaries with the experiment run. Now that we know how to run a simple experiment, let's learn how to log metrics and track results in the next section.

Logging metrics and tracking results

We already saw three useful features to track snapshot code, upload output artifacts, and register-trained model files in your Azure Machine Learning workspace. These features can be added to any existing experimentation and training Python script or notebook with a few lines of code. In the same way, we can extend the experimentation script to also track all kinds of variables, such as training accuracy and validation loss per epoch as well as the test set accuracy of the best model.

Using the **run.log()** method, you can track any parameter during training and experimentation. You simply supply a name and a value, and Azure will do the rest for you. The backend automatically detects if you send a list of values—hence multiple values with the same key when you log the same value multiple times in the same run—or a single value per run, for example, the test performance. In the Azure Machine Learning UI, these values will be automatically used to show your training performance. A list of values is used to visualize your run performance, while a single value per run will be used to show your experiment performance.

Let's look at an example where we use both types of metrics. Here is a simple snippet showing how you could track training, validation, and testing performance:

```
for i in range(epochs):
  model.fit(X_train, y_train)
  scores = model.evaluate(x_val, y_val)
  run.log('Validation loss', scores[0])
  run.log('Validation accuracy', scores[1])


# Evaluate trained model
scores = model.evaluate(x_test, y_test)
run.log('Test loss', scores[0])
run.log('Test accuracy', scores[1])
```

The preceding code logs the values to the ML workspace run. When you open the run in the UI in the Azure portal, the list values are automatically converted into line charts, as shown in *Figure 3.6*:

Figure 3.6: The status of running code in Azure Machine Learning, showing test accuracy, test loss, and val_loss in the chart

Another nifty feature is that the ML workspace experiment gives you a nice overview of all your runs. It automatically uses the numeric values that were logged per run and displays them on a dashboard. You can modify the displayed values and the aggregation method used to aggregate those values over the individual runs.

Figure 3.7 shows the minimum testing loss as well as the maximum testing accuracy directly on the experiment's dashboard:

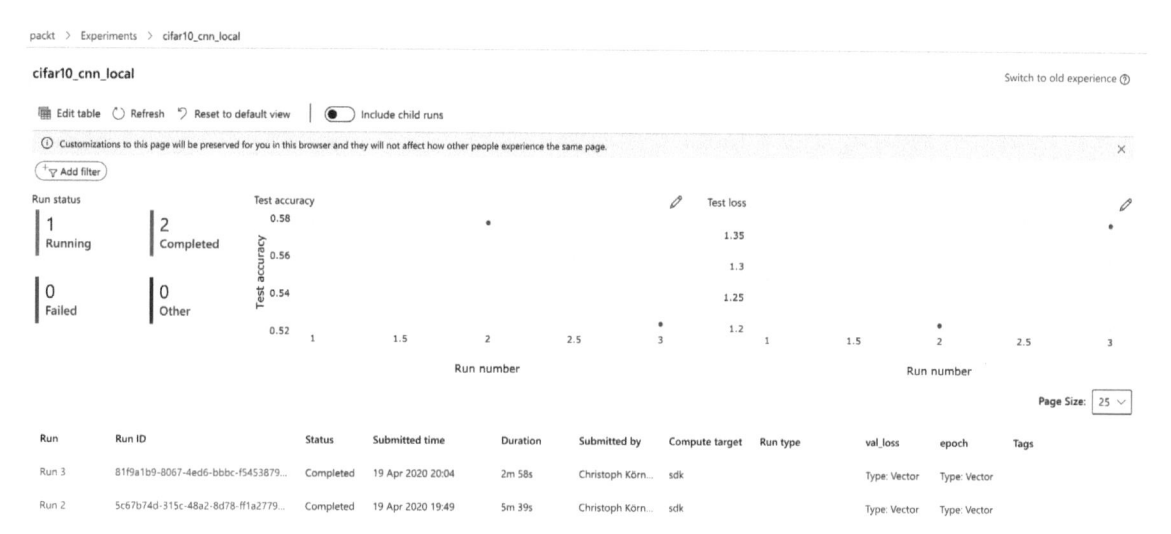

Figure 3.7: The experiment dashboard in Azure Machine Learning, showing the minimum testing loss and the maximum testing accuracy

This is the simplest method of tracking values from the runs and displaying them with the corresponding experiments. However, we can already see that these intelligent visualizations are also very helpful. It's worth mentioning that all this works by simply adding a few lines of code to your existing ML training scripts independently of which framework you are using.

The command for logging values to Azure Machine Learning can be easily transformed into a higher-level operator to extend your ML projects. One example would be a Keras callback to execute each epoch in a fit generator. We can write such a callback function similar to the built-in **RemoteMonitor** callback:

```
from keras.callbacks import Callback
import numpy as np


class AzureMlKerasCallback(Callback):

  def init (self, run):
    super(AzureMlKerasCallback, self). init ()
    self.run = run


  def on_epoch_end(self, epoch, logs=None):
    logs = logs or {}
    send = {} send['epoch'] = epoch
```

```
    for k, v in logs.items():

        if isinstance(v, (np.ndarray, np.generic)):
            send[k] = v.item()
        else:
            send[k] = v
    for k, v in send.items():
        if isinstance(v, list):
            self.run.log_list(k, v)
        else:
            self.run.log(k, v)
```

The preceding code implements a simple Keras callback function. It collects the metrics to send in a dictionary, either as an array or a single metric. Now, instead of manually logging each parameter, we simply use the callback function in the Keras training script as shown in the following code:

```
# Create an Azure Machine Learning monitor callback
azureml_cb = AzureMlKerasCallback(run)
model.fit(x_train, y_train,
    batch_size=batch_size,
    epochs=epochs,
    validation_data=(x_test, y_test),
    callbacks=[azureml_cb])
```

The preceding code extends Keras naturally using a callback function to track training and validation loss and accuracy in Azure Machine Learning. You can find the full working example in the source code provided with this book. Similar modules can be written for other ML libraries as well; we leave this as an exercise for you.

Scheduling and running scripts

In the previous section, we saw how you can annotate your existing ML experimentation and training code with a few lines of code, in order to track relevant metrics and run artifacts in your workspace. In this section, we move from invoking the training script directly to scheduling the training script to run on the local machine. You might immediately ask why this extra step is useful because there are not many differences between invoking the training script directly versus scheduling the training script to run locally.

The main motivation behind this exercise is that in the subsequent step, we can change the execution target to a remote target, and run the training code on a compute cluster in the cloud instead of the local machine. This will be a huge benefit as we can now easily test code locally and later deploy the same code to a highly scalable compute environment in the cloud.

One more difference is that when scheduling the training script instead of invoking it, the standard output and error streams, as well as all files in the **logs** directory will be streamed directly to the Azure Machine Learning workspace run. This gives you a great benefit—now, you can track the script output in real time in your ML workspace, even if your code is running on the compute cluster.

Let's implement this in an *authoring* script. We call it an *authoring* script (or *authoring* environment), when the script or environment's job is to schedule another training or experimentation script. We refer to the *execution* script (or *execution* environment) when we speak about the script or environment that actually runs and executes the training or experimentation script.

We need to define two things in the authoring script—a run configuration, **RunConfiguration**, that defines the execution environment and a run script configuration, **ScriptRunConfig**, that specifies the script that should be executed. Here is a code snippet that defines both:

```
from azureml.core.runconfig import RunConfiguration
from azureml.core import ScriptRunConfig
import os


run_local = RunConfiguration() run_local.environment.python.user_managed_dependencies = True
script_folder = os.path.join(os.getcwd(), 'examples')
src = ScriptRunConfig(source_directory=script_folder,
                      script='cifar10_cnn_remote.py',
                      run_config=run_local)
run = exp.submit(src)
run.wait_for_completion(show_output = True)
```

In the preceding code, we provide the **exp** object as in the previous sections. First, we create a local run configuration with user-managed dependencies to define the execution environment. This means that when we run locally, all dependencies are already provided. When we move this training run to the cloud afterward, we only have to change the run configuration.

In the next line, we define the directory and training file we want to execute locally. Finally, we submit the script, run it, and wait for its completion. Now we can follow the output of the script in the **Logs** section of the ML workspace run, as shown in *Figure 3.8*:

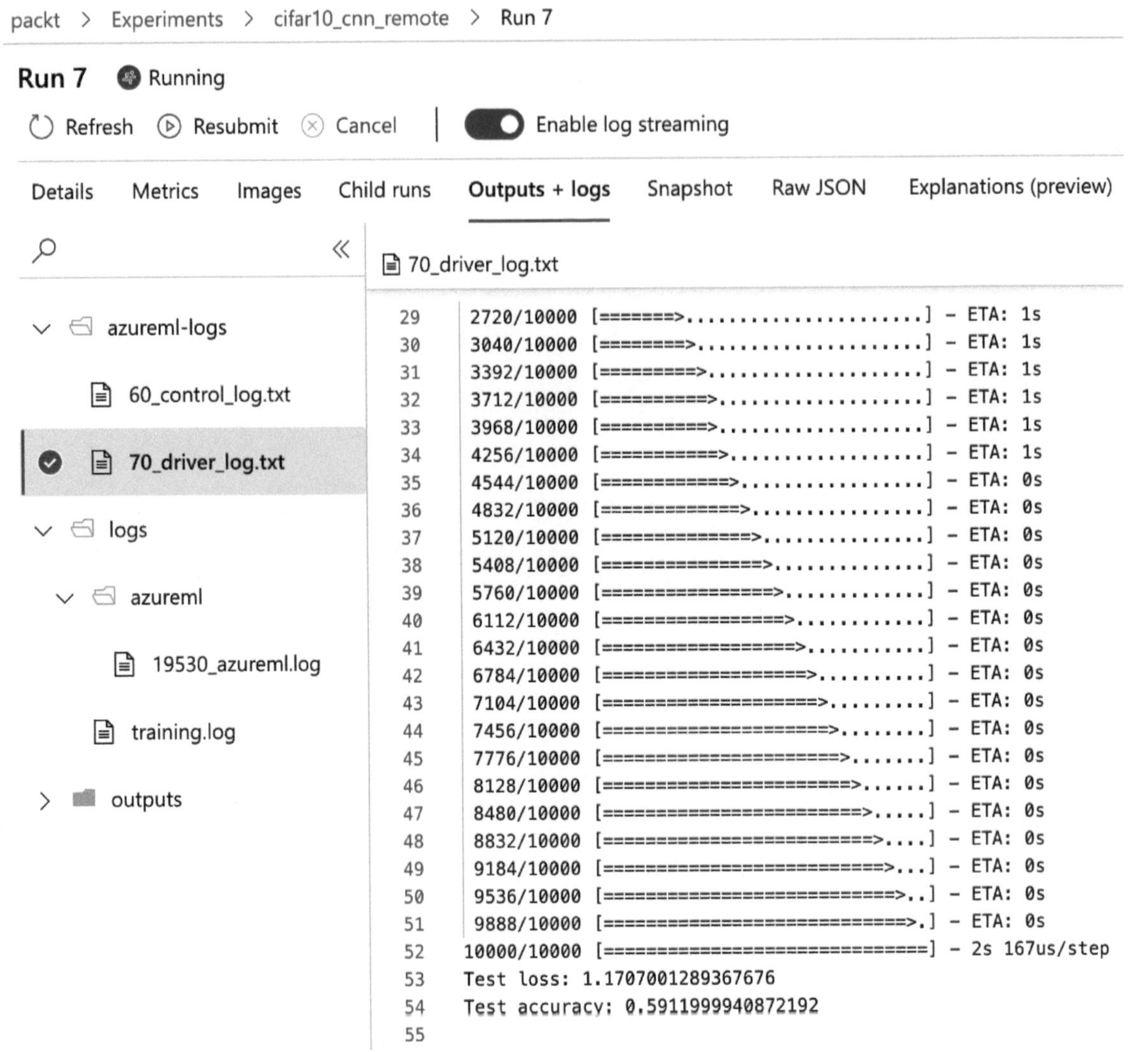

Figure 3.8: The Outputs + logs tab in the Azure Machine Learning workspace

This is very handy as, now, we don't really need to know where the code is ultimately executed. All we care about is seeing the output; the progress; and tracking all metrics, generated models, and all other artifacts. The link to the current run can be retrieved by calling the `print(run.get_portal_url())` method. However, instead of navigating to the Azure portal every time we run a training script, we can embed a widget in our notebook environment to give us the same (and more) functionality–directly within JupyterLab. To do so, we need to replace the `run.wait_for_completion()` line with the following snippet:

```
from azureml.widgets import RunDetails


RunDetails(run).show()
```

Finally, if we want to move to a remote execution environment, we need to infer the run context. In the execution script, we now load the **run** object from the current execution context instead of creating a new run as in the previous sections. We can change the **exp.start_logging** call with the following statement:

```
from azureml.core import Run


# Load the current run
run = Run.get_context()
```

In the preceding code, we replace the previous **start_logging()** method with code automatically inferring the run object from the current context. The **run** object will be automatically linked with the experiment when it was scheduled through the experiment. This is super-handy for remote execution as we don't need to explicitly specify the **run** object anymore.

Using the inferred **run** object, we can log values, upload files and folders, and register models exactly as in the previous sections. You can find a working example in the source code provided with this book.

Adding cloud compute to the workspace

In Azure Machine Learning, you can use two different types of compute targets in Azure—managed and unmanaged. Managed compute will be managed directly from within the ML workspace, whereas unmanaged compute will only be attached to your workspace. When an ML workspace is deleted, all managed compute targets will be deleted as well, while unmanaged (attached) compute targets will continue to exist.

The recommended compute target for training ML models in Azure is the managed Azure Machine Learning compute service—an auto-scaling compute cluster that is directly managed within your Azure subscription. If you have already used Azure for batch workloads, you will find it similar to Azure Batch and Azure Batch AI, with less configuration and tightly embedded in Azure Machine Learning. You can find it in the UI under the menu for **Compute** by clicking on **Training clusters**. In the SDK, we use the `Amlcompute` compute type (short for Azure Machine Learning Compute cluster) to define such a training cluster.

Let's use the Azure Machine Learning Python SDK to create a new compute target as an execution environment:

```
from azureml.core.compute import ComputeTarget, AmlCompute

compute_config = AmlCompute.provisioning_configuration(
  vm_size='STANDARD_D2_V2',
  max_nodes=4)

cpu_cluster = ComputeTarget.create(ws, cpu_cluster_name,
                                   compute_config)
cpu_cluster.wait_for_completion(show_output=True)
```

The preceding code creates an auto-scaling compute cluster optimized for ML directly in your Azure Machine Learning workspace using **STANDARD_D2_V2** VMs (2 CPUs, 7 GB RAM, and 100 GB HDD) as worker nodes. As you can see, we are tuning the maximum number of worker nodes as well as the required VM size, and many more parameters, such as VNet, Subnet, SSL, or load balancer configuration. You can even configure low-priority VMs for your compute cluster.

You can also define VM types with GPUs as your worker nodes—for example, **Standard_NC6** (6 CPUs, 56 GB RAM, 340 GB SSD, 1 GPU, and 12 GB GPU memory)—by simply changing the configuration. This is quite nice as, in contrast to other managed clusters such as Azure Databricks, you don't pay for a head or master node, only the worker nodes. We will go into a lot more detail about VM types for deep learning in *Chapter 8, Training deep neural networks on Azure*, and run distributed training on GPU clusters in *Chapter 10, Distributed machine learning on Azure*.

> **Note**
>
> It's worth noting that setting up and configuring your cluster can be also done using the Azure Machine Learning CLI or any other supported language of the Azure Machine Learning SDK.

You might ask yourself what VM types are available for Azure Machine Learning in a specific location. You can retrieve an up-to-date list using the **AmlCompute.supported_vmsizes()** method and passing your workspace and, optionally, your target location:

```
from azureml.core.compute import AmlCompute
AmlCompute.supported_vmsizes(workspace=ws, location='northeurope')
```

Now we go back to the authoring script and change the execution target to execute the training script on this remote compute cluster, **amldemocompute**. In this case, we load the compute target by name and wait until it is available—if it doesn't exist, we create it. The following script can be very handy when wrapped in a function taking the configuration as parameters and blocking execution until the cluster is created:

```
from azureml.core.compute import ComputeTarget, AmlCompute
from azureml.core.compute_target import ComputeTargetException


# Choose a name for your AML cluster
aml_cluster_name = "amldemocompute"


# Configure your compute cluster
vm_size='STANDARD_D2_V2'
max_nodes=4


# Verify that the cluster exists already
try:
    aml_cluster = ComputeTarget(workspace=ws, name=aml_cluster_name)
except ComputeTargetException:
    print('Cluster not '%s' found, creating one now.' % aml_cluster_name)
    compute_config = AmlCompute.provisioning_configuration(
        vm_size=vm_size, max_nodes=max_nodes)
    aml_cluster = ComputeTarget.create(ws, aml_cluster_name, compute_config)


# Wait until the cluster is ready aml_cluster.wait_for_completion(show_output=True)
```

In the preceding code, we re-use the functionality from before to create clusters and embed them in a function that either returns the cluster and starts it up if it exists, or creates an entirely new one.

Next, we have to configure the run configuration and hence the environment on the compute target in which we want to run our code. This means we need to configure all our libraries, frameworks, and services that the training script requires. This environment can be defined by a Docker base image as well as additional Conda packages:

```python
from azureml.core.runconfig import RunConfiguration
from azureml.core.conda_dependencies import CondaDependencies
from azureml.core.runconfig import DEFAULT_CPU_IMAGE

# Create a remote run configuration
run_amlcompute = RunConfiguration()

run_amlcompute.target = aml_cluster
run_amlcompute.environment.docker.enabled = True
run_amlcompute.environment.docker.base_image = DEFAULT_CPU_IMAGE

ds_packages = [
    'numpy', 'pandas', 'matplotlib', 'seaborn', 'scikit-learn', 'keras'
]

run_amlcompute.auto_prepare_environment = True
run_amlcompute.environment.python.user_managed_dependencies = False
run_amlcompute.environment.python.conda_dependencies = \
CondaDependencies.create(conda_packages=ds_packages)
```

In the preceding code, we create a new run configuration and specify the base Docker image, as well as additional Conda packages to be installed in this environment. We define common data science libraries and attach them to our Conda environment in the training cluster.

> **Note**
>
> Please note that once you create this run configuration for a job run, it will be loaded into your Container Registry, which is automatically added to your Azure Machine Learning workspace.

Finally, we modify the script configuration such that it uses the newly created run configuration as a compute target:

```
from azureml.core import ScriptRunConfig
from azureml.widgets import RunDetails


script = 'cifar10_cnn_remote.py'
script_folder = os.path.join(os.getcwd(), 'examples')


src = ScriptRunConfig (
  source_directory=script_folder,
  script=script,
  run_config=run_amlcompute)
run = exp.submit(src)
RunDetails(run).show()
```

The training script is now executed in the remote compute target on Azure. In the ML workspace, the collection snapshot, outputs, and logs look very similar to the local run. However, we can now also see the logs of the Docker environment build used for this run, as shown in *Figure 3.9*:

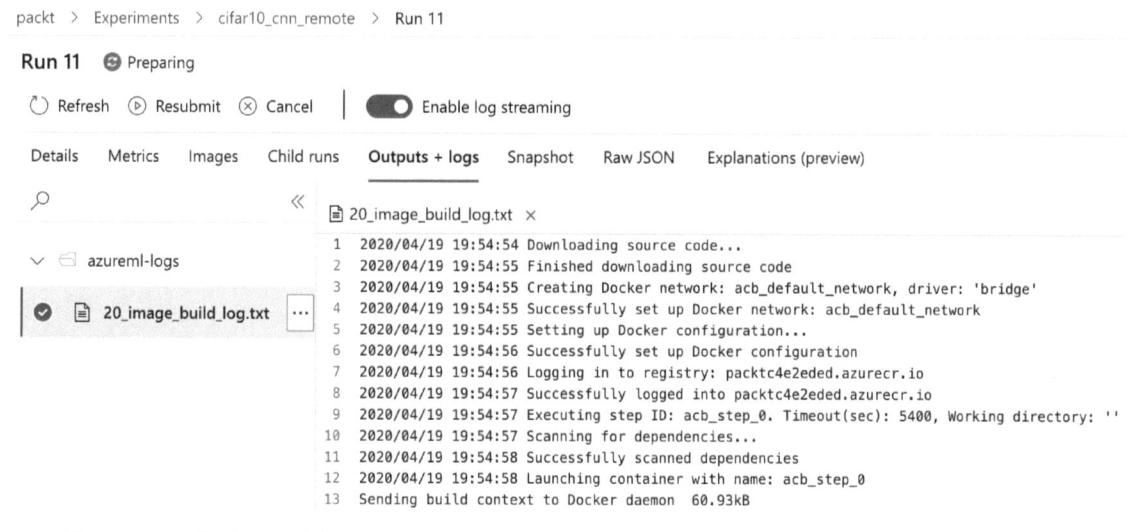

```
packt  >  Experiments  >  cifar10_cnn_remote  >  Run 11

Run 11    Preparing

  Refresh    Resubmit    Cancel    |    Enable log streaming

Details   Metrics   Images   Child runs   Outputs + logs   Snapshot   Raw JSON   Explanations (preview)


                          20_image_build_log.txt  ×

                        1   2020/04/19 19:54:54 Downloading source code...
 azureml-logs           2   2020/04/19 19:54:55 Finished downloading source code
                        3   2020/04/19 19:54:55 Creating Docker network: acb_default_network, driver: 'bridge'
                        4   2020/04/19 19:54:55 Successfully set up Docker network: acb_default_network
    20_image_build_log.txt  ...   5   2020/04/19 19:54:55 Setting up Docker configuration...
                        6   2020/04/19 19:54:56 Successfully set up Docker configuration
                        7   2020/04/19 19:54:56 Logging in to registry: packtc4e2eded.azurecr.io
                        8   2020/04/19 19:54:57 Successfully logged into packtc4e2eded.azurecr.io
                        9   2020/04/19 19:54:57 Executing step ID: acb_step_0. Timeout(sec): 5400, Working directory: ''
                       10   2020/04/19 19:54:57 Scanning for dependencies...
                       11   2020/04/19 19:54:58 Successfully scanned dependencies
                       12   2020/04/19 19:54:58 Launching container with name: acb_step_0
                       13   Sending build context to Docker daemon  60.93kB
```

Figure 3.9: The logs of the Docker environment in the Azure Machine Learning workspace

Let's capture again what happened when we submitted the run to Azure Machine Learning:

- Azure Machine Learning builds the configured environment in Docker, if it doesn't exist already.
- Azure Machine Learning registers your environment in the private container registry, so it can be reused for other scripts and deployments.
- Azure Machine Learning queues your script execution.
- Azure Machine Learning compute initializes and scales up a compute node.
- Azure Machine Learning compute executes the script.
- Azure Machine Learning compute captures logs, artifacts, and metrics and streams them to Azure Machine Learning.
- Azure Machine Learning stores all artifacts in Blob storage, and your metrics in Application Insights.
- Azure Machine Learning provides you with all the information about the run through the UI or API.
- Azure Machine Learning inlines all logs in the Juptyer notebook used as the authoring environment.
- Azure Machine Learning compute automatically scales down the cluster after x minutes of inactivity.

This is simply incredible. Given that it took us maybe 5 minutes to set up the Azure Machine Learning workspace, we get a full-fledged batch compute scheduling and execution environment for all your ML workloads. Many bits and pieces of this environment can be tuned and configured to your liking—and the best of all: everything can be automated through the Azure CLI or the Azure SDK. In the following chapters of this book, we will use the Python SDK to configure, start, scale, and delete clusters for training and scoring.

In the next chapter, we will learn how to perform dimensionality reduction to visualize high-dimensional datasets and automatically track them like metrics in Azure Machine Learning.

Visualizing high-dimensional data

One of the first steps when working with a new dataset should be to systematically look into the data, finding patterns, hypotheses, and insights by manually inspecting your dataset. While this advice might make sense to you at first, it will be hard to follow when your dataset contains thousands of numerical values in a spreadsheet. How should you navigate the data? What should you look for? And what insights can you get?

A great way to get quick insights and a good understanding of your data is to visualize it. This will also help you to identify clusters in your data and irregularities and anomalies—all things that need to be considered in all further data processing. But how can you visualize a dataset with 10, 100, 1,000 feature dimensions? And where should you keep the analysis?

In this section, we will answer all these questions. First, we will explore Azure Machine Learning functionality to register Matplotlib figures with your experiments. This will be extremely helpful for all your feature work, as you will be able to attach visualizations to all your experiments and hence help with understanding your data, models, and experiments at a later stage.

Then, we will look into the linear embedding techniques PCA—unsupervised dimensionality reduction—and LDA—a supervised technique to compute discriminant vectors in a dataset given the target labels too. Then, we will compare both techniques to two popular unsupervised non-linear embedding techniques, t-SNE and UMAP—a generalized and faster version of t-SNE. Having those four techniques in your toolchain will help you to understand datasets and create meaningful visualizations.

Tracking figures in experiments in Azure Machine Learning

In the previous section, we discovered how to track metrics and files for ML experiments using Azure Machine Learning. Other important outputs of your data transformation and ML scripts are visualizations, figures of data distributions, insights about models, and explaining results. Therefore, Azure Machine Learning provides a similar way to track metrics for images, figures, and Matplotlib references.

Let's take a look at a typical scenario; we will start at the simplest way to look at high-dimensional data: a two-dimensional grid visualizing all combinations of features. This visualization is also called a **pairplot** and is a standard visualization type in the visualization library **seaborn**.

Figure 3.10 shows the pairplot of the popular iris flower dataset which contains four feature dimensions (**sepal_length, sepal_width, petal_length**, and **petal_width**) and a target class (**species**). Within the grid cells, we visualize a tiny scatter plot of combinations of two feature dimensions. Along the diagonal, we simply plot the distribution of the feature dimension. As additional information, we encode the target class as hue in each cell:

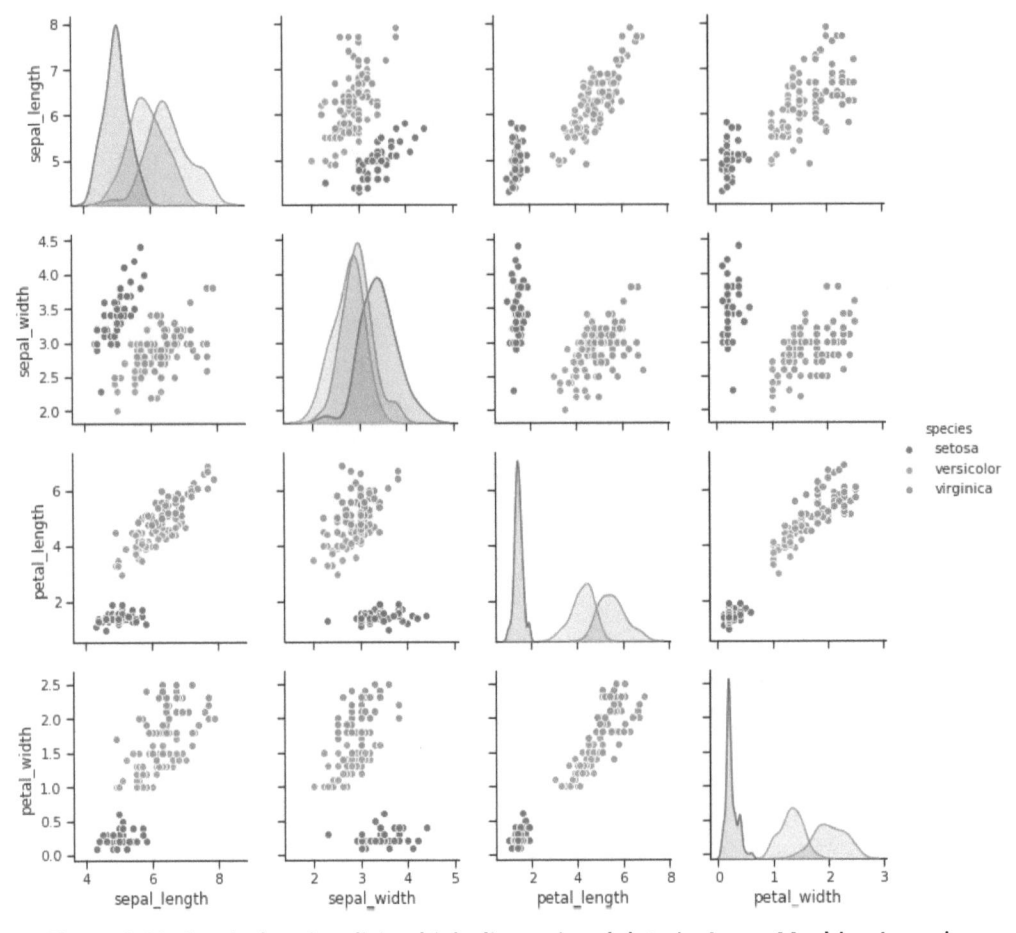

Figure 3.10: A pairplot visualizing high-dimensional data in Azure Machine Learning

To replicate this plot in a notebook, run the following snippet. First, we load the iris dataset packaged in the seaborn library, and next, we plot it calling the **pairplot()** method. This will return a Matplotlib figure and display it in a notebook environment:

```
import seaborn as sns
sns.set(style="ticks")


df = sns.load_dataset("iris")
sns.pairplot(df, hue="species")
```

The preceding code is interesting because it is a very simple way of visualizing high-dimensional data, similar to what you will do first when receiving a new dataset. While it is not really useful for very high-dimensional data, it serves as a good starting point for us. We will look into much more complicated techniques in the following sections.

What is more interesting is how we can automatically embed code like the preceding in our data experimentation and preparation script, and later, in the training and optimization pipelines. With a few lines of code, we can track all Matplotlib figures and attach them to our experimentation run. To do so, we only have to pass the Matplotlib reference to the **run.log_image()** method and give it an appropriate name. The following snippet shows how this would look in an experiment:

```
with exp.start_logging() as run:
    fig = sns.pairplot(df, hue="species")
    run.log_image("pairplot", plot=fig)
```

Now, this is the amazing part. By calling the function with the Matplotlib reference, Azure Machine Learning will render the figure, save it, and attach it to the experiment run. *Figure 3.11* shows the Azure Machine Learning UI with the **Images** tab clicked. You can see the **pairplot** image that we just created and registered attached to the run:

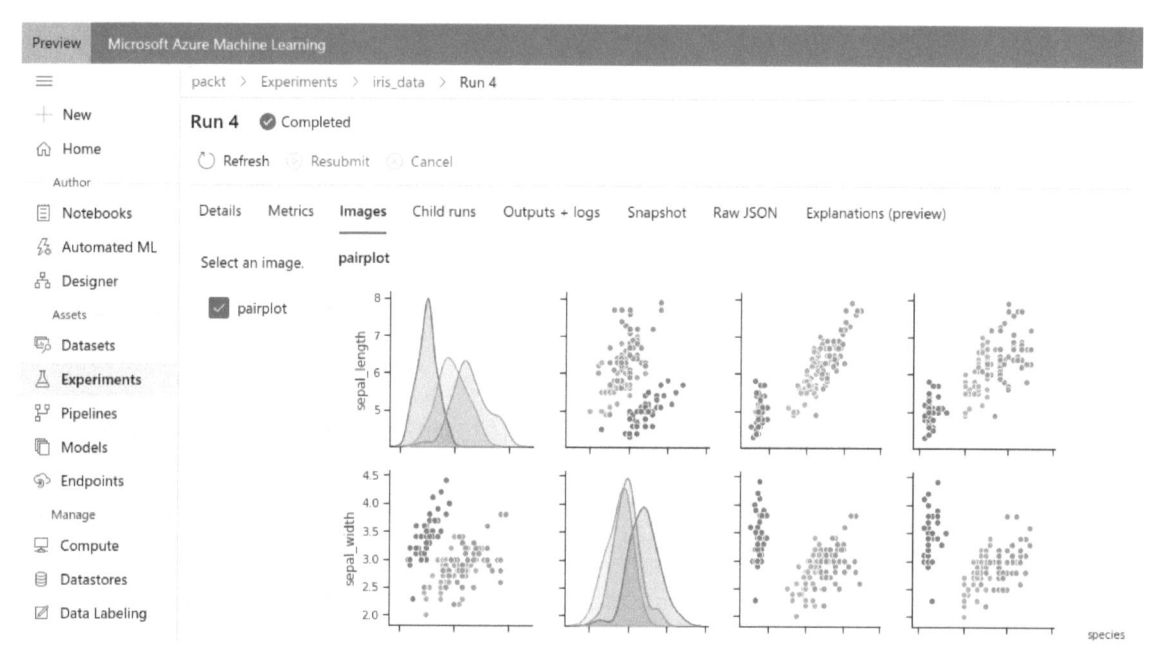

Figure 3.11: The Images tab, showing a pairplot in the Azure Machine Learning workspace

It seems like a tiny feature but it is insanely useful in real-world experimentation. Get used to automatically generating plots of your data, models, and results and attach them to your run. Whenever you are going through your experiments later, you'll have all the visualizations already attached to your run, metrics, and configuration.

Think about storing regression plots when training regression models, and confusion matrices and ROC curve when training classification models. Store your feature importance when training tree-based ensembles and activations for neural networks. You implement this once and add a ton of useful information to your data and ML pipelines.

> **Note**
>
> When using Azure Automated Machine Learning and HyperDrive to optimize parameters, preprocessing, feature engineering, and model selection, you will get a ton of generated visualizations out of the box to help you understand the data, model, and results.

Let's discover some algorithms that are useful for visualizing dataset insights and high-dimensional data. The code to generate the embeddings is omitted for brevity in this section, but can be found in the corresponding Github repository of this book.

Unsupervised dimensionality reduction with PCA

The most popular linear dimensionality reduction technique is PCA, as it is an unsupervised method and hence doesn't need any training labels. PCA embedding linearly transforms a dataset such that the resulting projection is uncorrelated. The axes of this project are called **principal components** and are computed in such a way that each of them has the next highest variance.

The principal components are the directions of the highest variance in the data. This means that the principal components or Eigenvectors describe the strongest direction of the dataset, and the next dimension shows the orthogonal difference from the previous direction. In NLP, the main components correspond with high-level concepts—in recommendation engines, they correspond with user or item traits.

PCA can be computed as Eigenvalue decomposition of the covariance or correlation matrix, or on a non-square matrix by using SVD. PCA and Eigenvalue decomposition are often used as a data experimentation step for visualization, whereas SVD is often used as dimensionality reduction for sparse datasets, for example, a Bag-of-Words model for NLP. We will see SVD being used in practice in Chapter 6, *Advanced feature extraction with NLP*.

An embedding technique can be used as dimensionality reduction by simply removing all but the first x components because these first—and largest—components explain a certain percentage of the variance of the dataset. Hence we remove data with a low variance to receive a lower-dimensional dataset.

To visualize data after PCA in two dimensions (or after any embedding technique) is to visualize the first two components of the transformed dataset – the two largest principal components. The resulting data is rotated along the axis—the principal components—scaled, and centered at zero. As you can see in the following figures, all visualizations have the highest variance projected at the x axis, and the second-highest across the y axis, and so on.

The figures show PCA applied to three datasets of increasing complexity:

- **The iris flower dataset**: three classes and four feature dimensions
- **The UCI wine recognition dataset**: three classes and thirteen feature dimensions
- **The MNIST handwritten digits dataset**: 10 classes and 784 feature dimensions (28 x 28 pixel images)

As a first observation, we should acknowledge that it is a great first step that we can show all these three datasets in only two dimensions, and immediately recognize clusters. If you go back to the iris flower pairplot visualization and look at the sepal width versus sepal length scatter plot, we wouldn't be able to see linear separable clusters in the data. However, by projecting the data across the first two principal components, we can see in the *Figure 3.12* on the left that all clusters look linearly separable (in two dimensions).

When looking at the UCI wine dataset on the right, we can already tell that the clusters are not extremely obvious anymore. Now, 13 feature dimensions are projected along the first two principal components, the highest variance along the x axis and the second-highest variance along the x axis. It's typical in PCA that the cluster shape is aligned with the x axis, because this is how the algorithm works:

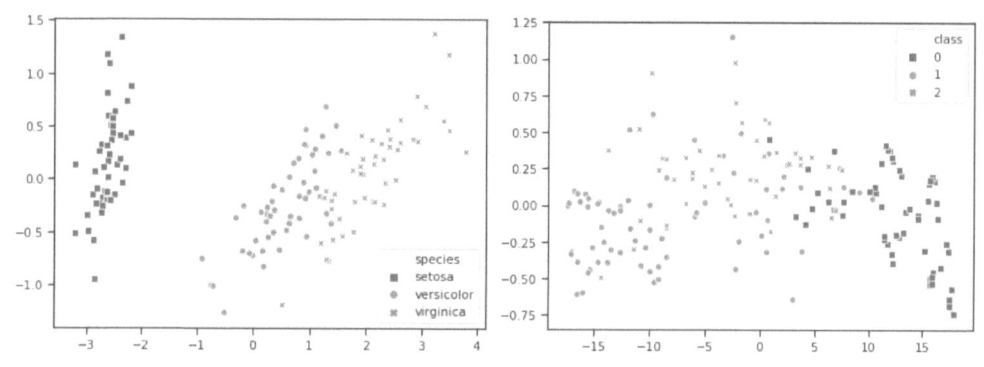

Figure 3.12: Projecting the iris flower and the UCI wine recognition dataset in two dimensions

Finally, when looking at the much more complex embedding of the MNIST handwritten digits dataset, we cannot see many clusters besides maybe the cluster for the digit 0 on top. The data is centered across zero and scaled to a range between -30 and 30 as shown in Figure 3.13. Hence, we can already tell the downsides of PCA—it doesn't take into account any target labels and hence doesn't optimize for separable classes:

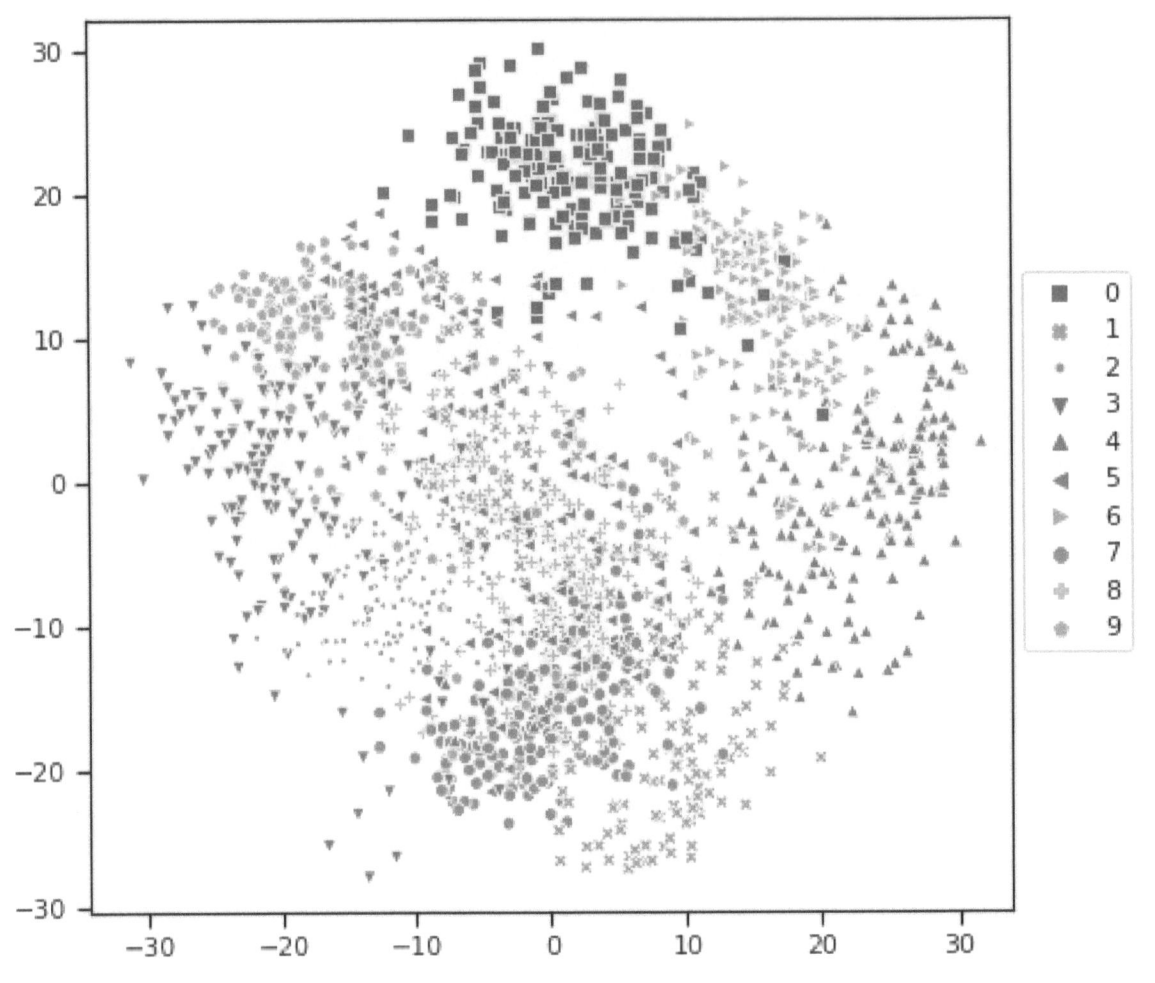

Figure 3.13: A complex embedding of the MNIST handwritten digits dataset

Let's look at a technique that takes target labels into account.

Using LDA for supervised projections

In LDA, we perform a linear transformation of the input data—similar to PCA—and optimize the transformation such that the resulting directions have the highest inter-cluster variance and the lowest intra-cluster variance. This means that the optimization tries to keep samples of the same cluster close to the cluster's mean, while at the same time, tries to keep the cluster's means as far apart as possible.

In LDA, we also receive a linear weighted set of directions as a resulting transformation. The data is centered around 0 and the directions are ordered by highest inter-cluster variance. Hence, in that sense, LDA is like PCA with taking target labels into account. Both LDA and PCA have no real tuning knobs, besides the number of components we want to keep in the projection and probably a random initialization seed.

Figure 3.14 shows the visualizations of the same datasets as in the previous section, we can see that the data is transformed into two dimensions in such a way that the cluster means are the farthest apart from each other across the x axis. We observe the same effect for both the iris (left) and the UCI wine (right) recognition dataset. Another interesting fact that we can observe in both embeddings is that the data also becomes linearly separable. We can almost put two straight lines in both visualizations to separate the clusters from each other:

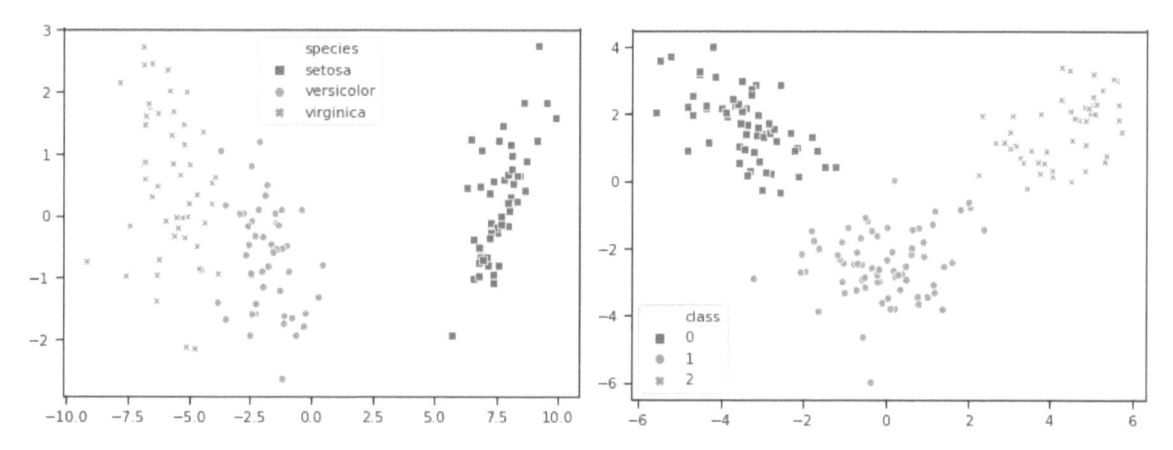

Figure 3.14: An LDA embedding of the iris (left) and UCI wine recognition (right) datasets

The LDA embedding for both of the preceding datasets looks quite good in terms of the separability of the data by classes. *Figure 3.14* gives a confident estimate that a linear classifier for both datasets should achieve great performance, for example, above 95% accuracy. While this might be just a ballpark estimate, we already know what to expect from a linear classifier with minimal analysis and data preprocessing. Unfortunately, most real-world embeddings look a lot more like *Figure 3.15* which is a lot less like the previous two:

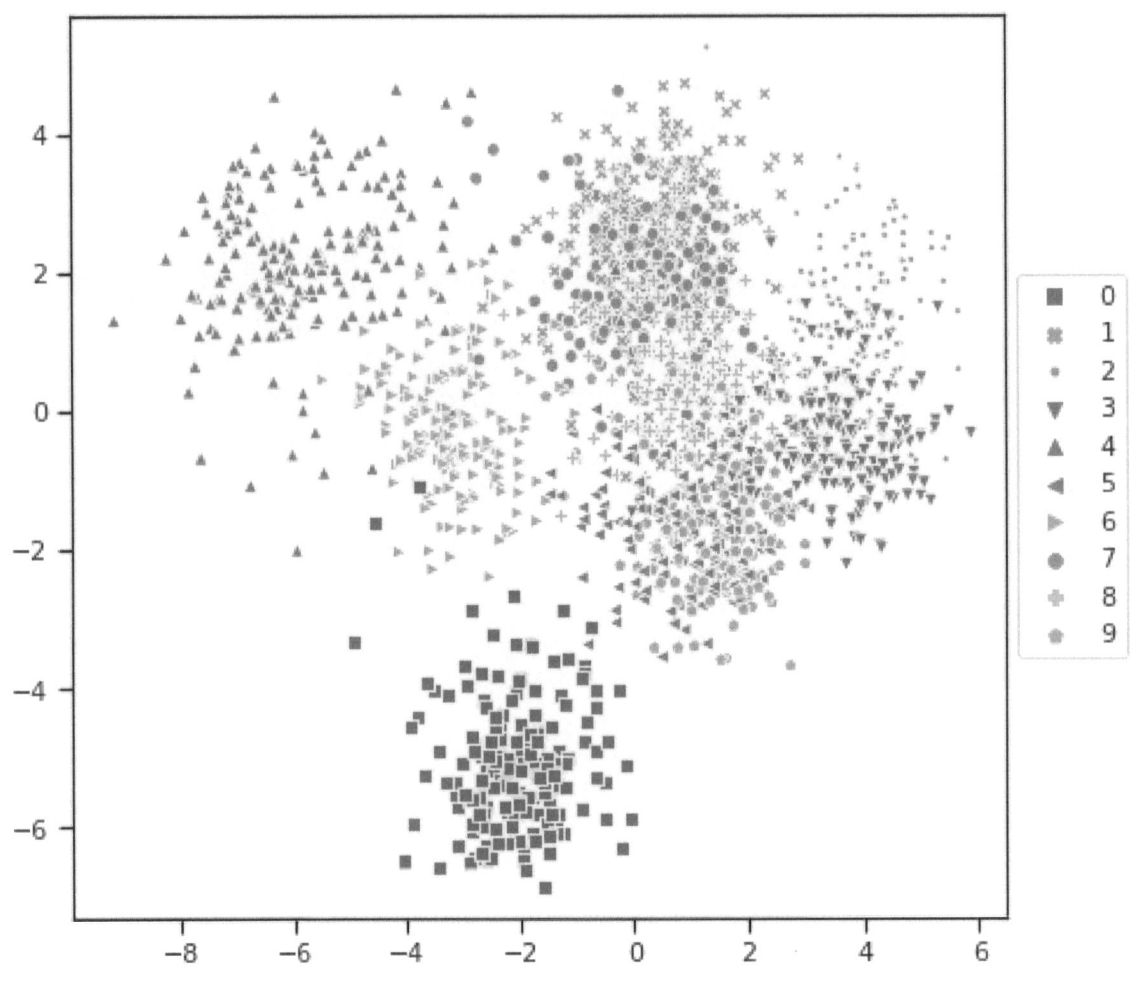

Figure 3.15: A non-separable, high-dimensional data visualization

Most real-world data is high-dimensional and often has above 10 or even 100 feature dimensions. In the preceding example, we again see a good separation of the cluster containing the 0 digits at the bottom and the two clusters of fours and sixes on the left side. All other clusters are drawn on top of each other and don't look to be linearly separable.

Hence, we could tell that a linear classifier won't perform well and will have maybe only around 30% accuracy—which is still a lot better than random. However, we can't really tell what performance we would expect from a complex non-linear model, maybe even a non- parametric model such as a decision tree-based ensemble classifier.

As we can see, LDA unsurprisingly performs a lot better than PCA as it takes class labels into account. It's a great embedding technique for linearly separable datasets with less than 100 dimensions and categorical target variables. An extension of LDA is **Quadratic Discriminant Analysis (QDA)**, which performs a non-linear projection using combinations of two variables.

If you are dealing with continuous target variables, you can use a very similar technique called **Analysis of variance (ANOVA)** to model the variance between clusters. The result of ANOVA transformations indicates whether the variance in the dataset is attributed to a combination of the variance of different components.

As we saw, both PCA and LDA didn't perform well on separating high-dimensional data such as image data. In the handwritten image dataset, we are dealing with *only* 784 feature dimensions from 28 x 28 pixel images. Imagine, your dataset consists of 1024 x 1024 pixel images – your dataset would have more than 1 million dimensions. Hence, we really need a better embedding technique for very high-dimensional datasets.

Non-linear dimension reduction with t-SNE

Projections of high-dimensional datasets into two or three dimensions were extremely difficult and cumbersome a couple of years ago. If you wanted to visualize image data on a two-dimensional graph, you could use any of the previously discussed techniques— if they could compute a result—or try exotic embeddings such as self-organizing maps.

However, in late 2012, t-SNE embedding was used by the team ranked first in the Merck Viz Kaggle competition—a rather unconventional way to release a great embedding algorithm. However, since the end of that competition, t-SNE has been used regularly in other Kaggle competitions and by large companies for embedding high-dimensional datasets with great success.

SNE projects high-dimensional features into two- or three-dimensional space while minimizing the difference of similar points in high-and low-dimensional space. Hence, high-dimensional feature vectors that are close to each other are very likely to be close to each other in the two-dimensional embedding.

Figure 3.16 shows t-SNE applied to the iris and UCI wine recognition dataset. As we can see, the complex non-linear embedding doesn't perform a lot better than the simple PCA or LDA techniques. However, its real power is highlighted on very large and high-dimensional datasets, up to 30 million observations of thousands of feature dimensions:

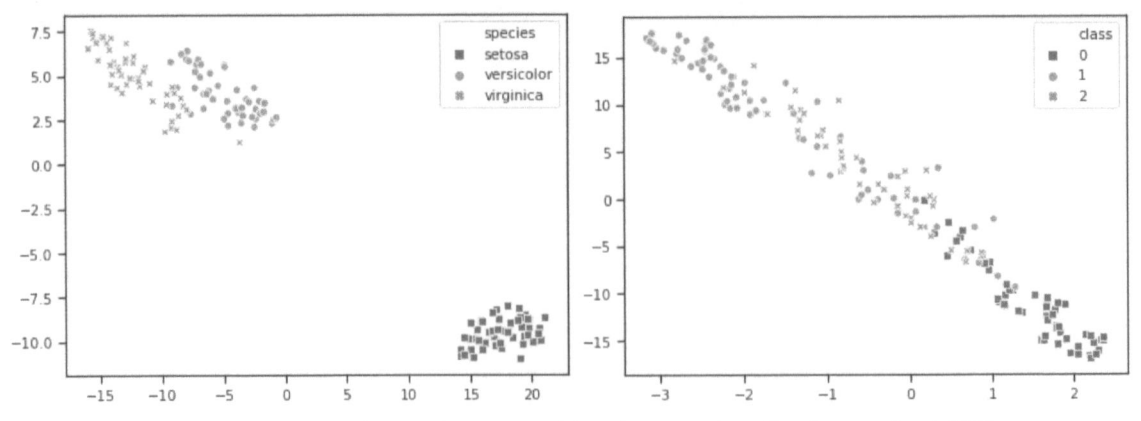

Figure 3.16: Iris and UCI wine recognition dataset visualizations using t-SNE

As we can see in *Figure 3.17*, t-SNE performs a lot better on the MNIST dataset and effortlessly separates the clusters of 10 handwritten digits. While it seemed impossible to separate the data in the two-dimensional LDA embedding—where the first two dimensions only explain 47% of the total variance—the t-SNE embedding suggests that 99% accuracy will be possible:

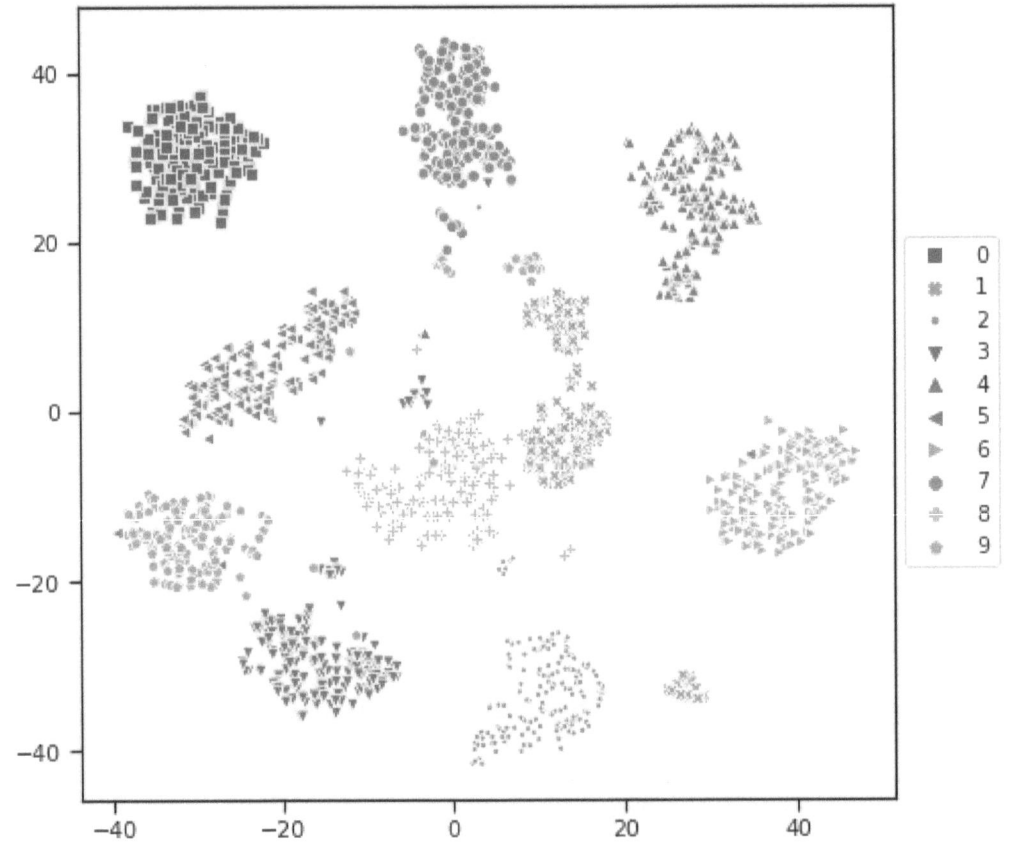

Figure 3.17: Achieving the highest accuracy using t-SNE embedding for data visualization

What is beautiful with this type of visualization is not only that we can see that the data is in fact separable, we can also imagine how the confusion matrix will look like when a classifier gets trained on the data—simply by looking at the preceding visualization. Here are some observations (which we couldn't easily identify in PCA or LDA embedding) about the data that we can infer from looking at the embedding:

- There are three clusters of ones where one cluster is further away from the mean.
- There are three clusters of nines where one cluster looks like ones and another looks like sevens.
- There is a cluster of threes that looks like eights.
- There is a small cluster of twos that looks like eights.
- The cluster of threes and nines are quite close so they might look similar.
- The clusters of zeros, fours, and sixes are distant from other clusters.

These are brilliant insights, as you now know what to expect and what to look for in your data when manually exploring samples. It also helps you to tune your feature engineering to, for example, try to differentiate ones, sevens, and nines as they will lead to most misclassification later on.

Generalizing t-SNE with UMAP

UMAP for dimension reduction is an algorithm for general-purpose manifold learning and dimension reduction. It is a generalization of t-SNE based on Riemannian geometry and algebraic topology.

In general, UMAP performs similar results to t-SNE with a topological approach, better scalability of feature dimensions, and faster computation at runtime. Due to the fact that it is faster and performs slightly better in terms of topological structure, it is quickly gaining popularity.

If we look again at embeddings of the iris and UCI wine recognition datasets, we see a similar effect as previously with t-SNE. As shown in *Figure 3.18*, the resulting embeddings look reasonable but not better than the linearly separable results of LDA. However, we can't measure computational performance by only comparing the results, and that's where UMAP really shines:

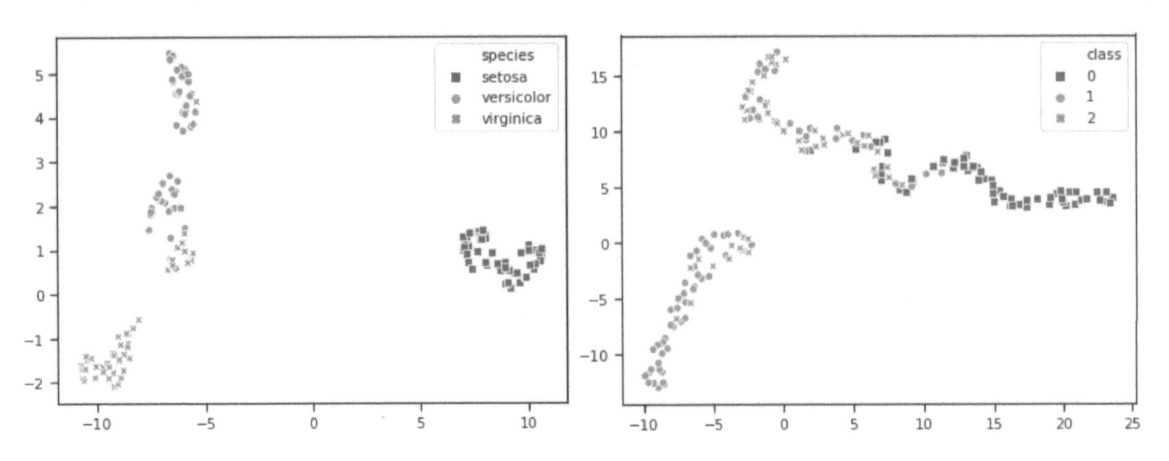

Figure 3.18: A high-dimensional data visualization using t-SNE with UMAP

When it comes to higher-dimensional data, such as the MNIST handwritten digits dataset, UMAP performs exceptionally well as a two-dimensional embedding technique. It reduces clusters to completely separable entities in the embedding, with minimal overlaps and a great distance between the clusters themselves. Similar observations such as clusters of classes 1 and 9 are still possible, but the clusters look a lot more separable in *Figure 3.19*:

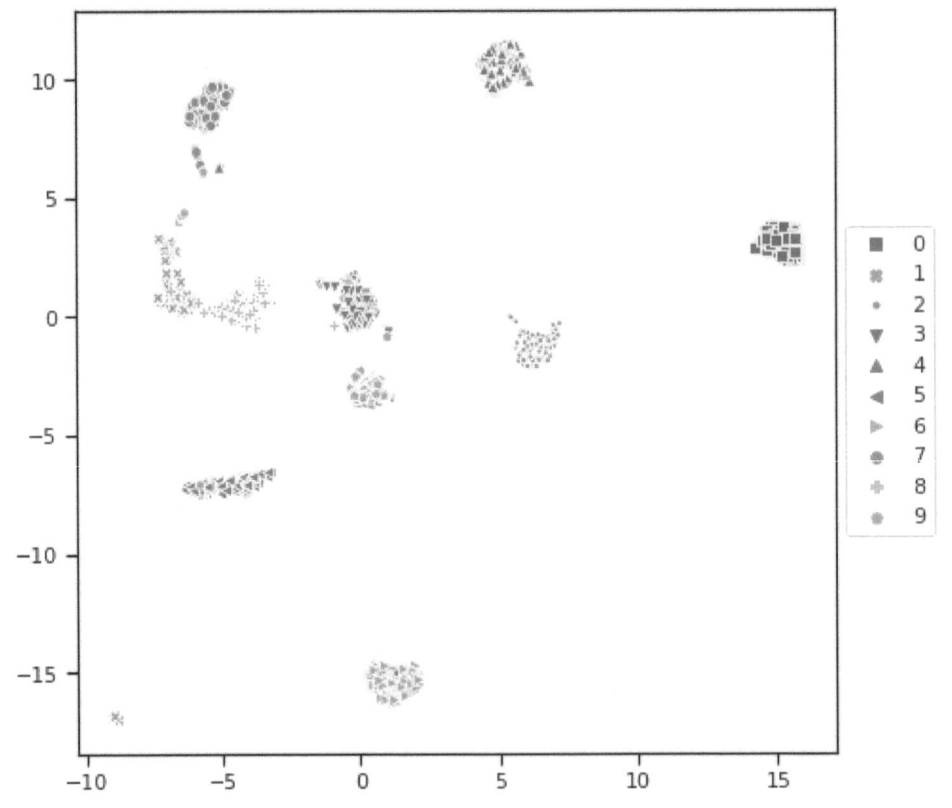

Figure 3.19: UMAP performance in the high-dimensional data visualization

From these data experimentation and visualization techniques, we would like you to take away the following key knowledge:

- Perform PCA to try to analyze Eigenvectors.
- Perform LDA or ANOVA to understand the variance of your data.
- Perform UMAP embedding if you have complex high-dimensional data.

Armed with this knowledge, we can dive right into data processing and feature engineering, knowing which data samples will be easy to handle and which samples will cause high mis-classification rates in the future.

Summary

In this chapter, we set up our Azure Machine Learning workspace, created our first Azure Machine Learning compute cluster (Amlcompute) and ran an initial experiment on the cluster. Everything is automated, from the setup of the workspace, to cluster creation and the submission of the training script.

Azure Machine Learning helps you keep track of experiments, metrics, training scripts, logs, trained models, artifacts, metrics, images, and much more. In this chapter, we started from a small ML script and, step by step, added additional functionality to take advantage of modern ML infrastructure and management techniques. We registered experiments, executed runs locally and on the compute cluster, stored a snapshot of the training folder with each run, collected training scores per epoch and a test score per run, and streamed the output directly back to the notebook environment. With a few lines of code, you can compare the trained model with all previously registered models. You can then register the model as a new version.

You then learned about dimensionality reduction techniques to visualize high-dimensional datasets. What's great about Azure Machine Learning is that you can also perform your data experimentation and analysis on the compute cluster and keep track of all generated figures and outputs. We compared unsupervised PCA to supervised LDA—both linear embeddings. Then, we compared linear techniques to non-linear dimensionality reductions such as t-SNE and the generalized form, UMAP. All these techniques are extremely useful for you to understand your data, the principal components, discriminant directions, and separability.

In the next chapter, using all the knowledge we've learned so far, we'll get started modeling our data by performing data loading (ETL), data preparation, and feature extraction. Try to make it a habit to create visualizations of your data and attach them as figures in your Azure Machine Learning experiments.

4
ETL, data preparation, and feature extraction

In this chapter, we will explore data preparation and **Extract, Transform, and Load** (**ETL**) techniques within Azure Machine Learning. We will start by looking behind the scenes of datasets and data stores, the abstraction for physical data storage systems. You will learn how to create data stores, upload data to the store, register and manage the data as Azure Machine Learning datasets, and later explore the data stored in these datasets. This will help you to abstract the data from the consumer and build separate parallel workflows for data engineers and data scientists.

In the subsequent section, we look at data transformations in Azure Machine Learning using Azure Machine Learning DataPrep, especially extracting, transforming, and loading the data. This enables you to build enterprise-grade data pipelines handling outliers, filtering data, and filling missing values.

The following topics will be covered in this chapter:

- Managing data and datasets in the cloud
- Preprocessing and feature engineering with Azure Machine Learning DataPrep

Managing data and datasets in the cloud

When you run an ML experiment or pipeline on your local development machine, you often don't need to manage your datasets as they are stored locally. However, as soon as you start training an ML model on remote compute targets, such as a VM in the cloud, you must make sure that the script can access the training data. And if you deploy a model that requires a certain dataset during scoring—for example, the lookup data for labels and the like—then this environment needs to access the data as well. As you can see, it makes sense to abstract the datasets for an ML project, both from the point of view of physical access and access permissions.

First, we will show how you can create a data store object to connect the Azure Machine Learning workspace to other data services, such as blob or file storage, data lake storage, and relational data stores, such as SQL Server and PostgreSQL. Once a data store is attached, we can register data from this data store—for example, a blob in blob storage, a file in file storage, or a table in a relational database—as a data store in Azure Machine Learning. By doing this, the dataset can be accessed from all execution environments, such as in the local development machine, on the Azure Machine Learning compute as a remote compute target, or in the scoring environment.

Next, we will look into a quick way to explore the datasets. Depending on the size of the dataset, you can access the data as an in-memory pandas dataframe or resilient distributed Spark dataframe. Finally, we will show how to write your datasets back to the original data store object.

Let's jump right in and find out how to move data to the cloud effectively.

Getting data into the cloud

Before we go into details about how to register data stores and datasets in Azure Machine Learning, I want to emphasize that you can load any data from any location to your experiment, data preparation, or ML script because you are running inside a Python interpreter. However, you would have to distribute the access keys and passwords to log in to the data sources and convert the data to the expected format.

By abstracting both the data storage (for example, file storage, blob storage, and relational database) and datasets (for example, file, folder, and table), you can provide a unified abstract view on the data to consume different datasets from various sources from a unified interface. This has many advantages, including unified access control and unified data format conversions. In this section, we will look at how to register a data store and dataset to consume data in multiple environments.

Organizing data in data stores and datasets

When creating an ML service workspace, you automatically deploy a blob storage to the same resource group. This storage is used internally for storing the code snapshots, outputs, and logs from experiment runs, but is also used as the default data store for datasets. However, in this section, we will create a new blob storage account to store all datasets:

1. Let's create a new blob storage account, **mldemoblob**. Please note that the name of each storage account must be unique. For the purpose of this book, we will create it as locally redundant storage (**Standard_LRS**) only. However, you can even deploy it as geo-redundant storage with read access on the replica. Once the account is created, we will extract and store the **Shared Access Signature (SAS)** in the **ACCOUNT_KEY** variable:

   ```
   $ az storage account create -n mldemoblob -g mldemo \
       --sku Standard_LRS --encryption-services blob
   
   $ ACCOUNT_KEY=$(az storage account keys list -n mldemoblob -g mldemo \
       | jq '.[0].value')
   ```

   In the preceding snippet, we use the CLI command **jq**. This is a very popular tool for parsing JSON responses and applying queries on top. If you don't have it installed, make sure that you install it now and make it available in your path.

2. Next, we create a container inside the blob storage account that will hold all our datasets later. We need to use the **ACCOUNT_KEY** variable to create the container:

   ```
   $ az storage container create -n data --account-name mldemoblob \
       --account-key ${ACCOUNT_KEY}
   ```

3. Finally, we can attach the blob storage container to the Azure Machine Learning workspace as a **datastore** under the name **mldemodatastore**. This allows us to use the abstract data store in the ML service without worrying about the storage technology under the hood. We also need an SAS to authorize the ML service to interact with the blob container. We could use either a container-specific or account-specific access token—in our case, we will use the same account SAS stored in the **ACCOUNT_KEY** variable:

   ```
   $ az ml datastore attach-blob -n mldemodatastore -a mldemoblob -c data \
       --account-key ${ACCOUNT_KEY}
   ```

   Now, we can start uploading data to this blob storage container and register this data as datasets in the ML service. The great benefit of this solution is that from now on, you can access your data from any ML service environment from this data store—be it your local machine, a remote distributed compute cluster, or even the container instance that runs your scoring service.

4. Let's go ahead and upload some data—in our case, we want to upload a local training folder to the **blob** storage account. You can achieve this using the command line or the cross-platform Azure Storage Explorer application:

   ```
   $ az storage blob upload-batch \
       --account-name mldemoblob --account-key ${ACCOUNT_KEY} \
       --destination "data/training" --source "./training"
   ```

5. Next, we open a Python authoring environment and register the data as **dataset**. First, we need to retrieve a reference to the **datastore** instance. Next, we can define the path of the data on this data store and load the data using the **Dataset.auto_read_files()** method. Finally, we can register the data as a new dataset in Azure Machine Learning. The **definition** attribute will show us the latest version of the dataset and the time it was updated:

   ```
   from azureml.core.datastore import Datastore
   from azureml.core.dataset import Dataset

   datastore_name = 'mldemodatastore'
   dataset_name = 'training.data.raw'

   # Retrieve the datastore
   datastore = Datastore.get(ws, datastore_name)
   datapath = datastore.path('training/raw_data.csv')
   dataset = Dataset.auto_read_files(datapath)
   ```

```
# Register the dataset

def = dataset.register(workspace=ws, name=dataset_name,
                       exist_ok=True, update_if_exist=True)

print(def.definition)
```

6. Ultimately, we can modify our pandas or Spark code to load the data using the Azure Machine Learning dataset instead of the direct connection, and it will handle data loading, authentication, and versioning automatically under the hood. Here is a snippet of how this is done in pandas:

```
# Access your dataset
dataset = Dataset.get(ws, dataset_name)

# Load in-memory Dataset to your local machine as Pandas dataframe
df = dataset.to_pandas_dataframe()
print(df.head())
```

If you are using PySpark instead of Python you can use the following snippet.

```
# Access your dataset
dataset = Dataset.get(ws, dataset_name)

# Load in-memory Dataset to your local machine as pandas dataframe
df = dataset.to_spark_dataframe()
df.show()
```

As you can see, by abstracting the dataset and data store, you can now analyze, prepare, and use your data in any environment automatically, be it your local machine, Azure Machine Learning compute cluster, Databricks-distributed Spark environment, or any compute target.

You have now learned how to load data into Azure Blob and register it as a dataset for further use in all other environments. This is a useful skill for a data engineer who will be responsible for cleaning and providing the data for business analysts, ML engineers, and data scientists.

Next, let's look at how to manage these datasets from a data steward's perspective.

Managing data in Azure Machine Learning

Despite the abstraction of data stores and datasets, there are many more advantages in Azure Machine Learning to using datasets. Once you are responsible for a large amount of data, you need to acquire skills to manage and organize datasets and data stores in the cloud. Fortunately, Azure Machine Learning provides a large set of functionalities to greatly facilitate working with the data and managing your data properly for transparent end-to-end ML processes.

For an end-to-end, fully reproducible ML workflow, you need to look at three large topics:

- Compute infrastructure
- Code
- Data

While an ML service helps to manage all three aspects, we will focus on the third point of data management in the following sections. We will specifically see how to update datasets using versions and definitions, how to manage the life cycle of datasets, and how to manage snapshots for reproducible ML processes.

First, we will take a look at how to abstract datasets and data stores to dataset definitions. This will help you to load data from a dataset definition without having to know anything about the data location, storage format, encoding, and access control. You can also version this dataset's definitions to keep your consumers up to date with the latest changes.

Then, we will discover a way to make ML run in a reproducible manner, namely by providing data snapshots. By having access to a vast amount of cheap and scalable data storage, it is a good practice to create data snapshots for smaller and mid-sized datasets. Dataset definitions makes this process very easy for you.

Finally, we will go through the life cycle of a dataset definition. This is a concept that you should put in place when managing more than three different datasets for more than three different data consumers. Your dataset definition can be easily compared to a public API, which also needs to be documented, versioned, updated, and deprecated– we will see the exact same for datasets.

Azure provides a fantastic way of abstracting and managing data stores and datasets. Let's take a look.

Versioning datasets and dataset definitions

Datasets in Azure Machine Learning can be versioned through dataset definitions. The version is a monotonically increasing number that is incremented whenever new data of the same dataset is registered using the `Dataset.register()` method and sets the `update_if_exist` parameter to `True`. If the dataset has the same name as an existing dataset, then the version of this dataset is incremented.

The version of each dataset is stored in its accompanying dataset definition:

```
# Register the dataset once
dataset_reg = dataset.register(workspace=ws, name=dataset_name,
                    exist_ok=True, update_if_exist=True)
print(dataset_reg.definition)
# > VersionID: 1, State: active, Created: 2019-06-17 20:54:37.026860+00:00,
Modified: 2019-06-17 20:54:37.026860+00:00, Notes: None


# Register the dataset with the same name a second time
dataset_reg = dataset.register(workspace=ws, name=dataset_name,
                    exist_ok=True, update_if_exist=True)
print(dataset_reg.definition)
# > VersionID: 2, State: active, Created: 2019-06-17 21:56:39.026860+00:00,
Modified: 2019-06-17 21:56:39.026860+00:00, Notes: None
```

As you can see, if you re-register a dataset of the same name, you will end up with a dataset with an incremented version number. Hence, once your data is registered as a dataset, it is automatically versioned and you can access specific versions of the data from your code through the dataset definitions:

```
# list all definitions for the dataset
dataset.get_definitions()
# > VersionID: 1, State: active, Created: 2019-06-17 ...
# > VersionID: 2, State: active, Created: 2019-06-17 ...


# get definition of version 1
dataset.get_definition(version_id=1)
# > VersionID: 1, State: active, Created: 2019-06-17 ...
```

You might want to ask yourself what exactly such a dataset definition represents, and why the version number is not assigned to the dataset directly. A dataset definition describes a set of transformations performed on the raw data. These transformations are automatically translated and applied to pandas or PySpark transformations when the data is accessed through these interfaces.

A good example would be if the raw data contains many fields that should not be exposed to the consumers of the data. Another common use case would be the renaming of existing columns to common column names and simple transformations and data assertions. Here is a small example of keeping just the relevant columns:

```
# Update the dataset definition to select only relevant columns
def = def.keep_columns(['id', 'A', 'B', 'C'])


# Update the dataset definition
dataset = dataset.update_definition(def, 'select relevant columns')
```

In the preceding code, we define a transformation via the **DatasetDefinition.keep_columns()** method. We will see more of these methods in a later section in this chapter. We can then use this definition to update the dataset and display only the relevant columns to each data consumer. Moreover, you can now make sure that all your ML pipelines always use the same dataset definition:

```
# Access your dataset
dataset = Dataset.get(ws, dataset_name)


# Get the dataset definition with version 1
def = dataset.get_definition(version_id=1)


# Get the Pandas dataframe from this definition
df = def.to_pandas_dataframe()
```

If the data in the data storage system is overwritten in its original location (for example, on blob storage) or changes (for example, on an RDBMS), then you cannot guarantee that the same data is used for all experiments and training. In this case, you can snapshot the dataset.

Taking data snapshots for reproducibility

For reproducibility, validation, and auditing purposes, you might want to take snapshots of datasets in your enterprise-grade ML pipeline. This will completely decouple the work of ML engineers and data scientists from the work of data engineers and data stewards. Both groups can work in parallel and run reproducible experiments while working on the ingesting, cleaning, and quality of the data.

By default, a snapshot in Azure Machine Learning creates and stores the dataset profile only—a summary of all column statistics. It uses the local compute (the current authoring environment) and stores it on the default data store—the blob storage account that was automatically deployed with Azure Machine Learning. Both the compute target and storage target can be configured. It's helpful to specify the compute target when you need to run profiling in parallel. For example with large Parquet datasets stored on a data lake, you want to use PySpark to parallelize execution rather than a single Python interpreter.

Here is a snippet on how to create such a local snapshot in the default data store:

```
# Name of the current snapshot
snapshot_name = 'experiment_1'


# Create a snapshot of the dataset
snapshot = dataset.create_snapshot(snapshot_name=snapshot_name)


# Monitor the snapshot process
snapshot.wait_for_completion(show_output=True, status_update_frequency=10)


# Return the snapshot
dataset.get_snapshot(snapshot_name)
```

As you can see in the preceding code, we simply pass a name for the snapshot and create it using the current Python interpreter. You can change both the compute environment and the storage location by passing additional arguments to the **Dataset.create_snapshot()** function.

Most importantly though, if you want to take a snapshot of the data as well, you need to set the **create_data_snapshot** argument to **True**. This will compute the data profile and store it together with the data to the configured data store.

If want to explore all snapshots from a dataset, we can list them using the following code snippet:

```
# Get all snapshots from a dataset
dataset.get_all_snapshots()
```

However, if we want to use the data from a specific snapshot (which has also saved a data snapshot), we can simply return the pandas or PySpark dataframe from this snapshot:

```
# Get snapshot from a dataset
dataset_snap = dataset.get_snapshot(snapshot_name)


# Get the Pandas dataframe from this snapshot
df = dataset_snap.to_pandas_dataframe()
```

In the preceding code, we load the pandas dataframe from the data snapshot. You can now use this functionality in your experiments, training, and validation pipelines in order to achieve reproducibility for all your ML processes.

The life cycle of a dataset

As you saw in the previous sections, datasets should be versioned, snapshotted, and managed together with the experiment code and environment (libraries, scripts, configurations, and more) that use them. The reason for this is because all data, by its very nature, is dynamic and changes over time. The life cycle management features of Azure Machine Learning datasets give you all the flexibility to handle these changes over time.

The most common situation is that datasets are reorganized and changes are done in their name, path, physical storage, and so on. Using Azure datasets, you can abstract the path (or table name in RDBMS) and physical storage via data stores. To modify the name of the dataset itself, you can use dataset life cycle management and deprecate the dataset in favor of a newer dataset.

Here is a slightly different example where you want to deprecate a certain version of a dataset in favor of a newer version:

```
# Dataset definition to deprecate
def = dataset.get_definition(version_id=1)


# Deprecate it by providing the replacement dataset definition
def.deprecate(deprecate_by_dataset_id=dataset.id,
              deprecated_by_definition_version=2)
```

Deprecating a dataset will warn the consumer of the dataset that there is a newer dataset version available that should be used instead. Another possibility is to archive a dataset when it is no longer used:

```
# Archive the dataset definition
def = dataset.get_definition(version_id=1)
def.archive()
```

To complete the life cycle, you can also reactivate the dataset definition and hence make it visible again to your consumers:

```
# Reactivate the dataset definition
def = dataset.get_definition(version_id=1)
def.reactivate()
```

Thus, you have learned how to manage your datasets over time using the life cycle management functionality on datasets in Azure Machine Learning.

Now that we have the data defined as datasets, data consumers need a way to navigate and explore these datasets. That's exactly what we will cover in the next section.

Exploring data registered in Azure Machine Learning

In this section, we will take a look at how to explore the data registered in Azure Machine Learning from the perspective of the data scientist. We assume that the data was previously loaded into Azure by a data engineer, and we now need to use the data as a data scientist.

A typical workflow would first list the different datasets available, and then dive into the dataset definition, profile, and samples to evaluate the data. You will learn how to implement this workflow in the following sections.

Exploring the datasets

First, as a data scientist, we want to know which datasets are available. Hence, we will explore the datasets from Azure Machine Learning from within a Jupyter Notebook. Please note that there are multiple ways to explore registered datasets, but for the purpose of this book, we will stick to the tools each data scientist is most likely familiar with and using already:

1. Let's explore the datasets from a workspace:

   ```
   # list all datasets from a workspace
   datasets = Dataset.list(ws)

   # Access your dataset
   dataset = Dataset.get(ws, dataset_name)
   ```

   In the preceding code, we first list all the available datasets.

2. Using the standard Python filter function, you can also limit the list of datasets. We then select a specific dataset given the dataset name and check all dataset definitions in the following code snippet:

   ```
   # List all definitions for the dataset
   definitions = dataset.get_definitions()

   # Get a specific dataset definition
   data_definition = dataset.get_definition(version_id=1)
   ```

   A dataset definition is a particular version of a dataset accompanied by an optional transformation, for example, dropped or renamed columns. When working on the dataset itself, you are always working on the latest dataset definition, hence the one with the largest version.

3. Dataset definitions are only tracking column transformations and not the data itself when it changes. To do so, we can take a look at all snapshots from a dataset, and specifically look for ones that snapshot the data as well along with the profile:

   ```
   # Get all snapshots from a dataset
   snapshots = dataset.get_all_snapshots()

   # Get snapshot from a dataset
   data_snapshot = dataset.get_snapshot(snapshot_name)
   ```

   In the preceding code, we list all snapshots and select a specific snapshot by name.

4. When you want to access the data from the dataset, definition or snapshot–you can do so directly by returning a pandas or PySpark dataframe, as shown in the following code snippet:

```
# Load dataframe from dataset
df = dataset.to_pandas_dataframe()

# Load dataframe from dataset definition
df = data_definition.to_pandas_dataframe()

# Load dataframe from dataset snapshot
df = data_snapshot.to_pandas_dataframe()
```

You can now explore datasets, data transformations as definitions, and data snapshots in Juptyer notebooks, or by using a Python interpreter. However, when the dataset is too big to fit in memory, you need to explore the data in a more efficient way. A common example is when pandas runs out of memory while attempting to parse a file that is larger than the available memory. In such a case, you need to split the file and read multiple chunks from multiple machines (scale out) or increase the RAM on your machine (scale up). We will go through these techniques in the next section.

Exploring the data

There are multiple ways to explore a large dataset without downloading the dataset on your local machine. The most common techniques are displaying the top N rows, returning a (stratified) sample of the data, or computing a dataset profile–a summary of the distribution of all columns. In this section, we will explore all three options.

1. Let's start with the easiest, returning the top N rows of a dataset. The function is called **dataset.head()** and works exactly as in pandas; it even returns a pandas dataframe containing the top N records:

```
# Return the first 10 records as pandas dataframe
df = dataset.head(10)
```

You can use the preceding function to return only a subset of records and load these records into local memory. However, if the records are sorted, then getting the first N values is not representative of the dataset. In order to retrieve a more representative sample of the dataset, you can use the **dataset.sample()** function. This function generates a new dataset as a sample from the original dataset, using the sampling strategy and parameters provided.

2. The general `sample()` function is defined as `sample (sample_strategy, arguments)`, where the `sample_strategy` parameter defines the sample, strategy (`top_n`, `simple_random` or `stratified`), and where `arguments` is a dictionary specifying the properties of the sampling strategy. Each sampling strategy has different properties. The output dataset is generated through the execution of a transformation pipeline defined by the dataset similar to a dataset definition. Hence, the return data will be sampled using the sampling strategy and parameters you defined. Once you return a sampled dataset, you can use the same methods as in the original dataset:

```
# Specify the sampling strategy top_n
sample_strategy = "top_n"
sample_props = {n: 10}

# Return a sampled dataset
sampled_dataset = dataset.sample(sample_strategy, sample_props)

# Get the Pandas dataframe of the dataset
sampled_dataset.to_pandas_dataframe()
```

In the preceding code, you can see that the sample function returns a new dataset with a sampling transformation. Hence, we can use `dataset.to_pandas_dataframe()` to convert the dataset to a pandas dataframe or PySpark dataframe.

3. You can use other sampling strategies as well to retrieve a more representative sample from the dataset. Here is an example configuration of retrieving a randomly sampled subset of the data:

```
# Specify the sampling strategy simple_random
sample_strategy = "simple_random"
sample_props = {probability: 0.7, seed: 1}

# Return a sampled dataset
sampled_dataset = dataset.sample(sample_strategy, sample_props)
```

4. If you need a subset with the same distribution as the original data, you can use stratified subsampling, as shown in the following example. You also have to define the columns and fractions for which the stratified split should be computed:

```
# Specify the sampling strategy stratified
sample_strategy = "stratified"
sample_props = {
    columns: ["A", "B", "C"],
    fractions: {("A", "B"): 0.6, ("C"): 0.4]},
    seed: 1
```

```
}

# Return a sampled dataset
sampled_dataset = dataset.sample(sample_strategy, sample_props)
```

The preceding code defines the stratified sampling strategy on the columns A, B, and C, using a fraction of 0.6 for columns A and B, and 0.4 for column C.

5. If you want to explore the data distribution without loading a sample of the data to local memory, you could also load the data profile. The profile is a summary of the value distribution for each column containing counts of unique values and missing values, as well as the min, max, and median. Here is an example of loading the dataset profile:

```
dataset.get_profile()
```

In this section, you have learned how to explore datasets in Python, how data is stored and registered in Azure Machine Learning, as well as data distribution.

In the next section, we will look at the data preparation techniques built into Azure Machine Learning.

Preprocessing and feature engineering with Azure Machine Learning DataPrep

In this section, we will dive deeper into the preprocessing and feature extraction process using Azure Machine Learning. We will first access and extract data with different data formats from different storage systems, such as text data and CSV data from blob storage, and tabular data from relational database systems.

Then, we will take a look at common data transformation techniques using Azure Machine Learning DataPrep, a Python library to build transformations on top of datasets directly in Azure Machine Learning. You will also learn common techniques of how to filter columns, split columns through expressions, fix missing values, convert data types, and even how to derive transformations through examples.

Finally, we will write the data back into data storage where it can be registered as a cleaned dataset in Azure Machine Learning. By doing this you can implement fully enterprise-grade ETL and data preparation pipelines within Azure Machine Learning.

Let's begin by parsing data that we previously moved to the cloud.

Parsing different data formats

There are different ways of loading data into Azure Machine Learning using the **DataPrep** SDK. The recommended way is to first upload data to blob storage in the cloud, and convert it into a supported format. Azure DataPrep allows data to be accessed from many different sources and to be used in various encodings.

> **Note**
>
> At the time of writing this book, Azure DataPrep cannot read from a versioned dataset definition. We recommend to first extract data from the source, then load the data into Azure Blob storage, read it using DataPrep, write the data back to Azure Blob storage, and then create versioned datasets out of the cleaned data.

Currently, Azure DataPrep can load data from local disk, blob storage, Azure Data Lake Storage, and SQL databases, such as Microsoft SQL Server and PostgreSQL. When accessing data files, Azure DataPrep currently supports delimiter-separated files, such as CSV, fixed-width files, binary formats such as Excel and Parquet, and complex nested JSON objects.

One fantastic feature of DataPrep is that it can automatically detect the schema and encoding of a file and infer all required settings for you using the **auto_read_file (path, include_path)** method. Here is a quick example for reading a text file from local disk:

```
import azureml.dataprep as dprep


dataflow = dprep.auto_read_file(path='./data/filename.txt')
```

Like most other **dataprep** statements, the preceding code defines a *lazy* transformation to read a file from a location on the local disk. This means that by calling this line, the execution engine doesn't actually load any data. This behavior is quite different to what you might be used to from pandas. However, this is the default behavior in reading and transforming **Resilient Distributed Dataframes (RDDs)** in Spark.

> **Note**
>
> Similar to Spark, all transformation are evaluated lazily in a **dataprep** flow. Hence, if you are not specifying an action, the transformations won't execute anything.

In fact, the `auto_read_file()` method might be the method that you will find yourself using most of the time because it works really well. Besides reading a single file, you can also define a pattern as the **path** argument and read multiple files at once. Setting the second parameter, **include_path**, to **True** will add an additional column to your dataset, specifying the path form where the rows were loaded.

However, if you need more control over the parsing of the data and you know the file types, then it's advisable to use file-specific functions that we are discussing in the following sections.

Loading delimiter-separated data

Most other libraries support complex rules on how to parse CSV and other delimiter-separated files. This is no different to Azure DataPrep providing an exhaustive list of options for parsing delimiters, quotes, data types, and so on, and to defining standard behavior for conversion errors (for example, dropping the row) and file headers (for example, assuming all files have the same header).

Here is a small example of reading a CSV file from local disk and inferring the column types of the dataset:

```
import azureml.dataprep as dprep


# Read CSV files
dataflow = dprep.read_csv(path='./data/*.csv', infer_column_types=True)
```

In the preceding code, we read a CSV file from disk and infer all the column types. To do so, the engine has to scan the first rows to extract a header type for each column in the dataset. You can access the data types using the **dataflow.dtypes** object.

> **Note**
>
> Azure DataPrep can also extract and read CSV files in zip archives.

Parsing JSON data

Reading and parsing nested JSON data is always a bit tricky. However, using Azure DataPrep, it is quite straightforward and similar to the CSV example from the preceding section. A common problem of parsing JSON is how to deal with nested arrays. In big data systems, nested arrays are usually either reduced to a single value, aggregated, or exploded and split over multiple rows.

The same can be done when reading JSON files in Azure DataPrep. With a single property setting `flatten_nested_arrays` to True, all nested arrays are exploded into additional rows in the dataset. All other columns are duplicated with the same content of the original row, but the values of the array are split across the newly created rows:

```
import azureml.dataprep as dprep

# Read JSON files
dataflow = dprep.read_json(path='./data/*.json')
```

The preceding code will read multiple JSON files and provide a lazily evaluated dataflow.

Loading binary column-store data in Parquet format

Azure DataPrep offers the functionality to load binary-encoded, column-store data, such as Parquet format. Parquet is a popular format for storing large amounts of data optimized for fast analytics and interactive querying. Parquet is also a great format for internal data pipelines as you automatically solve parsing issues and performance bottlenecks.

There are two ways to read Parquet files in Azure Machine Learning **DataPrep–read_parquet_file** and **read_parquet_dataset**. The former will read a single or multiple files defined via the path string similar to what we saw for CSV and JSON, whereas the latter will parse the whole directory as a big data dataset. This is somewhat confusing, but big data systems such as Hive and Spark usually write nested directories with Parquet files, where partition key names and values are encoded in the directory structure. Hence, the latter method is optimized for parsing these nested directory structures of Parquet. We will see an example in the following code snippet:

```
import azureml.dataprep as dprep

# Read single parquet files individually
dataflow = dprep.read_parquet_file(path='./data/filename.parquet')

# Read nested folders of parquet files
dataflow = dprep.read_parquet_dataset(path='./data/warehouse/telemetry')
```

In the preceding code, we use both functions to lazily load data that is either file-based or includes the entire partitioning directory structure. As a general advice, if you just drop a bunch of Parquet files into a flat folder structure for processing, use the former; if you are reading from a **Hadoop File System** (**HDFS**) or data generated by Hive or Spark, use the latter.

Thus, we have discussed how to load several data sources and types into Azure Machine Learning using the **DataPrep** SDK. In the next section, we will showcase how to transform the data using the same SDK.

Building a data transformation pipeline in Azure Machine Learning

Data transformations such as cleaning, preprocessing, filtering, imputing missing values, and feature extractions are the heart of every ETL pipeline. In the following sections, we are looking at the *transform* part of the ETL pipeline. It's worth mentioning that in cloud- or big data-based data pipelines, the order is usually ELT; in other words, extract from the source, load to the cloud, and transform in the cloud.

The **azureml-dataprep** package is not only useful for reading and writing data, but it also contains loads of functionality to transform data, whether that is adding columns, filtering out rows or columns, or imputing missing values. Before we dive into the concepts of transformations and actions in Azure, we want to quickly take a look at the dataflow object that was returned when reading the data.

If you have ever worked with Spark or TensorFlow 1, the concept of a dataflow might not be new to you. In both frameworks, you have also lazily evaluated **Directed Acyclic Graphs (DAGs)** of operations. In Spark, you might perform filters on an RDD, while in TensorFlow, you might compute the loss metric of a specific point in the graph. If the data is not displayed or the session is not executed, then the lazy transformations are not executed either.

Note that a dataflow is very similar to an RDD in Spark, as it is a DAG of lazy operations on a distributed dataset. Let's get started and explore different transformations provided in the Azure **dataprep** SDK.

Generating features through expression

First, we are going to look into the addition of features to a dataset. This is a common task when you need to extract information from a column, transform that information, and store it in a new column. The Azure **dataprep** SDK provides a range of expressions that allow you to extract data from existing columns and store it in new columns. The following expressions are available:

- **substring**: To compute the substring of all values of a column
- **length**: To compute the length of all values of a column
- **to_upper**: To convert all values of a column to uppercase
- **to_lower**: To convert all values of a column to lowercase
- **RegEx.extract_record**: To extract the capturing group from a regex matcher
- **create_datetime**: To create a date time object from the year, month, and day columns

- Algebraic operators
    - Addition +
    - Subtraction -
    - Division /
    - Multiplication *
    - Integer division //
    - Modulo %
    - Power **

Let's look at the **substring** method as an example for creating new columns through expressions.

The **substring(start, length)** expression can be used to extract a prefix from a column into a new column. You can also use **substring(start)** without specifying the length in the expression. If you pass the substring expression to the expression argument, it creates a new calculated column that executes the **expression** specified on every record of the column.

Let's look at an example. When you are given an **International Bank Account Number (IBAN)** field, you might want to split this code into its country code, bank identifier, branch, and account IDs. This can be achieved using the **substring** expression. In an example IBAN, **IE29 AIBK 9311 5212 3456 78**, we want to extract the first two characters as country code in order to incorporate additional country-specific information in the dataset:

```
substr_exp = dprep.col('iban').substring(0, 2)
country_code = dflow.add_column(expression=substr_exp,
   new_column_name='country_code', prior_column='iban',
   expression=substr_exp)
```

As you can see in the preceding code, we add the newly created column to the dataflow using the **add_column()** method. This method requires the expression, the name for the new column, **new_column_name**, and the name of the column, **prior_column**, after which the calculated column should be added as arguments. Let's continue with some data type conversions.

Data type conversions

When transforming data, you will often be confronted with the need to parse data into different data types. Therefore, the dataflow object contains the following methods to transform the data types of columns:

- to_bool()
- to_datetime()
- to_long()
- to_number()
- to_string()

The **to_long()** and **to_string()** functions don't take any additional parameters other than an array of column identifiers to be transformed. Let's look at the other functions.

The **to_bool()** method allows us to transform complex data structures into Boolean values. Similar to all the other functions, its first argument is a list of columns to be applied. The **true_values** and **false_values** arguments let us define a list of custom values that should be converted into **true** or **false**. Additionally, we can also specify what should happen when a value was not found in either of the two lists, using **MismatchAsOption.ASERROR**, **MismatchAsOption.ASTRUE**, or **MismatchAsOption.ASFALSE**. Let's take a look at an example:

```
from azureml.dataprep import MismatchAsOption
dflow = dflow.to_bool(['Survived'],
    true_values=['yes'], false_values=['no'],
mismatch_as=MismatchAsOption.ASFALSE)
```

In the preceding code, we convert the survived column of the string type into a Boolean data type. We define that the value **yes** should be converted to **true**, and the value no should be converted to **false**. Finally, we want any mismatches parsed as **false** values.

Next, we will convert strings into floating point numbers using the **to_number()** method. Again, we use the column names of the columns that will be transformed as a first argument. Additionally, we can specify the **decimal_point** argument to specify whether the source data uses a dot, **DecimalMark.DOT**, or a comma, **DecimalMark.COMMA**, to represent the decimal point:

```
from azureml.dataprep import DecimalMark
dflow = dflow.to_number(['Latitude', 'Longitude'],
decimal_point=DecimalMark.COMMA)
```

In the preceding code, we are transforming the two columns, **Latitude** and **Longitude**, from strings into floating-point numeric data types. We also specify the comma as a decimal point.

Let's take a look at the last conversion function, **to_datetime()**, which parses a string into a datetime format. The first argument is again an array of column names. Additionally, we can add a list of various datatime formats using the **date_time_formats** argument to be used for a conversion. This is very useful when your data source contains multiple different datetime string representations that should all be parsed at once. Another argument, **date_constant**, lets us specify a constant date as a string that will be appended to all values that only contain a time but not a date value:

```
dflow = dflow.to_datetime('Date', date_time_formats=['%d.%m.%Y %H:%M'])
```

The preceding code transforms the Date column from a string into a **datatype** format. In the following section, we will learn how to perform a similar transformation using examples.

Deriving columns by example

Next, we will look into a nifty way of deriving new columns through examples in Azure dataprep SDK. There are two methods that we can use to derive new columns:

- **split_column_by_example**: This splits columns into multiple columns using the examples provided.
- **derive_column_by_example**: This transforms columns into a new column using the examples provided.

These methods are extremely useful when you want to perform a complicated transformation or split that is much easier to define by a set of examples than through a set of rules. This is often the case when working with messy data or data from different sources. In our example, we will look into the **derive_column_by_example** method, but both methods work in the same way:

1. Create a builder object.
2. Add examples to the builder or modify a list of suggested examples.
3. Preview the transformation.
4. Apply the transformer.

Let's look at these steps in action. First, we create a builder directly from the **dflow** object using **dflow.builders.derive_column_by_example**. We also need to specify the source columns and the name for the new derived column using the **source_columns** and **new_column_name** arguments. In the following code snippet, we use the **Name** column of the Titanic dataset to derive the title of the passenger:

```
builder = dflow.builders.derive_column_by_example(
    source_columns=['Name'], new_column_name='Title')
```

Please see *Figure 4.1* which shows how the data in the **Name** column and the desired transformation to **Title** looks like:

Name	Title
Braund, Mr. Owen Harris	Mr
Cumings, Mrs. John Bradley (Florence Briggs Thayer)	Mrs
Heikkinen, Miss. Laina	Miss
Palsson, Master. Gosta Leonard	Master

Figure 4.1: Collating the names and titles of passengers

Now, we can add examples to the transformation using the **add_example** method. We need to specify the source data and the example transformation as arguments. Finally, we can preview the transformations on the first 10 records:

```
df = dflow.head()
builder.add_example(source_data=df.iloc[0], example_value='Mr')
builder.add_example(source_data=df.iloc[1], example_value='Mrs')
builder.add_example(source_data=df.iloc[2], example_value='Miss')
builder.add_example(source_data=df.iloc[3], example_value='Master')
builder.preview(count=10)
```

In the preceding example, we use the **df.iloc[index]** notation to specify the index of the example record for a specified transformation, very similar to the notation in Pandas. We then preview the first 10 records of the transformation. We can also use the **generate_suggested_examples**, **delete_example**, or **list_examples** methods to modify the list of example transformations.

Once we are happy with the transformation, we can apply the transformation and generate a new dataflow using the **to_dataflow** method:

```
dflow = builder.to_dataflow()
```

Imputing missing values

Next, we are looking into another important preprocessing technique: imputing missing values. In general, we can differentiate between two types of replacing missing values: constant replacement or learned replacement. Hence, we can either replace missing values in the dataset with a constant value or learn how to impute missing values based on the training data.

When you choose to replace values in your dataflow using constant replacements, you can use the following transformations:

- **replace**: To replace all values that match a specified value
- **replace_na**: To replace all custom-specified NaN values with nulls
- **fill_nulls**: To fill all nulls with a specified value
- **error**: To replace custom-specified values with an error code and message
- **fill_errors**: To fill all errors with a specified value

Often, constant replacement is not good enough. In these cases, you have to choose the imputation builder. The imputation builder works similar to the previously discussed derive-by-example builder. We have to define the following steps to define, learn, and impute missing values in the dataset:

1. Define column imputation arguments
2. Create a column imputation builder
3. Learn the imputation
4. Transform the dataflow

We start with the imputation arguments using the **ImputeColumnArguments** object. It takes the target column, **column_id**, as a first argument and lets you define either a constant value using **custom_impute_value** or a computed value using the **impute_function** argument. First, we define a simple static imputation and set the embarkation port in the Titanic dataset to 'S' (Southampton) for all null or empty values in the **Embarked** column – representing the port of embarkation for each passenger:

```
impute_embarked = dprep.ImputeColumnArguments(column_id='Embarked',
    custom_impute_value=S)
```

The preceding code is exactly the same as using `fill_nulls`. However, we can also create more complex imputation arguments. In the following code, we use **impute_function=ReplaceValueFunction.MEAN** to impute empty values in the Age column with the training set mean of the same column. We do the same for the Cabin column. Using the **StringMissingReplacementOption** option, we can define when the imputation should be applied, either for **EMPTY**, **NOTHING**, **NULLS**, or **NULLSANDEMPTY**. Let's define both imputations:

```
from azureml.dataprep import StringMissingReplacementOption

impute_cabin = dprep.ImputeColumnArguments(column_id='Cabin',
  impute_function=dprep.ReplaceValueFunction.MIN,
  string_missing_option=StringMissingReplacementOption.NULLSANDEMPTY)

impute_age = dprep.ImputeColumnArguments(column_id='Age',
  impute_function=dprep.ReplaceValueFunction.MEAN,
  string_missing_option=StringMissingReplacementOption.NULLSANDEMPTY)
```

As a next step, we create the imputation builder using the previously defined imputation arguments. What is great about this function is that it allows us to also define grouping columns that are used to compute the imputation function. In the following example, we define the **Sex** and **Pclass** columns as grouping columns and, hence, the aggregations for age and cabin are computed per sex and passenger class. This is much more accurate than just replacing the values with the mean of the entire training set:

```
impute_builder = dflow.builders.impute_missing_values(
  impute_columns=[impute_embarked, impute_cabin, impute_age],
  group_by_columns=['Sex', 'Pclass'])
```

Once the impute builder is constructed, we need to train it. This will compute the grouped imputation functions on the training data and store the values in an internal lookup dictionary:

```
impute_builder.learn()
```

Finally, we can apply the trained imputation function to the dataflow by calling the **to_dataflow** method:

```
dflow_imputed = impute_builder.to_dataflow()
```

Next, we will take a look into how we can encode categorical variables to numeric values.

Label and one-hot encoding

Using the Azure **dataprep** SDK, you can also encode categorical variables into numeric values. In this chapter, we will just look at transforming categorical values using label and one-hot encoding, but in the next chapter, *Chapter 6, Advanced feature extraction with NLP*, we will see many more advanced encoding techniques.

In label encoding, we replace all categorical values of a column with an integer label. If we apply the label encoder to the **Sex** column, the **male** value will be encoded as **0** and the **female** value as **1**. Let's look at the code example:

```
dflow = dflow.label_encode(
    source_column='Sex', new_column_name='Sex_Label')
```

Label encoding is great for high cardinal categorical or ordinal values. If your categorical columns contain a low amount of unique values and you are looking for an orthogonal embedding, you can choose one-hot encoding. Let's replace the values of the Embarked column with the orthogonal vectors **[1,0,0]**, **[0,1,0]**, and **[0,0,1]** for the values **S**, **C**, and **Q** using the following example:

```
dflow = dflow.one_hot_encode(
    source_column='Embarked', prefix='Embarked_')
```

In the preceding code, we create new columns prefixed with the **Embarked_** prefix; in total, as many columns as there are unique values in **Embarked**.

If your data contains many different but similar values, you can also group those similar values together using fuzzy grouping. In the Azure **dataprep** SDK, this operation is very simple using the **fuzzy_group_column** method. You need to define the source and destination columns, **source_column** and **new_column_name**, as well as the similarity threshold and column name for the similarity score, if required.

In the following example, we group all similar values from the **Ticket** column together using this fuzzy grouping approach:

```
dflow_grouped = dflow.fuzzy_group_column(source_column='Ticket',
    new_column_name='Ticket_Groups',
    similarity_threshold=0.75,
    similarity_score_column_name='similarity_score')
```

The preceding code will group similar values together and reduces the number of distinct categorical values in the **Ticket** column. Next, we continue with feature transformations for numeric values.

Transformations and scaling

It's often necessary to transform numeric data during the data preparation step. Instead of having an exact price for each **Fare** in our dataset, we may prefer a categorization of the fares into groups. To do so, we can use the quantile transformation, **quantile_transform**, which will group the source column into **quantiles_count** intervals.

Let's look at the code in action:

```
dflow = dflow.quantile_transform(source_column='Fare',
new_column='Fare_Normal',
  quantiles_count=5, output_distribution="Normal")
```

In the preceding code, we split the fares into five quantiles using a normal distribution. If we preferred a uniform split, we could also specify a **Uniform** distribution.

If we want to scale the range of a numeric column to a specific range, for example, for normalization, we can do so using the **min_max_scale** function. The function takes two additional arguments, **range_min** and **range_max**, to define the target range on which the source column should be scaled. Here is an example code for this transformation:

```
dflow_scaled = dflow.min_max_scale(column='Parch',
  range_min=0, range_max=1)
```

Once we have transformed the source columns into additional feature columns, we often need to remove the old columns from the dataflow. Now, let's look into some row and column filtering techniques.

Filtering columns and rows

The **dataprep** SDK also lets you filter columns and rows from your dataset using the following functions:

- **drop_columns**: To drop columns from a dataflow
- **filter**: To filter rows from a dataflow

While the **drop_columns** function only takes a list of column names as arguments, the **filter** function is a bit more complex and can use expressions to filter rows. Filter expressions can either be created through logical operators on the dataflow columns or by using the following filter functions:

- starts_with
- ends_with
- contains is_error
- is_null distinct
- distinct_rows

The resulting expression will evaluate each record when the data is processed and filter out data where the filter function returns **false**. Here are two examples of filtering the rows on a dataflow based on logical operators:

dflow.filter(dflow['a'] > dflow['b'])

dflow.filter(dprep.col('a') > 0)

Here are two examples involving the use of a filter function:

dflow.filter(dflow['a'].starts_with('prefix'))

dflow.filter(dflow['a'].ends_with('postfix'))

Often, the preceding functions are not enough when you need to create complex filters, such as a combination of two filter functions. To do so, Azure DataPrep provides the Boolean operators **f_not**, **f_and**, and **f_or**.

The following example uses a **filter** function to drop all non-null values from the dataflow:

dflow = dflow.filter(dprep.f_not(dprep.col('Survived').is_null()))

Using these filter expressions, as well as logical and Boolean operators, you can construct complex nested filter expressions. If this is not enough, you can also write custom transformations and filter functions. Let's now take a look how to write the output of a dataflow back to your blob storage.

Writing the processed data back to a dataset

In this last section, we will teach you how to write data back into a dataset using a dataflow and the DataPrep Python SDK. This is extremely useful, as this will make your data pipeline complete. Once the dataset is updated and has a new version and snapshot, it is ready to be used by data consumers for further analysis and ML.

First, we are going to write data to a delimited file–in this case, a **.csv** file–and use the **write_to_csv** function. This function can be used as shown in the following example:

```
from azureml.dataprep import LocalFileOutput


# Write dataflow to CSV
dataflow.write_to_csv(directory_path=LocalFileOutput('./outputs')).run_local()
```

The first parameter is the **directory_path**, which is the path to a directory in which we will store the output files. So, in the case of the Spark example, this needs to be empty.

The **separator** parameter defines the CSV column separator to use. The **na** argument is a string to use for null values, and **error** is a string to use for error values (in this case, we use the **ERROR** string for errors and **NA** for NaN values). The **write_to_csv** method returns the modified dataflow where the **write** operation is just another lazy step in the DAG. Hence, every execution of the returned dataflow will perform the **write** operation again:

```
# Create a new data flow using 'write_to_csv'
write_t = 
t.write_to_csv(directory_path=dprep.LocalFileOutput('./test_out/'))


# Run the current data flow using the local execution runtime
# to begin the write operation
write_t.run_local()


written_files = dprep.read_csv('./test_out/part-*')
written_files.head(5)
```

In the preceding code example, we write the CSV file to disk and load it back as a CSV file using Azure DataPrep. This could lead to errors while parsing the numeric columns, due to the numbers being parsed from strings containing **ERROR** and **NA** values.

CSV is useful only when you need to manually inspect the data. For most other cases, a binary-encoded format with an embedded data schema is a lot more efficient and will remove tons of potential parsing issues with CSV and text files in general. Hence, we recommend that you store your data in a Parquet format, a high-performance columnar data storage format with adapters and libraries in many languages.

Writing a dataflow to a Parquet file is quite similar to the `write_to_csv()` function. Let's look at a typesafe example of exporting a dataset using the Parquet writer:

```
dataflow.write_to_parquet(file_path='./outputs/train.parquet',
single_file=True).run_local()
```

In the preceding code, we write the data transformed by the dataflow back using Parquet format. We can specify the output destination using either the `file_path` or `directory_path` arguments. To output a single file, we additionally need to set the `single_file` argument to `true`.

Due to parallelization in the columnar data format, Parquet writes are often executed in parallel to create the output for a single dataset. This parallel execution will lead to multiple generated files for the dataset by default. Using the `single_file` parameter, you can force the creation of a single file while reducing the write throughput.

Dataflows, dataprep, datasets, and data stores are extremely useful concepts for managing your data and data pipelines, from hundreds of records to hundreds of thousands of files per dataset. Therefore, they are indispensable tools for building high-quality, end-to-end data pipelines in the cloud.

Summary

In this chapter, you have learned how to build enterprise-grade ETL pipelines and data transformations in Azure Machine Learning, as well as how to manage datasets.

You have learned how to load data into the cloud using blob storage and how to extract data from various other data formats. If you model your data in abstract data stores and datasets, then your users don't have to know where the data is located, how it is encoded, or what is the correct protocol and permission to access it. This is an essential part of an ETL pipeline. Another great way is to see your dataset definitions as contracts about what your users can expect from the data, very similar to an API. Therefore, it should make sense to follow a specific life cycle of creating datasets, updating and versioning them, before deprecating and archiving them if no longer used.

Using the Azure DataPrep SDK, you acquired the skills to write scalable data platforms using dataflows. We looked into how to create columns through simple transformations, how to impute missing values through grouped aggregations—such as mean encoding—and even generated a string parser using derived expressions through examples. You learned how to group categorical values together using fuzzy grouping and transform them using label and one-hot encoding.

Finally, we looked into writing the data back to a data store using Parquet, an efficient binary column-store format. Once the data is stored, you can again register it as dataset, and then version and snapshot it. This will allow your data scientists to access, explore, and use the data with the tools they are already familiar with.

In the next chapter, we will look into separating the data transformation script into individual steps using Azure Machine Learning pipelines.

5
Azure Machine Learning pipelines

In the previous chapters, we learned about many **extract, transform, and load** (ETL) preprocessing and feature-engineering approaches within the **Azure Machine Learning** using `Dataset`, `Datastore`, and `DataPrep`. In this chapter, you will learn how to use these transformation techniques to build reusable **machine learning** (ML) pipelines.

First, you will learn about the benefits of splitting your code into individual steps and wrapping them into a pipeline. Not only can you make your code blocks reusable through modularization and parameters, but you can also control the compute targets for individual steps. This helps to optimally scale your computations, save costs, and improve performance at the same time. Lastly, you can parameterize and trigger your pipelines through an HTTP endpoint or through a recurring or reactive schedule.

After that, we'll build a complex Azure Machine Learning pipeline in a couple of steps. We start with a simple pipeline; add data inputs, outputs, and connections between steps; and finally deploy the pipeline as a web service. You will also learn about advanced scheduling based on frequency and changing data, as well as exploring parallelizing pipeline steps for large volumes of data.

In the last part of the chapter, you will learn how to integrate Azure Machine Learning pipelines into other Azure services, such as Azure Machine Learning designer, Azure Data Factory, and Azure DevOps. This will help you to understand the commonalities and differences between the different pipeline and workflow services and how you can trigger ML pipelines.

In this chapter, we will cover the following topics:

- Benefits of pipelines for ML workflows
- Building and publishing an ML pipeline
- Integrating pipelines with other Azure services

Let's begin with a discussion of the benefits of using ML pipelines in your Azure projects.

Benefits of pipelines for ML workflows

Separating your workflow into reusable configurable steps and combining these steps to form an end-to-end pipeline provides many benefits for implementing end-to-end ML processes. Multiple teams can own and iterate on individual steps to improve the pipeline over time, while others can easily integrate each version of the pipeline into their current setup.

The pipeline itself doesn't only split code from execution—it also splits the execution from the orchestration. Hence, you can configure individual compute targets that can be used to optimize your execution and provide parallel execution, during which you don't have to touch the ML code.

We will take a quick look into Azure Machine Learning pipelines and why they should be your tool of choice when implementing ML workflows in Azure. In the following section, *Building and publishing an ML pipeline*, we will dive a lot deeper and explore the individual features by building such a pipeline.

Why build pipelines?

As a single developer doing mostly experimentation and working simultaneously on data, infrastructure, and modeling, pipelines don't add a ton of benefits to the developer's workflow. However, as soon as you perform enterprise-grade development across multiple teams that iterate on different parts of an ML system, you will greatly benefit from splitting your code into a pipeline of individual execution steps.

This modularization will give you great flexibility, and multiple teams will be able to collaborate efficiently. Teams can integrate your models and pipelines while you are iterating and building new versions of your pipeline at the same time. By using versioned pipelines and pipeline parameters, you can control how your data or model service pipeline should be called and ensure auditing and reproducibility.

Another important benefit of using workflows instead of running everything inside a single file is execution speed and cost improvements. Instead of running a single script on the same compute instance, you can run and scale steps individually on different compute targets. This gives you greater control over potential cost savings and better optimization for performance, and you only ever have to retry the parts of the pipeline that failed rather than the whole pipeline.

Through the scheduling of pipelines, you can make sure that all your pipeline runs are executed without any manual intervention on your part. You simply define triggers, such as the existence of new training data, that should execute your pipeline. Decoupling your code execution from triggering the execution gives you a ton of benefits, such as easy integration into many other services.

Finally, the modularity of your code allows for great reusability. By splitting your script into functional steps such as cleaning, preprocessing, feature engineering, training, and hyper-parameter tuning, you can version and reuse these steps for other projects as well.

Therefore, as soon as you want to benefit from one of these advantages, you can start organizing your code into pipelines so that they can be deployed, scheduled, versioned, scaled, and reused effectively. Let's find out how you can achieve this in Azure Machine Learning.

What are Azure Machine Learning pipelines?

Azure Machine Learning pipelines are workflows of executable steps in Azure Machine Learning that compose a complete ML workflow. You can combine data imports, data transformations, feature engineering, model training, and optimization, as well as deployment, as your pipeline steps.

Pipelines are resources in your Azure Machine Learning workspace that you can create, manage, version, trigger, and deploy. They integrate with all other Azure Machine Learning workspace resources, such as `Dataset` and `Datastore` for loading data, compute instances, models, and endpoints. Each pipeline run is executed as an experiment on your Azure Machine Learning workspace and gives you the same benefits that we covered in the previous chapters, such as tracking files, logs, models, artifacts, images, and more while running on flexible compute clusters.

Azure Machine Learning pipelines should be your first choice when implementing flexible and reusable ML workflows. By using pipelines, you can modularize your code into blocks of functionality, and you can version and share those blocks with other projects. This makes it easy to collaborate with other teams on complex end-to-end ML workflows.

Another great integration of Azure Machine Learning pipelines is the integration with endpoints and triggers in your workspace. With a single line of code, you can publish a pipeline as a web service or web service endpoint and use this endpoint to configure and trigger the pipeline from anywhere. This opens up the door for integrating Azure Machine Learning pipelines with many other Azure and third-party services.

However, if you need a more complex trigger, such as continuous scheduling or reactive triggering based on changes in the source data, you can easily configure this as well. The added benefit of using pipelines is that all orchestration functionality is completely decoupled from your training code.

As you can see, you get a lot of benefits by using Azure Machine Learning pipelines for your ML workflows. However, it's worth noting that this functionality does come with some extra overhead. Let's start by building our first pipeline.

Building and publishing an ML pipeline

Let's go ahead and use our knowledge from the previous chapters to build a pipeline for data processing. We will use the Azure Machine Learning Python SDK to define all pipeline steps as Python code so the pipeline can be easily managed, reviewed, and checked into version control as an authoring script.

We will define a pipeline as a linear sequence of steps. Each step will have an input and output defined as pipeline data sinks and sources. Each step will be associated with a compute target that defines both the execution environment and the compute resource for execution. We will set up an execution environment as a Docker container with all the required Python libraries and run the pipeline steps on a training cluster in Azure Machine Learning.

A pipeline runs as an experiment in your Azure Machine Learning workspace. We can either submit the pipeline as part of the authoring script, deploy it as web service and trigger it through a webhook, schedule it as a published pipeline similar to a cron job, or trigger it from a partner service such as Logic Apps.

In many cases, running a linear sequential pipeline is good enough. However, when the amount of data increases and the pipeline steps become slower and slower, we need to find a way of speeding up these large computations. A common solution for speeding up data transformations, model training, and scoring is parallelization. Hence, we will add a parallel execution step to our data transformation pipeline.

As we learned in the first section of this chapter, two of the main benefits of decoupling ML workflows into pipelines are modularity and reusability. By splitting a workflow into individual steps, we build the foundation for reusable computational blocks for common ML tasks, be it data analysis through visualizations and feature importance, feature engineering through **natural language processing** (**NLP**) and third-party data, or simply the scoring of common ML tasks such as automatic image tagging through object detection.

In Azure Machine Learning pipelines, we can use modules to create reusable computational steps from a pipeline. A module is a management layer on top of a pipeline step that allows you to version, deploy, load, and reuse pipeline steps with ease. The concept is very similar to Azure Machine Learning dataset definitions, which are used to version and manage data.

For any enterprise-grade ML workflow, the use of pipelines is essential. Not only does it help you decouple, scale, trigger, and reuse individual computational steps, but it also provides auditability and monitorability to your end-to-end workflow. Furthermore, splitting computational blocks into pipeline steps will set you up for a successful transition to MLOps—a **continuous integration/continuous deployment (CI/CD)** process for ML projects.

Let's get started and implement our first Azure Machine Learning pipeline.

Creating a simple pipeline

An Azure Machine Learning pipeline is a sequence of individual computational steps that can be executed in parallel or in series. Depending on the type of computation, you can schedule jobs on different compute targets, such as Azure Machine Learning or Azure Batch, or perform automated ML or HyperDrive experiments. Depending on the execution type, you may need to provide additional configuration.

Let's start with a simple pipeline that consists only of a single step. First, we need to define the type of execution for our pipeline step. While `PipelineStep` is the base class for any execution we can run in the pipeline, we need to choose one of the step implementations. The following steps are available at the time of writing:

- `PythonScriptStep`: Runs a Python script
- `AdlaStep`: Runs a U-SQL script using Azure Data Lake Analytics
- `DataTransferStep`: Transfers data between Azure storage accounts
- `DatabricksStep`: Runs a Databricks notebook
- `AzureBatchStep`: Runs a script on Azure Batch
- `EstimatorStep`: Runs an estimator
- `MpiStep`: Runs a **message passing interface (MPI)** job
- `HyperDriveStep`: Runs a HyperDrive experiment
- `AutoMLStep`: Runs an automated ML experiment

For our simple example, we want to run a single Python script wrapped into an estimator object in our pipeline, so we will choose **EstimatorStep** from the preceding list. We reuse the same script and estimator that we first saw in *Chapter 2, Choosing a machine learning service in Azure*. Let's make the example even simpler and start with a Python script that doesn't need any data input or output, or any configuration. We will add these separately in the following steps:

1. The pipeline steps are all attached to an Azure Machine Learning workspace. Hence, we start by loading the workspace configuration:

   ```
   from azureml.core import Workspace

   ws = Workspace.from_config()
   ```

2. Next, we need a compute target to execute our pipeline step on. Let's create an auto-scaling Azure Machine Learning training cluster as a compute target similar to what we created in *Chapter 2, Choosing a machine learning service in Azure*:

   ```
   from azureml.core.compute import ComputeTarget, AmlCompute

   compute_config = AmlCompute.provisioning_configuration(
       vm_size='STANDARD_D2_V2', max_nodes=4)
   cpu_cluster = ComputeTarget.create(ws, cpu_cluster_name, compute_config)
   cpu_cluster.wait_for_completion(show_output=True)
   ```

3. We can now define our estimator, which simply provides all the required configuration for a target ML framework:

   ```
   from azureml.train.estimator import Estimator

   estimator = Estimator(entry_script='train.py',
       compute_target=cpu_cluster, conda_packages=['tensorflow'])
   ```

4. Next, we configure the estimator step. If you recall, in *Chapter 2, Choosing a machine learning service in Azure*, we simply submitted the estimator as an experiment to the Azure Machine Learning workspace. However, now we will first wrap the single estimator into a pipeline step and instead submit the pipeline as an experiment. While this seems counterintuitive at first, we will see how we can then parametrize the pipeline and add more steps to it. But let's start with the first step, **EstimatorStep**:

   ```
   from azureml.pipeline.steps import EstimatorStep

   step = EstimatorStep(name="CNN_Train",
     estimator=estimator, compute_target=cpu_cluster)
   ```

5. The preceding step configuration looks very simple. As you can see, we are merely wrapping the estimator into an estimator step without any additional configuration. Don't worry, we will add some more configuration in the next section. But before we do this, we want to define and execute a pipeline:

   ```
   from azureml.pipeline.core import Pipeline

   pipeline = Pipeline(ws, steps=[step])
   ```

6. As you can see, the pipeline is defined simply through a series of pipeline steps and is linked to a workspace. In our example, we only define a single execution step, which makes the pipeline really simple. Let's also check whether we made any mistakes in configuring our pipeline through the built-in pipeline validation functionality:

   ```
   pipeline.validate()
   ```

7. All good–the pipeline is validated and ready to go. Let's submit it as an experiment to the Azure Machine Learning workspace:

   ```
   from azureml.core import Experiment

   exp = Experiment(ws, "simple-pipeline")
   run = exp.submit(pipeline)
   run.wait_for_completion(show_output=True)
   ```

Congratulations, you just ran your first very simple Azure Machine Learning pipeline.

> **Note**
>
> You can find many complete and up-to-date examples of using Azure Machine Learning pipelines in the official Azure repository: https://github.com/Azure/MachineLearningNotebooks/blob/master/how-to-use-azureml/machine-learning-pipelines/

While this simple pipeline doesn't add a ton of benefits to directly submitting the estimator as an experiment, we can now add additional steps to the pipeline and configure data inputs and outputs. Let's take a look!

Connecting data inputs and outputs between steps

Pipeline steps are the computational blocks of a workflow. In order to control the sequence of steps and thus the flow of data, we need to define the inputs and outputs for the pipeline and wire up the data inputs and outputs of individual steps. The data flow between the individual computational blocks will ultimately define the execution order for the blocks, and hence will turn a sequence of steps into a directed acyclic execution graph.

In most cases, a pipeline needs external inputs and connections between the individual blocks as well as persisted outputs. In Azure Machine Learning pipelines, we will use the following building blocks to configure this data flow:

- Pre-persisted pipeline inputs: `Dataset`
- Data between pipeline steps: `PipelineData`
- Persisting pipeline outputs: `PipelineData.as_dataset()`

In this section, we will look at all three types of data inputs and outputs. First, we'll take a look at how we pass data as input into a pipeline.

Inputting data to pipeline steps with Dataset

Let's start with adding a data input to the first step in a pipeline. To do so—or to pass any pre-persisted data to a pipeline step—we use a `Dataset` object, which we first learned about in *Chapter 4, ETL, data preparation, and feature extraction*. In Azure Machine Learning, `Dataset` is an abstract reference to data stored in a specified path with a specified encoding on a specified system. The storage system itself is abstracted as a `Datastore` object, a reference to the physical system with information about location, protocol, and access permissions.

If you recall from the previous chapters, we can access a dataset that was previously registered in our Azure Machine Learning workspace simply by referencing it by name:

```
from azureml.core.dataset import Dataset


train_dataset = Dataset.get(ws, 'training.data.raw')
```

The preceding code is very convenient when your data is initially organized and registered as datasets. As pipeline developers, we don't need to know the underlying data format (for example, CSV, ZIP, Parquet, JSON, and so on) or on which Azure Blob storage or Azure SQL Database instance the data is stored.

However, when passing new data into an Azure Machine Learning pipeline, we often don't have the data registered as datasets. In these cases, we can create a new dataset reference. In the following example, we convert a CSV file from our custom datastore, **mldemodatastore**, into a **Dataset** object:

```
from azureml.core.datastore import Datastore


# use default datastore 'ws.get_default_datastore()'
# or load a custom registered data store
datastore = Datastore.get(ws, 'mldemodatastore')
iris_dataset = Dataset.Tabular.from_delimited_files(
  datastore.path('iris.csv'))
```

The preceding code is probably what you will most likely use in your enterprise environment. It's quite common to have an ETL pipeline loading data into a blob storage location, and then have an ML pipeline pick up the data from there to extract features, re-train a model, or score a pre-trained model. Hence, using this technique, you can reference arbitrary data from your workspace and pass it to your pipelines as input.

Another possibility is accessing files that are hosted on a publicly available system. In this case, we don't need the datastore reference but solely the path to the desired files. Here is an example of creating a dataset from such data:

```
web_paths = [
  'https://.../mnist/train-images-idx3-ubyte.gz',
  'https://.../mnist/train-labels-idx1-ubyte.gz']
mnist_dataset = Dataset.File.from_files(path=web_paths)
```

As you can see, there are multiple ways to transform files and tabular data into **Dataset** objects. While this seems like a bit of complicated extra work instead of passing absolute paths to your pipelines directly, you will get a ton of benefits from following this convention. Most importantly, all compute instances in your Azure Machine Learning workspace will be able to access, read, and parse the data without any additional configuration. Imagine you are planning to manage local development and experimentation instances, and auto-scale training clusters and Kubernetes-based inferencing clusters, while also having to manually set up access control and more for all your datastores and systems—how painful.

Once we have obtained a reference to a **Dataset** object, we can pass the dataset to the pipeline step as input. There are two things to consider when passing a dataset to the computational step:

1. The name of the dataset to later reference it in the script–`as_named_input()`
2. The access type–`as_download()` or `as_mount()`

Let's see how this is done using the estimator step from the previous section:

```
step = EstimatorStep(name="CNN_Train",
    input=[mnist_dataset.as_named_input('mnist').as_mount()],
    estimator=estimator, compute_target=cpu_cluster)
```

As you can see in the preceding example, we can pass multiple datasets to the pipeline step as inputs. Using a specific name for this dataset will help us to differentiate between multiple inputs in the training script of this step. The access type tells the compute instance to either mount the datastore location (great for large files) or download the file to the local disk (great for small files).

Finally, let's look at the script file of this estimator that needs to load the data that was passed in the pipeline step configuration. To do so, we need to extend our script to retrieve the input datasets from the current **RunContext**. Here is an example of updating the estimator's training script, **train.py**, to access the dataset from the pipeline step configuration:

```
# in the training script 'train.py'
mnist_dataset = Run.get_context().input_datasets['mnist']
```

As you can see in the preceding snippet, your training file doesn't need to know anything about the path, location, or encoding of the data. However, the problem with this approach is that we can now run this estimator only as part of a pipeline step and cannot schedule it as a simple experiment, as we can't define data inputs in the same way. Therefore, there is a second way to pass datasets to pipeline steps through command-line arguments. Here is an example using arguments instead of the input definition:

```
step = EstimatorStep(name="CNN_Train", arguments=[
    '--train-data', mnist_dataset.as_named_input('mnist').as_mount()],
    estimator=estimator, compute_target=cpu_cluster)
```

Finally, in order to read the dataset from a command-line argument, we need to implement a small argument parser and parse the path from the dataset in the training script. The following example shows how this can be achieved:

```python
# in the training script 'train.py'
parser = argparse.ArgumentParser()
parser.add_argument('--train-data', type=str, dest='train_data')
args = parser.parse_args()
mnist_dataset = Dataset.File.from_files(args.train_data)
```

As you can see in the preceding snippet, we now only pass a reference to the dataset path to the training script and have to retrieve the dataset using this path. While this involves writing a bit more code than the previous example, this version lets you reuse the training script for manual execution, simple experiments, or HyperDrive runs without modification.

This is a great way to decouple a block of functionality from its input and helps you to build reusable blocks. We will see in the following section, *Reusing pipeline steps through modularization*, how we can turn these reusable blocks into shared modules.

Next, let's find out how to set up a data flow between individual pipeline steps.

Passing data between steps with PipelineData

When we define inputs to a pipeline step, we also often want to configure the outputs for the computations. By passing in input and output definitions, we completely separate the pipeline step from predefined data storage and avoid having to move data around as part of the computation step.

While pre-persisted inputs are defined as **Dataset** objects, data connections (inputs and outputs) between pipeline steps are defined using **PipelineData** objects. Let's look at an example of a **PipelineData** object used as the output of one pipeline step and as the input for another step:

```python
data_input = Dataset.get_by_name(ws, 'mnist_data')
data_output = PipelineData('mnist_results', datastore=datastore)

step1 = PythonScriptStep(name="Score", script_name="score.py",
    inputs=[data_input], outputs=[data_output])


step2 = PythonScriptStep(name="Validate", script_name="validate.py",
    inputs=[data_output])
```

Similarly to the previous section, instead of relying on pipeline inputs and outputs, we can generalize the data flows to command-line arguments. Here are the same two steps and data flow definitions using arguments instead:

```
step1 = PythonScriptStep(name="Score", script_name="score.py",
    arguments=["--input-path", data_input,
               "--output-path", data_output])


step2 = PythonScriptStep(name="Validate", script_name="validate.py",
    arguments=["--input-path", data_output])
```

Once we pass the expected output path to the scoring file, we need to parse the command-line arguments to retrieve the path. The scoring file looks like the following snippet, which will read the output path and output a pandas DataFrame to the desired output location:

```
# in the scoring script 'score.py'
parser = argparse.ArgumentParser()
parser.add_argument('--output-path', type=str, dest='output_path')
args = parser.parse_args()


# Create output directory
os.makedirs(os.path.dirname(args.output_path), exist_ok=True)


# Write Pandas dataframe to output path
df.to_csv(args.output_path)
```

As we can see in the previous example, we can read the output path from the command-line arguments and use it in the Python script as a standard file path. Hence, we need to make sure the file path exists and output some tabular data into the location. Next, we define the input for the second validation step that reads the newly created data:

```
# in the validation script 'validate.py'
parser = argparse.ArgumentParser()
parser.add_argument('--input-path', type=str, dest='input_path')
args = parser.parse_args()
dataset = Dataset.Tabular.from_delimited_files(args.input_path)
```

As we can see, the code looks very similar to standard data inputs from the previous section. We parse the data path from the command-line arguments and read the dataset from the specified location.

Finally, we will take a look at how to persist the output of a pipeline step for usage outside of the pipeline.

Persisting data outputs with PipelineData.as_dataset()

In this section, we want to look at the persisted outputs of a pipeline. It's quite common (as we will see in *Chapter 12, Deploying and operating machine learning models*) for a pipeline to be used to implement data transformation and hence expect a data output.

In the previous section, we learned about creating outputs from pipeline steps with **PipelineData**, mainly to connect these outputs to inputs of subsequent steps. However, we can use the same method to define a final persisted output of a pipeline.

Doing so is very simple once you know how to create, persist, and version datasets. The reason for this is that we can convert a **PipelineData** object into a dataset using the **as_dataset()** method. Once we have a reference to the **Dataset** object, we can go ahead and either export it to a specific datastore or register it as a dataset in the workspace.

Here is a snippet of how to convert a **PipelineData** object defined as output in a pipeline step to a dataset and register it in the Azure Machine Learning workspace:

```
step_output_ds = step_output_data.as_dataset()
step_output_ds.register(
    name="mnist_predictions", create_new_version=True)
```

By calling the preceding authoring code, you will be able to access the resulting predictions as a dataset in any compute instance connected with your workspace.

Next, we will take a look at the different ways to trigger pipeline execution.

Publishing, triggering, and scheduling a pipeline

After you have created your first simple pipeline, you have multiple ways of running the pipeline. One example that we have already seen was submitting the pipeline directly as an experiment to Azure Machine Learning. This would simply execute the pipeline from the same authoring script where the pipeline was configured. While this is a good start when executing a pipeline, there are other ways to trigger, parametrize, and execute it.

Common ways to execute a pipeline include the following:

- Publishing a pipeline as a web service
- Triggering a published pipeline using a webhook
- Scheduling a published pipeline to continuously run with a predefined frequency

In this section, we will look at all three methods to help you trigger and execute your pipelines with ease. Let's first start by publishing and versioning your pipeline as a web service.

Publish a pipeline as a web service

A common reason to split an ML workflow into a reusable pipeline is so that you can parametrize and trigger it for various tasks whenever needed. Good examples are common pre-processing tasks, feature engineering steps, and batch scoring runs. The latter will be tackled in more detail in Chapter 12, *Deploying and operating machine learning models*.

Hence, turning a pipeline into a parametrizable web service that we can trigger from any other application is a really great way of deploying your ML workflow. Let's get started and wrap and deploy the previously built pipeline as a web service.

As we want our published pipeline to be configurable through HTTP parameters, we need to first create these parameter references. Let's create a parameter to control the learning rate of our training pipeline:

```
from azureml.pipeline.core.graph import PipelineParameter


lr_param = PipelineParameter(name="lr_arg", default_value=0.01)
```

Next, we link the pipeline parameter with the pipeline step by passing it as an argument to the training script. We extend the step from the previous section:

```
step = EstimatorStep(name="CNN_Train", arguments=[
    '--train-data', mnist_dataset.as_named_input('mnist').as_mount(),
    '--learning-rate', lr_param],
    estimator=estimator, compute_target=cpu_cluster)
```

In the preceding example, we add the learning rate as a parameter to the list of command-line arguments. In the training script, we can simply parse the command-line arguments and read the parameter:

```
# in the scoring script 'score.py'
parser = argparse.ArgumentParser()
parser.add_argument('--learning-rate', type=float, dest='lr')
args = parser.parse_args()


# print learning rate
print(args.lr)
```

Next, the only step left is to publish the pipeline. To do so, we create a pipeline and call the `publish()` method. We need to pass a name and version to the pipeline, which will now be a versioned published pipeline:

```
pipeline = Pipeline(ws, steps=[step])
service = pipeline.publish(name="CNN_Train_Service", version="1.0")

service_id = service.id
service_endpoint = service.endpoint
```

That's all the code you need to expose a pipeline as a parametrized web service with authentication. If you want to abstract your published pipeline from a specific endpoint—for example, to iterate on the development process of your pipeline while letting other teams integrate the web service into their application—you can as well deploy pipeline webhooks as endpoints.

Let's look at an example where we take the previously created pipeline service and expose it through a separate endpoint:

```
from azureml.pipeline.core import PipelineEndpoint


application = PipelineEndpoint.publish(workspace=ws, pipeline=service,
    name="CNN_Train_Endpoint")


service_id = application.id
service_endpoint = application.endpoint
```

We have now deployed and decoupled the pipeline from the web service endpoint. Now, we can call and trigger the endpoint through the service endpoint. Let's take a look at this in the next section.

Triggering a published pipeline using a webhook

The published pipeline web service requires authentication. So, let's first retrieve an Azure Active Directory token before we call the web service:

```
from azureml.core.authentication import AzureCliAuthentication


cli_auth = AzureCliAuthentication()
aad_token = cli_auth.get_authentication_header()
```

Using the authentication token, we can now trigger and parametrize the pipeline by calling the service endpoint. Let's look at an example using the **requests** library. We can configure the learning rate through the **lr_arg** parameter, defined in the previous section, as well as the experiment name by sending a custom JSON body. If you recall, the pipeline will still run as an experiment in your Azure Machine Learning workspace:

```
import requests


response = requests.post(service_endpoint, headers=aad_token,
   json={"ExperimentName": "mnist-train",
       "ParameterAssignments": {"lr_arg": 0.05}})
```

We observe in the preceding code snippet that we call the pipeline webhook using a POST request and configure the pipeline run by sending a custom JSON body. For authentication, we also need to pass the authentication as an HTTP header.

In this example, we used a Python script to trigger the web service endpoint. However, you can use any other Azure service to trigger this pipeline now through the webhook, such as Azure Logic Apps, CI/CD pipelines in Azure DevOps, or any other custom application. If you want your pipeline to run periodically instead of having to trigger it manually, you can set up a pipeline schedule. Let's take a look at this in the next section.

Scheduling a published pipeline to continuously run with a predefined frequency

Setting up continuous triggers for workflows is a common use case when building pipelines. These triggers could run a pipeline and retrain a model every week or every day if new data is available. Azure Machine Learning pipelines support two types of scheduling techniques: continuous scheduling through a pre-defined frequency, and reactive scheduling and data change detection through a polling interval. In this section, we will take a look at both approaches.

Before we start scheduling a pipeline, we first explore a way to list all the previously defined pipelines of a workspace. To do so, we can use the **PublishedPipeline.list()** method, similar to the **list()** method from our Azure Machine Learning workspace resources. Let's print the name and ID of every published pipeline in the workspace:

```
from azureml.pipeline.core import PublishedPipeline


for pipeline in PublishedPipeline.list(ws):
    print("name: %s, id: %s" % (pipeline.name, pipeline.id))
```

To set up a schedule for a published pipeline, we need to pass the pipeline ID as an argument. Therefore, we can retrieve the desired pipeline ID from the preceding code snippet and plug it into the schedule declaration.

First, we look at continuous schedules that re-trigger a pipeline with a predefined frequency similar to cron jobs. To define the scheduling frequency, we need to create a **ScheduleRecurrence** object. Here is an example snippet to create a recurring schedule:

```
from azureml.pipeline.core.schedule import ScheduleRecurrence, Schedule

recurrence = ScheduleRecurrence(frequency="Minute", interval=15)

recurring_schedule = Schedule.create(ws, name="CNN_Train_Schedule",
    pipeline_id=pipeline_id, experiment_name="mnist-train",
    recurrence=recurrence, pipeline_parameters={})
```

The preceding code is all you need to set up a recurring schedule that continuously triggers your pipeline. The pipeline will run as the defined experiment in your Azure Machine Learning workspace. Using the **pipeline_parameters** argument, you can pass additional parameters to the pipeline runs.

Azure Machine Learning pipelines also support another type of recurring scheduling, namely polling for changes in a datastore. This type of scheduling is referred to as reactive scheduling and requires a connection to a **Datastore** object. It will trigger your pipeline whenever data changes in your datastore. Here is an example of setting up a reactive schedule:

```
from azureml.core.datastore import Datastore

# use default datastore 'ws.get_default_datastore()'
# or load a custom registered data store
datastore = Datastore.get(workspace, 'mldemodatastore')

# 5 min polling interval
polling_interval = 5

reactive_schedule = Schedule.create(ws, name="CNN_Train_OnChange",
    pipeline_id=pipeline_id, experiment_name="mnist-train",
    datastore=datastore, data_path_parameter_name="mnist_data"
    polling_interval=polling_interval, pipeline_parameters={})
```

As you can see, in the preceding example, we set up the reactive schedule using a datastore reference and a polling interval in minutes. Hence, the schedule will check each polling interval to see which blobs have changed and use those to trigger the pipeline. The blob names will be passed to the pipeline using the **data_path_parameter_name** parameter. Similar to the previous schedule, you can also send additional parameters to the pipeline using the **pipeline_parameters** argument.

Finally, let's take a look at how to programmatically stop a schedule once it has been enabled. To do so, we need a reference to the schedule object. We can get this—similar to any other resource in Azure Machine Learning—by fetching the schedules for a specific workplace:

```
for schedule in Schedule.list(ws):
    print(schedule.id)
```

We can filter this list using all available attributes on the schedule object. Once we've found the desired schedule, we can simply disable it:

```
schedule.disable(wait_for_provisioning=True)
```

Using the additional argument **wait_for_provisioning**, we ensure that we block code execution until the schedule is really disabled. You can easily re-enable the schedule using the **Schedule.enable** method. Now you can create recurring and reactive schedules, continuously run your Azure Machine Learning pipelines, and disable them if they're not needed anymore. Next, we will take a look at parallelizing execution steps.

Parallelizing steps to speed up large pipelines

It's inevitable in many cases that the pipeline will process more and more data over time. In order to parallelize a pipeline, you can run pipeline steps in parallel or sequence or parallelize a single pipeline step computation by using **ParallelRunConfig** and **ParallelRunStep**.

Before we jump into parallelizing a single-step execution, let's first discuss the control flow of a simple pipeline. We start with a simple pipeline that is constructed using multiple steps as shown in the following example:

```
pipeline = Pipeline(ws, steps=[step1, step2, step3])
```

When we submit this pipeline, how will these three steps be executed—in series, in parallel, or even in an undefined order? In order to answer the question, we need to look into the definitions of the individual steps. If all steps are independent and the compute target for each step is large enough, all steps are executed in parallel. However, if you defined **PipelineData** as the output of **step1** and the input of **step2**, **step2** will only be executed after **step1** has finished.

The data connections between the pipeline steps implicitly define the execution order of the steps. If no dependency exists between the steps, all steps are scheduled in parallel.

There is one exception to the preceding statement, which is enforcing a specific execution order of pipeline steps without a dedicated data object as a dependency. In order to do this, you can define these dependencies manually, as shown in the next code snippet:

```
step3.run_after(step1)
step3.run_after(step2)
```

The preceding configuration will first execute **step1** and **step2** in parallel before scheduling **step3**, thanks to your explicitly configured dependencies. This can be useful when you are accessing state or data in resources outside of the Azure Machine Learning workspace and hence the pipeline cannot implicitly create a dependency.

Now that we have answered the question of step execution order, we want to learn how we can execute a *single* step in parallel. A great use case for this is batch scoring a large amount of data. Rather than partitioning your input data as input for multiple steps, you want the data as input for a single step. However, to speed up the scoring process, you want a parallel execution of the scoring for the single step.

In Azure Machine Learning pipelines, you can use a **ParallelRunStep** step to configure parallel execution for a single step. To configure the data partitions and parallelization of the computation, you need to create a **ParallelRunConfig** object. The parallel run step is a great choice for any type of parallelized computation. Let's walk through an example of setting up parallel execution for a single pipeline step.

First, our training script needs a Python environment to run in. Therefore, we define a reusable environment for this batch scoring example. We choose a pre-existing curated environment and add the TensorFlow package:

```
from azureml.core import Environment
from azureml.core.conda_dependencies import CondaDependencies

# use a curated default environment
batch_env = Environment.get(ws, name="AzureML-Minimal")
conda_dep = CondaDependencies()
conda_dep.add_conda_package("tensorflow")

batch_env.python.conda_dependencies=conda_dep
```

Next, we need to set up a **ParallelRunConfig** instance, which will help us to split the input data into smaller partitions (also called *batches* or *mini-batches*) of data. We configure batch size as a pipeline parameter that can be set when calling the pipeline step:

```
from azureml.pipeline.core import PipelineParameter
from azureml.pipeline.steps import ParallelRunConfig


parallel_run_config = ParallelRunConfig(entry_script='score.py',
    mini_batch_size=PipelineParameter(name="batch_size",
        default_value="10"),
    output_action="append_row",
    append_row_file_name="parallel_run_step.txt",
    environment=batch_env,
    compute_target=cpu_cluster,
    process_count_per_node=2,
    node_count=2
)
```

The preceding snippet defines the run configuration for parallelizing the computation by splitting the input into mini-batches. We configure the batch size as a pipeline parameter, **batch_size**. We also configure the compute target and parallelism with the **node_count** and **process_count_per_node** parameters. Using the preceding settings, we can score four mini-batches in parallel.

The **score.py** script is a deployment file that needs to contain **init()** and **run(batch)** methods. The argument batch contains a list of filenames that will get extracted from the input argument of the step configuration. We will learn more about this file structure in *Chapter 12, Deploying and operating machine learning models*.

The **run** method in the **score.py** script should return the scoring results or write the data to an external datastore. Depending on this, the **output_action** argument needs to be set to either **append_row**, which means that all values will be collected in a result file, or **summary_only**, which means that the user will deal with storing the results. You can define the result file in which all rows will get appended using the **append_row_file_name** argument.

As you can see, setting up the run configuration for a parallel step is not simple and requires a bit of fiddling. However, once set up and configured properly, it can be used to scale out a computational step and run many tasks in parallel. Hence, we can now define **ParallelRunStep** with all the required inputs and outputs:

```
from azureml.pipeline.steps import ParallelRunStep
from azureml.core.dataset import Dataset
from azureml.core.datastore import Datastore

datastore = Datastore.get(workspace, 'mldemodatastore')

parallelrun_step = ParallelRunStep(
    name="ScoreParallel",
    parallel_run_config=parallel_run_config,
    inputs=[Dataset.get_by_name(ws, 'mnist_data')],
    output=PipelineData('mnist_results', datastore=datastore),
    allow_reuse=True
)
```

As you can see, we read from the **mnist_data** dataset, which references all the files in the datastore. We write the results to the **mnist_results** folder in our custom datastore. Finally, we can start the run and look at the results. To do so, we submit the pipeline as an experiment run to Azure Machine Learning:

```
from azureml.pipeline.core import Pipeline

pipeline = Pipeline(workspace=ws, steps=[parallelrun_step])
pipeline_run = exp.submit(pipeline)
pipeline_run.wait_for_completion(show_output=True)
```

Splitting a step execution into multiple partitions will help you to speed up the computation of large amounts of data. It pays off as soon as the time of computation is significantly longer than the overhead of scheduling a step execution on a compute target. Therefore, **ParallelRunStep** is a great choice for speeding up your pipeline with only a few changes in your pipeline configuration. Next, we will take a look into better modularization and reusability of pipeline steps.

Reusing pipeline steps through modularization

By splitting your workflow into pipeline steps, you are laying the foundation for reusable ML and data processing building blocks. However, instead of copying and pasting your pipelines, pipeline steps, and code into other projects, you might want to abstract your functionality into functional high-level modules.

Let's look at an example. We assume you are building a pipeline step that takes in a dataset of user and item ratings and outputs a recommendation of the top five items for each user. However, while you are fine-tuning the recommendation engine, you want to enable your colleagues to integrate the functionality into their pipeline. A great way would be to separate the implementation and usage of the code, define input and output data formats, and modularize and version it. That's exactly what modules do in the scope of Azure Machine Learning pipeline steps.

Let's create a module, the container that will hold a reference to the computational step:

```
from azureml.pipeline.core.module import Module


module = Module.create(ws, name="TopItemRecommender",
    description="Recommend the top 5 items for each user")
```

Next, we define inputs and outputs for the module using **InputPortDef** and **OutputPortDef** bindings. These are input and output references that later need to be bound to data references. We use these bindings to abstract all of our inputs and outputs:

```
from azureml.pipeline.core.graph import InputPortDef, OutputPortDef


in1 = InputPortDef(name="in1", default_datastore_mode="mount",
    default_data_reference_name=datastore.name, label="Ratings")
out1 = OutputPortDef(name="out1", default_datastore_mode="mount",
    default_datastore_name=datastore.name, label="Recommendation")
```

Finally, we can define the module functionality by publishing a Python script for this module:

```
module.publish_python_script("train.py", source_directory="./rec",
    params = {"numTraits": 5}, inputs=[in1], outputs=[out1],
    version="1", is_default=True)
```

That's all you need to do to enable others to reuse your recommendation block in their Azure Machine Learning pipelines. By using versioning and default versions, you can specify exactly what code is pulled by your users. As we can see, you can also define multiple inputs and outputs for each module, and define configurable parameters for modules. In addition to publishing functionality as Python code, we could as well publish an Azure Data Lake Analytics or Azure Batch step.

Next, we will take a look at how a module can be integrated into an Azure Machine Learning pipeline and executed together with custom steps. To do so, we first load the module that was previously created using the following command:

```
from azureml.pipeline.core.module import Module
```

```
module = Module.get(ws, name="TopItemRecommender")
```

Now, the great thing about this is that the preceding code will work in any Python interpreter or execution engine that has access to your Azure Machine Learning workspace. This is huge: there is no copying of code, no need to check out dependencies, and no need to define any additional access permissions for your application—everything is integrated with your workspace.

First, we need to wire up inputs and outputs for this pipeline step. Let's pass the inputs from the pipeline directly to the recommendation module and output everything to the pipeline outputs:

```
from azureml.pipeline.core import PipelineData


in1 = PipelineData("in1", datastore=datastore, output_mode="mount",
    is_directory=False)
input_wiring = {"in1": in1}
out1 = PipelineData("out1", datastore=datastore, output_mode="mount",
    is_directory=False)
output_wiring = {"out1": out1}
```

Now, we parametrize the module with the use of pipeline parameters. This lets us configure a parameter in the pipeline, which we can pass through to the recommendation module. In addition, we can define a default parameter for the parameter when used in this pipeline:

```
from azureml.pipeline.core import PipelineParameter


num_traits = PipelineParameter(name="numTraits", default_value=5)
```

We already defined the inputs and outputs for this pipeline, as well as the input parameters for the pipeline step. The only thing we are missing is bringing everything together and defining a pipeline step. Similar to the previous section, we can define a pipeline step that will execute the modularized recommendation block. To do so, instead of using **PythonScriptStep**, we will now use **ModuleStep**:

```
from azureml.core import RunConfiguration
from azureml.pipeline.steps import ModuleStep


step = ModuleStep(module= module, version="1",
    runconfig=RunConfiguration(), compute_target=aml_compute,
    inputs_map=input_wiring, outputs_map=output_wiring,
    arguments = ["--output_sum", first_sum,
                "--output_product", first_prod,
                "--num-traits", num_traits])
```

Finally, we can execute the pipeline by submitting it as an experiment to our Azure Machine Learning workspace. This code is very similar to what we saw in the previous section:

```
from azureml.core import Experiment
from azureml.pipeline.core import Pipeline


pipeline = Pipeline(ws, steps=[step])
exp = Experiment(ws, "item-recommendation")
run = exp.submit(pipeline)
run.wait_for_completion(show_output=True)
```

The preceding step executes the modularized pipeline as an experiment in your Azure Machine Learning workspace. However, you can also choose any other publishing method that we have discussed in the previous sections, such as publishing as a web service or scheduling the pipeline.

Splitting pipeline steps into reusable modules is extremely helpful when working with multiple teams on the same ML projects. All teams can work in parallel and the results can be easily integrated into a single Azure Machine Learning workspace. Let's take a look at how Azure Machine Learning pipelines integrate with other Azure services.

Integrating pipelines with other Azure services

It's rare that users use only a single service to manage data flows, experimentation, training, deployment, and CI/CD in the cloud. Other services provide specific benefits that make them a better fit for certain tasks, such as Azure Data Factory for loading data into Azure, as well as Azure Pipelines for CI/CD and running automated tasks in Azure DevOps.

The strongest argument for betting on a cloud provider is strong integration with the individual services. In this section, we will see how Azure Machine Learning pipelines integrate with other Azure services. The list for this section would be a lot longer if we were to cover every possible service for integration. As we learned in this chapter, you can trigger a published pipeline by calling a REST endpoint, and you can submit a pipeline using standard Python code. This means you can integrate pipelines anywhere where you can call HTTP endpoints or run Python code.

We will first look into integration with Azure Machine Learning designer. The designer lets you build pipelines using graphical blocks, and these pipelines, published pipelines, and pipeline runs will show up in the workspace just like any other pipeline that we have built in this chapter. Therefore, it is a good idea to take a quick look at the commonalities and differences.

Next, we will take a quick look at integrating Azure Machine Learning pipelines with Azure Data Factory, arguably an integration that is used the most. It's a very natural instinct to include ML pipelines with ETL pipelines, for scoring, enriching, or enhancing data during the ETL process.

Finally, we will compare Azure Machine Learning pipelines with Azure Pipelines for CI/CD in Azure DevOps. While Azure DevOps was used mainly for application code and app orchestration, it is now transitioning to provide fully end-to-end MLOps workflows. Let's start with the designer and jump right in.

Building pipelines with the Azure Machine Learning designer

The Azure Machine Learning designer is a graphical interface for creating complex ML pipelines through a drag-and-drop interface. You can choose functionality represented as blocks for data import (using `Datastore` and `Dataset` under the hood).

Figure 5.1 shows a simple pipeline for training and scoring a **Boosted Decision Tree Regression** model. As you can see, the block-based programming style requires less knowledge about the individual blocks, and it allows you to build complex pipelines without writing code:

```
                      ┌─ Enter Data Manually ─┐
                                │
┌─ Boosted Decision Tree Regression ─┐
                                    ┌─ Split Data ─┐
                ↓         ↓
            ┌─ Train Model ─┐
                        ↓         ↓
                    ┌─ Score Model ─┐
```

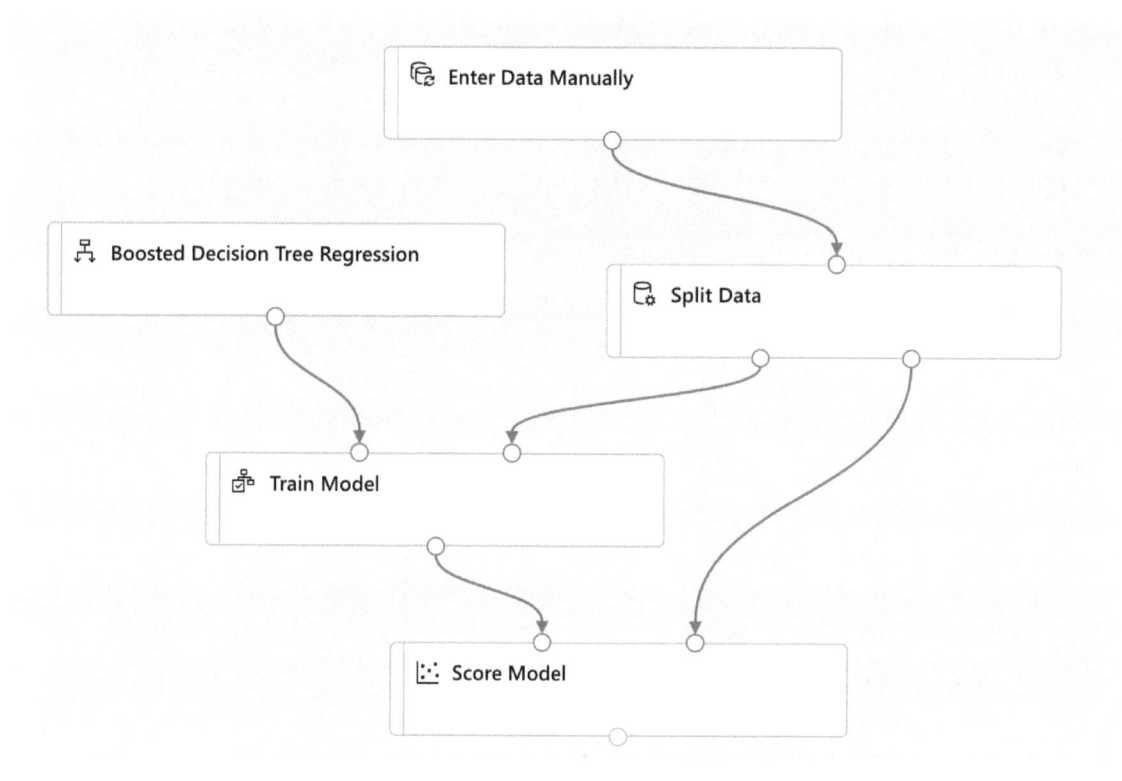

Figure 5.1. An Azure Machine Learning designer pipeline

> **Note**
>
> The Azure Machine Learning designer is a newer, better version of the deprecated Azure Machine Learning Studio (classic) product, which is now tightly integrated into your Azure Machine Learning workspace.

Some actions, such as connecting the output of one computation to the input of the next computation, are arguably more convenient to create in the visual UI than with code. Other actions, such as creating parallel executions of large data batches, are a bit easier to handle and maintain in a code environment. Due to our code-first approach for reproducibility, testability, and version control, we usually prefer code for authoring and execution.

It's worth noting that the functionality of pipelines in the designer and pipelines using code is not the same. While you have a broad set of preconfigured abstract functional blocks—such as the Boosted Decision Tree Regression block in *Figure 5.1*—you can't access these functionalities in code. However, you can use scikit-learn, PyTorch, TensorFlow, and more to reuse an existing functionality or build your own functionality in code.

Thanks to the first-class integration from the designer into the workspace, you can access all files, models, and datasets of the workspace from within the designer. An important takeaway is that all resources that are created in the workspace, such as pipelines, published pipelines, real-time endpoints, models, datasets, and more, are stored in a common system—independently of where they were created.

Azure Machine Learning pipelines in Azure Data Factory

When moving data and working with ETL and trigger computations in various Azure services, you will most likely come across Azure Data Factory. It is a very popular service for moving large amounts of data into Azure, performing processing and transformations, building workflows, and triggering many other Azure or partner services.

Azure Machine Learning pipelines integrate very well with Azure Data Factory and you can easily configure and trigger the execution of a published pipeline through Data Factory. To do so, you need to drag the **ML Execute Pipeline** activity to your Data Factory canvas and specify the pipeline ID of the published pipeline. In addition, you can specify pipeline parameters as well as the experiment name for the pipeline run.

Figure 5.2 shows how the **ML Execute Pipeline** step can be configured in Azure Data Factory. It uses a linked service to connect to your Azure Machine Learning workspace, which allows you to select the desired pipeline from a drop-down box:

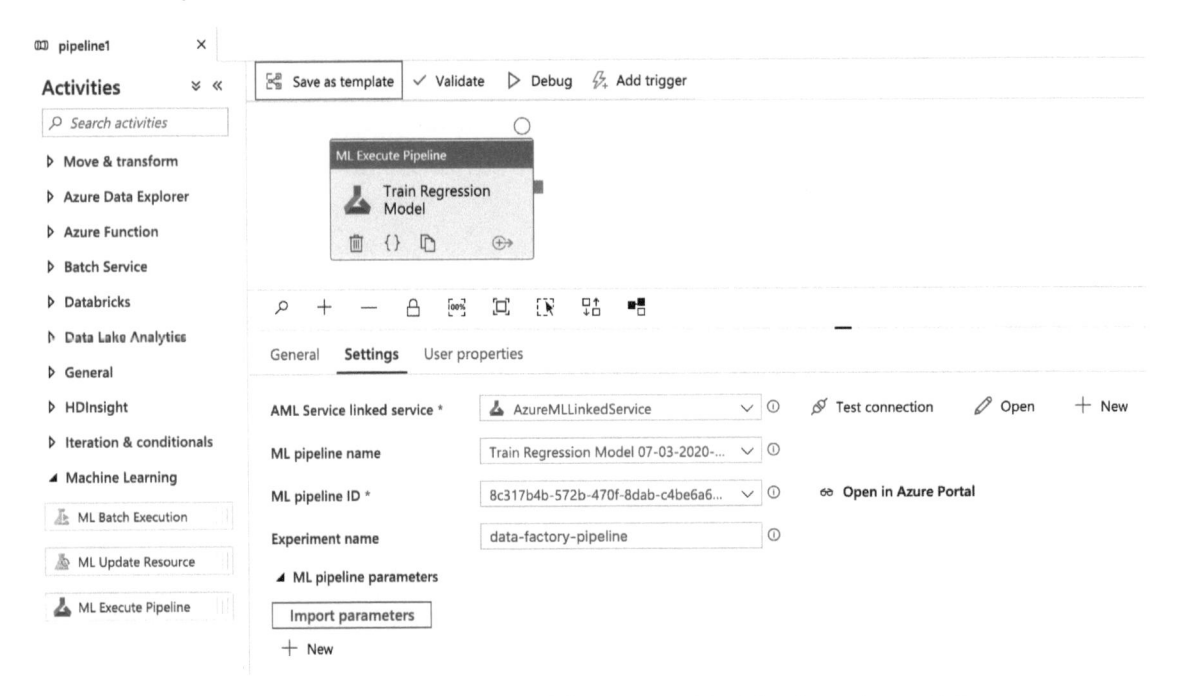

Figure 5.2. Azure Data Factory with an Azure Machine Learning activity

If you are configuring the computational steps using JSON, you can use the following snippet to create an **ML Execute Pipeline** activity with Azure Machine Learning as a linked service. Again, you must specify the pipeline ID and can pass an experiment name as well as pipeline parameters:

```
{
    "name": "Machine Learning Execute Pipeline",
    "type": "AzureMLExecutePipeline",
    "linkedServiceName": {
        "referenceName": "AzureMLService",
        "type": "LinkedServiceReference"
    },
    "typeProperties": {
        "mlPipelineId": "<insert pipeline id>",
        "experimentName": "data-factory-pipeline",
        "mlPipelineParameters": {
            "batch_size": "10"
        }
    }
}
```

Finally, you can trigger the step by adding triggers or outputs into the **ML Execute Pipeline** activity. This will finally trigger your published Azure Machine Learning pipeline and start the execution in your workspace. This is a great addition and makes it easy for other teams to reuse your ML pipelines during classical ETL and data transformation processes.

Azure Pipelines for CI/CD

Azure Pipelines is a feature of Azure DevOps that lets you run, build, test, and deploy code as a CI/CD process. Hence, they are flexible pipelines for code and app orchestration, with many advanced features such as approval queues and gated phases.

By allowing you to run multiple blocks of code, the best way to integrate Azure Machine Learning into Azure DevOps is by using Python script blocks. If you followed this book and used a code-first approach to author your experiments and pipelines, then this integration is very easy. Let's take a look at a small example.

First, let's write a utility function that returns a published pipeline given a workspace and pipeline ID as parameters. We will need this function in this example:

```
def get_pipeline(workspace, pipeline_id):
    for pipeline in PublishedPipeline.list(workspace):
        if pipeline.id == pipeline_id:
            return pipeline
    return None
```

Next, we can go ahead and implement a very simple Python script that allows us to configure and trigger a pipeline run in Azure. We initialize the workspace, retrieve the published pipeline, and submit the pipeline as an experiment to the Azure Machine Learning workspace, all configurable and all with only a few lines of code:

```
ws = Workspace.get(name=os.environ.get("WORKSPACE_NAME"),
    subscription_id=os.environ.get("SUBSCRIPTION_ID"),
    resource_group=os.environ.get("RESOURCE_GROUP"))


pipeline = get_pipeline(args.pipeline_id)
pipeline_parameters = args.pipeline_parameters


exp = Experiment(ws, name=args.experiment_name)
run = exp.submit(pipeline, pipeline_parameters=pipeline_parameters)


print("Pipeline run initiated %s" % run.id)
```

The preceding code demonstrates how we can integrate a pipeline trigger into an Azure pipeline for CI/CD. We can see that once the workspace is initialized, the code follows the exact same pattern as if we were submitting the published pipeline from our local development environment. In addition, we can configure the pipeline run through environment variables and command-line parameters. We will see this functionality in action in *Chapter 13, MLOps–DevOps for machine learning*.

Summary

In this chapter, you have learned how to use and configure Azure Machine Learning pipelines to split an ML workflow into multiple steps, and how to use pipelines and pipeline steps for estimators, Python execution, and parallel execution. You configured pipeline inputs and outputs using `Dataset` and `PipelineData` and managed to control the execution flow of a pipeline.

As another milestone, you deployed the pipeline as a `PublishedPipeline` instance to an HTTP endpoint. This lets you configure and trigger pipeline execution with a simple HTTP call. After that, you implemented automatic scheduling based on time frequency, and you used reactive scheduling based on changes in the underlying dataset. Now the pipeline can rerun your workflow when the input data changes without any manual interaction.

Finally, we also modularized and versioned a pipeline step, so it can be reused in other projects. We used `InputPortDef` and `OutputPortDef` to create virtual bindings for data sources and sinks. In the last step, we looked into the integration of pipelines into other Azure services, such as the Azure Machine Learning designer, Azure Data Factory, and Azure DevOps.

In the next chapter, we will look into more advanced preprocessing techniques, such as category embeddings and **natural language processing** (**NLP**), to extract semantic meaning from text features.

6
Advanced feature extraction with NLP

In the previous chapters, we learned about many standard transformation and preprocessing approaches within the **Azure Machine Learning** (**ML**) service and Azure Machine Learning pipelines. In this chapter, we want to go one step further to extract features from textual and categorical data—a problem that users often face when training ML models.

This chapter will describe the foundations of feature extraction with **Natural Language Processing** (**NLP**). This will help you to practically implement semantic embeddings using NLP for your ML pipelines.

First, we will take a look at the differences between textual, categorical, nominal, and ordinal data. This classification will help you to decide the best feature extraction and transformation technique per feature type. Later, we will look at the most common transformations for categorical values, namely label encoding and one-hot encoding. Both techniques will be compared and tested to understand the different use cases and applications for both techniques.

Next, we will tackle the numerical embedding of textual data. To achieve this, we will build a simple bag-of-words model, using a count vectorizer. To sanitize the input, you will build an NLP pipeline consisting of a tokenizer, stop-word removal, stemming, and lemmatization. We will learn how these different techniques affect a sample dataset step by step.

Then, we will replace the word count method with a much better word frequency weighting approach—the **term frequency-inverse document frequency (tf-idf)** algorithm. This will help you to compute the importance of words when given a whole corpus of documents by weighting the occurrence of a term in one document over the frequency in the corpus. We can improve this technique by using semantic word embeddings, such as **Global Vectors (GloVe)** and Word2Vec. Finally, we will take a quick look at current state-of-the-art language models that are based on sequence-to-sequence deep neural networks with over 100 million parameters.

The following topics will be covered in this chapter:

- Understanding categorical data Building
- A simple bag-of-words model
- Leveraging term importance and semantics
- Implementing end-to-end language models

Understanding categorical data

Categorical data comes in many forms, shapes, and meanings. It is extremely important to understand what type of data you are dealing with—is it a string, text, or numeric value disguised as a categorical value? This information is essential for data preprocessing, feature extraction, and model selection.

First, we will take a look at the different types of categorical data—namely ordinal, nominal, and text. Depending on the type, you can use different methods to extract information or other valuable data from it. Please keep in mind that categorical data is ubiquitous, either it is in an ID column, a nominal category, an ordinal category, or a free text field. It's worth mentioning that the more information you have on the data, the easier the preprocessing is.

Next, we will actually preprocess the ordinal and nominal categorical data by transforming it into numerical values. This is a required step when you want to use an ML algorithm later on that can't interpret categorical data, which is true for most algorithms except, for example, decision-tree-based approaches. Most other algorithms can only operate (for example, compute a loss function) on a numeric value and so a transformation is required.

Comparing textual, categorical, and ordinal data

Many ML algorithms, such as support vector machines, neural networks, linear regression, and so on, can only be applied to numeric data. However, in real-world datasets, we often find non-numeric columns, such as columns that contain textual data. The goal of this chapter is to transform textual data into numeric data as an advanced feature extraction step, which allows us to plug the processed data into any ML algorithm.

When working with real-world data, you will be confronted with many different types of textual and/or categorical data. To optimize ML algorithms, you need to understand the differences in order to apply different preprocessing techniques on the different types. But first, let's define the three different textual data types:

- **Textual data**: Free text
- **Categorical nominal data**: Non-orderable categories
- **Categorical ordinal data**: Orderable categories

The difference between textual data and categorical data is that in textual data we want to capture semantic similarities (the similarity in the meaning of the words), whereas in categorical data we want to differentiate between a small number of variables.

The difference between categorical nominal and ordinal data is that nominal data cannot be ordered (all categories have the same weight) whereas ordinal categories can be logically ordered on an ordinal scale.

Figure 6.1 shows an example dataset of comments on news articles, where the first column, named `statement`, is a textual field, the column named `topic` is a nominal category, and `rating` is an ordinal category:

statement	topic	rating
Great article!	international	good
Very interesting.	sports	very good
I don't like this.	sports	bad
Not accurate.	international	average
Good read.	politics	good

Figure 6.1: An example dataset comparing textual, categorical, and ordinal data

Understanding the difference between these data representations is essential for finding the proper embedding technique afterward. It seems quite natural to replace ordinal categories with an ordinal numeric scale and to embed nominal categories in an orthogonal space. On the contrary, it's not obvious how to embed textual data into a numerical space where the semantics are preserved—this will be covered in the later sections of this chapter dealing with NLP.

Please note that instead of categorical values, you will also see continuous numeric variables representing categorical information; for example, IDs from a dimension or look-up table. Although these are numeric values, you should consider treating them as categorical nominal values, if possible. Here is an example dataset as shown in *Figure 6.2*:

timestamp	sensorId	value
2019-01-01 00:01:00.000	1	18.5
2019-01-01 00:02:00.000	1	18.6
2019-01-01 00:03:00.000	1	18.4
2019-01-01 00:04:00.000	2	18.5
2019-01-01 00:05:00.000	2	18.6

Figure 6.2: An example dataset representing categorical data using numeric values

In the preceding example, we can see that the `sensorId` value is a numeric value that should be interpreted as a categorical nominal value instead of a numeric value by default because it doesn't have a numeric meaning. What do you get when you subtract `sensorId` 2 from `sensorId` 1? Is `sensorId` 10 10 times larger than `sensorId` 1? These are typical questions to ask to discover and encode these categorical values. We will see in *Chapter 7, Building ML models using Azure Machine Learning*, that by specifying that these values are categorical, a gradient boosted tree model can optimize these features instead of treating them as continuous variables.

Transforming categories into numeric values

Let's start by converting categorical variables (both ordinal and nominal) into numeric values. In this section, we will look at two common techniques for categorical encoding: label encoding and one-hot encoding (also called **dummy coding**). While label encoding replaces a categorical feature column with a numerical feature column, one-hot encoding uses multiple columns (the number of columns equals the number of unique values) to encode a single feature.

Both techniques are applied in the same way. During the training iteration, these techniques find all the unique values in a feature column and assigns them a specific numeric value (multidimensional for one-hot encoding). This look-up dictionary is stored, as a result, in the encoder. When the encoder is applied, the values in the applied column are transformed (replaced) using the look-up dictionary. If the list of possible values is known beforehand, most implementations allow the encoder to initialize the look-up dictionary directly from the list of known values, instead of finding the unique values in the training set. This has the benefit of specifying the order of the values in the dictionary and so orders the encoded values.

> **Note**
>
> Please note that it's often possible that certain categorical feature values in the test set don't appear in the training set and hence are not stored in the look-up dictionary. So, you should add a default category to your encoder that can also transform unseen values into numeric values.

Now, we will use two different categorical data columns, one ordinal and one nominal category, to showcase the different encodings. Figure 6.3 shows the dataset with nominal feature topic, which could represent a list of articles by a news agency:

id	topic	content
1	international	...
2	sports	...
3	sports	...
4	international	...
5	politics	...

Figure 6.3: An example dataset showing nominal feature topics

Advanced feature extraction with NLP

Figure 6.4 shows the dataset which contains the ordinal category rating; it could represent a feedback form for purchased articles on a website:

id	rating	comment
1	good	...
2	very good	...
3	bad	...
4	average	...
5	good	...

Figure 6.4: An example dataset representing feedback for purchased articles

First, we take a look at the label encoder. The label encoder assigns an incrementing value to each unique categorical value in a feature column. So, it transforms categories into a numeric value between 0 and N-1, where N represents the number of unique values.

Let's test the label encoder on the **topic** column in the first table. We train the encoder on the data and replace the **topic** column with a numeric topic ID. Here is an example snippet to train the label encoder and to transform the dataset:

```
from sklearn import preprocessing
data = load_articles()
enc = preprocessing.LabelEncoder()
enc.fit(data)
enc.transform(data)
```

The output of the preceding transformation looks similar to Figure 6.5:

id	topicId	content
1	0	...
2	1	...
3	1	...
4	0	...
5	2	...

Figure 6.5: Derived output on testing the label encoder

The generated look-up table for **topicId** looks like *Figure 6.6*:

topicId	topic
0	international
1	sports
2	politics

Figure 6.6: The lookup table for topicId

In the next example, we naively apply the label encoder to the **ratings** dataset. The encoder is trained by iterating the training data in order to create the look-up dictionary:

```
from sklearn import preprocessing
data = load_ratings()
enc = preprocessing.LabelEncoder()
enc.fit(data)
enc.transform(data)
```

The output looks similar to the following table shown in *Figure 6.7*:

id	ratingId	comment
1	0	...
2	1	...
3	2	...
4	3	...
5	0	...

Figure 6.7: The lookup dictionary created for the training data

From the original training data, the dictionary is generated as shown in *Figure 6.8*:

ratingId	rating
0	good
1	very good
2	bad
3	average

Figure 6.8: The dictionary based on the original training data

Do you see something odd in the auto-generated look-up dictionary? Due to the order of the categorical values in the training data, we created a numeric list with the following numeric order:

good < very good < bad < average

This is probably not what we anticipated when applying a label encoder on an ordinal categorical value. The ordering we would be looking for is something like the following:

very bad < bad < average < good < very good

In order to create a label encoder with the right order, we can pass the ordered list of categorical values to the encoder. This would create a more meaningful encoding, as shown in *Figure 6.9*:

id	rating	comment
1	3	...
2	4	...
3	1	...
4	2	...
5	3	...

Figure 6.9: An encoding based on the ordered list of categorical values

To achieve this in Python, we have to use pandas categorical ordinal variables, a special kind of label encoder that requires a list of ordered categories as input:

```
import pandas as pd
data = load_ratings()
categories = ['very bad', 'bad', 'average', 'good', 'very good']
data = pd.Categorical(data, categories=categories, ordered=True)
print(data.codes)
```

As shown in *Figure 6.10*, under the hood, we implicitly created the look-up dictionary for the encoder by passing the categories directly to it in order:

ratingId	rating
0	very bad
1	bad
2	average
3	good
4	very good

Figure 6.10: The lookup dictionary based on the ordered categories

> **Note**
>
> The key takeaway here is that the label encoder is great for encoding ordinal categorical data. You also saw that the order of elements matters, and so it is good practice to manually pass the categories to the encoder in the correct order.

Orthogonal embedding using one-hot encoding

In the second part of this section, we will take a look at the one-hot encoder. It will help us to create an equal-length encoding for nominal categorical values. The one-hot encoder replaces each unique categorical value in a feature column with a vector of size N, where N represents the number of unique values. This vector contains only zeroes, except for one column that contains 1 and represents the column for this specific value. Here is a snippet to apply the one-hot encoder to the **articles** dataset:

```
from sklearn import preprocessing

data = [load_articles()]

enc = preprocessing.OneHotEncoder()

enc.fit(data)

enc.transform(data)
```

The output of the preceding code will look similar to the following table shown in *Figure 6.11*:

id	topic_international	topic_sports	topic_politics
1	1	0	0
2	0	1	0
3	0	1	0
4	1	0	0
5	0	0	1

Figure 6.11: Orthogonal embedding using one-hot encoding

The look-up dictionary for one-hot encoding has N+1 columns, where N is the number of unique values in the encoded column. In *Figure 6.12*, we can see that all N-dimensional vectors in the dictionary are orthogonal and of an equal length, 1:

topic_international	topic_sports	topic_politics	topic
1	0	0	international
0	1	0	sports
0	0	1	politics

Figure 6.12: The lookup dictionary for one-hot encoding

Now, we apply the one-hot encoding technique to the ratings table:

id	rating_good	rating_very_good	rating_bad	rating_average
1	1	0	0	0
2	0	1	0	0
3	0	0	1	0
4	0	0	0	1
5	1	0	0	0

Figure 6.13: A rating table based on the one-hot encoding technique

We can see in *Figure* 6.33 that even if the original category values are ordinal, the encoded values cannot be sorted anymore and so this property is lost after the numeric encoding. So, we can conclude that one-hot encoding is great for nominal categorical values where the number of unique values is small.

So far, we learned how to embed nominal and ordinal categorical values to numeric values by using a look-up dictionary and 1- or N-dimensional numeric embedding. However, we saw that it is somewhat limited in many aspects, such as the number of unique categories and capabilities to embed free text. In the following sections, we will learn how to extract words using a simple NLP pipeline.

Categories versus text

It's worth understanding that a categorical value and a textual value are not the same. Although they both might be stored as a string and probably have the same data type, a categorical value usually represents a finite set of categories whereas a text value can hold any textual information.

Why is this distinction important? Once you preprocess your categorical data and embed it into a numerical space, nominal categories will often be implemented as orthogonal vectors. You will not automatically be able to compute a distance from category A to category B or create a semantic meaning between the categories.

However, with textual data, you usually start the feature extraction with a different approach that assumes that you have similar terms in different observations of your data. You can use this information to compute meaningful similarity scores between two textual columns; for example, to measure the number of words that are in common.

Therefore, we recommend you thoroughly check what kind of categorical values you have and how you are aiming to preprocess them. A great exercise is also to compute the similarity between two rows and to see whether it matches your prediction. Let's take a look at a simple textual preprocessing approach using a dictionary-based bag-of-words embedding.

Building a simple bag-of-words model

In this section, we will look at a surprisingly simple concept to tackle the shortcomings of label encoding for textual data with the *bag-of-words* concept, which will build a foundation for a simple NLP pipeline. Don't worry if these techniques look too simple when you read through it; we will gradually build on top of them with tweaks, optimizations, and improvements to build a modern NLP pipeline.

A naive bag-of-words model using counting

The main concept that we will build in this section is the bag-of-words model. It is a very simple concept; that is, modeling any document as a collection of words that appear in a given document with the frequency of each word. Hence, we throw away sentence structure, word order, punctuation, and so on and reduce the documents to a raw count of words. We can then vectorize this word count into a numeric vector representation, which can then be used for ML, analysis, document comparisons, and much more. While this word count model sounds very simple, we will encounter quite a few language-specific obstacles along the way that we will need to resolve.

Let's get started and define a sample document that we will transform throughout this section:

"Almost before we knew it, we had left the ground. The unknown holds its grounds."

Applying a naive word count on the document gives us a first (too simple) bag-of-words model as shown in *Figure 6.14*:

word	count
we	2
.	2
Almost	1
before	1
knew	1
it	1
,	1
had	1
left	1
the	1
ground	1
The	1
unknown	1
holds	1
its	1
grounds	1

Figure 6.14: A simple bag-of-words model based on the naïve word count

However, there are many problems with a naive approach such as the preceding one. We have mixed different punctuations, notations, nouns, verbs, adverbs, and adjectives in different declinations, conjugations, tenses, and cases. Hence, we have to build a pipeline to clean and normalize the data using NLP. In this section, we will build up a pipeline with the following cleaning steps before feeding the data into a *count vectorizer* that ultimately counts the word occurrences and collects them in a feature vector.

Tokenization – turning a string into a list of words

The first step in building the pipeline is to separate a corpus into documents and a document into words. This process is called **tokenization** because the resulting tokens contain words and punctuations. While splitting a corpus into documents, documents into sentences, and sentences into words sounds trivial, with a bit of **regular expression (RegEx)**, there are many non-trivial language-specific issues. Think about the different uses of periods, commas, and quotes and think about whether you would have thought about the following words in English: *don't, Mr. Smith, Johann S. Bach*, and so on. The **Natural Language Toolkit (NLTK)** Python package provides implementations and pre-trained transformers for many NLP algorithms, as well as for word tokenization. Let's split our document into tokens using `nltk`:

```
>>> from nltk.tokenize import word_tokenize
>>> nltk.download('punkt')
>>> tokens = word_tokenize(document)

>>> print(tokens)
['Almost', 'before', 'we', 'knew', 'it', ',', 'we', 'had',
 'left', 'the', 'ground', '.', 'The', 'unknown', 'holds', 'its',
 'grounds', '.']
```

You can see, in the preceding code, that `nltk` needs to download the pre-trained punctuation model in order to run the word tokenizer. The output of the tokenizer is the words and punctuation.

In the next step, we will remove the punctuation marks as they are not relevant for the subsequent stemming process. However, we will bring them back for lemmatization later in this section:

```
>>> words = [word.lower() for word in tokens if word.isalnum()]
>>> print(words)
['almost', 'before', 'we', 'knew', 'it', 'we', 'had', 'left',
 'the', 'ground', 'the', 'unknown', 'holds', 'its', 'grounds']
```

In the preceding code, we used the `word.islanum()` function to extract only alphanumeric tokens and make them all lowercase. The preceding list of words already looks much better than the initial naive model. However, it still contains a lot of unnecessary words, such as **the**, **we**, **had**, and so on, which don't convey any information.

In order to filter out the noise for a specific language, it makes sense to remove these words that appear often in texts and don't add any semantic meaning to the text. It is common practice to remove these so-called **stop words** using a pre-trained look-up dictionary. You can load and use such a dictionary by using the pre-trained `nltk` library in Python:

```
>>> from nltk.corpus import stopwords
>>> stopword_set = set(stopwords.words('english'))
>>> words = [word for word in words if word not in stopword_set]
>>> print(words)
['almost', 'knew', 'left', 'ground', 'unknown', 'holds', 'grounds']
```

The preceding code gives us a nice pipeline where we end up with only the semantically meaningful words. We can take this list of words to the next step and apply a more sophisticated transformation/normalization on each word. If we applied the count vectorizer at this stage, we would end up with the bag-of-words model as shown in *Figure 6.15*:

word	count
almost	1
knew	1
left	1
ground	1
unknown	1
holds	1
grounds	1

Figure 6.15: The bag-of-words model after applying the count vectorizer

You might ask: what qualifies a word as a stop word other than it occurring often in a text? Well, that's an excellent question! We can measure the importance of each word in the current context compared to its occurrences across the text using the **tf-idf method**, which will be discussed in the *Measuring the importance of words using tf-idf* section.

Stemming – rule-based removal of affixes

In the next step, we want to normalize affixes—word endings to create plurals and conjugations. You can see that with each step, we are diving deeper into the concept of a single language—English, in this case. However, when applying these steps to a different language, it's likely that completely different transformations need to be used. This is what makes NLP such a difficult field.

Removing the affixes of words to obtain the stem of a word is also called **stemming**. Stemming refers to a rule-based (heuristic) approach to transform each occurrence of a word into its word stem. Here is a simple example of some expected transformations:

```
cars -> car
saying ->
say flies -> fli
```

As we can see in the preceding example, such a heuristic approach for stemming has to be built specifically for each language. This is generally true for all other NLP algorithms as well. For the sake of brevity, we will only discuss English examples in this book.

A popular algorithm for stemming in English is Porter's algorithm, which defines five sequential reductions rules, such as removing -ed, -ing, -ate, -tion, -ence, -ance, and so on, from the end of words. The **nltk** library comes with an implementation of Porter's stemming algorithm:

```
>>> from nltk.stem import PorterStemmer
>>> stemmer = PorterStemmer()
>>> words = [stemmer.stem(word) for word in words]
>>> print(words)
['almost', 'knew', 'left', 'ground', 'unknown', 'hold', 'ground']
```

In the preceding code, we simply apply **stemmer** to each word in the tokenized document. The bag-of-words model after this step looks like *Figure 6.16*:

word	count
ground	2
almost	1
knew	1
left	1
unknown	1
hold	1

Figure 6.16: The bag-of-words model after stemming

While this algorithm works well with affixes, it can't help normalize conjugations and tenses. This will be our next problem to tackle using lemmatization.

Lemmatization – dictionary-based word normalization

When looking at the stemming examples, we can already see the limitations of the approach. What would happen, for example, with irregular verb conjugations—such as *are*, *am*, or *is*—that should all be normalized to the same word, *be*? This is exactly what lemmatization tries to solve using a pre-trained set of vocabulary and conversion rules, called **lemmas**. The lemmas are stored in a look-up dictionary and look similar to the following transformations:

```
are     ->  be
is      ->  be
taught  ->  teach
better  ->  good
```

There is one very important point to make when speaking about lemmatization. Each lemma needs to be applied to the correct word type, hence a lemma for nouns, verbs, adjectives, and so on. The reason for this is that a word can be either a noun or a verb in the past tense. In our example, **ground** could come from the noun *ground* or the verb *grind*; *left* could be an adjective or the past tense of *leave*. So, we also need to extract the word type from the word in a sentence—this process is called **Point of Speech** (**POS**) tagging.

Luckily, the **nltk** library has us covered once again. To estimate the correct POS tag, we also need to provide the punctuation:

```
>>> import nltk
>>> nltk.download('averaged_perceptron_tagger')
>>> tags = nltk.pos_tag(tokens)
>>> print(tags)
[('Almost', 'RB'), ('before', 'IN'), ('we', 'PRP'), ('knew', 'VBD'),
 ('it', 'PRP'), (',', ','), ('we', 'PRP'), ('had', 'VBD'),
 ('left', 'VBN'), ('the', 'DT'), ('ground', 'NN'), ('.', '.'),
 ('The', 'DT'), ('unknown', 'JJ'), ('holds', 'VBZ'),
 ('its', 'PRP$'), ('grounds', 'NNS'), ('.', '.')]
```

The POS tags describe the word type of each token in the document. You can find a complete list of tags using the `nltk.help.upenn_tagset()` command. Here is an example of doing so from the command line:

```
>>> import nltk
>>> nltk.download('tagsets')
>>> nltk.help.upenn_tagset()
CC: conjunction, coordinating
    & 'n and both but either et for less minus neither nor or plus
    so therefore times v. versus vs. whether yet
CD: numeral, cardinal

    mid-1890 nine-thirty forty-two one-tenth ten million 0.5 one
    forty- seven 1987 twenty '79 zero two 78-degrees eighty-four
    IX '60s .025 fifteen 271,124 dozen quintillion DM2,000 ...
DT: determiner
    all an another any both del each either every half la many
    much nary neither no some such that the them these this those
EX: existential there
    there
FW: foreign word
    gemeinschaft hund ich jeux habeas Haementeria Herr K'ang-si
    vous lutihaw alai je jour objets salutaris fille quibusdam pas
    trop Monte terram fiche oui corporis ...
IN: preposition or conjunction, subordinating
    astride among uppon whether out inside pro despite on by
    throughout below within for towards near behind atop around
    if like until below next into if beside ...
...
```

The POS tags also include tenses for verbs and other very useful information. However, for the lemmatization in this section, we only need to know the word type—**noun**, **verb**, **adjective**, or **adverb**. One possible choice of lemmatizer is the `WordNet` lemmatizer in `nltk`. WordNet (similar to ImageNet for images) is a lexical database of English words that groups them into groups of concepts and word types.

To apply the lemmatizer to the output of the stemming, we need to filter the POS tags by punctuation and stop words, similar to the previous preprocessing step. Then, we can use the word tags for the resulting words. Let's apply the lemmatizer using **nltk**:

```
>>> from nltk.corpus import wordnet
>>> from nltk.stem import WordNetLemmatizer
>>> nltk.download('wordnet')
>>> lemmatizer = WordNetLemmatizer()
>>> tag_dict = {"J": wordnet.ADJ, "N": wordnet.NOUN, "V": wordnet.VERB, "R": wordnet.ADV}
>>> pos = [tag_dict.get(t[0].upper(), wordnet.NOUN) for t in zip(*tags)[1]]
>>> words = [lemmatizer.lemmatize(w, pos=p) for w, p in zip(words, pos)]
>>> print(words)
['almost', 'know', 'leave', 'ground', 'unknown', 'hold', 'ground']
```

The preceding list of words looks beautiful; we could normalize the tenses of the verbs and transform them into their infinitive form. The resulting bag-of-words model would look like *Figure 6.17*:

word	count
ground	2
almost	1
know	1
leave	1
unknown	1
hold	1

Figure 6.17: The resulting bag-of-words model after the lemmatizer

A bag-of-words model in scikit-learn

Finally, we can put all our previous steps together to create a state-of-the-art NLP preprocessing pipeline to normalize input documents and run it through a count vectorizer to transform it into a numeric feature vector. Doing so for multiple documents lets us easily compare the semantics of the document in a numerical space. We could compute cosine similarities on the document's feature vectors to compute their similarity, plug them into a supervised classification method, or perform clustering on the resulting document concepts.

To recap, let's take a look at the final pipeline for the simple bag-of-words model. I want to emphasize that this model is only the start of our journey in feature extraction using NLP. We performed the following steps for normalization:

1. Tokenization
2. Removing punctuation
3. Removing stop-words
4. Stemming
5. Lemmatization with POS tagging

In the last step, we applied **CountVectorizer** in **scikit-learn**. It will count the occurrences of each word, create a global corpus of words, and output a sparse feature vector of word frequencies. Here is the sample code to pass the preprocessed data from **nltk** into **CountVectorizer**:

```
>>> from sklearn.feature_extraction.text import CountVectorizer
>>> count_vect = CountVectorizer()
>>> data = [" ".join(words)]
>>> X_train_counts = count_vect.fit_transform(data)
>>> print(X_train_counts)
  (0,0)         1
  (0,3)         1
  (0,4)         1
  (0,1)         2
  (0,5)         1
  (0,2)         1
>>> print(count_vect.vocabulary_)
{'almost': 0, 'know': 3, 'leave': 4, 'ground': 1, 'unknown': 5, 'hold': 2}
```

As we see in the preceding code, we transform the preprocessed document back into a string before passing it to **CountVectorizer**. The reason for this is that **CountVectorizer** comes with some configurable preprocessing techniques out of the box, such as tokenization, stop-word removal, and others. For this demonstration, we want to apply it to the preprocessed data. The output of the transformation is a sparse feature vector with the **(document id, term id) = term frequency** shape. The **vocabulary_ parameter** contains a look-up dictionary for the **ids** term.

Let's find out how we can combine multiple terms in semantic concepts.

Leveraging term importance and semantics

Everything we have done up to now has been relatively simple and based on word stems or so-called tokens. The bag-of-words model was nothing but a dictionary of tokens counting the occurrence of tokens per field. In this section, we will take a look at a common technique to further improve matching between documents using n-gram and skip-gram combinations of terms.

Combining terms in multiple ways will explode your dictionary. This will turn into a problem if you have a large corpus; for example, 10 million words. Hence, we will look at a common preprocessing technique to reduce the dimensionality of a large dictionary through **Singular Value Decomposition (SVD)**.

While this approach is, now, a lot more complicated, it is still based on a bag-of-words model that already works great on a large corpus, in practice. But, of course, we can do better and try to understand the importance of words. Therefore, we will tackle another popular technique in NLP to compute the term importance.

Generalizing words using n-grams and skip- grams

In the previous pipeline, we considered each word on its own without any context. However, as we all know, context matters a lot in language. Sometimes, words belong together and only make sense in context than on their own. To introduce this context into the same type of algorithm, we will introduce n-grams and skip-grams. Both techniques are heavily used in NLP for preprocessing datasets and extracting relevant features from text data.

Let's start with n-grams. An n-gram is the concatenation for N consecutive entities (characters, words, or tokens) of an input dataset. Here are some examples for computing the n-grams on a list of characters:

```
A, B, C, D -> 1-Gram: A, B, C, D
A, B, C, D -> 2-Gram: AB, BC, CD
A, B, C, D -> 3-Gram: ABC, BCD
```

Here is an example using the built-in **ngram_range** parameter in scikit-learn's **CountVectorizer** to generate multiple n-grams for the input data:

```
>>> from sklearn.feature_extraction.text import CountVectorizer
>>> count_vect = CountVectorizer(ngram_range=(1,2))
>>> X_train_counts = count_vect.fit_transform(data)
>>> print(count_vect.vocabulary_)
{'almost': 0, 'before': 2, 'we': 24, 'knew': 15, 'it': 11,
 'had': 7, 'left': 17, 'the': 19, 'ground': 4, 'unknown': 22,
 'holds': 9, 'its': 13, 'grounds': 6, 'almost before': 1,
 'before we': 3, 'we knew': 26, 'knew it': 16, 'it we': 12,
 'we had': 25, 'had left': 8, 'left the': 18, 'the ground': 20,
 'ground the': 5, 'the unknown': 21, 'unknown holds': 23,
 'holds its': 10, 'its grounds': 14}
```

In the preceding code, we can see that instead of the original words, we now also have a combination of two consecutive words in our trained vocabulary.

We can extend the concept of n-grams to also allow the model to skip words between each other. This way, we can define the distance of how much further the model can look for a word and how many words can be skipped in between. Here is an example using the same characters from before:

A, B, C, D -> 2-Gram (1 skip): AB, AC, BC, BD, CD

A, B, C, D -> 2-Gram (2 skip): AB, AC, AD, BC, BD, CD

Luckily, we find the generalized version of n-grams implemented in **nltk** as the **nltk.skipgrams** method. Setting the skip distance to **0** results in the traditional n-gram algorithm, we can apply it on our original dataset:

```
>>> list(nltk.skipgrams(document.split(' '), 2, 1))
[('Almost', 'before'), ('Almost', 'we'), ('before', 'we'),
 ('before', 'knew'), ('we', 'knew'), ('we', 'it,'), ('knew', 'it,'),
 ('knew', 'we'), ('it,', 'we'), ('it,', 'had'), ('we', 'had'),
 ('we', 'left'), ('had', 'left'), ('had', 'the'), ('left', 'the'),
 ('left', 'ground.'), ('the', 'ground.'), ('the', 'The'),
 ('ground.', 'The'), ('ground.', 'unknown'), ('The', 'unknown'),
 ('The', 'holds'), ('unknown', 'holds'), ('unknown', 'its'),
 ('holds', 'its'), ('holds', 'grounds.'), ('its', 'grounds.')]
```

In the preceding code, we can observe that skip-grams can generate a lot of additional useful feature dimensions for the NLP model. In real-world scenarios, both techniques are often used due to the fact that the individual word order plays a big role in the semantics.

However, the explosion of new feature dimensions could be devastating if the input documents are, for example, all websites from the web or large documents. Hence, we also need a way to avoid an explosion of the dimensions while capturing all the semantics from the input data. We will tackle this challenge in the next section.

Reducing word dictionary size using SVD

A common problem with NLP is the vast amount of words in a corpus and hence, exploding dictionary sizes. We saw in the previous example that the size of the dictionary defines the size of the orthogonal term vectors. Hence, a dictionary size of 20,000 terms would result in 20,000-dimensional feature vectors. Even without any n-gram enrichment, this feature vector dimension is too large to be processed on standard PCs.

Therefore, we need an algorithm to reduce the dimensions of the generated `CountVectorizer` while preserving the present information. Optimally, we would only remove redundant information from the input data and project it into a lower-dimensional space while preserving all the original information.

The **Principal Component Analysis** (**PCA**) transformation would be a great fit for our solution and help us to transform the input data to lower linearly-unrelated dimensions. However, computing the eigenvalues requires a symmetric matrix (the same number of rows and columns), which we don't have, in our case. Hence, we can use the SVD algorithm, which generalizes the eigenvector computation to non-symmetric matrices. Due to its numeric stability, it is often used in NLP and information retrieval systems.

The usage of SVD in NLP applications is also called **Latent Semantic Analysis** (**LSA**), as the principal components can be interpreted as concepts in a latent feature space. The SVD embedding transforms the high-dimensional feature vector into a lower-dimensional concept-space. Each dimension in the concept space is constructed by a linear combination of term vectors. By dropping the concepts with the smallest variance, we also reduce the dimensions of the resulting concept space to something that is a lot smaller and easier to handle. Typical concept spaces have 10s to 100s of dimensions, while word dictionaries usually have over 100,000.

Let's look at an example using the `TruncatedSVD` implementation from `sklearn`. The SVD is implemented as a transformer class and so we need to call `fit_transform` to fit a dictionary and transform it in the same step. The SVD is configured to keep only the components with the highest variance using the `n_components` argument. As it uses a randomized algorithm, we seed the pseudo-random number generator by setting a specific random state:

```
from sklearn.decomposition import TruncatedSVD
svd = TruncatedSVD(n_components=5, random_state=0)
X_lsa = svd.fit_transform(X_train_counts)
```

In the preceding code, we perform the LSA on the `X_train_counts` data and the output of the `CountVectorizer` using SVD. We configure the SVD to keep only the first five components with the highest variance.

By reducing the dimensionality of your dataset, you lose information. Thankfully, we can compute the amount of variance in the remaining dataset using the trained SVD object:

```
print(svd.explained_variance_ratio_.sum())
```

In the preceding code, we can see that we can compute the value of how much variance of the data is preserved with the configured number of components. Hence, we can now reduce the number of dimensions while keeping x percent of the information from the data. This is a very helpful operation and is used in many practical NLP implementations.

We are still using the original word dictionary from the bag-of-words model. One particular downside of this model is that the more often a term occurs, the higher its count (and therefore weight) will get. This is a problem because now any term that is not a stop word and appears often in the text will receive a high weight—independent of the importance of the term to a certain document. Therefore, we introduce another extremely popular preprocessing technique—**tf-idf**.

Measuring the importance of words using tf-idf

One particular downside of the bag-of-words approach is that we simply count the absolute number of words in a context without checking whether the word generally appears often in the whole corpus. Hence, an important technique in text mining is to compute the importance of a certain word in a given context.

Instead of an absolute count of terms in a context, we want to compute the count of terms in the context relative to a corpus of documents. By doing so, we will give higher weight to terms that appear only in a certain context, and reduced weight to terms that appear in many different documents. Figure 6.18 shows exactly what the tf-idf algorithm does to compute a weight (w) for a term (t) in a document (d):

$$w(t, d) = f_t(t, d) \times \log\left(\frac{N}{f_d(t)}\right)$$

Figure 6.18: The formula for tf-idf measure

While the term frequency (f_t) counts all the terms in a document, the inverse document frequency is computed by dividing the total number of documents (N) by the counts of a term in all documents (f_d). The IDF term is usually log-transformed as the total count of a term across all documents can get quite large.

In the following example, we will not use the **tf-idf** function directly, but instead, use **TfidVectorizer**, which does the counting and then applies the **tf-idf** function on the result in one step. Again, the function is implemented as a sklearn transformer and hence we call **fit_transform** to fit and transform the dataset:

```
from sklearn.feature_extraction.text import TfidfVectorizer vect = TfidfVectorizer()
data = [" ".join(words)]
X_train_counts = vect.fit_transform(data)
print(X_train_counts)
#   (0, 2)         0.3333333333333333
#   (0, 5)         0.3333333333333333
#   (0, 1)         0.6666666666666666
#   (0, 4)         0.3333333333333333
#   (0, 3)         0.3333333333333333
#   (0, 0)         0.3333333333333333
```

In the preceding code, we apply **TfidfVectorizer** directly, which returns the same result as using **CountVectorizer** and **TfidfTransformer** combined. We transform a dataset containing the words of the bag-of-words model and return the **tf-idf** values. We can also return the terms for each **tf-idf** value:

```
print(vect.get_feature_names())
# ['almost', 'ground', 'hold', 'know', 'leave', 'unknown']
```

We can see that in this example, **ground** gets a tf-idf value of `0.667`, whereas all the other terms receive a value of `0.333`. This count would now scale relatively when more documents are added to the corpus—hence, if the word *hold* were to be included again, the tf-idf value would actually decrease.

In any real-world pipeline, we would always use all the techniques presented in this chapter—tokenization, stopword removal, stemming, lemmatization, n-grams/skip-grams, tf-idf, and SVD—combined in a single pipeline. The result would be a numeric representation of n-grams/skip-grams of tokens weighted by importance and transformed to a latent semantic space. Using these techniques for your first NLP pipeline will get you quite far as you can now capture a lot of information from your textual data.

So far, we have learned how to numerically encode many kinds of categorical and textual values using either 1- or N-dimensional labels or counting and weighting word stems and character combinations. While many of these methods work well in many situations where you require simple numeric embedding, they all have a serious limitation—they don't encode semantics. Let's take a look at how we can extract the semantic meaning of text in the same pipeline.

Extracting semantics using word embeddings

When computing the similarity of news, you would imagine that topics such as tennis, Formula 1, or soccer would be semantically more similar to each other than topics such as politics, economics, or science. Yet, for all previously discussed techniques, all encoded categories are equally different from each other. In this section, we will discuss a simple method of semantic embedding, also called **word embedding**.

The previously discussed pipeline using LSA transforms multiple documents into terms and those terms into semantic concepts that can be compared with other documents.

However, the semantic meaning is based on the term occurrences and importance—there is no measurement of semantics between individual terms.

Hence, what we are looking for is an embedding of terms into numerical multi-dimensional space such that each word represents one point in this space. This allows us to compute a numerical distance between multiple words in this space in order to compare the semantic meaning of two words. The most interesting benefit of word embeddings is that algebra on the word embeddings is not only numerically possible but also makes sense. Consider the following example:

```
King - Man + Woman = Queen
```

We can create such an embedding by mapping a corpus of words on an N-dimensional numeric space and optimizing the numeric distance based on the word semantics—for example, based on the distance between words in a corpus. The resulting optimization outputs a dictionary of words in the corpus and their numeric N-dimensional representation. In this numeric space, words have the same, or at least similar, properties as in the semantic space. A great benefit is that these embeddings can be trained unsupervised and so no training data has to be labeled.

One of the first embeddings is called **Word2Vec** and is based on a continuous bag-of-words or a continuous skip-gram model to count and measure the words in a window. Let's try this functionality and perform a semantic word embedding using Word2Vec:

1. The best Python implementation for word embeddings is **gensim**, which we will use here as well. We need to feed our tokens into the model in order to train it:

   ```
   from gensim.models import Word2Vec
   
   model = Word2Vec(words, size=100, window=5)
   vector = model.wv['ground']
   ```

   In the preceding code, we load the **Word2Vec** model and initialize it with the list of tokens from the previous sections, which is stored in the **words** variable. The **size** attribute defines the dimension of the resulting vectors and the **window** parameter decides how many words we should consider per window. Once the model is trained, we can simply look up the word embedding in the model's dictionary.

   The code will automatically train the embedding on the set of tokens we provided. The resulting model stores the word to vector mapping in the **wv** property. Optimally, we also use a large corpus or pre-trained model that is either provided by **gensim** or other NLP libraries, such as **NLTK**, to train the embedding and fine-tune it with a smaller dataset.

2. Next, we can use the trained model to embed all the terms from our document using the **Word2Vec** embedding. However, this will result in multiple vectors as each word returns its own embedding. Therefore, you need to combine all vectors into a single one using the mean of all embeddings, which has a similar meaning to the concept in LSA. Also, other reduction techniques are possible; for example, weighting the individual embedding vectors using their tf-idf:

   ```
   dim = len(model.wv.vectors[0])
   X = np.mean([model.wv[w] for w in words if w in model.wv] or
       [np.zeros(dim)], axis=0)
   ```

In the preceding function, we compute the mean from all word embedding vectors of the terms—this is called a **mean embedding** and it represents the concept of this document in the embedding space. If a word is not found in the embedding, we need to replace it with zeros in the computation.

You can use such a semantic embedding for your application by downloading a pre-trained embedding; for example, on the Wikipedia corpus. Then, you can loop through your sanitized input tokens and look up the words in the dictionary of the numeric embedding.

GloVe is another popular technique for encoding words as numerical vectors, developed by Stanford University. In contrast to the continuous window-based approach, it uses the global word-word co-occurrence statistics to determine linear relationships between words:

1. Let's take a look at the pre-trained 6 B tokens embedding trained on Wikipedia and the Gigaword news archive:

    ```
    # download pre-trained dictionary from
    # http://nlp.stanford.edu/data/glove.6B.zip
    glove = {}
    with open('glove.6B.100d.txt') as f:
        for line in f:
            word, coefs = line.split(maxsplit=1)
            coefs = np.fromstring(coefs, 'f', sep=' ')
            glove[word] = coefs
    ```

    In the preceding code, we only open and parse the pre-trained word embedding in order to store the word and vectors in a look-up dictionary.

2. Then, we use the dictionary to look up tokens in our training data and merge them by computing the mean of all GloVe vectors:

    ```
    X - np.mean([glove[w] for w in words if w in glove] or
        [np.zeros(dim)], axis=0)
    ```

    The preceding code works very similar to before and returns one vector per word, which is aggregated by taking their mean at the end. Again, this corresponds with a semantic concept using all the tokens of the training data.

Gensim provides other popular models for semantic embeddings, such as doc2word, fastText, and GloVe. The `gensim` Python library is a great place for utilizing these pre- trained embeddings or for training your own models. You can now replace your bag-of- words model with a mean embedding of the word vectors to also capture word semantics. However, your pipeline is still built out of many tunable components. In the next section, we will take a look at building an end-to-end language model and reusing some of the language features from Azure Cognitive Services.

Implementing end-to-end language models

In the previous sections, we trained and concatenated multiple pieces to implement a final algorithm where most of the individual steps need to be trained as well. Lemmatization contains a dictionary of conversion rules. Stop words are stored in the dictionary.

Stemming needs rules for each language and word that the embedding needs to train— tf- idf and SVD are computed only on your training data but independent of each other.

This is a similar problem to the traditional computer vision approach that we will discuss in more depth in *Chapter 8, Training deep neural networks on Azure*, where many classic algorithms are combined into a pipeline of feature extractors and classifiers. Similar to breakthroughs of end-to-end models trained via gradient descent and backpropagation in computer vision, deep neural networks—especially sequence-to-sequence models—replaced the classical approach, a few years ago.

First, we will take a quick look at improving our previous model using custom embedding and a **Long Short-Term Memory** (**LSTM**) implementation to model a token sequence. This will give you a good understanding of how we are moving from an individual preprocessor-based pipeline to a fully end-to-end approach using deep learning.

Sequence-to-sequence models are models based on encoders and decoders that are trained on a variable set of inputs. This encoder/decoder architecture is used for a variety of tasks, such as machine translation, image captioning, and summarization. A nice benefit of these models is that you can reuse the encoder part of this network to convert a set of inputs into a fixed-set numerical representation of the encoder. We will look at the state-of-the-art language representation models and discuss how they can be used for feature engineering and the preprocessing of your text data.

Finally, we will also look at reusing Azure Cognitive Services APIs for text analytics to carry out advanced modeling and feature extraction, such as text or sentence sentiment, key words, or entity recognition. This is a nice approach because you can leverage the know- how and amount of training data from Microsoft to perform complex text analytics using a simple HTTP request.

End-to-end learning of token sequences

Instead of concatenating different pieces of algorithms to a single pipeline, we want to build and train an end-to-end model that can train the word embedding, pre-form latent semantic transformation, and capture sequential information in the text in a single model. The benefit of such a model is that each processing step can be fine-tuned for the user's prediction task in a single combined optimization process:

1. The first part of the pipeline will look extremely similar to the previous sections. We will build a tokenizer that converts documents into sequences of tokens that are then transformed into a numerical model based on the token sequence. Then, we use **pad_sequences** to align all the documents to the same length:

    ```
    from keras.preprocessing.text import Tokenizer
    from keras.preprocessing.sequence import pad_sequences

    num_words = 1000
    tokenizer = Tokenizer(num_words=num_words)
    tokenizer.fit_on_texts(X_words)
    X = tokenizer.texts_to_sequences(X_words)
    X = pad_sequences(X, maxlen=2000)
    ```

2. In the next step, we will build a simple model using Keras, an embedding layer and an LSTM layer to capture token sequences. The embedding layer will perform a similar operation to GloVe, where the words will be embedded into a semantic space. The LSTM cell will ensure that we are comparing sequences of words instead of single words at a time. We then use a dense layer with a **softmax** activation to implement a classifier head:

    ```
    from keras.layers import Embedding, LSTM, Dense
    from keras.models import Sequential

    embed_dim = 128
    lstm_out = 196

    model = Sequential()
    model.add(Embedding(num_words, embed_dim,
        input_length=X.shape[1]))
    model.add(LSTM(lstm_out, recurrent_dropout=0.2, dropout=0.2))
    model.add(Dense(len(labels), activation='softmax'))
    model.compile(loss='categorical_crossentropy',
                  optimizer='adam',
                  metrics=['categorical_crossentropy'])
    ```

As you can see in the preceding function, we build a simple neural network using three layers and a `softmax` activation for classification. This means that in order to train this model, we would also need a classification problem to be solved at the same time. Hence, we do need labeled training data to perform analysis using this approach. In the next section, we will see how sequence-to-sequence models are used on input-output text sequences to learn an implicit text representation.

State-of-the-art sequence-to-sequence models

In recent years, another type of model has replaced the traditional NLP pipelines—transformer-based models. These types of models are fully end-to-end and use sequence-to-sequence mapping, positional encoding, and multi-head attention layers. As you might be able to tell, these models are fairly complicated and usually have well over 100 million parameters.

Popular models at the time of writing are the unidirectional **Generative Pre-trained Transformer (OpenAI GPT)** model, the shallowly bidirectional ELMo model, **Bidirectional Encoder Representations from Transformers (BERT)**, TransformerXL, and MT-DNN. Models based on the BERT architecture seem to perform particularly well, but might already have been outperformed by a new tuned or modified architecture when you are reading this text.

The key takeaway from these models is that they use an encoder/decoder-based architecture, which allows us to simply borrow the encoder to embed text into a semantic numerical feature space. Hence, a common approach is to download the pre-trained model and perform a forward pass through the encoder part of the network. The fixed-sized numerical output can now be used as a feature vector for any other model. This is a common preprocessing step and a good trade-off for using a state-of-the-art language model for numerical embedding.

We won't look at any code in this section as the tools, frameworks, and implementations are changing rapidly. However, at the time of writing, the Hugging Face transformers library seems to be the best one regarding pre-trained models and compatibility with TensorFlow and PyTorch.

Text analytics using Azure Cognitive Services

A good approach in many engineering disciplines is not to reinvent the wheel when many other companies have already solved the same problem much better than you will ever be able to solve it. This might be the case for basic text analytics and text understanding tasks that Microsoft has developed, implemented, and trained and now offers as a service.

What if I told you that when working with Azure, text understanding features such as sentiment analysis, key phrase extraction, language detection, named entity recognition, and extraction of **Personal Identifiable Information (PII)** is just one request away? Azure provides the Text Analytics API as part of Cognitive Services, which will solve all these problems for you.

This won't solve the need to transform text into numerical values, but it will make it easier to extract semantics from your text. One example would be to perform a key phrase extraction or sentiment analysis using Cognitive Services as an additional feature engineering step, instead of implementing your own NLP pipeline.

Let's implement a function that returns the sentiment for a given document using the Text Analytics API of Cognitive Services. This is great when you want to enrich your data with additional attributes, such as overall sentiment, in the text:

```
import requests


def cs_sentiment_analyze(text, key, region='westus', lang='en'):
    endpoint = 'https://%s.api.cognitive.microsoft.com' % region
    baseurl = '%s/text/analytics/v3.0-preview.1/sentiment' %endpoint
    headers = {'Content-Type': 'application/json',
        'Ocp-Apim-Subscription-Key': key}
params = {'showStats': False}
payload = {'documents': ['id': 1, 'text': text, 'language': lang]}

r = requests.post(baseurl, json=payload,
    params=params, headers=headers)
return r.json()


text = 'Hello world. This is some input text that I love.'
key = '<insert subscription key>'
res = cs_sentiment_analyze(url, key, features=features) print(res)
```

The preceding code looks very similar to the computer vision example that we saw in Chapter 2, *Choosing a machine learning service in Azure*. In fact, it uses the same API but just a different endpoint for Text Analytics and, in this case, sentiment analysis functionality.

Let's run this code and look at the output, which looks very similar to the following snippet:

```
{
  "documents": [
    {
      "id": "1",
      "sentiment": "positive",
      "documentScores":
      {
        "positive": 0.998519241809845,
        "neutral": 0.0009635657188483,
        "negative": 0.000517153472174
      }
    }
  ]
}
```

We can observe that the JSON response contains a sentiment classification for each document (**positive**, **neutral**, and **negative**) as well as numeric confidence scores for each class. You can also see that the resulting documents are stored in an array and marked with an id value. Hence, you can also send multiple documents to this API using an ID to identify each document.

Using custom pre-trained language models is great, but for standardized text analytics, we can simply reuse Cognitive Services. Microsoft has invested tons of resources into the research and production of these language models, which you can use for your own data pipelines for a relatively small amount of money. Hence, if you prefer using a managed service instead of running your customer transformer model, you should try this Text Analytics API.

Summary

In this chapter, you learned how to preprocess textual and categorical nominal and ordinal data using state-of-the-art NLP techniques.

You can now build a classical NLP pipeline with stop-word removal, lemmatization and stemming, n-grams, and count term occurrences using a bag-of-words model. We used SVD to reduce the dimensionality of the resulting feature vector and to generate lower-dimensional topic encoding. One important tweak to the count-based bag-of-words model is to compare the relative term frequencies of a document. You learned about the `tf-idf` function and can use it to compute the importance of a word in a document compared to the corpus.

In the following section, we looked at Word2Vec and GloVe, pre-trained dictionaries of numeric word embeddings. You can now easily reuse a pre-trained word embedding for commercial NLP applications with great improvements and with accuracy due to the semantic embedding of words.

Finally, we finished the chapter by looking at a state-of-the-art approach to language modeling, using end-to-end language representations, such as OpenAI GPT, ELMo, BERT, or TransformerXL, which are trained as sequence-to-sequence models. The great benefit of this model is that you can reuse the encoder part of the model to transform a sequence of text into a numerical representation—very similar to the bag-of-words approach or the mean embedding of GloVe vectors.

In the next chapter, we will look at training an ML model using Azure Machine Learning, applying everything we have learned so far.

Section 3: Training Machine Learning Models

In the third part of the book, the reader will learn all about training and optimizing traditional machine learning models as well as deep learning models on Azure. The reader will implement and train different **Deep Neural Networks (DNNs)** on Azure using the capabilities of Azure Machine Learning.

This section comprises the following chapters:

- Chapter 7, *Building ML models using Azure Machine Learning*
- Chapter 8, *Training deep neural networks on Azure*
- Chapter 9, *Hyperparameter tuning and Automated Machine Learning*
- Chapter 10, *Distributed machine learning on Azure*
- Chapter 11, *Building a recommendation engine in Azure*

7
Building ML models using Azure Machine Learning

In the previous chapter, we learned how to extract features from textual and categorical columns using NLP techniques. In this chapter, we will use the knowledge we have gained so far to create and train a powerful tree-based ensemble classifier.

First, we will look behind the scenes of popular ensemble classifiers such as random forest, XGBoost, and LightGBM. These classifiers perform extremely well in practical real-world scenarios, and all are based on decision trees under the hood. By understanding their main benefits, you will be able to spot problems that can be solved with ensemble decision tree classifiers easily.

We will also learn the difference between gradient boosting and random forest and what makes these tree ensembles useful for practical applications. Both techniques help to overcome the main weaknesses of decision trees and can be applied to many different classification and regression problems.

Finally, we will train a LightGBM classifier on a sample dataset using all the techniques we have learned so far. We will write a training script that automatically logs all parameters, evaluation metrics, and figures, and is configurable with command-line arguments. Then, we will schedule the training script on an Azure Machine Learning Compute cluster that we'll generate in two lines of Python code.

In this chapter, we will cover the following topics:

- Working with tree-based ensemble classifiers
- Training an ensemble classifier model using LightGBM

Working with tree-based ensemble classifiers

Supervised tree-based ensemble classification and regression techniques have proved very successful in many practical real-world applications in recent years. Hence, they are widely used today in various applications such as fraud detection, recommendation engines, tagging engines, and many more. Your favorite OS (mobile and desktop), office program, and audio or video streaming service will use them heavily every day.

Therefore, we will dive into the main reasons and drivers for their popularity and performance, both for training and scoring, in this section. If you are an expert on traditional ML algorithms and know the difference between boosting and bagging, you might as well jump right to the *Training an ensemble classifier model using LightGBM* section—otherwise, I encourage you to read this section carefully.

We will first look at decision trees, a very simple technique that is decades old. I encourage you to follow along even with the simple methods as they build the foundation of today's state-of-the-art classical supervised ML approaches. We will also explore the advantages of tree-based classifiers in great detail to help you choose a classical approach over a deep learning-based ML model.

A single decision tree also has a lot of disadvantages and is always used in an ensemble model and never as an individual model; we will take a closer look at the disadvantages later in this section. Afterwards, we will discover methods to combine multiple weak individual trees into a single strong ensemble classifier that builds upon the strengths of tree-based approaches and transforms them into what they are today—powerful multi- purpose supervised ML models that are integrated into almost every off-the-shelf ML platform.

Understanding a simple decision tree

Let's first discuss what a decision tree is and how it works. A decision tree estimator is a supervised ML approach that learns to approximate a function with multiple nested `if/else` statements. This function can be a continuous regressor function or a decision boundary function. Hence, like many other ML approaches, decision trees can be used for learning both regression and classification problems.

From the preceding description, we can immediately spot a few important advantages of decision trees:

- One is the flexibility to work on different data distributions, data types, and ML problems.

- Another advantage and one of the reasons they compete with more complicated models is their interpretability. Tree-based models and ensembles can be visualized and even printed out on paper to explain the decision (output) from a scoring result.

- The third advantage lies in their practical use for training performance, model size, and validity. Integrating a pre-trained decision tree into a desktop, web, or mobile application is a lot less complex and is faster than a deep learning approach.

> **Note**
>
> Please note that we don't intend to sell tree-based ensembles as the solution to every ML problem and to downplay the importance of deep learning approaches. We rather want to make you aware of the strengths of traditional approaches so you can evaluate the right approach for your problem.

Figure 7.1 shows an example of a decision tree used to decide whether a person is fit or not:

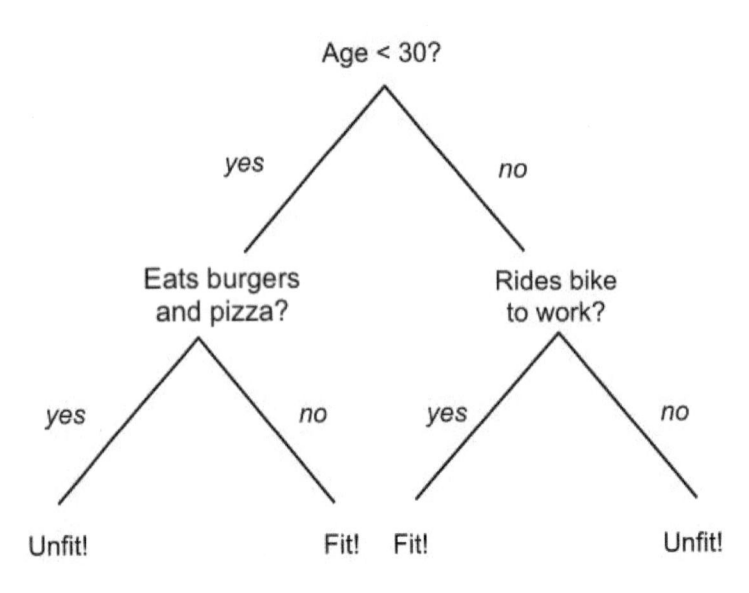

Figure 7.1: Decision tree

This is an example of a trained decision tree, where we can score the model by simply walking through each node and arriving at a class label at the leaf of the tree.

Advantages of a decision tree

Decision tree-based ML models are extremely popular due to their great strengths when working on real-world applications where data is messy, biased, and incomplete. The key advantages are the following:

- Support for a wide range of applications
- They require little data preparation
- The interpretability of the model
- Fast training and fast scoring

First, let's focus on the flexibility of decision trees, which is one of their major strengths as opposed to many other classical/statistical ML approaches. While the general framework is very flexible and supports classification, regression, as well as multi-output problems, it gained a lot of popularity due to the fact that it can handle both numerical and categorical data out of the box. Thanks to nested **if-else** trees, it can also handle nominal categories as well as **NULL** or missing values in data. Decision trees are popular because they don't require massive preprocessing and data cleansing beforehand.

While data preparation and cleaning are important steps in every ML pipeline, it's still very nice to have a framework that naturally supports categorical input data out of the box.

Some ensemble tree-based classifiers are built on top of this advantage, for example, CatBoost—a gradient boosted trees implementation from Yandex Research with native support for categorical data.

Another important advantage of tree-based models, especially from a business perspective, is the interpretability of the model. Unlike other ML approaches, the output of a decision tree classifier model is not a huge parametric decision boundary function. Trained deep learning models often generate a model with more than 10-100 million parameters and hence behave like a black box—especially for business decision makers. While it is possible to gain insights and reason about the activations in deep learning models, it's usually very hard to reason about the effect of an input parameter on the output variable.

Interpretability is where tree-based approaches shine. In contrast to many other traditional ML approaches (such as SVM, logistic regression, or deep learning), a decision tree is a non- parametric model and therefore, doesn't use parameters to describe the function to be learned. It uses a nested decision tree that can be plotted, visualized, and printed out on paper. This allows decision makers to understand every decision (output) of a tree-based classification model—it may require a lot of paper but it is always possible.

While speaking about interpretability, I want to mention another important aspect, which is the influence of a single variable (dimension) on the output. This is something that works really well in linear regression (without correlated inputs) where we can interpret the absolute value of the coefficient as a measurement of importance.

> **Note**
>
> Please note that many other approaches, such as SVM and deep learning, don't give you the notion of feature importance for the individual input dimensions of the model.

However, decision tree-based approaches excel at this as they internally create each individual split (decision) based on an importance criterion. This results in an inherent understanding of how and which feature dimensions are important to the final model.

We are in such a good flow, let's add another great advantage to the mix. Decision trees have many practical benefits over traditional statistical models derived from the non-parametric approach. Tree-based models generally yield good results on a wide variety of input distributions and even work well when the model assumptions are violated. On top of that, the size of the trained tree is small compared to deep learning approaches, and inference/scoring is fast.

Disadvantages of a decision tree

As everything in life comes with advantages and disadvantages, the same is true for decision trees. There are quite a few severe disadvantages of individual decision trees, which should make you feel like never using a single decision tree classifier in your ML pipeline. The main weakness of a decision tree is that the tree is fitted on all training samples and hence is very likely to overfit. The reason for this is that the model itself tends to build complex `if-else` trees to model a continuous function. Another important point is that finding the optimal decision tree even for simple concepts is an **NP-hard problem** (lesser-known as a **nondeterministic polynomial time-hard problem**). Therefore, it is solved through heuristics and the resulting single decision is usually not the optimal one.

Overfitting is bad – very bad – and leads to a serious complication in machine learning. Once a model overfits, it doesn't generalize well and hence has very poor performance on unseen data. Another related problem is that small changes in the training data can lead to very different nested trees and hence, the training convergence is unstable. Single decision trees are extremely prone to overfitting. On top of that, a decision tree is very likely to be biased toward the training class with the largest number of samples.

You can overcome the disadvantages of single trees, such as overfitting, instability, and non-optimal trees, by combining multiple decision trees through bagging and boosting to an ensemble model. There are also many tree-based optimizations like tree pruning to improve generalization. Popular models using these techniques are random forests and gradient boosted trees, which overcome most of the problems of an individual decision tree while keeping most of their benefits. We will look at these two methods in the next section.

> **Note**
>
> There are some more fundamental disadvantages that sometimes come up even with tree-based ensemble methods that are worth mentioning. Due to the nature of decision trees, tree-based models have difficulties learning complicated functions, such as the XOR problem. For these problems, it's better to use neural networks and deep learning approaches.

Combining classifiers with bagging

One key disadvantage of a single decision tree is overfitting to training data and hence poor generalization performance and instability due to small changes in the training data. A bagging (also called **bootstrap aggregation**) classifier uses the simple concept of combining multiple independent models into a single ensemble model trained on a subset of the training data (random picks with replacement) to overcome this exact problem. The output is either selected through a majority vote for classification or mean aggregation for regression problems.

By combining independent models, we can reduce the variance of the combined model without increasing the bias and hence greatly improve generalization. However, there is another great benefit of using individual models, parallelization. Due to the fact that each individual model uses a random subset of the training data, the training process can easily be parallelized and split into multiple compute nodes. Therefore, bagging is a popular technique when training a large number of tree-based classifiers on a large dataset.

Figure 7.2 shows how each classifier is trained independently on the same training data—each model uses a random subset with replacements. The combination of all individual models makes up the *Ensemble Model*:

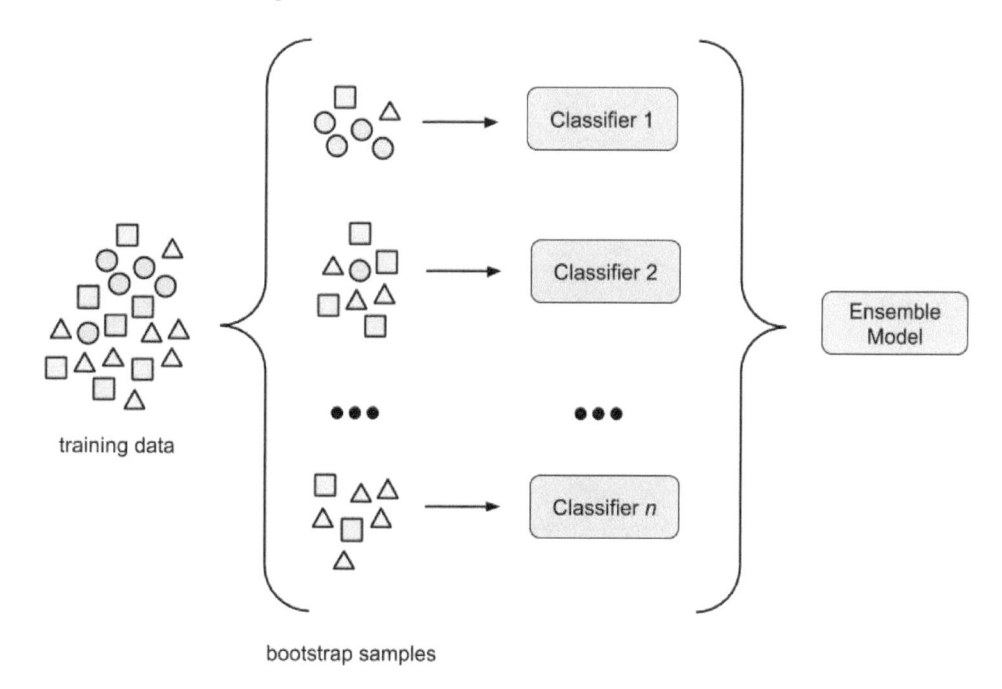

Figure 7.2: Ensemble model

Bagging can be used to combine any ML model; however, it is often used with tree-based classifiers as they suffer most from overfitting. The idea of random forest builds on top of the bagging method combined with a random subset of features for each split (decision). When a feature is selected at random, the optimal threshold for the split is computed such that a certain information criterion is optimized (usually GINI or information gain). Hence the random forest uses a random subset of the training data, random feature selection, and an optimal threshold for the split.

Random forests are widely used for their simple decision tree-based model combined with much better generalization and easy parallelization. Another benefit of taking a random subset of features is that this technique also works really well with very high-dimensional inputs. Hence, when dealing with classical ML approaches, random forests are often used for large-scale tree ensembles.

Another popular tree-based bagging technique is the extra-trees (extremely randomized trees) algorithm, which adds another randomization step on the split dimension. For each split, thresholds are drawn at random and the best one is selected for that decision. Hence, in addition to random features, extra-trees also uses random split thresholds to further improve generalization.

Figure 7.3 shows how all tree ensemble techniques are used for inferencing. Each tree computes an individual score while the result of each tree is aggregated to yield the final result:

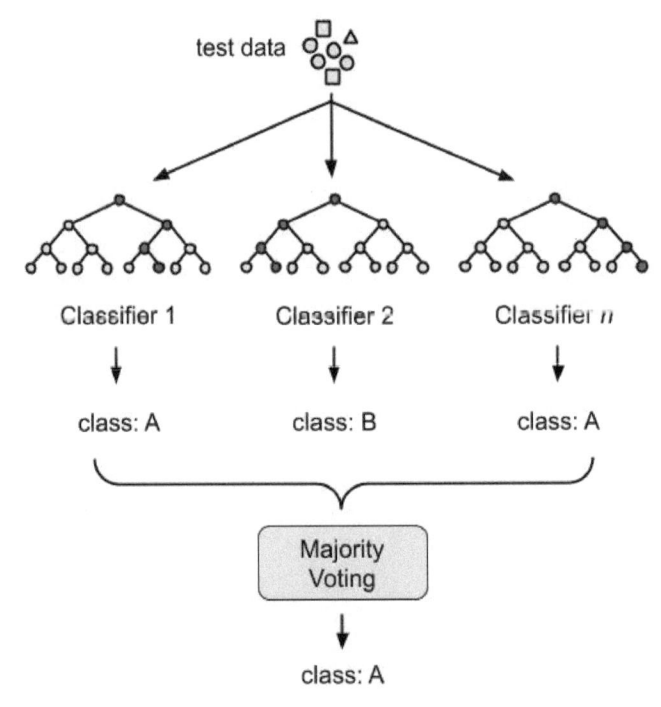

Figure 7.3: Inferencing using a tree ensemble

You can find tree-based bagging ensembles such as random forest, and sometimes also extra-trees, in many popular ML libraries, such as scikit-learn, Spark MLlib, ML.NET, and many others.

Optimizing classifiers with boosting rounds

Often in computer science problems, we can replace a random greedy approach with a more complex but more optimal approach. The same holds true for tree ensembles and builds the foundation for boosted tree ensembles.

The basic idea behind boosting is quite simple:

1. We start to train an individual model on the whole training data.
2. Then we compute the predictions of the model on the training data and start weighting training samples that yield a wrong result higher.
3. Next, we train another decision tree using the weighted training set. We then combine both decision trees into an ensemble and again predict the output classes for the weighted training set. As you might have guessed, we further increase the weights on the wrongly classified training samples for the next boosting round.
4. We continue this algorithm until a stopping criterion is reached.

Figure 7.4 shows how the training error using boosting optimization decreases each iteration (boosting round) with the addition of a new tree:

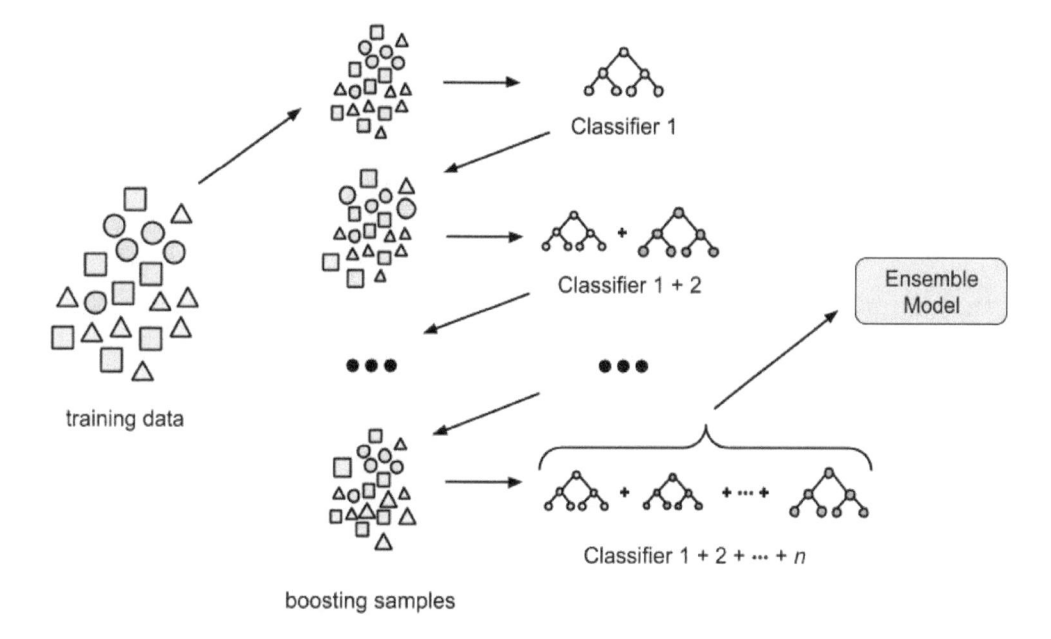

Figure 7.4: Optimizing classifiers with boosting rounds

The first boosting algorithm was AdaBoost, which combined multiple weak models into an ensemble by fitting it on a weighted training set that adapts each iteration through a learning rate. The notion of this approach was to add individual trees that focus on predicting something the previous trees couldn't predict.

One particular successful technique of boosting is gradient boosted trees (or gradient boosting). In gradient boosting, you combine the gradient descent optimization technique with boosting in order to generalize boosting to arbitrary loss functions. Now, instead of tuning the dataset samples using weights, we can compute the gradient of the loss function and select the optimal weights—the ones that minimize the loss function—during each iteration. Thanks to the usage of optimization, this technique yields very good results, adding to the existing advantages of decision trees.

Gradient boosted tree-based ensembles are included in many popular ML libraries such as scikit-learn, Spark ML, and others. However, some individual implementations, such as XGBoost and LightGBM, have gained quite a lot of popularity and are available as standalone libraries and as plugins for scikit-learn and Spark.

Training an ensemble classifier model using LightGBM

Both random forest and gradient boosted trees are pretty powerful ML techniques due to their simple basis of decision trees and ensembles of multiple classifiers. In this example, we will use a popular library from Microsoft to implement both techniques on a test dataset: *LightGBM*, a framework for gradient boosting that incorporates multiple tree-based learning algorithms.

For this section, we will follow a typical best-practice approach using Azure Machine Learning and perform the following steps:

1. Register the dataset in Azure.
2. Create a remote compute cluster.
3. Implement a configurable training script.
4. Run the training script on the compute cluster.
5. Log and collect the dataset, parameters, and performance.
6. Register the trained model.

Before we start with this exciting approach, we'll take a quick look at why we chose LightGBM as a tool for training bagged and boosted tree ensembles.

LightGBM in a nutshell

LightGBM uses many optimizations of classical tree-based ensemble techniques to provide excellent performance on both categorical and continuous features. The latter is profiled using a histogram-based approach and converted into discrete bins of optimal splits, which reduces memory consumption and speeds up training. This makes LightGBM faster and more memory efficient than other boosting libraries that use pre-sort-based algorithms for computing splits, and hence is a great choice for large datasets.

Another optimization in LightGBM is that trees are grown vertically, leaf after leaf, whereas other similar libraries grow trees horizontally, layer after layer. In a leaf-wise algorithm, the newly added leaf always has the largest decrease in loss. This means that these algorithms tend to achieve less loss compared to level-wise algorithms. However, greater depth also results in overfitting, and therefore you must limit the maximum depth of each tree. Overall, LightGBM produces great results using default parameters on a large set of applications.

In *Chapter 6*, *Advanced feature extraction with NLP*, we learned a lot about categorical feature embedding and extracting semantic meanings from textual features. We looked at common techniques for embedding nominal categorical variables, such as label encoding and one-hot encoding, and others. However, to optimize the split criterion in tree-based learners for categorical variables, there are better encodings to produce optimal splits. Therefore, we don't encode categorical variables at all but simply tell LightGBM which of the used variables are categorical.

One last thing to mention is that LightGBM can take advantage of GPU acceleration, and training can be parallelized both in a data-parallel or model-parallel way. We will learn more about distributed training in *Chapter 10*, *Distributed machine learning on Azure*. However, keep in mind that LightGBM is a great choice for a tree-based ensemble model especially for very large datasets.

We will use LightGBM with the **lgbm** namespace throughout this book. We can then call different methods from the namespace directly by typing four characters less—a best-practice approach among data scientists in Python:

```
import lightgbm as lgbm


# Construct a LGBM dataset
lgbm.Dataset(..)


# Train a LGBM predictor
clf = lgbm.train(..)
```

What is interesting to note is that all algorithms are trained via the `lgbm.train()` method and we use different parameters to specify algorithm, application type, and loss function, as well as additional hyperparameters for each algorithm. LightGBM supports multiple decision-tree based ensemble models for bagging and boosting. These are the options of algorithms that you can choose from as well as their names to identify them for the **boosting** parameter:

- **gbdt**: Traditional gradient boosting decision tree
- **rf**: Random forest
- **dart**: Dropouts meet multiple additive regression trees
- **goss**: Gradient-based one-side sampling

The first two options, namely gradient boosting decision tree (**gbdt**)—which is the default choice of LightGBM—and random forest (**rf**) are classical implementations of the boosting and bagging techniques, explained in the first section of this chapter, with LightGBM specific optimizations. The other two techniques, dropouts meet multiple additive regression trees (**dart**) and gradient-based one-side sampling (**goss**), are specific to LightGBM and provide more optimizations for better results in a trade-off for training speed.

The **objective** parameter—which is one of the most important parameters—specifies the application type of the model, and hence the ML problem you're trying to solve. In LightGBM, you have the following standard options, which are similar to most other decision-tree based ensemble algorithms:

- **regression**: For predicting continuous target variables
- **binary**: For binary classification tasks
- **multiclass**: For multiclass classification problems

Besides the standard choices, you can also choose between the following more specific objectives: **regression_l1, huber, fair, poisson, quantile, mape, gamma, tweedie, multiclassova, cross_entropy, cross_entropy_lambda, lambdarank,** and **rank_xendcg**.

Directly related to the **objective** parameter of the model is the choice of loss function to measure and optimize the training performance. Also here, LightGBM gives us the default options that are also available in most other boosting libraries, which we can specify via the **metric** parameter:

- **mae**: Mean absolute error
- **mse**: Mean squared error
- **binary_logloss**: Loss for binary classification
- **multi_logloss**: Loss for multi-classification

Apart from these loss metrics, other metrics are supported as well, such as **rmse**, **quantile**, **mape**, **huber**, **fair**, **poisson**, and many others. In our classification scenario, we will choose **dart** (dropouts meet multiple additive regression trees), with the **binary** objective and **binary_logloss** metric.

> **Note**
>
> You can also use older versions of the LightGBM algorithm as an **sklearn** estimator. To do so, call the **LGBMModel**, **LGBMClassifier**, or **LGBMRegressor** model from the **lightgbm** namespace. However, the latest features are only available through the **LightGBM** interface: **clf = lgbm.LGBMModel()**.

Now, knowing how to use LightGBM, we can start with the implementation of the data preparation and authoring script.

Preparing the data

In this section, we will read and prepare the data and register the cleaned data as a new dataset in Azure Machine Learning. This will allow us to access the data from any compute target connected with the workspace without the need to manually copy data around, mount disks, or set up connections to datastores. All of the setup, scheduling, and operations will be done from an authoring environment—a Jupyter notebook on a compute instance of Azure Machine Learning.

For the classification example, we will use the Titanic dataset, a popular dataset for machine learning practitioners to predict the binary survival probability for each passenger on the Titanic. The features of this dataset describe the passengers and contain the following attributes: passenger ID, class, name, sex, age, number of siblings or spouse on the ship, number of children or parents on the ship, ticket identification number, fare, cabin number, and embarked port.

> **Note**
>
> The details about this dataset, as well as the complete preprocessing pipeline, can be found in the source code that comes with this book.

Without knowing any more details, we'll roll up our sleeves and set up the workspace and experiment in an Azure Machine Learning compute instance:

1. We import **Workspace** and **Experiment** from **azureml.core** and specify the name **titanic-lgbm** for this experiment:

   ```
   from azureml.core import Workspace, Experiment

   # Configure workspace and experiment
   ws = Workspace.from_config()
   exp = Experiment(workspace=ws, name="titanic-lgbm")
   ```

2. Next, we load the dataset using pandas, and start cleaning and preprocessing the data:

   ```
   import pandas as pd

   # Read the data
   df = pd.read_csv('data/titanic.csv')

   # Transform attributes
   df.loc[df['Sex'] == 'female', 'Sex'] = 0
   df.loc[df['Sex'] == 'male', 'Sex'] = 1

   # Perform all data pre-paraption, feature extraction and cleaning
   # ...

   # Register the data
   df_to_dataset(ws, df, 'titanic_cleaned',
      'data/titanic_cleaned.csv')
   ```

In the preceding example, we replaced the values of the **Sex** feature with labels 0 and 1. Ultimately, we take the pandas **DataFrame** and register the dataset as a newly cleaned dataset with the name **titanic_cleaned**. We write a small utility function, **df_to_dataset()**, which will help us to store pandas DataFrames and register them as Azure datasets, in order to reuse them with ease anywhere in the Azure Machine Learning environment.

3. Then, we register a new version for the dataset:

```
import os
from azureml.core import Dataset

def df_to_dataset(ws, df, name, data_dir='./data'):
    data_path = os.path.join(data_dir, "%s.csv" % name)

    # save data to disk
    df.to_csv(data_path)

    # get the default datastore
    datastore = ws.get_default_datastore()

    # upload the data to the datastore
    datastore.upload(src_dir=data_dir,
      target_path=data_dir)

    # create a dataset
    dataset = Dataset.Tabular.from_delimited_files(
      datastore.path(data_path))

    # register the dataset
    dataset.register(workspace=ws, name=name,
      create_new_version=True)
    return dataset
```

The first step in the preceding function is to save the cleaned and preprocessed pandas DataFrame to disk. Next, we retrieve a reference to the default datastore of our ML workspace—this is the Azure Blob Storage that was created when we first set up the workspace. Next, we upload the dataset to this default datastore, just to reference it from there using a tabular dataset. This dataset holds the reference to the Azure datastore, and hence we can call the **register(create_new_version=True)** method.

4. Once the preceding steps are done, the dataset is registered in Azure and can be accessed anywhere in the Azure Machine Learning workspace. If we now go to the UI and click on the **Datasets** menu, we will find the `titanic_cleaned` dataset. In the UI, we can also easily inspect and preview the data as shown in *Figure 7.5*:

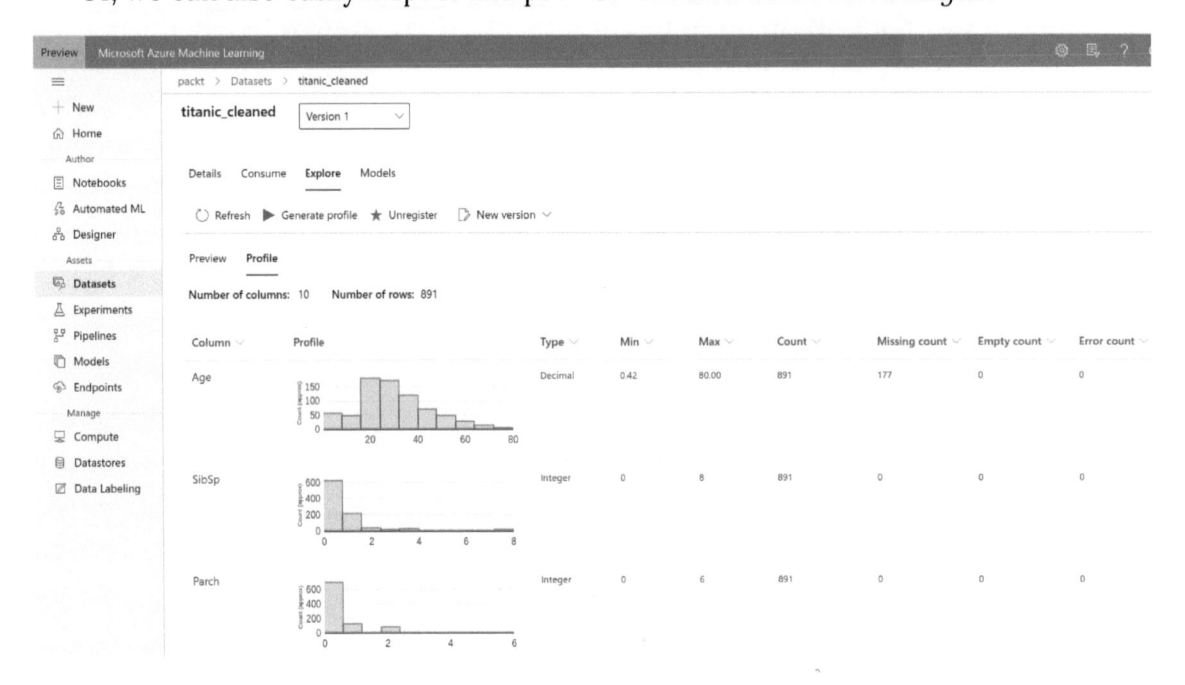

Figure 7.5: The Datasets preview in the Azure Machine Learning workspace

> **Note**
>
> One thing worth mentioning is that we will first encode categorical variables to integers using label encoding, but later tell LightGBM which variables contain categorical information in the numeric columns. This will help LightGBM to treat these columns differently when computing the histogram and optimal parameter splits.

The great benefit of having the dataset registered is that we can now simply run the following snippet to retrieve the dataset as a pandas DataFrame in any execution environment in Azure Machine Learning:

```
from azureml.core import Dataset

# Get a dataset by name
df = Dataset.get_by_name(workspace=ws,
    name='titanic_cleaned').to_pandas_dataframe()
```

The preceding code can now be placed in any training script that is scheduled in Azure Machine Learning or anywhere with access to the Azure Machine Learning workspace and it will return the cleaned dataset. Moreover, the data is versioned, and hence starting from now, data engineers and data scientists can work in parallel on the same version of the dataset. Let's create a cluster that we can finally train a LightGBM classifier on.

Setting up the compute cluster and execution environment

Before we can start training the LightBGM classifier, we need to set up our training environment, and also our training cluster and training image with all the required Python libraries. For this ML model, we choose a CPU cluster with up to four nodes of type **STANDARD_D2_V2**. To do so, we call two helper functions, which we will define in a second:

1. First, we create the Azure Machine Learning compute cluster and then configure a Python image with all the required pip packages, including `lightgbm`:

    ```
    # Create a compute cluster
    aml_cluster = get_aml_cluster(ws,
        cluster_name="amldemocompute", vm_size="STANDARD_D2_V2")

    # Create a remote run configuration
    run_amlcompute = run_config(aml_cluster, [
        'numpy', 'pandas', 'matplotlib', 'seaborn', 'scikit-learn', 'lightgbm'
    ])
    ```

    The two functions used in the preceding snippets are very useful. The longer you work with Azure Machine Learning, the more abstractions you will build to easily interact with Azure Machine Learning.

2. We then retrieve an existing cluster, or create a new cluster, and return the cluster once it is started:

```python
from azureml.core.compute import ComputeTarget, AmlCompute
from azureml.core.compute_target import ComputeTargetException

def get_aml_cluster(ws, cluster_name,
  vm_size='STANDARD_D2_V2', max_nodes=4)
  try:
    cluster = ComputeTarget(workspace=ws, name=cluster_name)
  except ComputeTargetException:
    compute_config = AmlCompute.provisioning_configuration(
    vm_size=vm_size, max_nodes=max_nodes)
    cluster = ComputeTarget.create(ws, cluster_name,
    compute_config)
  cluster.wait_for_completion(show_output=True)
  return cluster
```

We have already seen the preceding script in the previous chapters, where we called **AmlCompute.provisioning_configuration()** to provision a new cluster. It is extremely helpful that you can define all your infrastructure within your authoring environment. The same is true for your Python interpreter and packages.

3. Next, we configure the **run_config()** function to return a remote execution target with a Python configuration:

```python
from azureml.core.runconfig import RunConfiguration
from azureml.core.conda_dependencies import CondaDependencies
from azureml.core.runconfig import DEFAULT_CPU_IMAGE

def run_config(target, packages=None):
  packages = packages or []
  config = RunConfiguration()
  config.target = target
  config.environment.docker.enabled = True
  config.environment.docker.base_image = DEFAULT_CPU_IMAGE
```

```
azureml_pip_packages = [
 'azureml-defaults', 'azureml-contrib-interpret',
 'azureml-core', 'azureml-telemetry',
 'azureml-interpret', 'sklearn-pandas', 'azureml-dataprep'
]
config.auto_prepare_environment = True config.environment.python.user_
managed_dependencies = False
config.environment.python.conda_dependencies =
   CondaDependencies.create(
   pip_packages=azureml_pip_packages + packages)

return config
```

In the preceding script, we set a couple of options on the **RunConfiguration** objects, such as to enable Docker and to specify the Azure Machine Learning default CPU image. Then, we defined the required packages for Azure Machine Learning, such as the **core**, **defaults**, and **dataprep** packages. Finally, we added all custom-defined packages and passed them to the **pip_packages** argument.

Using the preceding configuration, Azure Machine Learning will set up the proper Docker images and register them in the Container Registry automatically for us—as soon as we schedule a job using this configuration. Let's first construct the training script and then schedule it to the cluster. It's quite cool to see that you can spin up an auto-scaling compute cluster and your custom Docker execution environments with all but two function calls and a couple of lines of code.

Let's take a look at the training script that we can then schedule on the newly created cluster.

Building a LightGBM classifier

Now that we have the dataset ready, and we've set up the environment and cluster for the training of the LightGBM classification model, we can set up the training script. The code from the preceding section was written in a Jupyter notebook. The following code in this section will now be written and stored in a Python file called `train_lgbm.py`. We will start building the classifier using the following steps:

1. Let's start again with the basics of Azure Machine Learning. We configure **run** and extract the **workspace** configuration from **run**. Then, we can reference the cleaned dataset and load it to memory using the `to_pandas_dataframe()` method:

   ```
   from azureml.core import Dataset, Run

   # Load the current run and ws
   run = Run.get_context()
   ws = run.experiment.workspace

   # Get a dataset by name
   dataset = Dataset.get_by_name(workspace=ws, name='titanic_cleaned')

   # Load a TabularDataset into pandas DataFrame
   df = dataset.to_pandas_dataframe()
   ```

2. Having loaded the dataset as a pandas DataFrame, we can now start splitting the training data into training and validation sets. We will also split the target variable, **Survived**, from the training dataset into its own variable:

   ```
   import lightgbm as lgbm
   from sklearn.model_selection import train_test_split

   # Target labels
   y = df.pop('Survived')

   # Train / validation split
   X_train, X_test, y_train, y_test = train_test_split(df, y, test_size=0.2, random_state=42)
   ```

3. Next, we tell LightGBM about categorical features—that are actually already transformed into numeric variables—but need special treatment to compute the optimal split values:

```python
# Convert to LGBM dataset for training
categorical_features = ['Alone', 'Sex', 'Pclass', 'Embarked']
train_data = lgbm.Dataset(data=X_train, label=y_train,
    categorical_feature=categorical_features, free_raw_data=False)
test_data = lgbm.Dataset(data=X_test,
    label=y_test, categorical_feature=categorical_features,
    free_raw_data=False)
```

In contrast to scikit-learn, we cannot work directly with pandas DataFrames in LightGBM but need to use a wrapper class, `lgbm.Dataset`. This will give us access to all required optimizations and features, such as distributed training, optimization for sparse data, and meta-information about categorical features.

4. Next, we set up an argument parser to parse command-line parameters into LightGBM parameters:

```python
parser = argparse.ArgumentParser()
parser.add_argument('--boosting', type=str, dest='boosting',
    default='dart')
parser.add_argument('--num-boost-round', type=int,
    dest='num_boost_round', default=500)
parser.add_argument('--early-stopping', type=int,
    dest='early_stopping_rounds', default=200)
parser.add_argument('--drop-rate', type=float,
    dest='drop_rate', default=0.15)
parser.add_argument('--learning-rate', type=float,
    dest='learning_rate', default=0.001)
parser.add_argument('--min-data-in-leaf', type=int,
    dest='min_data_in_leaf', default=20)
parser.add_argument('--feature-fraction', type=float,
    dest='feature_fraction', default=0.7)
parser.add_argument('--num-leaves', type=int,
    dest='num_leaves', default=40)
args = parser.parse_args()
```

> **Note**
>
> This is not really required in the beginning, but we strongly advise to make your training scripts configurable. If you use the preceding method to pass arguments to your training scripts, you will be able to automatically tune the hyperparameters without changing a line of code in your training script.

5. Having parsed the command-line arguments, we now pass them into a parameter dictionary, which will then be passed to the LightGBM training method:

   ```
   lgbm_params = {
     'application': 'binary',
     'metric': 'binary_logloss',
     'learning_rate': args.learning_rate,
     'boosting': args.boosting,
     'drop_rate': args.drop_rate,
     'min_data_in_leaf': args.min_data_in_leaf,
     'feature_fraction': args.feature_fraction,
     'num_leaves': args.num_leaves,
   }
   ```

6. In order to keep track of all our experiments, and which parameters were used for training, we are tracking the parameters by logging them with the run method. This will attach all the parameters to each run we execute and will be extremely helpful in the future:

   ```
   # Log the parameters
   for k, v in lgbm_params.items():
       run.log(k, v)
   ```

   Gradient boosting is an iterative optimization approach with a variable number of iterations and an optional early stopping criterion. Therefore, we also want to log all metrics for each iteration of the training script. Throughout this book, we will use a similar technique for all ML frameworks—namely, using a callback function that logs all available metrics to your Azure Machine Learning workspace. Let's write such a function using LightGBM's specification for custom callbacks.

7. Here, we create a **callback** object, which iterates over all the evaluation results and logs them for run:

   ```
   def azure_ml_callback(run):
       def callback(env):
           if env.evaluation_result_list:
               for data_name, eval_name, result, _ in
                 env.evaluation_result_list:
                   run.log("%s (%s)" % (eval_name, data_name), result)
       callback.order = 10
       return callback
   ```

8. After we have set the parameters for the LightGBM predictor, we can configure the training and validation procedure using the `lgbm.train()` method. We need to supply all arguments, parameters, and callbacks:

   ```
   clf = lgbm.train(train_set=train_data,
       params=lgbm_params,
       valid_sets=[train_data, test_data],
       valid_names=['train', 'val'],
       num_boost_round=args.num_boost_round,
       early_stopping_rounds=args.early_stopping_rounds,
       callbacks = [azure_ml_callback(run)])
   ```

   What's great about the preceding code is that by supplying the generic **callback** function, all training and validation scores will be logged to Azure automatically. Hence we can follow the training iterations in real time either in the UI or via the API—for example, inside a Jupyter widget that automatically collects all run information.

9. In order to evaluate the final score of the training, we use the trained classifier to predict a couple of default classification scores, such as **accuracy**, **precision**, and **recall**, as well as the combined **f1** score:

   ```
   from sklearn.metrics import accuracy_score, recall_score,
   precision_score, f1_score

   y_pred = clf.predict(X_test)
   run.log("accuracy (test)", accuracy_score(y_test, y_pred))
   run.log("precision (test)", precision_score(y_test, y_pred))
   run.log("recall (test)", recall_score(y_test, y_pred))
   run.log("f1 (test)", f1_score(y_test, y_pred))
   ```

   We could already run the script and see all metrics and the performance of the model in Azure. But this was just the start – we want more!

10. Let's compute **feature importance** and track a plot of it and run it in Azure Machine Learning. That's easy – we can do this in a few lines of code:

    ```
    import matplotlib.pyplot as plt
    fig = plt.figure()
    ax = plt.subplot(111)
    lgbm.plot_importance(clf, ax=ax)
    run.log_image("feature importance", plot=fig)
    ```

    Once this snippet is added to the training script, each training run will also store a feature importance plot. This is really helpful to see how different metrics influence feature importance.

11. There is one more step we would like to add. Whenever the training script runs, we want to upload the trained model and register it in the model registry. By doing so, we can later take any training run and manually or automatically deploy the model to a container service. However, this can only be done by saving the training artifacts of each run:

    ```
    from sklearn.externals import joblib
    joblib.dump(clf, 'outputs/lgbm.pkl')
    run.upload_file('lgbm.pkl', 'outputs/lgbm.pkl')
    run.register_model(
        model_name='lgbm_titanic', model_path='lgbm.pkl')
    ```

    In the preceding snippet, we use the **joblib** object from the **sklearn.externals** package to save the classifier to disk. While LightGBM provides its own functionality for exporting and importing models, we prefer using the **sklearn** library for reproducible results across multiple Python versions.

That's it – we have written the whole training script. It's not extremely long, it's not super-complicated. The trickiest part is understanding how to pick some of the parameters of LightGBM and understanding gradient boosting in general–and that's why we dedicated the first half of the chapter to that topic. Let's fire up the cluster and submit the training script.

Scheduling the training script on the Azure Machine Learning cluster

We are logically jumping back to the authoring environment, the Jupyter Notebook. The code from the previous section is stored as a **train_lgbm.py** file, and we'll now get ready to submit it to the cluster. One great thing is that we made the training script configurable via command-line arguments, so we can tune the base parameters of the LightGBM model using CLI arguments. In the following steps, we will configure the authoring script to execute the training process:

1. Let's define the parameters for this model–we will use dart, with a standard learning rate of 0.01 and a dropout rate of 0.15:

    ```
    script_params = [
      '--boosting', 'dart',
      '--learning-rate', '0.01',
      '--drop-rate', '0.15',
    ]
    ```

    We specified the boosting method, **dart**. As we learned in the previous section, this technique performs very well but is not extremely performant and is a bit slower than the other options–**gbdt**, **rf**, and **goss**.

> **Note**
>
> This is also the same way that hyperparameters are passed by HyperOpt—the hyperparameter tuning tool in Azure Machine Learning—to the training script. We will learn a lot more about this in *Chapter 9, Hyperparameter tuning and Automated Machine Learning*.

2. Next, we can finally pass the parameters to **ScriptRunConfig** and kick off the training script. Let's bring all the pieces together:

   ```
   from azureml.core import ScriptRunConfig

   script = 'train_lightgbm.py'
   script_folder = os.getcwd()

   src = ScriptRunConfig(
     source_directory=script_folder,
     script=script,
     run_config=run_amlcompute,
     arguments=script_params)
   ```

   In the preceding code, we specify the file of our classifier, which is stored relative to the current authoring script. Azure Machine Learning will upload the training script to the default datastore, and make it available on all cluster nodes that run the script.

3. Finally, let's submit the run configuration and execute the training script:

   ```
   from azureml.widgets import RunDetails

   run = exp.submit(src)
   RunDetails(run).show()
   ```

   The **RunDetails** method gives us a nice interactive widget with real-time logs of the remote computing service. We can see the cluster getting initialized and scaled up, the Docker images getting built and registered, and ultimately, also the training script logs.

> **Note**
>
> If you prefer other methods than an interactive Jupyter widget, you can also trail the logs using **run.wait_for_completion(show_output=True)** or **print(run.get_portal_url())** to get the URL to the experiment run in Azure.

4. Let's switch over to the Azure Machine Learning UI and look for the run in the experiment. Once we click on it, we can navigate to the **Metrics** section and find a nice overview of all our logged metrics. It's great to see in *Figure 7.6*, how metrics that are logged multiple times with the same name get converted into vectors and displayed as line charts:

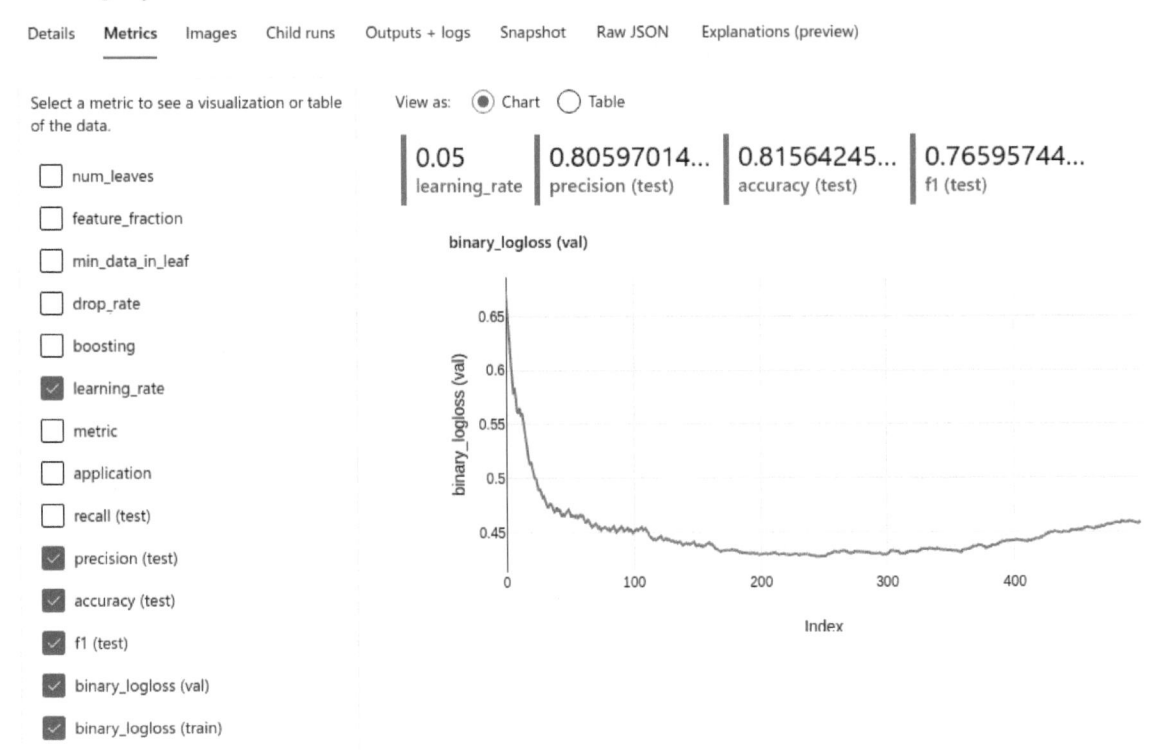

Figure 7.6: The Metrics tab in the Azure Machine Learning workspace, showing the logged metrics of the running experiment

Then, click on the **Images** section. As we expect, when we do so, we are presented with the feature importance that we created in the training script. *Figure 7.7* shows how this looks in the Azure Machine Learning UI:

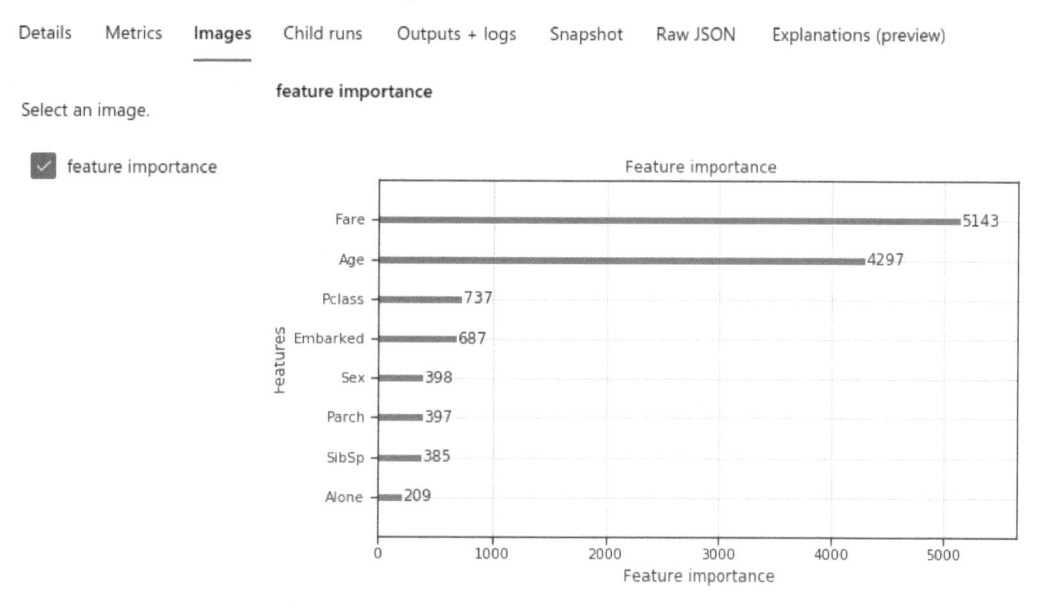

Figure 7.7: The Images tab in the Azure Machine Learning workspace, showing the feature importance of the running experiment

We saw how one can train a LightGBM classifier in Azure Machine Learning, taking advantage of an auto- scaling Azure Machine Learning compute cluster. Logging metrics, figures, and parameters keeps all information about the training run in a single place. Together with saving snapshots of the training script, outputs, logs, and the trained model, this is invaluable for any professional, large-scale ML project.

What you should remember from this chapter is that gradient boosted trees are a very performant and scalable classical ML approach, with many great libraries, and support for distributed learning and GPU acceleration. LightGBM is one alternative offered by Microsoft that is well embedded in both the Microsoft and open source ecosystem. If you have to choose a classical, fast, and understandable approach, our advice is to go with LightGBM.

Summary

In this chapter, you learned how to build a classical ML model in Azure Machine Learning.

You learned about decision trees, a popular technique for various classification and regression problems. The main strengths of decision trees are that they require little data preparation as they work well on categorical data and different data distributions. Another important benefit is their interpretability, which is especially important for business decisions and users. This helps you to understand when a decision-tree-based ensemble predictor is appropriate to use.

However, we also learned about a set of weaknesses, especially regarding overfitting and poor generalization. Luckily, tree-based ensemble techniques such as bagging (bootstrap aggregation) and boosting help to overcome these problems. While bagging has popular methods such as random forests that parallelize very well, boosting—especially gradient boosting—has efficient implementations such as XGBoost and LightGBM.

You implemented and trained a decision tree-based classifier in Azure Machine Learning using the LightGBM library. LightGBM is developed at Microsoft and delivers great performance and training time through a couple of optimizations. These optimizations help LightGBM to keep a small memory footprint, even for larger datasets, and yield better losses with fewer iterations. You used Azure Machine Learning not only to execute your training script but also to track your model's training performance, and the final classifier.

In the following chapter, we will take a look at some popular deep learning techniques and how to train them using Azure Machine Learning.

8
Training deep neural networks on Azure

In the previous chapter, we learned how to train and score classical **machine learning** (**ML**) models using non-parametric tree-based ensemble methods. While these methods work well on many small and medium-sized datasets with categorical variables, they don't generalize well on large datasets.

In this chapter, we will train complex parametric models using **deep learning** (**DL**) for even better generalization with large datasets. This will help you understand which situations **Deep Neural Networks** (**DNNs**) perform better in than traditional models.

First, we will give a short and practical overview of why and when DL works well. We will focus more on understanding the general principles and rationale rather than a theoretical approach. This will help you to assess which use cases and datasets have a need for DL and how it works in general.

We will then take a look at the most popular application domain for DL–computer vision. Then, we will train a simple **Convolutional Neural Network (CNN)** architecture for image classification using Azure Machine Learning and additional Azure infrastructure. We will compare the performance to a model that was fine-tuned on a pre-trained **Residual Network (ResNet)** model. This will show you how to overcome situations where not enough training data is provided.

The following topics will be covered in this chapter:

- Introduction to deep learning
- Training a CNN for image classification

Introduction to deep learning

DL has revolutionized the ML domain recently and is constantly outperforming classical statistical approaches, and even humans, in various tasks, such as image classification, object detection, segmentation, speech transcription, text translation, text understanding, sales forecasting, and much more. In contrast to classical models, DL models use many millions of parameters, clever weight sharing, optimization techniques, and implicit feature extraction to outperform all previously hand-crafted feature detectors and ML models when trained with enough data.

In this section, we will help you understand why and when DL models make sense for certain domains and datasets. If you are already an expert in DL, feel free to skip this section and go directly to the more practical sections. However, if you are new to DL, I strongly encourage you to stay for this section in order to understand the practical and business need for larger, more capable models, as well as a bit of non-theoretical background.

Why DL?

Many traditional optimization, classification, and forecasting processes have worked well over the past years on classical ML approaches, such as k-nearest neighbor, linear/logistic regression, naive Bayes, and tree-based ensemble models. They worked well on various types of data (transactional, time-series, operational, and so on) and data types (binary, numerical, and categorical) for small to mid-sized datasets.

However, in some domains, data generation has exploded and classical ML models couldn't improve performance even with an increasing amount of training data. This especially affected the domains of computer vision and **natural language processing (NLP)** around late 2010. That's when researchers started to look again into neural networks (or **multilayer perceptrons (MLPs)**), a technique used in the late 80s, to capture the vast amount of features in a large image dataset by using multiple nested layers.

The following chart captures this idea pretty well. While traditional ML approaches work very well on small and medium-sized datasets, their performance does not improve with more training data. However, DL models are massive parametric models and can capture a vast amount of detail from training data. Hence, we can see that their prediction performance increases as the amount of data increases:

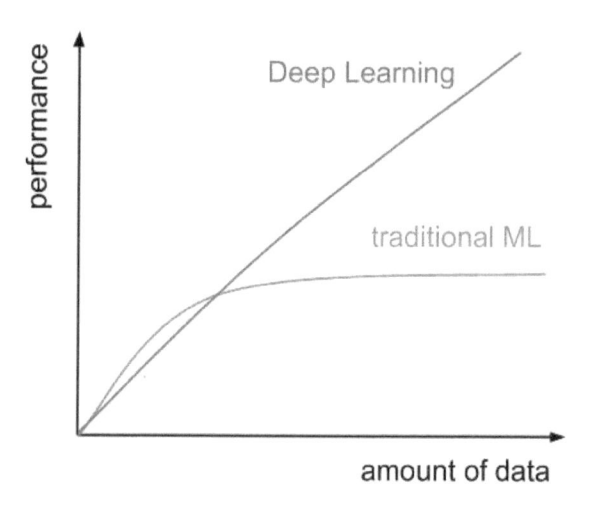

Figure 8.1: A chart illustrating prediction performance based on the amount of training data

Traditional models tend to use pre-engineered features and so are optimized for datasets of various data types and ranges. We saw in the last chapter that gradient-boosted trees perform extremely well on categorical data. However, in domains with highly structured data or data of variable lengths, many traditional models reached their limits. This was especially true for pixel information in two- and three-dimensional images and videos, as well as waveforms in audio data and characters in text data. ML models used to process such data would have complex feature extractors, such as **histogram of oriented gradients** (**HOG**) filters, **scale-invariant feature transform** (**SIFT**) features, or **Local Binary Patterns** (**LBPs**)—just to name a few.

What makes this data so complicated is that no obvious linear relation between the input data (for example, a single pixel) and the output exists—seeing a single pixel of an image won't help, in most cases, to determine the brand of a car in that image. Therefore, there was an increasing need to train larger and more capable parametric models that use raw, unprocessed data as input to capture these relations from an input pixel to a final prediction.

It's important to understand that the need for deeper models with many more parameters comes from the vastly increasing amount of highly structured training data in specific domains, such as vision, audio, and language. These new models often have tens of millions of parameters to capture the massive amounts of raw and augmented training data and to develop an internal generalized conceptual representation of the training data. Keep this in mind when choosing an ML approach for your use case.

In many cases, you can make a direct relation from the data store of your training data to the ML model. If your data is stored on a SQL database or in Excel files, then you should usually look into classical ML approaches, such as parametric statistical (linear regression, SVM, and so on) or non-parametric (decision-tree based ensembles) approaches. If your data is so big that it is stored in **Hadoop Distributed Filesystem (HDFS)**, a blob, or a file storage server, then you might need to use a DL approach.

From neural networks to DL

Various sources exist that explain neural networks and how they work in great detail; for example, Stanford's courses on DL, or Andrew Ng's courses on Coursera, and many more. This section will provide you with an intuitive understanding of their evolution from classical perceptrons in the 1950s to **artificial neural networks (ANNs)** and CNNs in the 1980s, and to DL in the last decade.

As you might have heard, the foundation of neural networks—the perceptron—is a concept that is over half a century old. The perceptron was introduced to model a cell from the human brain as a weighted sum of all inputs and activation functions that fires if the output is higher than a defined threshold. While this biological analogy of a brain cell is a great way to model the brain, it is a poor model to describe its internal state and the transformation of the input signal.

Rather than neurons in the brain, we prefer a much simpler approach to think about the perceptron, MLPs (that is, ANNs), and CNNs—namely, a very clean, geometric approach. This method requires you to only understand the equation of a line in two dimensions and the same equation in a higher-dimensional coordinate space. Hence, the equation of a plane will be in three dimensions and a hyperplane in n dimensions.

If we look at a single perceptron, it solely describes a weighted sum of its inputs plus a static bias with an activation function. Do you know what is also described as a weighted sum of its inputs? A line equation:

$$y = k * x + b$$

Figure 8.2: The line equation

OK, to be fair, this line equation only has a single input (x), hence a single dimension. However, if x is a vector, the very same equation describes a plane. I am sure you would have seen this equation at some point in your secondary math curriculum. A nice property of this equation is that when inserting a point's coordinate into this equation, it yields 0 = 0, or simply 0 when moved to one side.

What happens if we add a point into the line equation that is not on the line? Well, the result will be either positive or negative but certainly not 0. Another nice property of the line equation is that the absolute value of this result describes the shortest distance to the line (using the trigonometric formula) and the sign of the result describes the side of the line. Hence, the point can be either on the left or the right side of the line.

In the *Figure 8.3*, we see two points and their distance to the line. If we insert both points' coordinates into the two-dimensional equation of a line, then one point would result in a positive distance, whereas the other point would result in a negative distance from the line:

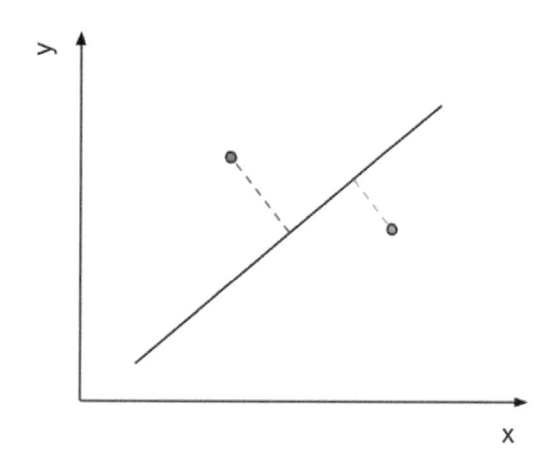

Figure 8.3: The shortest distance between a point and a line

Let's assume we would first insert a point's coordinates into a line equation and then apply the result with a step function between -1 and 1, or simply the sign function. The result would tell us which side of the line the point lies on. This is a fantastic geometric description of the perceptron or a very simple classifier. The trained perceptron is equal to the line equation (actually a hyperplane), which separates a space into left and right. So, this line is the decision boundary for a classification. A point is an observation. By inserting a point into the line equation and applying the step function, we return the resulting class of the observation, which is left or right. This exactly describes a binary classifier.

However, it gets even better. How do we train such a decision boundary? Well, we look at the training samples and the distance from the samples to a randomly initialized decision boundary. Then, we move the decision boundary in a way that the sample is classified correctly. We then look at the next sample and continue this process. The optimal vector to move the decision boundary is if we move it along the negative gradient, such that the distance between the point and the line reaches a minimum. By using a learning rate factor, we iterate this process a few times and end up with a perfectly aligned decision boundary, if the training samples are linearly separable.

Therefore, a single perceptron (also called a **neuron**) plus an activation function simply describes a small classifier consisting of a hyperplane that defines the decision boundary. Multiple perceptrons stacked in parallel layers are simply multiple hyperplanes combined–for example, they are used to find a sample that is on the right side of the first line but on the left side of a second line.

While a single stack of perceptrons only describes a linear combination of inputs and outputs, researchers began to stack these perceptrons into multiple consecutive layers, where each layer was followed by an activation function. This is called **MLP**, or simply a neural network. While it is quite difficult to understand this multi-layer approach from a biological standpoint, we can again use our geometric model. In a geometric model, we would simply stack multiple hyperplane equations into more complicated objects.

This exact geometric phenomenon is also described by many other resources as higher-level features of DL models. While the first layers of a network describe very low-level features, such as the left or right side of a line (an edge), the higher levels describe complicated nested combinations of these low-level features; for example, four lines build a square, five squares build a shape, and a combination of those shapes looks like a human nose. Hence, we just built a nose detector using a 3 layer neural network.

In *Figure 8.4*, we visualize how a DNN sees an image in the individual layers and tries to match it to features that each layer has learned. The image on the left is the original image and the three images on the right show a representation of this image in a specific layer in a DNN. We can see how the earlier layer focuses mostly on lines and edges (the second image from the left), whereas the middle layer sees shapes (the third image from the left), and the last layer activates on specific high-level features in the image (the fourth image from the left):

Figure 8.4: The minimized loss of an input image for individual layers

Using multiple high-dimensional hyperplane equations, where each output feeds into each input of the following layer, requires a very high number of parameters. While a high number of parameters is required to model a massive amount of complex training data, a so-called fully connected neural network is not the best way to describe these connections. So, what's the problem?

In a fully connected network, each output is fed to each neuron of the consecutive layer as input. In each neuron, we require a weight for each input, and therefore, as many weights as input dimensions. This number quickly explodes when we start stacking multiple layers of perceptrons. Another problem is that the network cannot generalize because it learns individual weights for individual dimensions.

To fight this problem, CNNs were introduced. Their purpose was to reduce the number of connections and hence parameters on a single layer to a fixed set of parameters, independent of the number of input dimensions. Therefore, the parameters of the layer are now shared within all the inputs. The idea of this approach came from signal processing, where filters are applied to a signal through a convolution operation. Convolution means applying a single set of weights, such as a window function, to multiple regions of the input and later summing up all signal responses of the filter for each location.

This was the same idea for convolution layers on CNNs. By using a fixed-sized filter that is convolved with the input, we can greatly reduce the number of parameters for each layer and so add more nested layers to the network. By using a so-called pooling layer, we can also reduce the image size and apply filters to a downscaled version of the input. As we stated earlier, this was all developed in the 80s.

There were three reasons why CNNs didn't reach a similar hype in the 80s as they did in the late 2010s:

- Only a small amount of labeled training data was available
- Convergence of the training process was difficult due to exploding and vanishing gradients
- Computational performance was low

However, when researchers looked into those models in 2012, a massive amount of labeled image training data was available through the ImageNet project; high-performance parallel processing was possible through GPUs, even for desktop machines, and some final tweaks, such as normalization and rectifiers, helped the training process to converge.

From then on, researchers started doing the following:

- Stacking more layers horizontally (see ResNet-152) and vertically (see GoogLeNet)
- Developing more efficient layer groups (SqueezeNet, Inception v3, and so on)
- Developing new layers (LSTM, and so on) as well as training (GAN)
- Optimizing techniques (RMSProp, Adam, and so on)

Today, DL is applied in almost any domain where there is sufficient data at hand.

Comparing classical ML and DL

Let's take a look at the main differences between classical ML and DL approaches and find out what DL models do with so many more parameters and how they benefit from them.

When we look at the image or audio processing domain before 2012, ML models were usually not trained on the raw data itself. Moreover, the raw data went through a manually crafted feature extractor to be converted into a lower-dimensional feature space. If we are dealing with images of 256 x 256 x 3 dimensions (RGB)—which corresponds to a 196,608- dimensional feature space—and convert these to, say, a 2,048-dimensional feature embedding as input for the ML models, we greatly reduce the computational requirements for these models. Interestingly, the extracted image and audio features often used a convolution operator and a specific filter (such as edge detector, blob detector, spike/dip detector, and so on). However, the filter was usually constructed manually.

The classical ML models developed in the past 50+ years are still the ones we are successfully using today. Among those are tree-based ensemble techniques, linear and logistic regression, **support vector machines** (**SVMs**), and MLPs. The MLP model is also known as a fully connected neural network with hidden layers and still serves as a classification/regression head in some of the early DL models.

Figure 8.5 shows the typical pipeline of a classical ML approach in the computer vision domain:

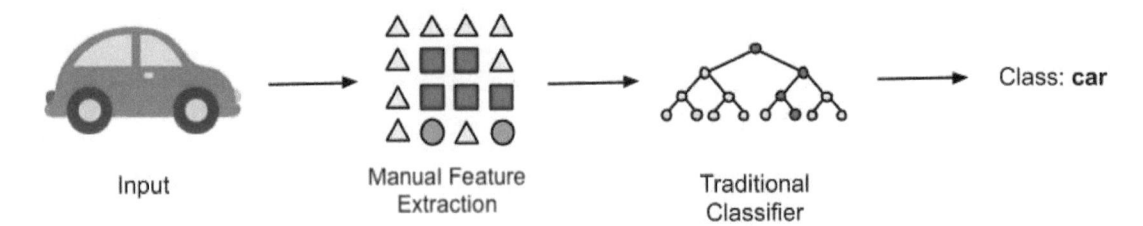

Figure 8.5: The pipeline of a classical ML approach

First, the raw data is converted into a lower-dimensional feature embedding using hand- crafted image filters (SIFT, SURF, Haar filters, and so on). Then, feature embedding is used to train an ML model; for example, a multi-layer, fully connected neural network.

When it is difficult for a human being to express a relationship between an input image and an output label in simple rules, then it is also difficult for a classical computer vision and ML approach to learn these rules. The reason for this is that DL models are trained on raw input data instead of manually extracted features. Due to the fact that convolution layers are the same as randomized and trained image filters, these filters for feature extraction are implicitly learned by the network.

Figure 8.6 shows a DL approach to image classification—similar to the previous diagram for the classical ML approach:

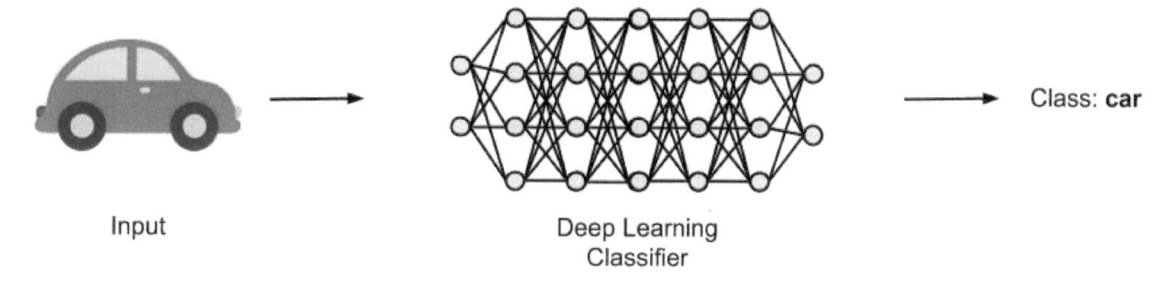

Figure 8.6: The DL approach to image classification

As we can see, the raw input data of the image is fed directly to the network, which outputs the final image label. This is why we often refer to a DL model as an end-to-end model because it creates an end-to-end connection between the input data (literally, the pixels) and the output data.

> **Note**
>
> A key takeaway is that you should look at the type of data as well before choosing your ML model. If you are dealing with images, videos, audio, time series, language, or text, you might use a DL model or feature extractor for embedding, clustering, classification, or regression. If you are working with operational or business data, then maybe a classic approach would be a better fit.

In many cases, especially when you have small datasets or not enough compute resources or knowledge to train end-to-end DL models, you can also reuse a pre-trained DL model as a feature extractor. This can be done by loading a pre-trained model and performing a forward pass until the classification/regression head. It returns a multi-dimensional embedding (a so-called latent space representation) that you can directly plug in to a classical ML model.

Here is an example of such a hybrid approach. We use the **IncpetionV3** model as a feature extractor, pre-trained on the **imagenet** data. The DL model is only used for transforming the raw input image data into a lower-dimensional feature representation. Then, an SVM model is trained on top of the image features. Let's look at the source code for this example:

```
import numpy as np
from keras.applications import InceptionV3


def extract_features(img_data, IMG_SIZE): IMG_SHAPE =
    (IMG_SIZE, IMG_SIZE, 3)
    model = InceptionV3(input_shape=IMG_SHAPE, include_top=False,
    weights='imagenet', pooling='avg')
    predictions = model.predict(img_data) return
    np.squeeze(predictions)
    labels = [] # loaded previously features =
    extract_features(image_data)
    X_train, X_test, y_train, y_test = train_test_split(features,
    labels) from sklearn.svm import SVC
    clf = SVC(kernel='linear', C=1)
    clf.fit(X_train, y_train)
```

In the preceding code, we use TensorFlow to load the **InceptionV3** model with the **imagenet** weights but without any classification or regression head. This is done by setting the **include_top** property to **False**. We then squeeze the output of the prediction into a single vector. Finally, we train an SVM on the image features using scikit-learn and a default train/test split.

We started with the classical approach, where feature extraction and ML were separated into two steps. However, the filters in the classical approach were hand-crafted and applied directly to the raw input data. In a DL approach, we implicitly learn the feature extraction.

Training a CNN for image classification

Once we have a good understanding of why and when to use DL models, we can start to actually implement one using Azure Machine Learning. We will start with a task that DL performed very well with over the past years, computer vision, or more precisely, image classification. If you feel that this is too easy for you, you can replace the actual training script with any other computer vision technique and follow along with the steps in this section:

- First, we will power up an Azure Machine Learning compute instance, which serves as our Jupyter Notebook authoring environment. We will first write a training script and execute it in the authoring environment to verify that it works properly, checkpoints the model, and logs the training and validation metrics. We will train the model for a few epochs to validate the setup, the code, and the resulting model.

- Once this is set up, we will try to improve the algorithm by adding data augmentation to the training script. While this seems like an easy task, I want to reiterate that this is necessary and strongly recommended for any DL-based ML approach. Image data can be easily augmented to improve generalization and therefore model scoring performance. However, through this technique, the training of the model will take even longer than before because more training data is used for each epoch.

- In the next step, we move the training script from the authoring environment to a GPU cluster—a remote compute environment. We will do all this—upload the data, generate the training scripts, create the cluster, execute the training script on the cluster, and retrieve the trained model—from within the authoring environment in Azure Machine Learning. If you are already training ML models yourself on your own server, then this section will show you how to move your training scripts to a remote execution environment and how to benefit from dynamically scalable compute (both vertically and horizontally, hence larger and more machines), auto scaling, cheap data storage, and much more.

- Once you have successfully trained a CNN from scratch, you want to move on to the next level in terms of model performance and complexity. A good and recommended approach is to fine-tune pre-trained DL models rather than train them from scratch. Using this approach, we can often also use a pre-trained model from a specific task, drop the classification head (usually the last one or two layers) from the model and reuse the feature extractor for another task by training our own classification head on top. This is called transfer learning and is widely used for training state-of-the-art models for various domains.

Let's dive into it!

Training a CNN from scratch in your notebook

Let's train a CNN on Jupyter on Azure Machine Learning. As a first step, we want to simply train a model in the current authoring environment, and so use the compute (CPU and memory) from the compute instance. This is a standard Python/Jupyter environment and so it is no different from training an ML model on your local machine. So, we go ahead and create a new compute instance in our Azure Machine Learning workspace, and then open the Jupyter environment:

1. Before we begin creating our CNN model, we need some training data. As we train the ML model on the authoring computer, the data needs to be on the same machine. For this example, we will use the MNIST image dataset:

    ```
    import os
    import urllib
    os.makedirs('./data/mnist', exist_ok=True)

    urllib.request.urlretrieve(
    'http://yann.lecun.com/exdb/mnist/train-images-idx3-ubyte.gz', filename = './data/mnist/train-images.gz')

    urllib.request.urlretrieve( 'http://yann.lecun.com/exdb/mnist/train-labels-idx1-ubyte.gz', filename = './data/mnist/train-labels.gz')

    urllib.request.urlretrieve( 'http://yann.lecun.com/exdb/mnist/t10k-images-idx3-ubyte.gz', filename = './data/mnist/test-images.gz')

    urllib.request.urlretrieve( 'http://yann.lecun.com/exdb/mnist/t10k-labels-idx1-ubyte.gz', filename = './data/mnist/test-labels.gz')
    ```

    We can see, in the preceding code, that we load the training and testing data and put it in the data directory on the current environment where the code executes. We will see in the subsequent section how to make the data available on any compute in the ML workspace.

2. Next, we load the data, parse it, and store it in multi-dimensional NumPy arrays. We use a helper function, load, which is defined in the accompanying source code of this chapter. We preprocess the training data by normalizing the pixel values to a range between **0** and **1**:

```
X_train = load('./data/mnist/train-images.gz', False) / 255.0 X_test =
load('./data/mnist/test-images.gz', False) / 255.0

y_train = load('./data/mnist/train-labels.gz', True).reshape(-1) y_test =
load('./data/mnist/test-labels.gz', True).reshape(-1)
```

Using the reshape method, we check that the training and testing labels are one-dimensional vectors with a single label per training and testing sample.

> **Note**
>
> Once we have the training data, it is time to decide which Python framework to use to train neural network models. Actually, you should have thought about this already before starting to write code for your ML experiment. While you are not limited to any specific framework in Azure Machine Learning, it is recommended you use either TensorFlow (with Keras) or PyTorch for training neural networks and DL models. TensorFlow and Keras are great choices when training and deploying standard models for production.
>
> PyTorch is a great choice for tinkering with exotic models and custom layers and debugging customized models. In my opinion, PyTorch is a bit easier to get started with, whereas TensorFlow is more complex and mature and has a bigger ecosystem. In this chapter, we will use TensorFlow due to its large ecosystem, Keras integration, great documentation, and good support in Azure Machine Learning.

3. Having chosen an ML framework, we can start to construct a simple CNN. We use **keras** to construct a sequential model:

```
from keras.models import Sequential
from keras.layers import Conv2D, MaxPooling2D, Flatten, Dense

model = Sequential()
model.add(Conv2D(filters=16, kernel_size=3, padding='same',
activation='relu', input_shape=(28,28,1)))
model.add(MaxPooling2D(pool_size=2))
model.add(Conv2D(filters=32, kernel_size=3, padding='same',
activation='relu'))
model.add(MaxPooling2D(pool_size=2))
model.add(Flatten())
model.add(Dense(256, activation='relu'))
model.add(Dense(10, activation='softmax'))
```

In the preceding code, we took advantage of the `keras.Sequential` model API to construct a simple CNN model. We go with the default initialization of the weights and solely specify the model structure here. You can also see the typical combination of a feature extractor until the `Flatten` layer, and the MLP classification head outputting 10 probabilities using the `softmax` activation function at the end. Let's take a quick look at the model, which has, in total, 409,322 parameters. Please note that we specifically constructed a simple CNN from a tiny image size of 28 x 28 grayscale images. The *Figure 8.7* shows the compact structure of the model defined. We can observe that the largest number of parameters is the fully connected layer after the feature extractor, containing 98% of the parameters of the total model:

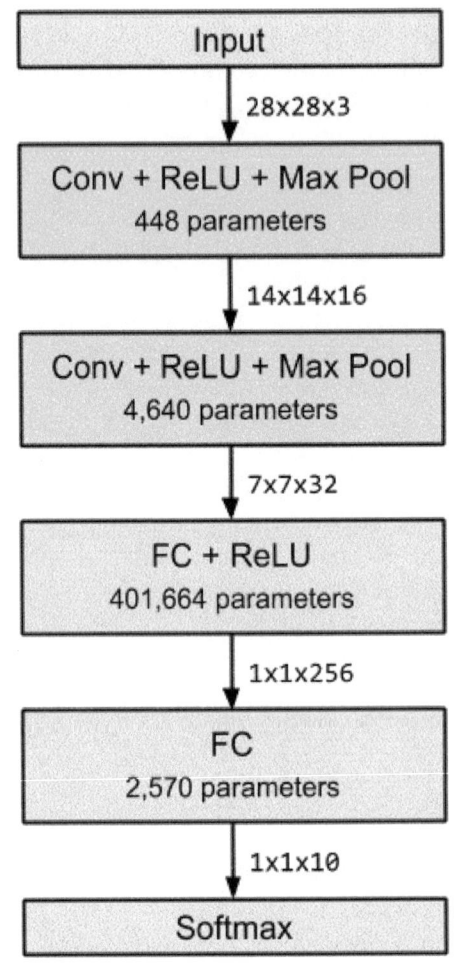

Figure 8.7: A visual representation of the model structure

After defining a model structure, we need to define the loss metric that we are trying to optimize and specify an optimizer. The optimizer is responsible for computing the changes for all weights per training iteration, given the total and backpropagated loss. With Keras and TensorFlow, we can easily choose a state-of-the-art optimizer and use a default metric for classification:

```
model.compile(loss='categorical_crossentropy', optimizer='adam',
metrics=['accuracy'])
```

In the preceding code, we define a `categorical_crossentropy` loss and `adam` optimizer for training the CNN. We also track another metric besides the loss, which is accuracy. This makes it easier to estimate and measure the performance of the CNN during training.

4. One more step before we start training is to define a model checkpoint. This is quite important in allowing us to pause and resume training at any given time after an epoch. Using Keras, it is quite simple to implement the following:

```
from keras.callbacks import ModelCheckpoint

checkpoint_path = "./mnist_cnn.bin" checkpoint_cb =
ModelCheckpoint(checkpoint_path)
```

5. Finally, we can start the training locally by invoking the fit method on the Keras model. We supply the training data as well as the batch size and number of epochs (iterations) for training. We also pass the previously created callback model checkpoint so we can save the model after each epoch:

```
model.fit(X_train, y_train, batch_size=16, epochs=10,
callbacks=[checkpoint_cb])
```

6. Finally, we can use the trained model of the last epoch to compute the final score on the test set:

```
from keras.models import load_model model = load_model(checkpoint_path)
scores = model.evaluate(X_test, y_test, verbose=1)

print('Test loss:', scores[0]) print('Test accuracy:', scores[1])
```

We can see, in the preceding code, that training a CNN on a compute instance in Azure Machine Learning is straightforward and similar to training a model on the local machine. The only difference is that we have to be sure that all required libraries (and required versions) are installed and that the data is made available.

Generating more input data using augmentation

DL models usually have many millions of parameters to represent the model with the training set distribution. Hence, when dealing with DL, be it in custom vision using cognitive services, Azure Machine Learning designer, or custom models in Azure Machine Learning, you should always implement data augmentation.

Data augmentation is a way of creating more training data by slightly modifying the available data and providing the modified data to the ML algorithm. Depending on the use case, this could include mirroring, translating, scaling, or skewing images; or changing the brightness, luminosity, or color information of images. These modifications strongly improve the generalization of the model, such as enabling better scale, translation, rotation, and transformation invariance.

The benefit of using TensorFlow and Keras is that data augmentation is a built-in capability. We first create an **ImageDataGenerator** object, which stores all our modifications and can generate iterators through the augmented dataset. The data augmentation techniques for this generator can be configured during the initialization of the generator. However, we want to use the generator to simply iterate through the training images without augmentation and add augmentation once we have connected all the pieces:

1. Let's implement an image data generator in Keras using the **ImageDataGenerator** object:

    ```
    datagen = ImageDataGenerator()
    ```

2. In the next step, we can return a data iterator from the image data generator by passing the original training image data and labels to the generator. Before we sample images from the generator, we need to compute the training set statistics that will be required for further augmentations. Similar to the scikit-learn **BaseTransformer** interface, we need to call the fit method on the generator:

    ```
    datagen.fit(x_train)
    ```

3. Next, we can create an iterator by using the **flow** method:

    ```
    it = datagen.flow(X_train, y_train, batch_size=16)
    ```

4. If instead of loading the images into NumPy arrays beforehand, we wanted to read individual images from a folder, we can use a different generator function to do so, as seen in the following snippet:

    ```
    it = datagen.flow_from_directory(directory='./data/mnist', target_size=(28, 28), batch_size=16, class_mode='categorical')
    ```

    However, in our example, the training images are combined into a single file and so we don't need to load the image data ourselves.

5. The iterator can now be used to loop through the data generator and yield new training samples with each iteration. To do so, we need to replace the fit function with the **fit_generator** function, which expects an iterator instead of a training dataset:

    ```
    model.fit_generator(it,
        steps_per_epoch=256, epochs=10, callbacks=[checkpoint_cb])
    ```

As we can see, we can pass the same arguments for epoch and callback to the **fit_generator** function as we did to the fit function. The only difference is that now we need to fix a number of steps per epoch so that the iterator yields new images. Once we add augmentation methods to the generator, we could theoretically generate unlimited modifications of each training image per epoch. Hence, with this argument, we define how many batches of data we train each epoch with, which should roughly correspond with the number of training samples divided by the batch size.

Finally, we can configure the data augmentation techniques. The default image data generator supports a variety of augmentations through different arguments:

- Translation or shifts
- Horizontal or vertical flips
- Rotations
- Brightness
- Zoom

Let's go back to the image data generator and activate data augmentation techniques. Here is an example generator that is often used for data augmentation in image processing:

```
datagen = ImageDataGenerator(
    featurewise_center=True,
    featurewise_std_normalization=True,
    rotation_range=20,
    width_shift_range=0.2,
    height_shift_range=0.2,
    horizontal_flip=True)
```

By using this data generator, we can now train the model with augmented image data and further improve the performance of the CNN. As we saw before, this is a crucial and strongly recommended step in any DL training pipeline.

Let's move all the code that we have developed so far into a file called **scripts/train.py**. We will use this file in the next section to schedule and run it on a GPU cluster.

Moving training to a GPU cluster using Azure Machine Learning compute

Once we have a training script ready, have verified that the script works, and have added data augmentation, we can move this training script to a more performant execution environment. In DL, many operations, such as convolutions, pooling, and general tensor operators, can benefit from parallel execution. Therefore, we will execute the training script on a GPU cluster and track its status in the authoring environment.

A great aspect of Azure Machine Learning is that we can set up and run everything in Python from the authoring environment, that is the Jupyter notebook running on the Azure Machine Learning compute instance:

1. First, we will configure our Azure Machine Learning workspace, which is a single statement without arguments on the compute instance:

    ```
    from azureml.core.workspace import Workspace ws = Workspace.from_config()
    ```

    > **Note**
    >
    > Please note that you are requested to authenticate this application with your Azure account through an URL outputted from the configuration method.

2. Next, we will load or create a GPU cluster with autoscaling for the training process:

    ```
    from azureml.core.compute import ComputeTarget, AmlCompute from azureml.core.compute_target import ComputeTargetException
    cluster_name = "gpu-cluster" vm_size = "STANDARD_NC6" max_nodes = 3
    try:
        compute_target = ComputeTarget(workspace=ws, name=cluster_name) print('Found existing compute target.')
    except ComputeTargetException: print('Creating a new compute target...')
        compute_config = AmlCompute.provisioning_configuration(vm_size=vm_size, max_nodes=max_nodes)
        # create the cluster and wait for completion
        compute_target = ComputeTarget.create(ws, cluster_name, compute_config) compute_target.wait_for_completion(show_output=True)
    ```

Wasn't that very simple? Creating a GPU cluster with autoscaling in three lines of code within Jupyter is pretty cool. Great, now we have our cluster up and running. However, how do we choose the VM size and the number of nodes for the GPU cluster?

In general, you can decide between the NC, ND, and NV types from the N-series VMs in Azure. A later version number (for example, v2 or v3) usually means updated hardware, hence a newer CPU and GPU, and better memory. For a little help, you can think of the different N-series versions in terms of applications (NC, where C means compute; ND, where D means deep learning; and NV, where V means video). Here is a table to compare the different N-series VM types and their particular GPU configurations. Most machines can be scaled up to four GPUs per VM. The *Figure 8.8* shows an Azure VM N-series comparison:

VM type	GPU	GPU memory	TFlops (FP32)	Cost (per hour)
NC	½ Tesla K80	12 GB	2.0	$0.90
NCv2	1 Tesla P100	16 GB	9.3	$2.07
NCv3	1 Tesla V100	16 GB	14.0	$3.06
ND	1 Tesla P40	24 GB	11.8	$2.07
NDv2	8 Tesla V100 (NVLINK)	16 GB	-	$12.24
NV	½ Tesla M60 (GRID)	8 GB	4	$1.092
NVv3	½ Tesla M60 (GRID)	8 GB	4	$1.14

Figure 8.8: Azure VM N-series comparison

The prices in the preceding table represent pay-as-you-go prices for Linux VMs in the West US2 region (except NVv3 in West US and NDv2 in East US) for September 2019. Please note that these prices may have changed by the time you are reading this, but it should give you an indication of the different options and configurations to choose from.

In order to get a better understanding of the costs and performance, we can look at a typical workload for training a ResNet-50 model on the ImageNet dataset. The *Figure 8.9*, provided by Nvidia, shows that it makes sense to choose the latest GPU models as their performance increase is much better and the costs are actually cheaper:

GPU	Training time	VM type	Cost/instance	Total cost (USD)
8X V100	6h	2 x Standard_NC24s_v3	$13.712/hour	$164.54
8X P100	18h	2 x Standard_NC24s_v2	$9.972/hour	$358.99
8X K80	38h	4 x Standard_NC24	$4.336/hour	$659.07

Figure 8.9: A table showing GPU models and the associated costs of training

As we can see in the preceding table, the performance increase visible in the lower training duration for the same task pays off and results in a much lower cost for the overall task.

Hence, the **STANDARD_NC6** model is a great starting point, from a pricing perspective, for experimenting with GPUs and CNNs in Azure. The only thing that we have to make sure is that our model can fit into the available GPU memory of the VM. A common way to calculate this is to compute the number of parameters for the model, times it by 2 for storing gradients (times it by 1 when we do only inferencing), times it by the batch size, and times it by 4 for the single- precision size in bytes (use 2 for half-precision).

In our example, the CNN architecture requires 1.63 MB to store the trainable parameters (weights and biases). To also store backpropagated losses for a batch size of 16, we require around 52.6 MB of GPU memory in order to perform the whole end-to-end training on a single GPU. This also fits perfectly in our 12 GB of GPU memory in the smallest NC instance.

> **Note**
>
> Please note that while these numbers seem pretty small and reasonable for our test case, you will usually deal with larger models (around 1 to 10 million parameters) and larger image sizes. To put that into perspective, ResNet-152, trained on image dimensions of 224 x 224 x 3, has approximately 60 million parameters and a size of 240 MB. On the STANDARD_NC6 instance, we could train, at most, at a batch size of 24, according to our equation. In reality, however, we also need to store additional blobs in GPU memory, which makes this calculation quite sharp.

By adding more GPUs or nodes to the cluster, we have to introduce a different framework to take advantage of the distributed setup. We will discuss this in more detail in *Chapter 10, Distributed machine learning on Azure*. However, we can add more nodes with autoscaling to the cluster, such that multiple people can submit multiple jobs simultaneously. The number of maximum nodes can be easily computed by simultaneous models/node * number of peak models to be trained simultaneously. In our test scenario, we go with a cluster size of 3 so we can schedule a few models at the same time.

> **Note**
>
> Keep in mind that this becomes a more important issue when doing parallel hyperparameter tuning—we will take a closer look at this in the next chapter.

3. OK, we decided on a VM size and GPU configuration and can continue with the training process. Next, we need to make sure that the cluster can access the training data. To do so, we use the default datastore on the Azure Machine Learning workspace. This is blob storage that is automatically deployed with each workspace and has configured access control for your container instance:

    ```
    ds = ws.get_default_datastore() ds.upload(src_dir='./data/mnist', target_path='mnist',
    show_progress=True)
    ```

    In the preceding code, we copy the training data from the local machine to the default datastore, the blob storage account. As we have discussed in previous chapters, there are also other ways to upload your data to blob storage or to another storage system. However, using the datastore API in Azure Machine Learning has a great benefit—mounting the storage to the cluster.

    Mounting blob storage to a machine, or even a cluster, is usually not a straightforward task. Yes, you could have an NAS and mount it as a network drive on every node in the cluster, but this is tedious to set up and scale. Using the datastore API, we can simply request a reference to the datastore, which can be used to mount the correct folder on every machine that needs to access the data:

    ```
    ds_data = ds.as_mount()
    ```

    The preceding command returns a Datastore Mount object, which doesn't look particularly powerful. However, if we pass this reference as a parameter to the training script through the estimator, it can automatically mount the datastore and read the content from the datastore. If you have ever played with mount points or **fstab**, you will understand that this magical one-liner can really speed up your daily workflow.

4. Now, we can create an Azure ML estimator. An estimator is an abstraction over a compute target, a highly configurable execution environment (for example, Docker, Python 3, Conda, or TensorFlow), and your training script. While you can run any Python script on an abstract estimator, there are a few preconfigured estimators to work with TensorFlow, PyTorch, Chainer, scikit-learn, and others. Let's create such an estimator so that we can schedule it on the cluster:

```python
from azureml.train.dnn import TensorFlow
script_params={
'--data-dir': ds_data
}
estimator= TensorFlow(
    source_directory='./scripts',
    compute_target=compute_target,
    script_params=script_params,
    framework_version='1.13',
    entry_script='train.py')
```

5. In order to read the data from the specified default datastore, we need to parse the argument in the train.py script. Let's go back to the script and replace the file loading with the following code block:

```python
import argparse
parser = argparse.ArgumentParser()
parser.add_argument('--data-dir', type=str, dest='data_dir') args = parser.parse_args()
X_train = load(... % args.data_dir, False) / 255.0 X_test = load(... % args.data_dir, False) / 255.0
y_train = load(... % args.data_dir, True).reshape(-1) y_test = load(... % args.data_dir, True).reshape(-1)
```

6. That leaves us to schedule and run the script on the GPU cluster. However, before doing so, we want to make sure that all runs are tracked in the Azure Machine Learning workspace. Therefore, we also add Run to the train.py file and reuse the Keras callback for Azure Machine Learning from *Chapter 3, Data experimentation and visualization using Azure*. Here is what the training script will look like:

```python
from azureml.core import Run
# Get the run configuration run = Run.get_context()

# Create an Azure Machine Learning monitor callback azureml_cb = AzureMlKerasCallback(run)

model.fit_generator(it, steps_per_epoch=256, epochs=10, callbacks=[azureml_
```

```
    cb, checkpoint_cb])

# Load the best model
model = load_model(checkpoint_path)

# Score trained model
scores = model.evaluate(X_test, y_test, verbose=1) print('Test loss:',
scores[0])run.log('Test loss', scores[0]) print('Test accuracy:',
scores[1])
run.log('Test accuracy', scores[1])
```

As we can see in the preceding code, we add the Run configuration and the Keras callback to track all metrics during the epochs. We also collect the final test set metric and report it to the Azure Machine Learning workspace. You can find the complete runnable example in the code provided with this book.

Improving your performance through transfer learning

In many cases, you don't have a dataset of hundreds of millions of labeled training samples, and that's completely understandable. However, how can you still benefit from all the previous work and benchmarks? Shouldn't a feature extractor trained on recognizing animals also perform well on recognizing faces? The classifier would certainly be different, but the visual features extracted from images should be similar.

This is the exact idea behind **fine-tuning** pre-trained models or, more generally speaking, **transfer learning**. To fine-tune, we can simply reuse a feature extractor from a pre-trained DL model (for example, pre-trained on the ImageNet dataset, the faces dataset, the CoCo dataset, and so on) and attach a custom classifier to the end of the model. Transfer learning means that we can transfer the features from a model from one task to another task; for example, from classification to object detection. It seems a bit confusing at first whether we would want to reuse features for a different task. However, if a model learned to identify patterns of geographical shapes in images, this could certainly be reused for any image- related task in the same domain.

One cool property of this is that the task for transfer learning doesn't necessarily need to be a supervised ML task and so it is often not required to have annotated training data for the base task. A popular unsupervised ML technique is called auto-encoders, where an ML model tries to generate a similar-looking output given an input using a feature extractor and an upsampling network. By minimizing the error between the generated output and the input, the feature extractor learns to efficiently represent the input data. Auto-encoders are popular for pre-training network architectures before reusing the pre-trained weights for the actual task.

Therefore, we need to make sure that the pre-trained model was trained on a dataset of the same domain. Images of biological cells look very different from faces and clouds look very different from buildings. In general, the `ImageNet` dataset covers a broad spectrum of photograph-style images for many standard visual features, such as buildings, cars, animals, and so on. Therefore, it is a good choice for many pre-trained models.

One more thought worth mentioning is that transfer learning is not only tied to image data and models dealing with computer vision. Transfer learning has proven valuable in any domain where datasets are sufficiently similar, such as human voice or written text. Hence, whenever you are implementing a DL model, do your research on what datasets could be used for transfer learning and to ultimately improve the model's performance.

Let's dive into some code. We saw a similar example earlier in this chapter, where we piped the output of the feature extractor to an SVM. In this section, we want to achieve something similar but with a single resulting DL model. Therefore, in this example, we will solely build a network architecture for the new model consisting of a pre-trained feature extractor and a newly initialized classification head:

1. First, we define the number of output classes and the input shape and load the base model from Keras:

   ```
   from keras.applications.resnet50 import ResNet50 num_classes = 10
   input_shape = (224, 224, 3)
   # create the base pre-trained model
   base_model = ResNet50(input_shape=input_shape, weights='imagenet',
   include_top=False, pooling='avg')
   ```

   In the preceding code, most of the magic for pre-training happens thanks to Keras. We first specify the image dataset used for training this model using the weights argument, which will automatically initialize the model weights with the pre-trained `imagenet` weights. With the third argument, `include_top=False`, we tell Keras to only load the feature extractor part of the model. Using the `pooling` argument, we can also specify how the last pooling operation should be performed. In this case, we choose average pooling.

2. Next, we freeze the layers of the model by setting their trainable property to False. To do so, we simply loop over all the layers in the model:

   ```
   for layer in base_model.layers: layer.trainable=False
   ```

3. Finally, we can attach any network architecture to the model we want. In this case, we will attach the same classifier head used in the CNN network of the previous section. Finally, we construct the final model class by using the new architecture and output at the classifier output layer:

```
from keras.models import Model
from keras.layers import Flatten, Dense
clf = base_model.output
clf = Dense(256, activation='relu')(clf) clf = Dense(10, activation='softmax')(clf)
model = Model(base_model.input, clf)
```

That's it! You have successfully built a model combining a ResNet50 feature extractor pre- trained on ImageNet with your own custom classification head. You can now use this Keras model and plug it into your preferred optimizer and send it off to the GPU cluster. The output of the training will be one single model that can be managed and deployed as any other custom model.

> **Note**
>
> I want to mention that you are not limited to freezing all the layers of the original network at all times. A common approach is also to unfreeze later layers in the network, decrease the learning rate by at least a factor of 10, and continue training. By repeating this procedure, we could even retrain (or fine-tune) all the layers of the network in a step-by-step approach with a decreasing learning rate.

Independently of your choice and use case, you should add transfer learning to your standard repertoire of tricks for training DL models. Treat it as similar to data augmentation, which in my opinion should always be used as well in all cases.

Summary

In this chapter, we learned when and how to use DL to train an ML model on Azure. We used both compute instance and a GPU cluster from within Azure Machine Learning to train a model using Keras and TensorFlow.

First, we found out that DL works very well on highly structured data with non-obvious relations from the raw input data to the resulting prediction. Good examples are image classification, speech-to-text, or translation. However, we also saw that DL models are parametric models with a large number of parameters and so we often need a large amount of labeled or augmented input data. In contrast to traditional ML approaches, the extra parameters are used to train a fully end-to-end model, also including feature extraction from the raw input data.

Training a CNN using Azure Machine Learning is not difficult. We saw many approaches, from prototyping in Jupyter to augmenting the training data to running the training on a GPU cluster with autoscaling. The difficult part in DL is preparing and providing enough high-quality training data, finding a descriptive error metric, and optimizing between costs and performance. We looked at an overview of how to decide on the best VM and GPU size and configuration for your job, something that I recommend you do before starting your first GPU cluster.

In the next chapter, we go one step further and look into hyperparameter tuning and automated ML, a feature in Azure Machine Learning that lets you train and optimize stacked models automatically.

9
Hyperparameter tuning and Automated Machine Learning

In the previous chapter, we learned how to train convolutional and more complex **deep neural networks (DNNs)**. When training these models, we are often confronted with complex choices when parametrizing them, involving various parameters such as the number of layers, the order of layers, regularization, batch size, learning rate, the number of epochs, and more. This is not only true for DNNs; the same problem arises with selecting the correct preprocessing steps, features, models, and parameters in statistical ML approaches.

In this chapter, we will take a look at optimizing the training process in order to take away some of those error-prone human choices from machine learning. These necessary tuning tricks will help you to train better models faster and more efficiently. First, we will take a look at hyperparameter tuning (also called **HyperDrive** in Azure Machine Learning), a standard technique for optimizing all parameter choices in a machine learning process. By evaluating different sampling techniques for hyperparameter tuning such as random sampling, grid sampling, and Bayesian optimization, you will learn how to efficiently trade off runtime and model performance.

In the second half of this chapter, we will move from hyperparameter optimization to automating the complete end-to-end machine learning training process using **automated machine learning**, which is often referred to as **automated machine learning**. Using Azure Automated Machine Learning, we can simply optimize preprocessing, feature engineering, model selection, hyperparameter tuning, and model stacking all in one simple abstract pipeline.

One great benefit of Azure Machine Learning is that the concepts of both hyperparameter tuning and automated machine learning are supported in the same general way. This means we can deploy a Bayesian optimization experiment to a remote auto-scaling GPU cluster the same way as we would an Azure Automated Machine Learning experiment. The best model is returned in the same generic way, which can then be stored to disk, registered in the model stored, or deployed to Kubernetes in an instant, without ever leaving your notebook environment.

The following topics will be covered in this chapter:

- Hyperparameter tuning to find the optimal parameters
- Finding the optimal model with Azure Automated Machine Learning

Hyperparameter tuning to find the optimal parameters

In machine learning, we typically deal with parametric or non-parametric models. These models represent the distribution of the training data in order to make predictions for unseen data from the same distribution. While parametric models (such as linear regression, logistic regression, and neural networks) represent the training data distribution by using a learned set of parameters, non-parametric models describe the training data through other traits such as decision trees (all tree-based classifiers), training samples (k- nearest neighbors), or weighted training samples (support vector machine).

The *Figure 9.1* outlines a few of the key differences between parametric and non-parametric models:

Parametric model	Non-parametric model
Constant number of parameters, independent of training data	Number of parameters grows with the number of training samples
Strong assumption about the training data	No assumption about the training data
Fewer training samples required	Many training samples required
Fast training, fast inference	Slow training and slow inference
Examples: Linear regression and logistic regression	Examples: Decision trees and k-nearest neighbors

Figure 9.1: The difference between parametric and non-parametric models

The term **hyperparameter** refers to all parameters that are used to configure and tune the training process of parametric or non-parametric models. Here is a list of some typical hyperparameters in a neural network:

- The number of hidden layers
- The number of units per layer
- The batch size
- Depth dimensions
- The learning rate Regularization
- Dropout
- The loss metric

The number of hyperparameters and choices of possible values for training a simple ML model are huge. Have you ever found yourself manually tweaking a setting in your training process, for example, the number of splits in a decision-based classifier or the number of units in a neural network classifier? You are not alone, and many beginners do this! However, it's very important to accept that given the number of possible parameter choices, it is not feasible to try all combinations.

Not only can we not possibly try all distinct combinations of parameters manually, but, in many cases, we also can't possibly predict the outcome of a tweak in a hyperparameter. In such scenarios, we can start looking into finding the optimal set of parameters automatically. This process is called **hyperparameter tuning** or **hyperparameter search**.

Hyperparameter tuning entails the automated testing of a model's performance against different sets of hyperparameter combinations and ultimately choosing the best combination of hyperparameters. The definition of the *best performance* depends on the chosen metric and validation method. For example, stratified-fold cross-validation with the f1-score metric will yield a different set of winning parameters than the accuracy metric with k-fold cross-validation.

One reason why we discuss hyperparameter tuning (and also automated machine learning) in this book is that we have a competitive advantage by using elastic cloud compute infrastructure. While it is difficult to train hundreds of models in series on your laptop, it is super easy to train thousands of models in parallel in the cloud using cheap auto-scaling compute. Also, using cheap cloud storage, we can persist all potentially good models for later analysis. Many of the more recent ML papers have shown that we can often achieve better results by using more compute.

Before we begin tuning hyperparameters, I want to remind you of the importance of a baseline model. For many practical ML models, you should be able to achieve good performance using a single tree-based ensemble classifier or a pre-trained neural network with default parameters. If this is not the case, hyperparameter tuning won't magically output a top-performing model. In this case, it would be better to go back to data preprocessing and feature engineering in order to build a good baseline model first, before tuning batch sizes, the number of hidden units, or the number of trees.

Another issue to avoid with hyperparameter tuning is overfitting and focusing on the wrong performance metric or validation method. As with any other optimization technique, hyperparameter tuning will yield the best parameter combination according to a given metric. Therefore, it is essential to validate your performance metric before starting hyperparameter tuning.

As with most other techniques in machine learning, there are multiple ways to find the best hyperparameters for a model. The most popular techniques are grid search, random search, and Bayesian optimization. In this chapter, we will take a look at all three of them and discuss their strengths and weaknesses.

Sampling all possible parameter combinations using grid search

Grid search (or grid sampling) is a popular technique for finding the optimal hyperparameters from a parameter grid by trying every possible parameter combination of a multi-dimensional grid. For every parameter (continuous and categorical), we need to define all values that should be tested. Popular ML libraries provide tools to create these parameter grids efficiently.

There are two properties differentiating grid search from other hyperparameter sampling methods:

- All parameter combinations are assumed to be independent of each other and hence can be tested in parallel. Therefore, given a set of 100 possible parameter combinations, we can start 100 models to test all combinations in parallel.
- By testing all possible parameter combinations, we make sure that we search for a global optimum rather than a local optimum.

Grid search works perfectly for smaller machine learning models with only a few hyperparameters but grows exponentially with every additional parameter because it adds a new dimension to the parameter grid.

Let's take a look into how grid search can be implemented using Azure Machine Learning. In Azure Machine Learning, the hyperparameter tuning functionality lives in the hyperdrive package. Here is what we are going to do in the following steps:

1. Create a grid sampling configuration.
2. Define a primary metric to define the tuning goal.
3. Create a hyperdrive configuration.
4. Submit the hyperdrive configuration as an experiment to Azure Machine Learning.

We will now look at the steps in more detail:

1. First, we define the parameter choices and ranges for grid sampling, as shown in the following code block:

    ```
    from azureml.train.hyperdrive import GridParameterSampling from azureml.train.hyperdrive.parameter_expressions import *
    grid_sampling = GridParameterSampling( {
            "--first-layer-neurons": choice(16, 32, 64, 128),
            "--second-layer-neurons": choice(16, 32, 64, 128),
            "--batch-size": choice(16, 32)
        }
    )
    ```

    In the preceding code, we defined a parameter grid using discrete parameter choices along three parameter dimensions—the number of neurons in the first layer, the number of neurons in the second layer, and the training batch size.

2. The parameter names are written as command-line arguments because they will be forwarded as arguments to the training script. Hence, in your training script, you should make all your training parameters configurable via command-line arguments. Here is a snippet showing how this could look in your training example:

   ```
   import argparse

   parser = argparse.ArgumentParser()
   parser.add_argument('--batch-size', type=int, dest='batch_size', default=50)
   parser.add_argument('--epochs', type=int, dest='epochs', default=30)
   parser.add_argument('--first-layer-neurons', type=int, dest='n_hidden_1', default=100)
   parser.add_argument('--second-layer-neurons', type=int, dest='n_hidden_2', default=100)
   parser.add_argument('--learning-rate', type=float, dest='learning_rate', default=0.01)
   parser.add_argument('--momentum', type=float, dest='momentum', default=0.9)
   args = parser.parse_args()
   ```

   With grid sampling, we will test all possible combinations of these parameters. This will result in a total of 32 runs (4 x 4 x 2) that we could theoretically run in parallel, as the training runs and parameter configurations are not dependent on each other. It might seem obvious, in this case, how many runs we have to perform and that we can run all parameter configurations in parallel, but we will see later that this is not the case for random sampling and Bayesian optimization. There, the number of training runs won't be fixed, and the number of parallel runs will affect the optimization process. Therefore, it is great to stop for a moment and appreciate the simplicity of this solution of grid sampling for a small number of discrete parameters.

3. Next, we need to define a metric that measures the performance of each parameter combination. This metric can be any numeric value that is logged by the training script. Please note that this metric does not need to be the same as the loss function—it can just be any measurement that you would like to use to compare different parameter pairs. Have a look at the following example. Let's decide to maximize the accuracy metric for this example. We define the following parameters:

   ```
   from azureml.train.hyperdrive import PrimaryMetricGoal primary_metric_name = "accuracy"
   primary_metric_goal = PrimaryMetricGoal.MAXIMIZE
   ```

In the preceding case, we choose the accuracy metric, which is what we want to maximize. You can see that we simply specify any metric name. In order to use this metric to evaluate hyperparameter optimization runs, the training script needs to log a metric with this name. We have already seen this in the previous chapters, where we solely wanted to collect a metric in the Azure Machine Learning runs tab and compare them for an experiment.

4. We use the same name of **primary_metric_name** to define and log a metric that can be picked up by hyperdrive to evaluate the run in the training script:

   ```
   from azureml.core.run import Run
   run = Run.get_context() run.log("accuracy", float(val_accuracy))
   ```

5. Before we continue, recall the estimator configuration from the previous chapters. We reuse a CPU-based Azure Machine Learning cluster defined in **compute_target** that we saw in *Chapter 7, Building ML models using Azure Machine Learning*:

   ```
   from azureml.train.dnn import TensorFlow

   estimator = TensorFlow( "training", compute_target=compute_target, entry_script="train.py",
   conda_packages=['scikit-learn', 'keras'])
   ```

6. Now, we can initialize the **hyperdrive** configuration, consisting of the estimator, the sampling grid, the optimization metric, and the number of runs and concurrent runs:

   ```
   from azureml.train.hyperdrive import HyperDriveConfig

   hyperdrive_run_config = HyperDriveConfig(
           estimator=estimator,
           hyperparameter_sampling=grid_sampling,
           primary_metric_name=primary_metric_name,
           primary_metric_goal=primary_metric_goal,
           max_total_runs=32, max_concurrent_runs=4)
   ```

In grid sampling, the number of runs should correspond with the number of possible parameter combinations. As it is a required attribute, we need to compute this value and pass it here. The maximum number of concurrent runs in grid sampling is limited only by the number of nodes in your Azure Machine Learning cluster. We are using a four-node cluster, so we set the number to **4** to maximize concurrency.

7. Finally, we can submit the **hyperdrive** configuration to an experiment, which will execute all the concurrent child runs on the specified compute target:

   ```
   from azureml.core.experiment import Experiment
   experiment = Experiment(workspace, experiment_name) hyperdrive_run = experiment.submit(hyperdrive_run_config) print(hyperdrive_run.get_portal_url())
   ```

   The preceding snippet will kick off the training process, building and registering any new Docker images if needed, initializing and scaling up nodes in the cluster, and finally running the training scripts on the cluster. Each script will be parameterized using a unique parameter combination from the sampling grid.

8. The *Figure 9.2* shows the resulting experiment run when we click on the link that is returned from the preceding code snippet:

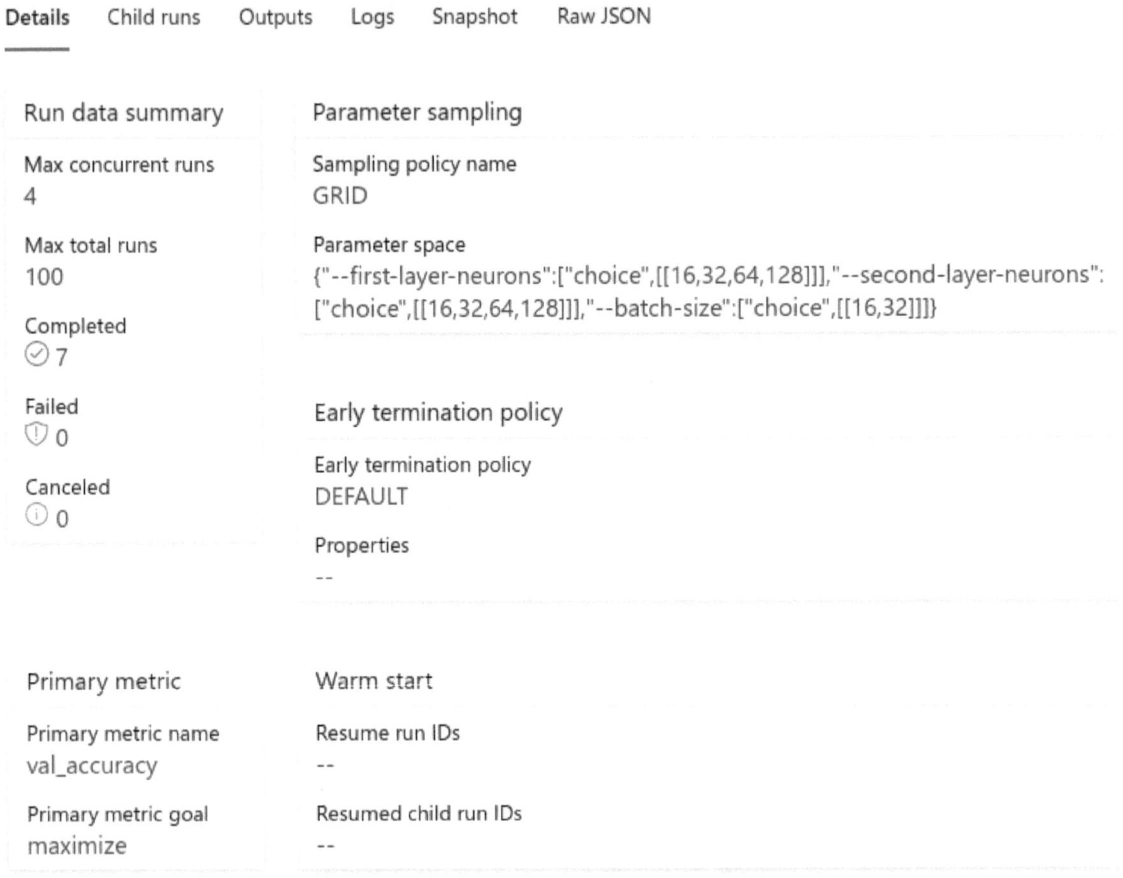

Details | Child runs | Outputs | Logs | Snapshot | Raw JSON

Run data summary	Parameter sampling
Max concurrent runs 4	Sampling policy name GRID
Max total runs 100	Parameter space {"--first-layer-neurons":["choice",[[16,32,64,128]]],"--second-layer-neurons":["choice",[[16,32,64,128]]],"--batch-size":["choice",[[16,32]]]}
Completed ✓ 7	
Failed ⓪ 0	Early termination policy
Canceled ⓘ 0	Early termination policy DEFAULT
	Properties --
Primary metric	Warm start
Primary metric name val_accuracy	Resume run IDs --
Primary metric goal maximize	Resumed child run IDs --

Figure 9.2: The result of the experiment run

We can see that the sampling policy is set to **GRID**, as well as seeing the spawned parameter space. These parameters will be applied as command-line arguments to the training script.

However, as you might have guessed already, not everything is great with sampling all possible parameter combinations from a multi-dimensional grid. As the number of hyperparameters grows, so do the dimensions of the grid. And each dimension of parameters adds a magnitude of new parameter configurations that need to be tested. And don't forget, testing a parameter configuration usually means performing training, cross- validation, and test set predictions on your model, which can take a significant amount of resources.

Imagine that you want to search the best parameter combination for 5 parameters with 10 different values for each parameter. Let's assume the following:

- We test 105 (10*10*10*10*10) parameter combinations
- One training run takes only 2 minutes
- We perform 4-fold cross-validation

Then, we would end up with 2 minutes * 4 * 10^5 = 10,00,000 minutes = 555 days of required runtime. While you probably could perform training in parallel, there exist other methods that are better suited to large amounts of parameters.

Let's see how we can limit the required runtime of the parameter optimization search by sampling parameter configurations at random.

Trying random combinations using random search

Random search is another popular hyperparameter sampling method similar to grid search. The main difference is that instead of testing all possible parameter combinations, only a few combinations are randomly selected and tested in random search. The main idea is that grid search often samples parameter configurations that have little effect on model performance. Therefore, we waste a lot of time chasing similar solutions where we could use the time instead to try many diverse and hopefully more successful configurations.

When dealing with large amounts of hyperparameters (for example, more than 5), random search will find a good set of hyperparameters much faster than grid search–however, it might not be the optimal result given all possible choices. Even so, in many cases, it will be a reasonable trade-off to use random search over grid search to improve prediction performance with hyperparameter tuning.

In random search, parameters are usually sampled from a continuous distribution instead of using discrete values. This leads to a slightly different way of defining the parameter grid. Instead of providing precise value choices for continuous variables, we can define a distribution function for each parameter to draw random values from.

Like grid search, all parameter combinations are completely independent if drawn without replacement and hence can be fully parallelized. If a parameter grid with 10,000 distinct configurations is provided, we can run and test all x models in parallel. The variable x stands for any number of different random combinations that should be tested.

Let's look into random search in Azure Machine Learning:

1. As with all other hyperparameter optimization methods, we find the random sampling method in the hyperdrive package. As discussed previously, we can now define probability distribution functions such as normal and uniform for each parameter instead of choosing only discrete parameters:

   ```
   from azureml.train.hyperdrive import RandomParameterSampling from azureml.train.hyperdrive.parameter_expressions import *
   random_sampling = RandomParameterSampling( { "--learning-rate": normal(10, 3),
           "--momentum": uniform(0.5, 1.0),
           "--batch-size": choice(16, 32, 64)
       }
   )
   ```

   Using continuous parameter ranges is not the only difference in random sampling. Due to the fact that we can now sample an infinite amount of parameter configurations from a continuous range, we need a way to specify the duration of the search. We can use the **max_total_runs** and **max_duration_minutes** parameters to define the expected runtime in minutes or to limit the amount of sampled parameter configurations.

2. Let's test 25 different configurations in this sample and run the hyperparameter tuning process for a maximum of 60 minutes. We set the following parameters:

   ```
   max_total_runs = 25
   max_duration_minutes = 60
   ```

3. We reuse the same metric that we defined in the previous section, namely accuracy. The hyperdrive configuration looks as follows:

   ```
   from azureml.train.hyperdrive import HyperDriveConfig hyperdrive_run_config = HyperDriveConfig(
       estimator=estimator,
       hyperparameter_sampling=random_sampling,
       primary_metric_name=primary_metric_name,
       primary_metric_goal=primary_metric_goal,
       max_total_runs=max_total_runs,
       max_duration_minutes=max_duration_minutes)
   ```

4. Similar to before, we can submit the hyperdrive configuration to Azure Machine Learning from the authoring runtime, which will schedule all the optimization runs on the compute target:

```
from azureml.core.experiment import Experiment
experiment = Experiment(workspace, experiment_name) hyperdrive_run = experiment.submit(hyperdrive_run_config) print(hyperdrive_run.get_portal_url())
```

Random sampling is a good choice for large amounts of tunable hyperparameters or sampling values from a continuous range. However, instead of optimizing the parameter configurations step by step, we simply try all those configurations at random and compare how they perform.

> **Note**
>
> If you are asking yourself now whether there is no better (or more elegant way) to solve this, I encourage you to continue to the Optimizing parameter choices using Bayesian optimization section.

Converging faster using early termination

Both the grid and random sampling techniques will test models for poor parameter choices and hence spend precious compute resources on fitting a poorly parameterized model to your training data. Early termination is a technique used to stop a training run early if the intermediate results look worse than other models.

In general, you should always try to use early termination when using either grid or random sampling. You get no benefit from training such models if the results are a lot worse than for some of the existing models.

Once we agree on the idea of canceling poor-performing runs, we need to find a way to specify a threshold of when a run performs well and when a run should be canceled. Azure Machine Learning provides a few termination policies, namely **bandit**, **median stopping**, and **truncation selection**. Let's take a look at them and see what their differences are.

Before we get into the details, though, let's first take a look into how to configure early termination. In Azure Machine Learning, we can parameterize the different early termination policies with two global properties, namely `evaluation_interval` and `delay_evaluation`. These parameters control how often the early termination policy is tested. An example of using these parameters follows:

```
evaluation_interval = 1
delay_evaluation = 10
```

The unit of both parameters is in intervals. An **interval** is whenever we log a metric in an experiment run and hence whenever we call `run.log()`. For example, when training a neural network, an interval will equal one training epoch. The `delay_evaluation` parameter controls how many intervals we want to wait from the start to test the early termination policy for the first time. In the preceding example, we configured it to `10`, and hence we wait for 10 epochs before testing the early termination policy.

Then, every other test of the policy is controlled using the `evaluation_interval` parameter. It describes how many iterations should pass until the next test. In the preceding example, we set `evaluation_interval` to `1`, which is also the default value. This means that we test the early termination policy every interval after the `delay_evaluation` interval—here, every 1 iteration. Let's look into the three termination policies.

The median stopping policy

We start with the easiest of the three, the median stopping policy. It takes no other arguments than the two default arguments, which control when and how often the policy should be tested. The median stopping policy keeps track of the running average of the primary metric across all experiment runs. Whenever the median policy is evaluated, it will test whether the current metric is above the median of all running experiments and stop those that are below. Here is an example of how to create a median stopping early termination policy for any hyperparameter tuning script:

```
from azureml.train.hyperdrive import MedianStoppingPolicy early_termination_policy = MedianStoppingPolicy(
    evaluation_interval=evaluation_interval,
    delay_evaluation=delay_evaluation)
```

As we can see in the preceding example, it's quite simple to construct a median stopping policy as it is only configured by the two default parameters. Due to its simplicity, it is a very effective method of reducing the runtime of your hyperparameter optimization script. The early termination policy is then applied to the **hyperdrive** configuration file using the policy parameter. Let's now look at the truncation selection policy.

The truncation selection policy

Unlike the median stopping policy, the truncation selection policy will always kill runs when evaluated. It will kill all runs whose primary metric is at the lowest configured percentage. This percentage is defined using the `truncation_percentage` parameter:

```
truncation_percentage = 10
evaluation_interval = 5
delay_evaluation = 10
```

In the preceding example, we set the **truncation_percentage** value to 10%. This means that whenever the early termination policy is executed, it will kill the worst-performing 10% of runs. We also increase the **evaluation_interval** value to 5, as we don't want to kill runs every epoch, as shown:

```
from azureml.train.hyperdrive import TruncationSelectionPolicy
early_termination_policy = TruncationSelectionPolicy(
    truncation_percentage=truncation_percentage,
    evaluation_interval=evaluation_interval,
    delay_evaluation=delay_evaluation)
```

This early termination policy makes sense when only very little training resources are available and we want to aggressively prune the number of runs each time the early termination policy is evaluated. Let's take a look at the final policy, the bandit policy.

The bandit policy

The bandit policy works similarly but inverse to the truncation policy. Instead of stopping the X% worst performing runs, it kills all runs that are X% worse than the best current run. However, the bandit policy is not configured using a percentage value, but rather a **slack_factor** or **slack_amount** parameter. The **slack_factor** parameter describes the relative deviation from the best metric, whereas the **slack_amount** parameter describes the absolute deviation from the best primary metric.

Let's look at an example. We configure hyperdrive with the following configuration of a **slack_factor** parameter of **0.2** and test an accuracy value (bigger is better). As before, we set the **evaluation_interval** value to **5** and the **evaluation_delay** value to **10** intervals:

```
slack_factor = 0.2
evaluation_interval = 5
delay_evaluation = 10
from azureml.train.hyperdrive import BanditPolicy early_termination_policy = BanditPolicy(
slack_factor = slack_factor, evaluation_interval=evaluation_interval, delay_evaluation=delay_evaluation)
```

Let's say the best-performing run yields an accuracy of 0.8 after epoch 10, when the early termination policy gets applied for the first time. Now, all runs that are performing up to 20% worse than the best metric are killed. We can compute the relative deviation from 0.8 accuracy by using the following function: 0.8/(1 + 0.2) = 0.67. Hence, all runs that yield a performance lower than 0.67 will get canceled by the early termination policy.

A HyperDrive configuration with termination policy

In order to create a HyperDrive configuration, we need to pass the early termination policy using the policy parameter. Here is an example using grid search sampling and the previously defined bandit policy:

```
from azureml.train.hyperdrive import HyperDriveConfig
hyperdrive_run_config = HyperDriveConfig( estimator=estimator,
    hyperparameter_sampling=grid_sampling,
    policy=early_termination_policy,
    primary_metric_name="accuracy",
    primary_metric_goal=PrimaryMetricGoal.MAXIMIZE)
```

The bandit policy is a good trade-off between the median stopping and the truncation selection policy that works well in many cases. You can be rest assured that only a well- performing subset of all hyperparameter configurations will be run and tested for multiple intervals.

Let's submit this HyperDrive configuration as the experiment to Azure Machine Learning. We can use the **RunDetails** method that we saw in *Chapter 7, Building ML models using Azure Machine Learning*, to output additional information about the hyperparameter tuning experiment—such as scheduling and parameter information, a visualization of the training performance, and a parallel coordinate chart showing the parameter dimensions:

```
from azureml.widgets import RunDetails
hyperdrive_run = exp.submit(hyperdrive_run_config) RunDetails(hyperdrive_run).show()
```

If you run the preceding code, you will see a nice visualization showing the sampled parameters on a parallel coordinates plot. Here you can see which parameter combinations yield high model accuracy. You can also select different plots such as two- and three- dimensional scatter plots to view the same information:

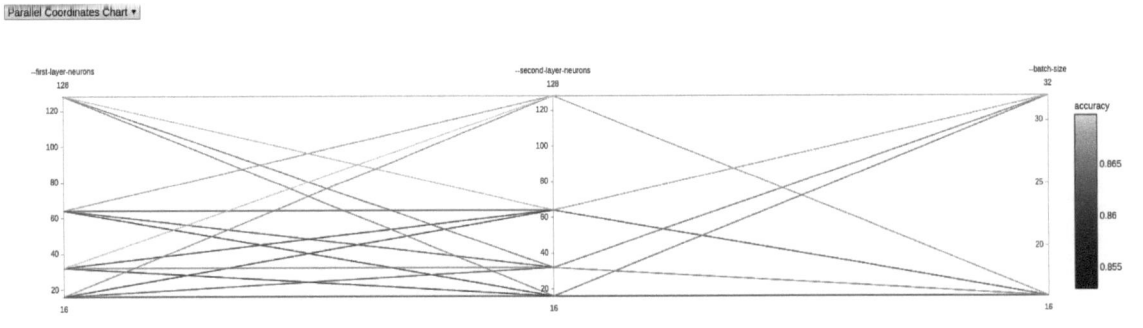

Figure 9.3: A parallel coordinates chart showing parameters and accuracy

By reading through this section, you have learned that applying an early termination policy to your hyperparameter optimization script is quite simple but extremely effective in Azure Machine Learning. With just a few lines of code, we can reduce the number of training runs to a minimum and only finish those that are yielding promising results.

> **Note**
>
> When using hyperparameter optimization with random or grid sampling, always use an early termination policy.

Optimizing parameter choices using Bayesian optimization

Until now, we have solely been evaluating different parameter configurations sampled from a grid or at random without many strategies. This had the benefit that all configurations were independent and could run concurrently. However, imagine using an ML model to help us find the best parameter combination for a large multi-dimensional parameter space. That's exactly what Bayesian optimization does in the domain of hyperparameter tuning.

The job of an optimization method is to find the optimal value (that is, a minimum or maximum) of a predefined objective function. In hyperparameter tuning, we are faced with a very similar problem: we want to find the parameter configuration that yields the best- predefined evaluation metric for an ML model.

So, how does this work? We first define a hyperplane, a multi-dimensional grid to sample our parameter configurations. In the following diagram, we show such a plane for two parameters along the x and y axes. The z axis represents the performance of the model that is tested using the parameters at this specific location:

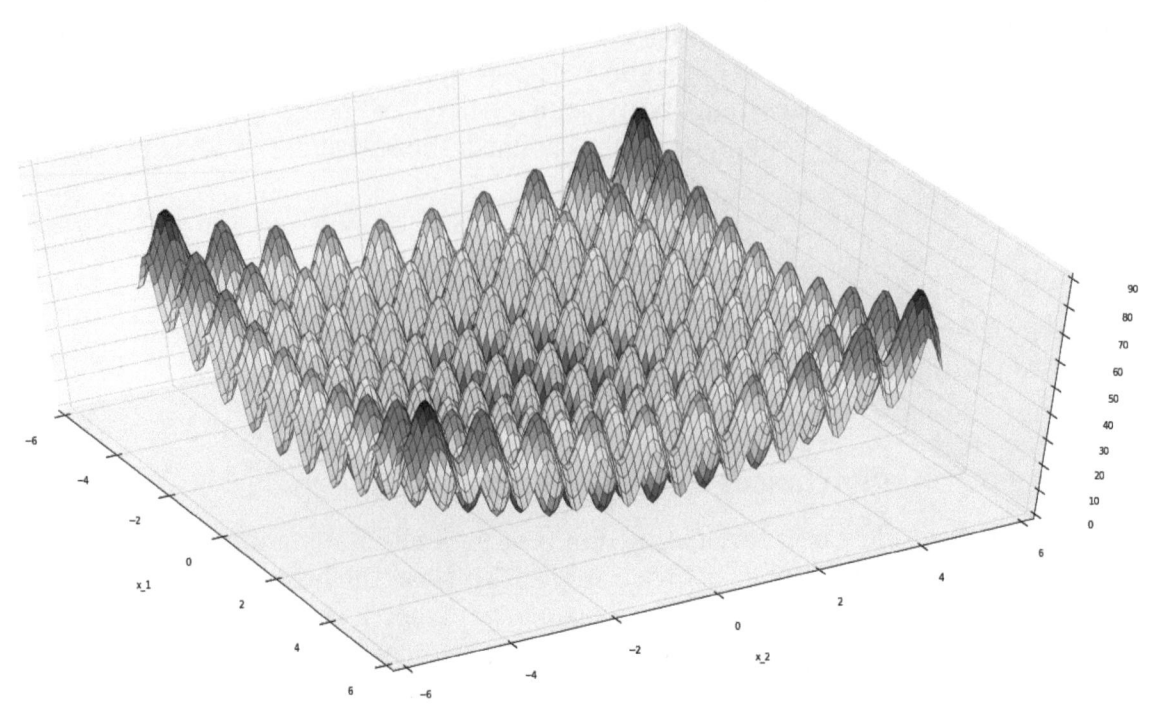

Figure 9.4: The two-dimensional Rastrigin function

The preceding diagram shows the two-dimensional Rastrigin function, as an example of something that is extremely hard to optimize. In hyperparameter tuning, we often face a similar problem in that finding the optimal solution is really difficult—just like finding the global minimum in the preceding function.

We then sample points from this plane and test the first (few) parameter configurations. Our assumption is that the parameters are not independent and the model will have similar performances when using similar parameters. However, each evaluation only yields a noisy value of the true model performance. Using these assumptions, we can use Gaussian processes to combine the model evaluations to a multi-variate continuous Gaussian. Next, we can compute the points for the highest expected improvements on this Gaussian. These points will yield the new samples to test with our model.

Luckily, we don't have to implement the algorithm ourselves, but many ML libraries provide a hyperparameter optimization algorithm out of the box. In Azure Machine Learning, we can use the Bayesian sampling method, which helps us to pick good parameter configurations in order to optimize the pre-defined metric.

The parameter grid is defined similarly to the random sampling technique by using a continuous or discrete parameter space for all parameter values, as shown in the following code block:

```
from azureml.train.hyperdrive import BayesianParameterSampling from azureml.train.hyperdrive.parameter_expressions import *
bayesian_sampling = BayesianParameterSampling( { "--learning-rate": normal(10, 3),
       "--momentum": uniform(0.5, 1.0),
       "--batch-size": choice(16, 32, 64)
    }
)
```

Before we continue, we need to keep one thing in mind. The Bayesian sampling technique tries to predict well-performing parameter configurations based on the results of the previously tested parameters. This means that the parameter choices and runs are not independent anymore. We can't run all experiments concurrently at the same time, as we need the results of some experiments to sample new parameters. Therefore, we need to set an additional parameter to control how many training runs should run concurrently.

We do this using the **max_concurrent_runs** parameter. In order to let the Bayesian optimization technique converge, it is recommended to set this value to a small value, for example, in the range of **2-10**. Let's set the value to **4** for this experiment and the number of total runs to **100**. This means that we are using **25** iterations for the Bayesian optimization method where we explore four parameter configurations concurrently at a time:

```
max_concurrent_runs = 4
max_total_runs = 100
```

Let's kick off the experiment with Bayesian sampling:

```
from azureml.train.hyperdrive import HyperDriveConfig from azureml.core.experiment import Experiment
hyperdrive_run_config = HyperDriveConfig( estimator=estimator, hyperparameter_sampling=bayesian_sampling, primary_metric_name=primary_metric_name, primary_metric_goal=primary_metric_goal, max_total_runs=max_total_runs, max_concurrent_runs=max_concurrent_runs)
experiment = Experiment(workspace, experiment_name) hyperdrive_run = experiment.submit(hyperdrive_run_config) print(hyperdrive_run.get_portal_url())
```

It's easy to see that this technique can't be parallelized to thousands of machines in order to finish faster. However, due to the optimization step, it generally yields good results in a relatively short amount of time. Another issue is that the optimization technique used in Bayesian sampling requires each result of each run with the defined parameter configuration to compute the new parameter choices. Therefore, we can't use early termination together with Bayesian sampling, as the training would be stopped earlier, and therefore no accurate metric could have been computed.

Once you've played with the technique of using machine learning to optimize an ML model, a certain question might come to you: why should we stop at optimizing hyperparameters, and why shouldn't we optimize model choices, network structures, or model stacking altogether?

And this is a perfectly valid thought. No human can possibly test all variations of different ML models, different parameter configurations, and different nested models together.

Therefore, as a next step, we will look into the domain of Azure Automated Machine Learning in the next section.

Finding the optimal model with Azure Automated Machine Learning

Automated machine learning is an exciting new trend that many (if not all) cloud providers follow. The aim is to provide a service to users that automatically preprocesses your data, selects an ML model, and trains and optimizes the model to optimally fit your training data given a specific error metric. In this way, it will create and train a fully automated end-to-end ML pipeline that only needs your labeled training data as input. Here is a list of steps that Azure Automated Machine Learning optimizes for you:

- Data preprocessing
- Feature engineering
- Model selection
- Hyperparameter tuning
- Model ensembling

While most experienced machine learning engineers or data scientists would be very cautious about the effectiveness of such an automated approach, it still has a ton of benefits, which will be explained in this section. If you like the idea of hyperparameter tuning, then you will definitely find a lot of value in Azure Automated Machine Learning.

A good way to think about Azure Automated Machine Learning is that it performs a hyperparameter search over the complete end-to-end ML pipeline, similar to Bayesian optimization, but over a much larger parameter space. The parameters are now individual steps in the end-to-end ML pipeline, which should be automated. The great thing about Azure Automated Machine Learning is that instead of going through the dumb sampling of all possible parameter choices, it will predict how well certain preprocessing steps and models will perform on a dataset before actually training a model. This process is called **meta-learning** and will help the optimization process to yield great candidate solutions for the pipeline.

Advantages and benefits of Azure Automated Machine Learning

Let's evaluate the advantages of Azure Automated Machine Learning. If we look at the list of automated steps mentioned earlier, each one requires multiple days for an experienced data scientist to explore and apply it, even if they would end up only with the best-practice approach for each category, for example, replacing categorical variables with a label encoder. Even steps such as selecting the correct model, such as either LightGBM or XGBoost for gradient-based tree ensemble classification, are non-trivial, as they require experience and knowledge of both tools. Moreover, we all know that those two are only a tiny subset of all the possible options for a classification model. If we go up all the way to hyperparameter tuning and model stacking, we can immediately tell that the amount of work required to build a great ensemble model is non-trivial.

I want to emphasize that this is not only a knowledge problem. The key aim of Azure Automated Machine Learning is to replace manual steps with automated best practices, applying continuously improving rules and heavily optimizing every possible human choice. It's very similar to hyperparameter tuning but for the complete end-to-end process. A machine will find the best parameters much faster than a human simply by using optimization.

You are now through more than half of this book and you have learned the tips and tricks for how to build end-to-end ML pipelines on your own. We can also look at Azure Automated Machine Learning from a different perspective, namely as **machine learning as a service** (**MLaaS**). By now, you should be aware that each step of building an end-to-end ML pipeline is a thorough and complicated task. Even when you can choose the correct model and tuning parameters using Bayesian optimization, the cost of building this infrastructure and operating it is significant. In this case, choosing MLaaS would provide you with a machine learning infrastructure for a fraction of the usual cost.

There is another reason why the idea of Azure Automated Machine Learning is very interesting. It abstracts the machine learning part from your problem and leaves you with what every business should know best—data. Similar to using a managed service in the cloud (for example, a managed database), which lets you focus on implementing business logic rather than operating infrastructure, Azure Automated Machine Learning will allow you to use a managed ML pipeline built on best practices and optimization.

This also leads to the reason why Azure Automated Machine Learning is still a great fit for many (mature) companies—it reduces a prediction problem to the most important tasks:

- Data acquisition
- Data cleansing
- Data labeling
- Selecting an error metric

We don't want to blame anyone, but some machine learning engineers love to simply skip these topics and dive right into the fun parts, namely feature engineering, model selection, parameterization, and tuning. Therefore, a good start for every ML project is to actually start with Azure Automated Machine Learning, because you have to focus only on the data side and not worry at all about the machine learning side. After achieving a good initial score, you can always go ahead and start further feature engineering and build your own model if needed.

If you now agree that the Azure Automated Machine Learning trend is reasonable and that you could benefit from it in one way or another, we will now dive deep into some examples and code. We will look at the different capabilities of Azure automated machine learning, a product of Azure Machine Learning, as applied in a standard end-to-end ML pipeline.

Before we jump into the code, let's take a look at what problem Azure automated machine learning can tackle. In general, we can decide between classification, regression, and time- series forecasting in Azure Automated Machine Learning. As we know from the previous chapters, time-series forecasting is simply a variant of regression where all predicted values are in the future.

Hence, the most important task after choosing the correct ML task is choosing the proper error metric that should be optimized. The following table lists all error metrics that are supported right now:

Classification	Regression	Time-Series Forecasting
accuracy	spearman_correlation	spearman_correlation
AUC_weighted	normalized_root_mean_squared_error	normalized_root_mean_squared_error
average_precision_score_weighted	r2_score	r2_score
norm_macro_recall	normalized_mean_absolute_error	normalized_mean_absolute_error
precision_score_weighted		

Figure 9.5: A list of the error metrics

You should be familiar with most of these metrics as they are variants of the most popular error metrics for classification and regression. Once we have chosen our metric, we continue with preprocessing.

For completeness, here is a table of all possible models per task at the time of writing. The great thing about a managed service in the cloud is that this list will most likely grow in the future to add the most recent state-of-the-art models. However, this table should be thought of just as additional information for you, since the idea of Azure Automated Machine Learning is that the models are automatically chosen for you. However, according to the user's preferences, individual models from the list can be included or excluded for Azure Automated Machine Learning:

Classification	Regression	Time-Series Forecasting
LogisticRegression	ElasticNet	ElasticNet
SGD	GradientBoosting	GradientBoosting
MultinomialNaiveBayes	DecisionTree	DecisionTree
BernoulliNaiveBayes	KNN	KNN
SVM	LassoLars	LassoLars
LinearSVM	SGD	SGD
KNN	RandomForest	RandomForest
DecisionTree	ExtremeRandomTrees	ExtremeRandomTrees
RandomForest	LightGBM	LightGBM
ExtremeRandomTrees	TensorFlowLinearRegressor	TensorFlowLinearRegressor
LightGBM	TensorFlowDNN	TensorFlowDNN
GradientBoosting		Arima
TensorFlowDNN		Prophet
TensorFlowLinearClassifier		

Figure 9.6: A list of all supported models

With all this in mind, let's now look at a classification example using Azure Automated Machine Learning.

A classification example

When using new technology, it's always good to take a step back and think about what the technology could be theoretically capable of. Let's use the same approach to figure out how automated preprocessing could help us in a typical ML project and where its limitations will be.

Azure Automated Machine Learning is great in applying best-practice transformations to your dataset: applying date/time transformations, the normalization and standardization of your data when using linear regression, handling missing data or dropping low-variance features, and so on. There is a long list of features provided by Microsoft that is expected to grow in the future.

Let's recall *Chapter 6, Advanced feature extraction with NLP*. While Azure Automated Machine Learning can detect free text and convert it into a numeric feature vector, it won't be able to understand the semantic meaning of the data in your business domain. Therefore, it will be able to transform your textual data, but if you need semantic encoding of your text or categorical data, you have to implement that yourself.

Another thing to remember is that Azure Automated Machine Learning will not try to infer any correlations of different feature dimensions in your training data. Hence, if you want to combine two categorical columns into a combined feature column (for example, using one-hot-encoding, mean embedding, and so on), then you will have to implement this on your own.

In Azure Automated Machine Learning, there are two different sets of preprocessors—the **simple** ones and the **complex** ones. Simple preprocessing is just referred to as **preprocessing**. The *Figure 9.7* shows all simple preprocessing techniques that will be evaluated during Azure Automated Machine Learning training if the **preprocess** argument is specified. If you have worked with scikit-learn before, then most of the following preprocessing techniques should be fairly familiar to you:

Preprocessing Step	Description
StandardScaler	Normalization: mean subtraction and scaling feature to unit variance.
MinMaxScaler	Normalization: scaling feature to minimum and maximum.
MaxAbsScaler	Normalization: scaling feature by maximum absolute value.
RobustScaler	Normalization: scaling feature to quantile range.
PCA	Linear dimensionality reduction based on **principal component analysis** (**PCA**).
TruncatedSVD	Linear dimensionality reduction-based truncated **singular value decomposition** (**SVD**). Contrary to PCA, this estimator does not center the data beforehand.
SparseNormalizer	Normalization: each sample is normalized independently.

Figure 9.7: A list of supported preprocessing techniques

Complex preprocessing is referred to as **featurization**. These preprocessing steps are more complicated and apply various tasks during Azure Automated Machine Learning optimization. As a user of Azure automated machine learning, you can expect this list to grow and include new state-of-the- art transformations as they become available. The *Figure 9.8* lists the various featurization steps:

Featurization Step	Description
Drop high cardinality or no variance features	Drops high cardinality (for example, hashes, IDs, or GUIDs) or no variance (for example, all values missing or the same value across all rows) features.
Impute missing values	Imputes missing values for numerical features (mean imputation) and categorical features (mode imputation).
Generate additional features	Generates additional features derived from date/time (for example, year, month, day, day of the week, day of the year, quarter, week of the year, hour, minute, and second) and text features (term frequency based on n-grams).
Transform and encode	Encodes categorical features using one-hot encoding (low cardinality) and one-hot-hash encoding (high cardinality). Transforms numeric features with few unique values into categorical features.
Word embeddings	Uses a pre-trained embedding model to convert text into aggregated feature vectors using mean embeddings.
Target encodings	Performs target encoding on categorical features.
Text target encoding	Performs target encoding on text features using a bag-of-words model.
Weight of evidence	Calculates the correlation of categorical columns to the target column through the weight of evidence and outputs a new feature per column per class.
Cluster distance	Trains a k-means clustering model on all numerical columns and computes the distance of each feature to its centroid and outputs a new feature per column per cluster.

Figure 9.8: A list of supported featurization steps

Let's start with a simple classification task that also uses preprocessing:

1. We start by defining a dictionary containing the Azure Automated Machine Learning configuration. To enable standard preprocessing such as scaling, normalization, and PCA/SVD, we need to set the **preprocess** property to true. For advanced preprocessing and feature engineering, we need to set the featurization property to auto. The following code block shows all the settings:

    ```
    automl_settings = { "experiment_timeout_minutes" : 15,
    "n_cross_validations": 3, "primary_metric": 'accuracy', "featurization":
    'auto', "preprocess": True, "verbosity": logging.INFO,
    }
    ```

2. Using this configuration, we can now load a dataset using pandas. As you can see in the following snippet, we load the **titanic** dataset and specify the target column as a string. This column is required later for the Azure Automated Machine Learning configuration:

    ```
    import pandas as pd
    df = pd.read_csv("train.csv")
    target_column = "survival"
    ```

    > **Note**
    >
    > When using Azure Automated Machine Learning and the local execution context, you can use a pandas DataFrame as the input source. However, when you execute the training on a remote cluster, you need to wrap the data in an Azure Machine Learning dataset.

3. Whenever we use a black-box classifier, we should also hold out a test set to verify the test performance of the model in order to validate generalization. Therefore, we split the data into train and test sets:

    ```
    from sklearn.model_selection import train_test_split df_train, df_test =
    train_test_split(df, test_size=0.2)
    ```

4. Finally, we can supply all the required parameters to the Azure Automated Machine Learning configuration constructor. In this example, we use a local execution target to train the Azure Automated Machine Learning experiment. However, we can also provide an Azure Machine Learning dataset and submit the experiment to our training cluster:

   ```
   from azureml.train.automl import AutoMLConfig automl_config = AutoMLConfig(
       task='classification',
       debug_log='debug.log',
       compute_target=local_target,
       training_data=df_train,
       label_column_name=target_column,
       **automl_settings)
   ```

5. Let's submit the Azure Automated Machine Learning configuration as an experiment to the defined compute target and wait for completion. We can output the run details:

   ```
   from azureml.widgets import RunDetails

   automl_run = experiment.submit(automl_config, show_output = False)
   RunDetails(automl_run).show()
   ```

   Similar to **HyperDriveConfig**, we can see that **RunDetails** for Azure Automated Machine Learning shows a lot of useful information about your current experiment. Not only can you see all of your scheduled and running models, but you also get a nice visualization for the trained models and their training performance. The *Figure 9.9* shows the accuracy of the first 14 runs of the Azure Automated Machine Learning experiment:

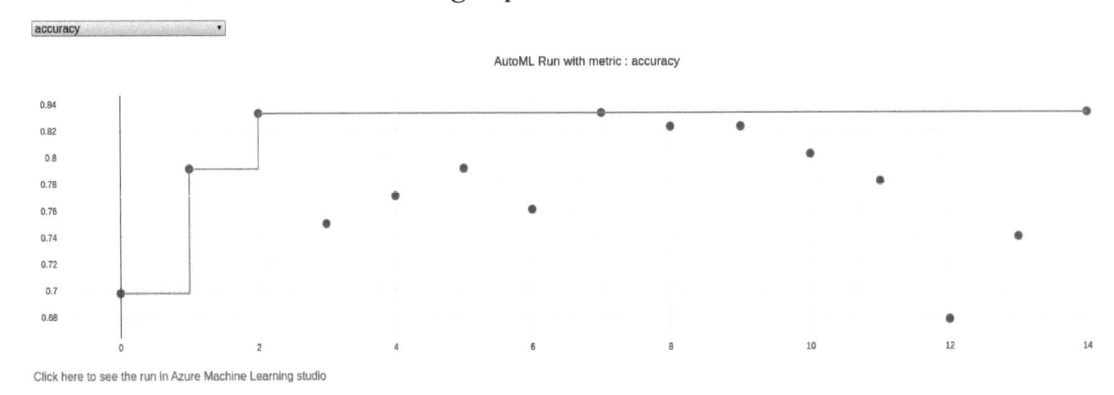

Figure 9.9: The accuracy of the first 14 runs of Azure Automated Machine Learning

6. Finally, after 15 minutes, we can retrieve the best ML pipeline from the Azure Automated Machine Learning run. From now on, we will refer to this pipeline simply as the **model**, as all preprocessing steps are packed into the model, which itself is a pipeline of operations. We use the following code to retrieve the pipeline:

   ```
   best_run, best_model = remote_run.get_output()
   ```

7. The resulting fitted pipeline (called **best_model**) can now be used exactly like a scikit-learn estimator. We can store it to disk, register it to the model store, deploy it to a **Container** instance, or simply evaluate it on the test set. We will see this in more detail in *Chapter 12, Deploying and operating machine learning models*. Finally, we want to evaluate the best model. To do so, we take the testing set that we separated from the dataset beforehand and predict the output on the fitted model:

   ```
   from sklearn.metrics import accuracy_score

   y_test = df_test[target_column]
   X_test = df_test.drop(target_column, axis=1) y_pred = fitted_model.
   predict(X_test)

   accuracy_score(y_test, y_pred)
   ```

In the preceding code, we used the **accuracy_score** function from scikit-learn to compute the accuracy of the final model. These steps are all you need to perform classification on a dataset using automatically preprocessed data and fitted models.

Summary

In this chapter, we introduced hyperparameter tuning (through HyperDrive) and Azure Automated Machine Learning. We observe that both techniques can help you to efficiently retrieve the best model for your ML task.

Grid sampling works great with classical ML models, and also when the number of tunable parameters is fixed. All values on a discrete parameter grid are evaluated. In random sampling, we can apply a continuous distribution for the parameter space and select as many parameter choices as we can fit into the configured training duration. Random sampling performs better on a large number of parameters. Both sampling techniques can/should be tuned using an early stopping criterion.

Unlike random and grid sampling, Bayesian optimization probes the model performance in order to optimize the following parameter choices. This means that each set of parameter choices and the resulting model performance are used to compute the next best parameter choices. Therefore, Bayesian optimization uses machine learning to optimize parameter choices for your ML model. Due to the fact that the underlying Gaussian process requires the resulting model performance, early stopping does not work with Bayesian optimization.

We learned that Azure Automated Machine Learning is a generalization of Bayesian optimization on the complete end-to-end ML pipeline. Instead of choosing only hyperparameters, we also choose pre-processing, feature engineering, model selection, and model stacking methods and optimize those together. Azure Automated Machine Learning speeds up this process by predicting which models will perform well on your data instead of blindly trying all possible combinations. Both techniques are essential for a great ML project; Azure Automated Machine Learning lets you focus on the data and labeling first, while hyperparameter tuning lets you optimize a specific model.

In the next chapter, we will take a look at training deep neural networks where the data or the model parameters don't fit into the memory of a single machine anymore, and therefore distributed learning is required.

10
Distributed machine learning on Azure

In the previous chapter, we learned about hyperparameter tuning, through search and optimization using HyperDrive as well as Azure Automated Machine Learning, as a special case of hyperparameter optimization, involving feature engineering, model selection, and model stacking. Automated machine learning is **machine learning as a service** (**MLaaS**) where the only input is your data, a ML task, and an error metric. It's hard to imagine running all the experiments and parameter combinations for Azure Automated Machine Learning on a single machine or a single CPU/GPU—we are looking into ways to speed up the training process through parallelization and distributed computing.

In this chapter, we will take a look into distributed and parallel computing algorithms and frameworks for efficiently training ML models in parallel. The goal of this chapter is to build an environment in Azure where you can speed up the training process of classical ML and **deep learning** (**DL**) models by adding more machines to your training environment, thereby scaling out the cluster.

First, we will take a look at the different methods and fundamental building blocks for distributed ML. You will grasp the difference between training independent models in parallel, as done in HyperDrive and Azure Automated Machine Learning, and training a single model ensemble on a large dataset in parallel by partitioning the training data. We then will look into distributed ML for single models and discover the data-distributed and model-distributed training methods. Both methods are often used in real-world scenarios for speeding up or enabling the training of large **deep neural networks (DNNs)**.

After that, we will discover the most popular frameworks for distributed ML and how they can be used in Azure and in combination with Azure Machine Learning compute. The transition between execution engines, communication libraries, and functionality for distributed ML libraries is smooth but often hard to understand. However, after reading this chapter, you will understand the difference between running Apache Spark in Databricks with MLlib and using Horovod, Gloo, PyTorch, and TensorFlow parameter server.

In the final section, we will take a look at two practical examples of how to implement the functionality we'll be covering in Azure and integrate it with Azure Machine Learning compute.

This chapter covers the following topics:

- Exploring methods for distributed ML
- Using distributed ML in Azure

Exploring methods for distributed ML

The journey of implementing ML pipelines is very similar for a lot of users, and is often similar to the steps described in the previous chapters. When users start switching from experimentation to real-world data or from small examples to larger models, they often experience a similar issue: training large parametric models on large amounts of data—especially DL models—takes a very long time. Sometimes, epochs last hours and training takes days to converge.

Waiting hours or even days for a model to converge means precious time wasted for many engineers, as it makes it a lot harder to interactively tune the training process. Therefore, many ML engineers need to speed up their training process by leveraging various distributed computing techniques. The idea of distributed ML is as simple as speeding up a training process by adding more compute resources. In the best case, the training performance improves linearly by adding more machines to the training cluster (scaling out). In this section, we will take a look at the most common patterns of distributed ML and try to understand and reason about them. In the next section of this chapter, we will also apply them to some real-world examples.

Most modern ML pipelines use some of the techniques discussed in this chapter to speed up the training process once their data or models become larger. This is similar to the need for big data platforms—like Spark, Hive, and so on—for data preprocessing, once the data gets large. Hence, while this chapter seems overly complex, I would recommend revisiting the chapter anytime you are waiting for your model to converge or want to produce better results faster.

There are generally three patterns for leveraging distributed computing for ML:

- Training independent models in parallel
- Training copies of a model in parallel on different subsets of the data
- Training different parts of the same model in parallel

Let's take a look at each of these methods.

Training independent models on small data in parallel

We will first look at the easiest example, training (small) independent models on a (small) dataset. A typical use case for this parallel training is performing a hyperparameter search or the optimization of a classic ML model or a small neural network. This is very similar to what we covered in the previous chapter. Even Azure Automated Machine Learning—where multiple individual independent models are trained and compared—uses this approach under the hood. In parallel training, we aim to speed up the training of multiple independent models with different parameters by training these models in parallel.

Figure 10.1 shows this case, where instead of training the individual models in sequence on a single machine, we train them in parallel:

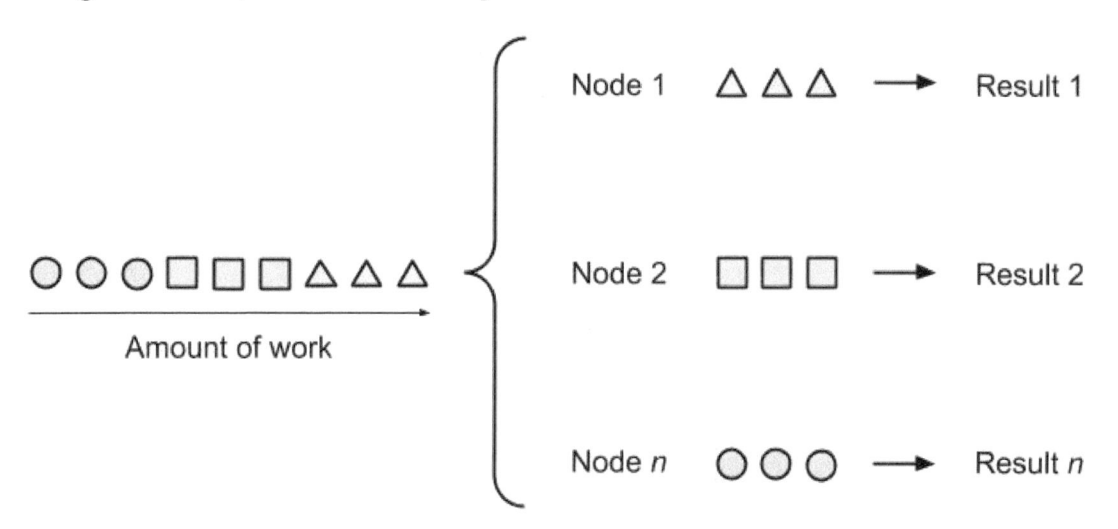

Figure 10.1: Training the model in parallel

You can see that no communication or synchronization is required during the training process of the individual models. This means that we can train either on multiple CPUs/GPUs on the same machine or on multiple machines.

When using Azure Machine Learning for hyperparameter tuning, this parallelization is easy to achieve by configuring an Azure Machine Learning compute target with multiple nodes and selecting the number of concurrent runs through the **max_concurrent_runs** parameter of the HyperDrive configuration. In Azure Machine Learning HyperDrive, all it takes is to specify an estimator and **param_sampling**, and submit the HyperDrive configuration as an experiment in order to run the individual task in parallel, as shown here:

```
from azureml.train.hyperdrive import HyperDriveConfig hyperdrive_run_config = HyperDriveConfig(estimator=estimator,
    hyperparameter_sampling=param_sampling,
    primary_metric_name="accuracy",
    primary_metric_goal=PrimaryMetricGoal.MAXIMIZE,
    max_total_runs=100,
    max_concurrent_runs=4)
from azureml.core.experiment import Experiment = Experiment(workspace, experiment_name)
hyperdrive_run = experiment.submit(hyperdrive_run_config)
```

Here are some formulas to compute the value for **max_concurrent_runs** for HyperDrive or any other distributed computing setup:

- For CPU-based training, we can train at least N_{total} models concurrently if every node has enough memory for the training data and model parameters using the following equation:

$$N_{total} = N_{cores} \times (N_{nodes} - 1), \text{if } (N_{nodes} - 1) \times M_{model} + M_{data} < M_{node}$$
$$N_{cores} = number\ of\ cores\ per\ node$$
$$N_{nodes} = number\ of\ nodes$$
$$M_{model} = memory\ consumed\ per\ model$$
$$M_{data} = memory\ for\ training\ data$$
$$M_{node} = total\ memory\ per\ node$$

Figure 10.2: The number of models for CPU-based training

- For GPU-based training, the number of concurrent models, N_{total}, is computed in the same way, given that each node has enough GPU memory available:

$N_{total} = N_{cores} \times (N_{nodes} - 1), \text{if } (N_{nodes} - 1) \times M_{model} + M_{data} < M_{node}$
$N_{cores} = \textit{number of cores per node}$
$N_{nodes} = \textit{number of nodes}$
$M_{model} = \textit{GPU memory consumed per model}$
$M_{data} = \textit{GPU memory for training data}$
$M_{node} = \textit{total GPU memory per node}$

Figure 10.3: The number of models for GPU-based training

Here is a guide to how to estimate how much memory a single model will consume in memory:

- Size of a single parameter:

    Half-precision float: 16 bits (2 bytes)

    Single-precision float: 32 bits (4 bytes)–this is often the default

    Double-precision float: 64 bits (8 bytes)

- Number of parameters required for a model:

    Parametric model: *sum of all parameters*

    Non-parametric model: *number of representations (for example, decision trees) * number of a representation's parameters*

- Then you multiply additional factors:

    Models using backpropagation: *overall memory * 2*

    Models using batching: *overall memory * batch size*

    Models using (recurrent) states: *memory per state * number of recurrent steps*

While this use case seems very similar, let's move on to the next use case where we are given a large dataset that cannot be copied onto every machine.

Training a model ensemble on large datasets in parallel

The next thing we will discuss is a very common optimization within ML, particularly when training models on large datasets. In order to train models, we usually require a large amount of data, which rarely all fits into the memory of a single machine. Therefore, it is often required to split the data into chunks and train multiple individual models on the different chunks.

The *Figure 10.4* shows two ways of splitting data into smaller chunks—by splitting the rows horizontally (left) or by splitting the columns vertically (right):

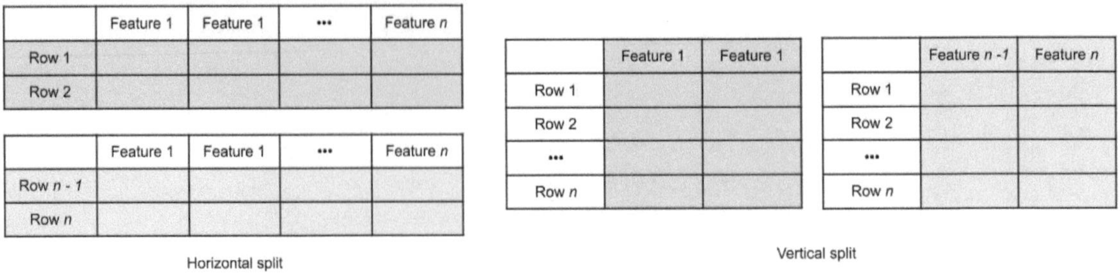

Figure 10.4: Horizontal versus vertical partitioning

You could also mix both techniques to extract a subset from your training data. Whenever you are using tools from the big data domain, such as MapReduce, Hive, or Spark, partitioning your data will help you to speed up your training process or enable training over huge amounts of data in the first place.

A good example for performing data-distributed training is to train a massive tree ensemble of completely separate decision tree models, also called a **random forest**. By splitting the data into many thousands of randomized chunks, you can train one decision tree per chunk of data and combine all of the trained trees into a single ensemble model. Apache Hivemall is a library based on Hive and Spark that does exactly this on either of the two execution engines. Here is an example of training multiple XGBoost multi-class ensemble models on Hive using HiveQL and Apache Hivemall:

```
-- explicitly use 3 reducers
-- set mapred.reduce.tasks=3;

create table xgb_softmax_model as select
train_xgboost(features, label,
'-objective multi:softmax -num_class 10 -num_round 10') as (model_id, model)
from (
select features, (label - 1) as label from data_train
cluster by rand(43) -- shuffle data to reducers
) data;
```

In the preceding function, we use the **cluster** keyword to randomly move rows of data to the reducers. This will partition the data horizontally and train an XGBoost model per partition on each reducer. By defining the number of reducers, we also define the number of models trained in parallel. The resulting models are stored in a table where each row defines the parameters of one model. In a prediction, we would simply combine all individual models and perform average-voting criterion to retrieve the final result.

Another example of this approach would be a standard Spark pipeline that trains multiple independent models on vertical and horizontal data partitions. When we've finished training the individual models, we can use average-voting criterion during inference to find the optimal result for a prediction task. Here is a small example script of training multiple models on horizontally partitioned data in parallel using Python, PySpark, and scikit-learn:

```
# read the input data
df = spark.read.parquet("data/")


# define your training function
from sklearn.ensemble import RandomForestClassifier def train_model(data):
    clf = RandomForestClassifier(n_estimators=10)
    return clf.fit(data['train_x'], data['train_y'])


# split your data into partitions and train models num_models = 100

models = df.rdd.repartition(num_models)
    .mapPartitions(train_model)
    .collect()
```

In the preceding function, we can now load almost any amount of data and repartition it such that each partition fits into the local memory of a single node. If we have 1 TB of training data, we could split it into 100 partitions of 10 GB chunks of data, which we distribute over 10 12-core worker nodes with 128 GB RAM each. The training time will, at most, take a couple of seconds for the training of the 100 models in parallel. Once all the models are trained, we use the **collect()** function to return all trained models to the head node.

We could have also decided to just store the models from each individual worker to disk or in a distributed filesystem, but it might be nicer to just combine the results on a single node. You see, in this example, we have the freedom to choose either of the two methods, because all models are independent of each other. This is not true for cases where the models are suddenly dependent on each other, for example, when minimizing a global gradient, or splitting a single model over multiple machines, which are both common use cases when training DNNs in the same way. In this case, we need some new operators to steer the control flow of the data and gradients. Let's look into these operators in the following section.

Fundamental building blocks for distributed ML

As we saw in the previous example, we need some fundamental building blocks or operators to manage the data flow in a distributed system. We call these operators **collective algorithms**. These algorithms implement common synchronization and communication patterns for distributed computing and are required when training ML models. Before we jump into distributed training methods for DNNs, we will have a quick look into these patterns to understand the foundations.

The most common communication patterns in distributed systems are as follows:

- One-to-one
- One-to-many (also called *broadcast* or *scatter*)
- Many-to-one (also called *reduce* or *gather*)
- Many-to-many (also called *all reduce* or *all gather*)

Figure 10.5 gives a great overview of these patterns and shows how the data flows between the individual actors of the system:

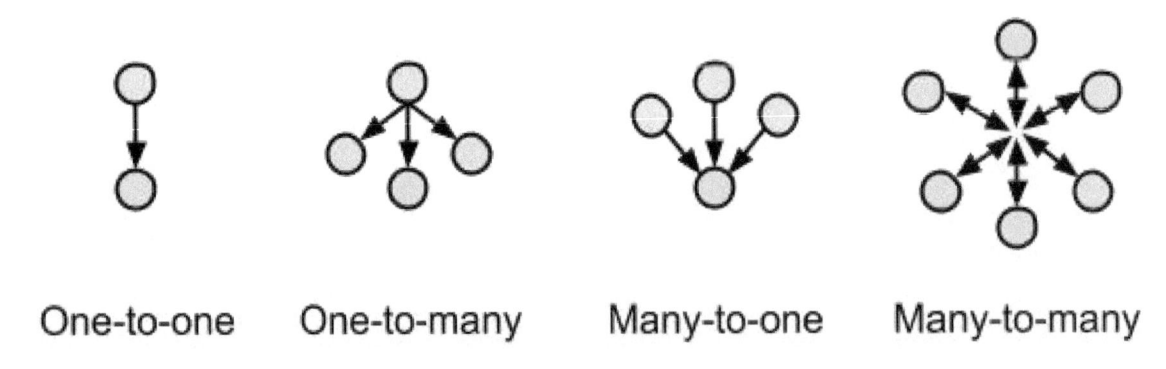

Figure 10.5: An overview of distributed communication primitives

We can immediately think back to the hyperparameter optimization technique of Bayesian optimization. First, we need to **broadcast** the training data from the master to all worker nodes. Then we can choose parameter combinations from the parameter space on the master and **broadcast** those to the worker nodes as well. Finally, we perform the training on the worker nodes, before then **gathering** all the model validation scores from the worker nodes on the master. By comparing the scores and applying Bayes' theorem, we can predict the next possible parameter combinations and repeat **broadcasting** them to the worker nodes.

Did you notice something in the preceding algorithm? How can we know that all worker nodes finished the training process and we gathered all scores from all worker nodes? To do this, we will use another building block called **synchronization**, or **barrier synchronization**. With barrier synchronization, we can schedule the execution of a task such that it needs to wait for all other distributed tasks to be finished. The following *Figure 10.6* shows a good overview of the synchronization pattern in multi-processors:

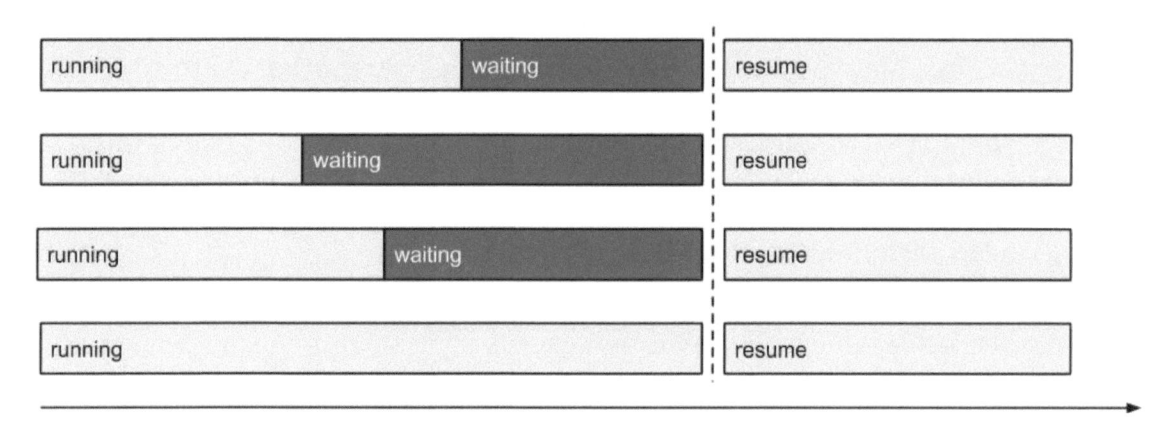

Figure 10.6: Synchronization pattern in multi-processors

As you can see, we implicitly used these algorithms already in the previous chapter, where they were hidden from us behind the term **optimization**. Now we will use them explicitly by changing the optimizers in order to train a single model over multiple machines.

As you might have already realized, these patterns are not new and are used by your operating system many times per second. However, in this case, we can take advantage of these patterns and apply them to the execution graph of a distributed training process, and through specialized hardware (for example, by connecting two GPUs together using InfiniBand).

In order to use this collective algorithm with a different level of hardware support (GPU support and vectorization), you need to select a communication backend. These backends are libraries that often run as a separate process and implement communication and synchronization patterns. Popular libraries for collective algorithms include Gloo, MPI, and NCCL.

Most DL frameworks, such as PyTorch or TensorFlow, provide their own higher-level abstractions on one of these communication backends, for example, PyTorch RPC and TensorFlow parameter server. Instead of using a different execution and communication framework, you could also choose a general-purpose framework for distributed computing, such as Spark.

As you can see, the list of possible choices is endless and multiple combinations are possible. We haven't even talked about Horovod, a framework used to add distributed training to other DL frameworks through distributed optimizers. The good part is that most of these frameworks and libraries are provided in all Azure Machine Learning runtimes as well as being supported through the Azure Machine Learning SDK. This means you will often only specify the desired backend, supply your model to any specific framework, and let Azure Machine Learning handle the setup, initialization, and management of these tools. We will see this in action in the second half of this chapter.

Speeding up DL with data-parallel training

Another variation of distributed data-parallel training is very common in DL. In order to speed up the training of larger models, we can run multiple training iterations with different chunks of data on distributed copies of the same model. This is especially crucial when each training iteration takes a significant amount of time (for example, multiple seconds), which is a typical scenario for training large DNNs where we want to take advantage of multi-GPU environments.

Data-distributed training for DL is based on the idea of using a distributed gradient descent algorithm:

1. Distribute a copy of the model to each node.
2. Distribute a chunk of data to each node.
3. Run a full pass through the network on each node and compute the gradient.
4. Collect all gradients on a single node and compute the average gradient.
5. Send the average gradient to all nodes.
6. Update all models using the average gradient.

The *Figure 10.7* shows this in action for multiple models, running the forward/backward pass individually and sending the gradient back to the parameter server:

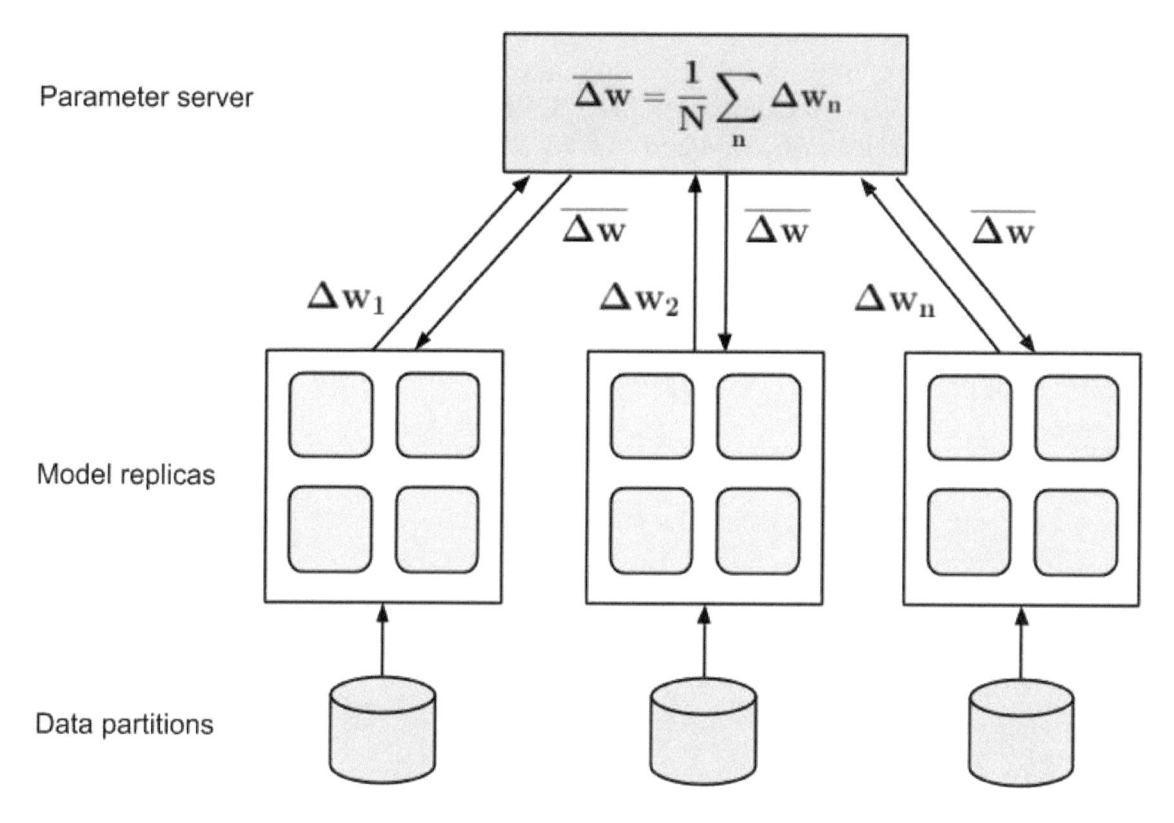

Figure 10.7: Distributed gradient descent using a parameter server

As seen here, the server computes the average gradient, which is sent back to all other nodes. We can immediately see that, all of a sudden, communication is required between the worker nodes and a master node (let's call it the parameter server), and that synchronization is required too while waiting for all models to finish computing the gradient.

A great example of this use case is speeding up the training process of DL models by parallelizing the backpropagation step and combining the gradients from each node to an overall gradient. TensorFlow currently supports this distribution mode using a so-called **parameter server**. The Horovod framework developed at Uber provides a handy abstraction for distributed optimizers and plugs into many available ML frameworks or distributed execution engines, such as TensorFlow, PyTorch, and Apache Spark. We will take a look at practical examples of using Horovod and Azure Machine Learning in the *Horovod – a distributed DL training framework* section.

Training large models with model-parallel training

Lastly, another common use case in DL is to train models that are larger than the provided GPU memory of a single GPU. This approach is a bit more tricky as it requires the model execution graph to be split among different GPUs or even different machines. While this is not a big problem in CPU-based execution, and is often done in Spark, Hive, or TensorFlow, we also need to transfer the intermediate results between multiple GPU memories. In order to do this effectively, extra hardware and drivers such as InfiniBand (GPU-to-GPU communication) and GPUDirect (efficient GPU memory access) is required.

The *Figure* 10.8 displays the difference between computing multiple gradients in parallel (on the left) and computing a single forward pass of a distributed model (on the right):

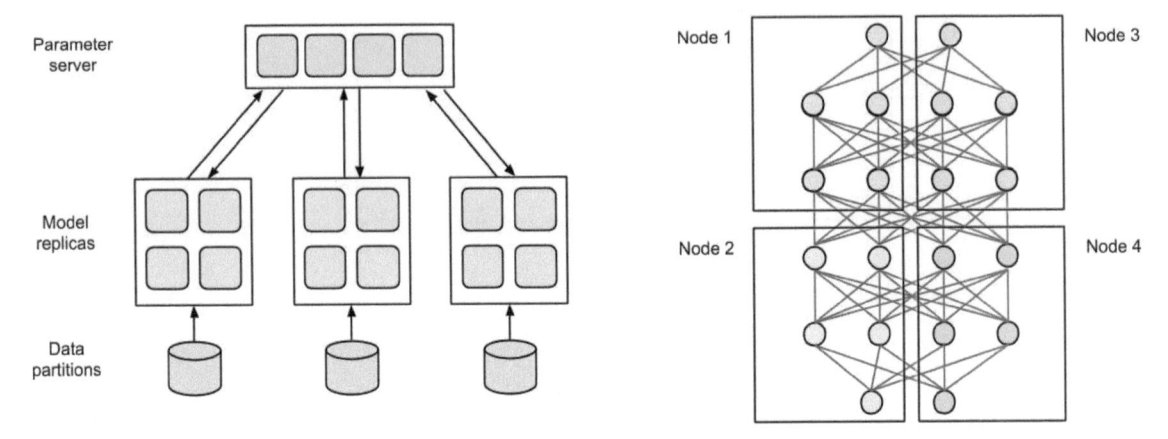

Figure 10.8: The difference between distributed gradient descent and a distributed model

The latter is a lot more complicated as data has to be exchanged during forward and backward passes between multiple GPUs and/or multiple nodes.

In general, we choose between two scenarios: multi-GPU training on a single machine and multi-GPU training on multiple machines. As you might expect, the latter is a lot more difficult, as it requires communication between and the synchronization of multiple machines over a network.

Here is a simple Python script to train a small model on multiple GPUs using PyTorch:

```python
import torch
import torch.nn as nn
import torch.optim as optim
class ParallelModel(nn.Module):
    def init (self):
        super(ParallelModel, self). init ()
        self.net1 = torch.nn.Linear(10, 10).to('cuda:0')
        self.relu = torch.nn.ReLU()
        self.net2 = torch.nn.Linear(10, 5).to('cuda:1')
    def forward(self, x):
        x = self.relu(self.net1(x.to('cuda:0')))
        return self.net2(x.to('cuda:1'))
model = ParallelModel() loss_fn = nn.MSELoss()
optimizer = optim.SGD(model.parameters(), lr=0.001)
optimizer.zero_grad()
outputs = model(torch.randn(20, 10))
labels = torch.randn(20, 5).to('cuda:1')
loss_fn(outputs, labels).backward()
optimizer.step()
```

As you can see, we now split individual layers to run on multiple GPUs, while the data between these layers needs to be transferred during forward and backward passes. We observe in the preceding code example that we now apply code changes to the model itself, in order to specify which parts of the model should run on which GPU.

> **Note**
> Please note that we could also make this split dynamic, such that we split the model into x consecutive subgraphs that are executed on x GPUs.

It's interesting to note that many of the techniques discussed in this chapter can be combined. We could, for example, train one multi-GPU model per machine, while partitioning the data into chunks and computing multiple parts of the gradient on multiple machines—hence adopting a data-distributed model-parallel approach.

Using distributed ML in Azure

The *Exploring methods for distributed ML* section contained an overwhelming amount of different parallelization scenarios, various communication backends for collective algorithms, and code examples using different ML frameworks and even execution engines. The amount of choice when it comes to ML frameworks is quite large and making an educated decision is not easy. This choice gets even more complicated when some frameworks are supported out of the box in Azure Machine Learning while others have to be installed, configured, and managed by the user.

In this section, we will go through the most common scenarios, learn how to choose the correct combination of frameworks, and implement a distributed ML pipeline in Azure.

In general, you have three choices for running distributed ML in Azure:

- The first obvious choice is using Azure Machine Learning, the Notebook environment, the Azure Machine Learning SDK, and Azure Machine Learning compute clusters. This will be the easiest solution for many complex use cases. Huge datasets can be stored on Azure Blob storage and models can be trained as data-parallel and/or model-parallel models with different communication backends. Everything is managed for you by wrapping your training script with an estimator abstraction.

- The second choice is to use a different authoring and execution engine for your code instead of Azure Machine Learning notebooks and Azure Machine Learning compute clusters. A popular option is Azure Databricks with integrated interactive notebooks and Apache Spark as a distributed execution engine. Using Databricks, you can use the pre-built ML images and auto scaling clusters, which provides a great environment for running distributed ML training.

- The third choice is to build and roll out your own custom solution. To do so, you need to build a separate cluster with virtual machines or Kubernetes and orchestrate the setup, installation, and management of the infrastructure and code. While this is the most flexible solution, it is also, by far, the most complex and time consuming to set up. For this book, we will first look into Horovod optimizers, Azure Databricks, and Apache Spark before diving deeper into Azure Machine Learning.

Horovod—a distributed DL training framework

Horovod is a framework for enabling distributed DL and was initially developed and made open source by Uber. It provides a unified way to support the distributed training of existing DL training code for the following supported frameworks—TensorFlow, Keras, PyTorch, and Apache MXNet. The design goal was to make the transition from single node training to data-parallel training extremely simple for any existing project, and hence enable these models to train faster on multiple GPUs in a distributed environment.

Horovod is an excellent choice as a drop-in replacement for optimizers in any of the supported frameworks for data-parallel training. It integrates nicely with the supported frameworks through initialization and update steps or update hooks, by simply abstracting the GPUs from the DL code. From a user's perspective, only minimal code changes have to be done to support data-parallel training for your model. Let's take a look at an example using Keras and implement the following steps:

1. Initialize Horovod.
2. Configure Keras to read GPU information from Horovod.
3. Load a model and split training data.
4. Wrap the Keras optimizer as a Horovod distributed optimizer.
5. Implement model training.
6. Execute the script using horovodrun.

The detailed steps are as follows:

1. The first step is very similar for any script using Horovod—we first need to load **horovod** from the correct package and initialize it:

    ```
    import horovod.keras as hvd hvd.init()
    ```

2. Next, we need to perform a custom setup step, which varies depending on the framework used. This step will set up the GPU configuration for the framework, and ensure that it can call the abstracted versions through Horovod:

    ```
    from keras import backend as K
    import tensorflow as tf
    # pin GPU to be used to process local rank (one GPU per process) config = tf.ConfigProto()
    config.gpu_options.allow_growth = True config.gpu_options.visible_device_list = str(hvd.local_rank()) K.set_session(tf.Session(config=config))
    ```

3. Now, we can simply take our single-node, single-GPU Keras model and define all the parameters, and the training and validation data. There is nothing special required during this step:

   ```
   # standard model and data
   batch_size = 10
   epochs = 100
   model = load_model(...)
   x_train, y_train = load_train_data(...) x_test, y_test = load_test_
   data(...)
   ```

4. Finally, we arrive at the magical part, where we wrap the framework optimizer—in this case, **Adadelta** from Keras—as a Horovod distributed optimizer. For all subsequent code, we will simply use the distributed optimizer instead of the plain one. We also need to adjust the learning rate to the number of used GPUs, as the resulting gradient will be averaged from the individual changes. This can be done using the following code:

   ```
   # adjust learning rate based on number of GPUs opt = keras.optimizers.
   Adadelta(1.0 * hvd.size())

   # add Horovod Distributed Optimizer opt = hvd.DistributedOptimizer(opt)
   ```

5. The remaining part looks fairly simple. It involves compiling the model, fitting the model, and evaluating the model, just like the single-node counterpart. It's worth mentioning that we need to add a callback to initialize all gradients during the training process:

   ```
   model.compile(loss=keras.losses.categorical_crossentropy, optimizer=opt,
   metrics=['accuracy'])
   callbacks = [
       hvd.callbacks.BroadcastGlobalVariablesCallback(0),
   ]
   model.fit(x_train, y_train,
       batch_size=batch_size,
       callbacks=callbacks, epochs=epochs,
       verbose=1 if hvd.rank() == 0 else 0,
       validation_data=(x_test, y_test))
   score = model.evaluate(x_test, y_test)
   print('Test loss:', score[0])
   print('Test accuracy:', score[1])
   ```

When looking at the preceding code, it's fair to say that Horovod is not over-promising on making it easy to extend your code for distributed execution using a data-parallel approach and distributed gradient computation. If you have looked into the native TensorFlow or PyTorch versions, you will see that this requires far fewer code changes and is a lot more readable and portable than a parameter server or RPC framework.

The Horovod framework uses an MPI communication backend to handle collective algorithms under the hood, and usually requires one running process per GPU per node. However, it can also run on top of the Gloo backend or a custom MPI backend through a configuration option. Here is a sample snippet of how to use the **horovodrun** command to start a training process on two machines, **server1** and **server2**, each using four separate GPUs:

```
$ horovodrun -np 8 -H server1:4,server2:4 python train.py
```

Running and debugging Horovod on your own cluster can still be painful when you only want to speed up your training progress by scaling out your cluster. Therefore, Azure Machine Learning compute provides a wrapper that does all the heavy lifting for you, requiring only a training script with Horovod annotations. We will see this in the *Running Horovod on Azure Machine Learning compute* section.

Model-parallel training can be combined with Horovod by using the model-parallel features of the underlying framework and using only one Horovod process per machine instead of per GPU. However, this is a custom configuration and is currently not supported in Azure Machine Learning.

Implementing the HorovodRunner API for a Spark job

In many companies, ML is an additional data processing step on top of existing data pipelines. Therefore, if you have huge amounts of data and you are already managing Spark clusters or using Azure Databricks to process that data, it is easy to also add distributed training capabilities.

As we have seen in the *Exploring methods for distributed ML* section of this chapter, we can simply train multiple models using parallelization, or by partitioning the training data. However, we could also train DL models and benefit from distributed ML techniques to speed up the training process.

When using the Databricks ML runtime, you can leverage Horovod for Spark to distribute your training process. This functionality is available through the **HorovodRunner** API and is powered by Spark's barrier mode execution engine to provide a stable communication backend for long-running jobs. Using **HorovodRunner** on the head node, it will send the training function to the workers and start the function using the MPI backend. This all happens under the hood within the Spark process.

Again, this is one of the reasons why Horovod is quite easy to use, as it is literally just a drop-in replacement for your current optimizer. Imagine that you usually run your Keras model on Azure Databricks using the PySpark engine. However, you would like to add Horovod to speed up the training process by leveraging other machines in the cluster and splitting the gradient descent over multiple machines. In order to do so, you would have to add literally only two lines of code to the example from the previous section, as seen here:

```
hr = HorovodRunner(np=2)
def train():
    # Perform your training here..
    import horovod.keras as hvd
    hvd.init()
    ...
hr.run(train)
```

In the preceding code, we observe that we only need to initialize **HorovodRunner()** with the number of worker nodes. Calling the **run()** method with the training function will automatically start the new workers, the MPI communication backend, send the training code to the workers, and execute the training in parallel. Therefore, you can now add data- parallel training to your long-running Spark ML jobs.

Running Horovod on Azure Machine Learning compute

One of the benefits of moving to a cloud service is that you can consume functionality as a service rather than managing infrastructure on your own. Good examples are managed databases, lambda functions, managed Kubernetes, or container instances, where choosing a managed service means that you can focus on your application code, while the infrastructure is managed for you in the cloud.

Azure Machine Learning sits in a similar spot where you can consume many of the different functionalities through an SDK (such as model management, optimization, training, and deployments) so you don't have to maintain an ML cluster infrastructure. This brings a huge benefit when it comes to speeding up DNNs through distributed ML. If you have stuck with Azure Machine Learning compute until now, then moving to data-parallel training is as difficult as adding a single parameter to your training configuration—for any of the various choices discussed in this chapter.

Let's think about running the Keras training script in data-parallel mode using a Horovod optimizer in a distributed environment. You need to make sure all the correct versions of your tools are set up (from CUDA to cuDNN, GPUDirect, MPI, Horovod, TensorFlow, and Keras) and play together nicely with your current operating system and hardware. Then, you need to distribute the training code to all machines, start the MPI process, and then call the script using Horovod and the relevant command-line argument on every machine in the cluster. And we haven't even talked about authentication, data access, or auto-scaling.

With Azure Machine Learning, you get a ML environment that just works and will be kept up to date for you. Let's take a look at the previous Horovod and Keras training script, which we store in a **train.py** file. Now, similar to the previous chapters, we create an estimator to wrap the training call for the Azure Machine Learning SDK. To enable multi-GPU data-parallel training using Horovod and the MPI backend, we simply add the relevant parameters. The resulting script looks like the following snippet:

```
from azureml.train.dnn import TensorFlow, Mpi

estimator = TensorFlow(source_directory=project_folder,
    compute_target=compute_target, entry_script='train.py',
    script_params=script_params, node_count=2,
    distributed_training=Mpi(process_count_pernode=1),
    pip_packages=['keras'],
    framework_version='1.13',
    use_gpu=True)
```

Using the **use_gpu** flag, we can enable GPU-specific machines and their corresponding images with pre-compiled binaries for our Azure Machine Learning compute cluster. Using **node_count** and **process_count_per_node**, we specify the level of concurrency for the data-parallel training, where **process_count_per_node** should correspond with the number of GPUs available per node. Finally, we set the **distributed_backend** parameter to **mpi**, to enable the MPI communication backend for this estimator. Another possible option would be using **ps** to enable the TensorFlow **ParameterServer** backend.

Finally, to start up the job, we simply submit the experiment, which will automatically set up the MPI session on each node and call the training script with the relevant arguments for us. I don't know how you feel about this, but for me, this is a really big step forward from the previous manual examples. The following line shows how you can submit the experiment:

```
run = experiment.submit(estimator)
```

Wrapping your training as part of an Azure Machine Learning estimator gives you the benefit of fine- tuning your training script configuration for multiple environments, be it multi-GPU data- parallel models for distributed gradient descent training or single-node instances for fast inference. By combining distributed DL with Azure Machine Learning compute auto-scaling clusters, you can get the most from the cloud by using pre-built managed services, instead of manually fiddling with infrastructure and configurations.

Summary

Distributed ML is a great approach to scaling out your training infrastructure in order to gain speed in your training process. It is applied in many real-world scenarios and is very easy to use with Horovod and Azure Machine Learning.

Parallel execution is similar to hyperparameter search, while distributed execution is similar to Bayesian optimization, which we discussed in detail in the previous chapter. Distributed executions need methods to perform communication (such as one-to-one, one- to-many, many-to-one, and many-to-many) and synchronization (such as barrier synchronization) efficiently. These so-called collective algorithms are provided by communication backends (MPI, Gloo, and NCCL) and allow efficient GPU-to-GPU communication.

DL frameworks build higher-level abstractions on top of communication backends to perform model-parallel and data-parallel training. In data-parallel training, we partition the input data to compute multiple independent parts of the model on different machines and add up the results in a later step. A common technique in DL is distributed gradient descent, where each node performs gradient descent on a partition of the input batch, and a master collects all the separate gradients to compute the overall average gradient of the combined model. In model-parallel training, you distribute a single model over multiple machines. This is often the case when a model doesn't fit into the GPU memory of a single GPU.

Horovod is an abstraction on top of existing optimizers of other ML frameworks, such as TensorFlow, Keras, PyTorch, and Apache MXNet. It provides an easy-to-use interface to add data-distributed training to an existing model without many code changes. While you could run Horovod on a standalone cluster, Azure Machine Learning provides good integration by wrapping its functionality as an estimator object. You learned how to run Horovod on an Azure Machine Learning compute cluster to speed up your training process through distributed ML with a few lines of Horovod initialization and a wrapper over the current optimizer.

In the next chapter, we will use all the knowledge from the previous chapters to train recommendation engines on Azure. Recommendation engines often build on top of other NLP feature extraction or classification models and hence combine many of the techniques we have learned about so far.

11
Building a recommendation engine in Azure

In the previous chapter, we discussed distributed training methods for **machine learning** (**ML**) models, and you learned how to train distributed ML models efficiently in Azure. In this chapter, we will dive into traditional and modern recommendation engines, which often combine technologies and techniques covered in the previous chapters.

First, we will take a quick look at the different types of recommendation engines, what data is needed for each type, and what can be recommended using these different approaches.

This will help you understand when to choose from non-personalized, content-based, or rating-based recommenders.

After this, we will dive into content-based recommendations, namely item-item and user- user recommenders based on feature vectors and similarity. You will learn about cosine distance to measure the similarity between feature vectors and feature engineering techniques to avoid common pitfalls while building content-based recommendation engines.

Subsequently, we will discuss rating-based recommendations that can be used once enough user-item interaction data has been collected. You will learn the difference between implicit and explicit ratings, develop your own implicit metric function, and think about the recency of user ratings.

In the section following this, we will combine both content-and rating-based recommenders into a single hybrid recommender and learn about state-of-the-art techniques for modern recommendation engines. You will implement two hybrid recommenders using Azure Machine Learning, one using Python and one using Azure Machine Learning designer—the graphical UI of Azure Machine Learning.

In the last section, we will look into an online recommender system as a service using reinforcement learning—Azure Personalizer. Having understood both content- and rating- based methods, you will learn how to improve your recommendations on the fly using a fitness function and online learning.

The following topics will be covered in this chapter:

- Introduction to recommender engines
- Content-based recommendations
- Collaborative filtering—a rating-based recommendation engine
- Combining content and ratings in hybrid recommendation engines
- Automatic optimization through reinforcement learning

Introduction to recommender engines

In today's digital world, recommendation engines are ubiquitous among many industries. Many online businesses, such as streaming, shopping, news, and social media, rely at their core on recommending the most relevant articles, news, and items to their users. How often have you clicked on a suggested video on YouTube, scrolled through your Facebook feed, listened to a personalized playlist on Spotify, or clicked on a recommended article on Amazon?

If you ask yourself what the term *relevant* means for the different services and industries, you are on the right track. In order to recommend relevant information to the user, we need to first define a relevancy metric, and a way to describe and compare different items and their similarity. These two properties are the key to understanding the different recommendation engines. We will learn more about this in the following sections of this chapter.

While the purpose of a recommendation engine is clear to most people, the different approaches are usually not. Hence, in order to better understand this, in this chapter, we will compare the different types of recommender systems and give some examples of them that you might have seen in the wild. It's also worth mentioning that many services implement more than one of these approaches to produce great recommendations.

The easiest recommendation engines and methods are *non-personalized* recommendations. They are often used to show global interest (for example, Twitter global trends, popular Netflix shows, and a news website's front page) or trends where no user data is available. A good example is the recommendations of any streaming service that appear when you register and log into the service for the first time.

Once you log into a web service and start using it moderately, you are usually confronted with *content-based* recommendations. Content-based recommenders look for similar items or items of similar users based on the item and user profile features. User profile items could include the following:

- Age
- Gender
- Nationality
- Country of residence
- Mother tongue

Imagine logging into Amazon without having bought anything there yet. Most recommended items will be similar to the ones you just viewed or the ones matching your demographics and location.

Once enough interaction data is available, you will start seeing *rating-based* recommendations, a method that is also called collaborative filtering. In rating-based recommenders, the users' interactions with items are transformed into explicit or implicit ratings. Based on these ratings, recommendations are made based on similar recommendations given by other users. Rating a movie on Netflix is an explicit rating, while watching a full 20-minute documentary on YouTube is an implicit rating. Therefore, a user will be shown movies liked by other people who also liked the movie that you just rated. And similarly, YouTube will show videos watched by other users who also watched the video you just saw.

> **Note**
>
> Microsoft provides many different implementations for popular recommendation engines in their GitHub repository at https://github.com/Microsoft/Recommenders. This makes it easy to get started, pick the right algorithm, and implement, train, and deploy a recommendation engine on Azure.

The next natural step is to combine both content and rating-based recommenders into a single *hybrid recommendation* engine that can deal with both user ratings and cold-start users who are users, without ratings. The benefit of this approach is that both recommender systems are optimized together and create a combined recommendation. Azure Machine Learning designer provide the building blocks to train and deploy the Matchbox Recommender, an online Bayesian hybrid recommendation engine built by Microsoft Research.

The most exciting new development in the past year was the introduction of hybrid online recommender optimization based on reinforcement learning. By providing a fitness function for the user rating, the algorithm can continuously learn to optimize this function. In the last section of this chapter, we will take a look at Azure Personalizer, a reinforcement learning-based recommendation engine as a service.

Let's dive right into the methods discussed and develop some example solutions for scalable recommendation engines in Azure.

Content-based recommendations

We first start with content-based recommendations, as they are the most similar to what we previously discussed in this book. The term *content* refers to the usage of only an item's or user's content information in the shape of a (numeric) feature vector. The way to arrive at a feature vector from an item (an article in a web shop) or a user (a browser session in a web service) is through data mining, data pre-processing and feature engineering—skills you learned in *Chapter 4, ETL, data preparation, and feature extraction*, and *Chapter 6, Advanced feature extraction with NLP*.

Using users' and items' feature vectors, we can divide content-based recommendations into roughly two approaches:

- Item-item similarity
- User-user similarity

Hence, recommendations are based on the similarity of items or the similarity of users. Both approaches work great in cases where little to no interaction data between user and items is available for example, a user with no purchase history on Amazon, no search history on YouTube, or no movies yet watched on Netflix—the so-called cold-start problem.

You will always have to deal with the cold-start problem the moment you decide to roll out recommendations or the moment a new user starts using your service. In both cases, you don't have sufficient user-item interactions (so-called ratings) available and need to recommend items based on content only.

For the first approach, we design a system that recommends similar items to the one a user interacts with. The item similarity is based on the similarity of the item's feature vectors—we see in the subsequent section how to compute this similarity. This approach can be used when absolutely no user interaction data is available. The *Figure 11.1* visualizes this approach of recommending similar items based on content features and a single user interaction:

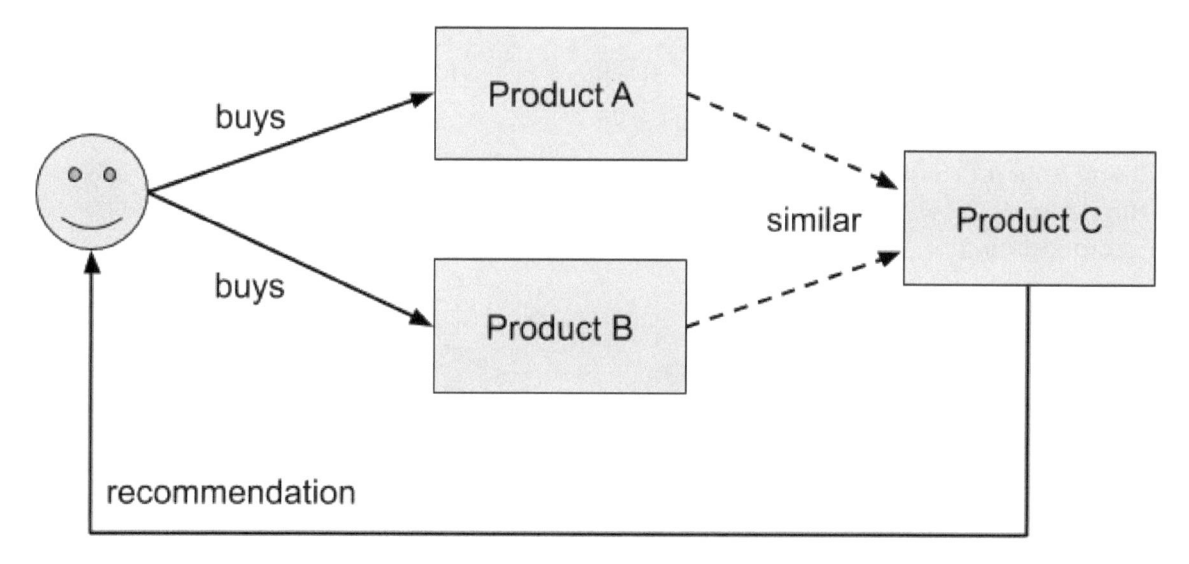

Figure 11.1: Recommendation based on content features

Creating a playlist on Spotify will yield a box with recommended songs in the bottom, as shown in *Figure 11.2*. We can see that the recommended songs are based on the songs in the playlist—hence, similar content:

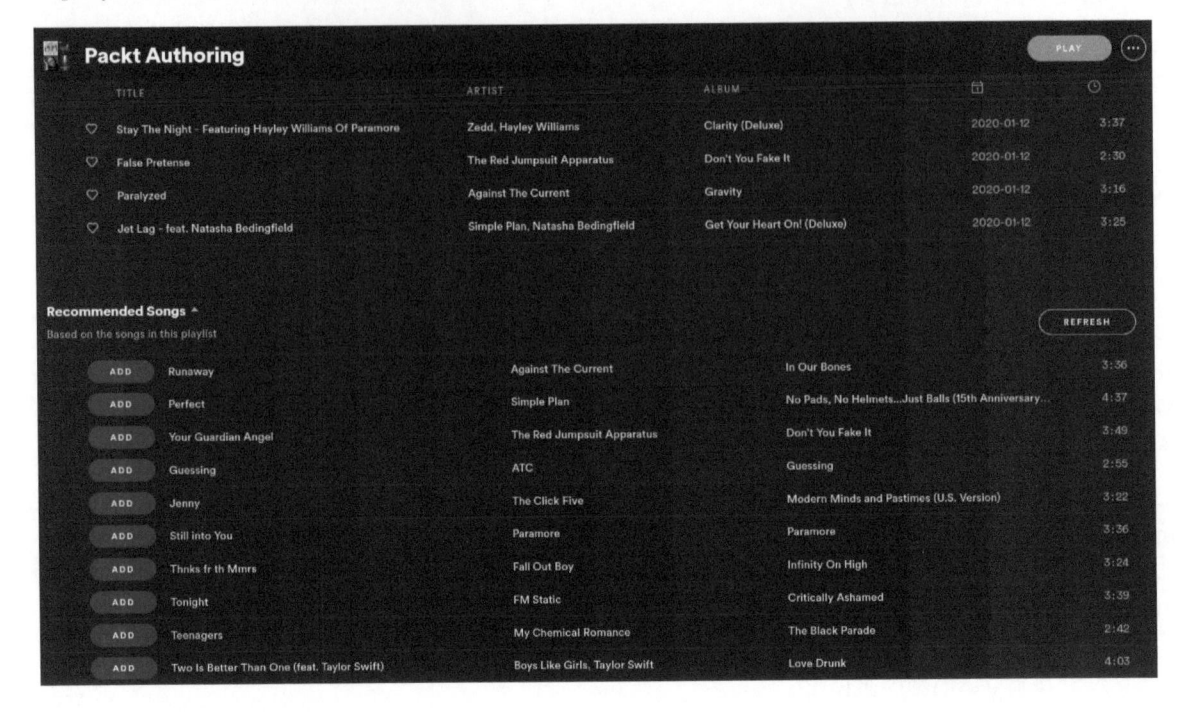

Figure 11.2: An example of content-based recommendation: Spotify-recommended songs for a playlist

We can see songs listed that are similar to the ones in the playlist—similar in terms of genre, style, artists, and many more features.

Clicking on a product on Amazon will yield a box with related products on the bottom of the page, as shown in *Figure 11.3*. Again, similar products means it is a content-based recommendation:

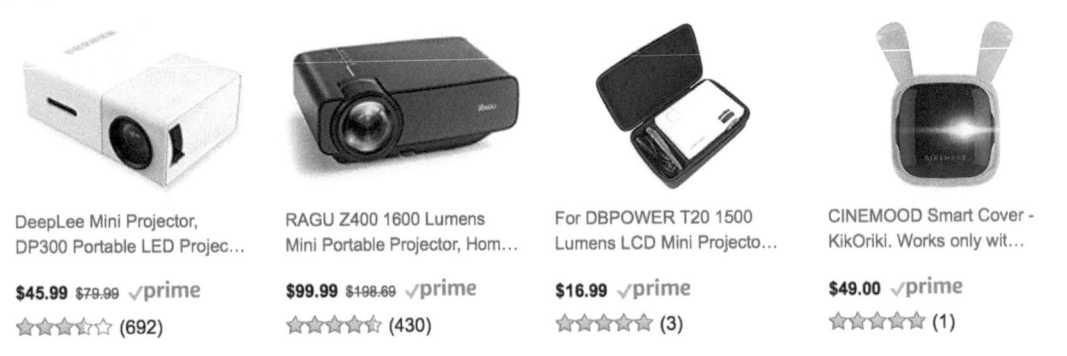

Figure 11.3: An example of content-based recommendation: related products on Amazon

This recommendation has nothing to do with your previous shopping experience and can be displayed even when no user-purchase history is found.

In the second approach, the system recommends similar users based on a user profile. From those similar users, we can then select the favorite items and present it as a recommendation. Please note that in digital systems, the user profile can be implicitly defined via location (for example, through an IP address), language, demographic, and device fingerprinting. This technique can be used when user-item interaction data is available from other users but not for the current user. The *Figure 11.4* visualizes this recommendation of the purchases of a similar user based on user features:

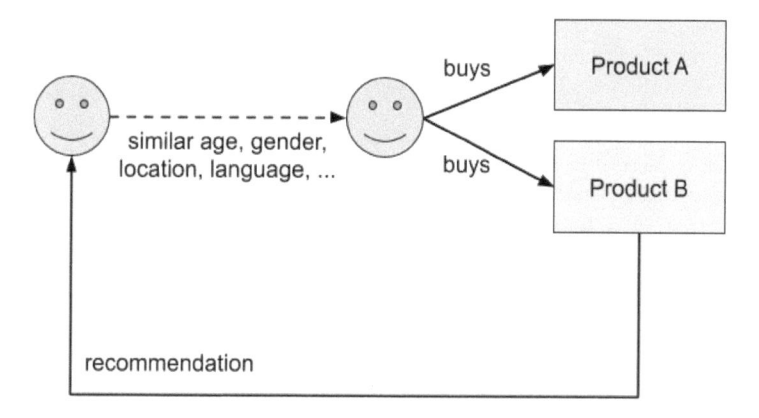

Figure 11.4: Recommendation based on user features

From a user's perspective, it is usually hard to distinguish between this kind of recommendation and a non-personalized recommendation, for example, the top products in your location for your demographic or your language—all properties that can be extracted from your browser's fingerprint.

Measuring similarity between items

The crucial part of training a content-based recommendation engine is to specify a metric that can measure and rank the similarity between two items. A popular choice is to use the cosine distance between the items' feature vectors to measure the similarity between two items. The cosine distance is computed as $1 - \cos(f_1, f_2)$ between two vectors or 1 minus the cosine similarity. The *Figure 11.5* shows two numeric feature vectors and the cosine distance between them:

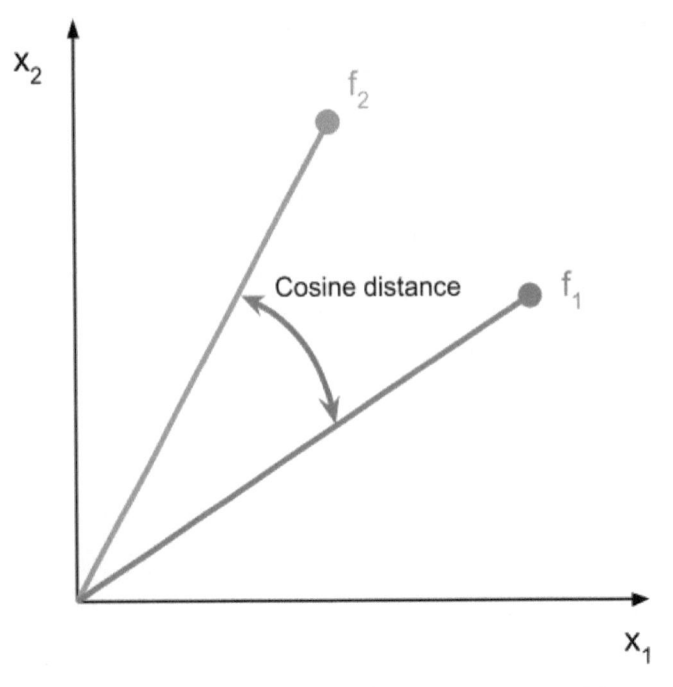

Figure 11.5: A representation of two numeric feature vectors and the cosine distance

Hence, the cosine distance of two feature vectors yields a value between 0, where both vectors are pointing in the same direction, and 1, where both vectors are orthogonal to each other. We conclude that at value 0, the feature vectors are the same, whereas at value 1, the feature vectors are completely different.

If you are unsure, you can always compute the cosine distance between two feature vectors using the following code (make sure that your DataFrame **df** has no additional id column and all columns are numeric):

```
from scipy import spatial
f1 = df.iloc[0, :]
f2 = df.iloc[1, :]
# compute the cosine distance between the first 2 rows
cosine_d = spatial.distance.cosine(f1, f2)
print(cosine_d)
```

Looking at the preceding snippet, I recommend you pick a few rows from your dataset, estimate their similarity (0 if they are the same, 1 if they are completely different), and then compute the cosine distance using the aforementioned approach. If your guess and the computed approach are very different and you don't understand the reason, you'd better go back to data pre-processing and feature engineering. In the next section, you will learn the most common mistakes in feature engineering for recommender systems.

Feature engineering for content-based recommenders

Training a content-based recommendation engine is very similar to training a classical ML model. For the end-to-end ML pipelines, all the steps, such as data preparation, training, validation, optimization, and deployment, are exactly the same and use very similar or even the same tools and libraries as any traditional embedding, clustering, regression, or classification technique.

As for most other ML algorithms, great feature engineering is the key for good results from the recommendation engine. The difficulty for clustering-based recommenders is that most of the embeddings and similarity metrics only work in numeric space. While other techniques, such as tree-based classifiers, give you more freedom in the structure of the input data, many clustering techniques require numeric features.

Another important factor for training content-based recommenders is the semantic meaning of categorical features. Therefore, you most likely want to use advanced NLP methods to embed categorical features into numerical space to capture this semantic meaning and provide it for the recommendation engine. The reason for the effect of categorical features in recommendation systems is based on the way similarity is measured.

As we discussed in the previous section, similarity is often expressed/measured as cosine similarity, and hence computing the cosine between two feature vectors. Therefore, even if there is only a single different character between two categorical values, those categorical values would yield a similarity of 0 using one-hot encoding– although they are semantically very similar. Using simple label encoding, the results are even less obvious. With label encoding, the resulting similarity is now not only 0, but a non-interpretable value different from 0.

Therefore, we recommend semantic embedding of nominal/textual variables in order to capture their semantic meaning in numeric space and avoid common pitfalls with categorical embeddings leaking into the similarity metric.

In general, there are two possible ways to implement content-based recommenders. If you are looking for a pure similarity search, you can use any non-supervised embedding and clustering technique for finding similar items or users. The second possibility is to implement the recommender as a regression or classification technique. With this, you can predict a discrete or continuous value of relevance for all items, solely considering item features or combinations of item and user features. We will take a look at an example method in the subsequent section.

Content-based recommendations using gradient boosted trees

For our content-based model, we will use the Criteo dataset to predict the **click-through rate (CTR)** per article based on some article features. We will use the predicted CTR to recommend articles with the highest predicted CTR. As you can see, it's very simple to formulate a content-based recommendation engine as a standard classification or regression problem.

For this example, we will use a gradient-boosted tree regressor from LightGBM. The model to predict the CTR is very similar to any regression model previously trained in this book. Let's get started:

1. First, we define the parameters for the LightGBM model:

    ```
    params = {
        'task': 'train',
        'boosting_type': 'gbdt',
        'num_class': 1,
        'objective': "binary",
        'metric': "auc",
        'num_leaves': 64,
        'min_data': 20,
        'boost_from_average': True,
        'feature_fraction': 0.8,
        'learning_rate': 0.15,
    }
    ```

2. Next, we define the training and test set as LightGBM datasets:

    ```
    lgb_train = lgb.Dataset(x_train, y_train.reshape(-1), params=params)
    lgb_test = lgb.Dataset(x_test, y_test.reshape(-1), reference=lgb_train)
    ```

3. Using this information, we can now train the model:

    ```
    lgb_model = lgb.train(params, lgb_train, num_boost_round=100)
    ```

4. Finally, we can evaluate the model performance by predicting the CTR and computing the area under the ROC curve as an error metric:

    ```
    y_pred = lgb_model.predict(x_test)
    auc = roc_auc_score(np.asarray(y_test.reshape(-1)), np.asarray(y_pred))
    ```

Great—you have learned to create recommendations based on item similarities. However, these recommendations have a poor diversity and will only recommend similar items.

Therefore, they can be used when no user-item interaction data is available, but will perform poorly once the user is active on your service. A better recommendation engine would recommend a variety of different items to help users explore and discover new and unrelated items they might like. This is exactly what we will do with collaborative filtering in the next section.

Collaborative filtering—a rating-based recommendation engine

By recommending only similar items or items from similar users, your users might get bored of the recommendations provided due to the lack of diversity and variety. Once a user starts interacting with a service, for example, watching videos on YouTube, reading and liking posts on Facebook, or rating movies on Netflix, we want to provide them with great personalized recommendations and relevant content to keep them happy and engaged. A great way to do so is to provide a good mix of similar content and new content to explore and discover.

Collaborative filtering is a popular approach for providing such diverse recommendations by comparing user-item interactions, finding other users who interact with similar items, and recommending items that those users also interacted with. It's almost as if you were to build many custom stereotypes and recommend other items consumed from the same stereotype. *Figure 11.6* illustrates this example:

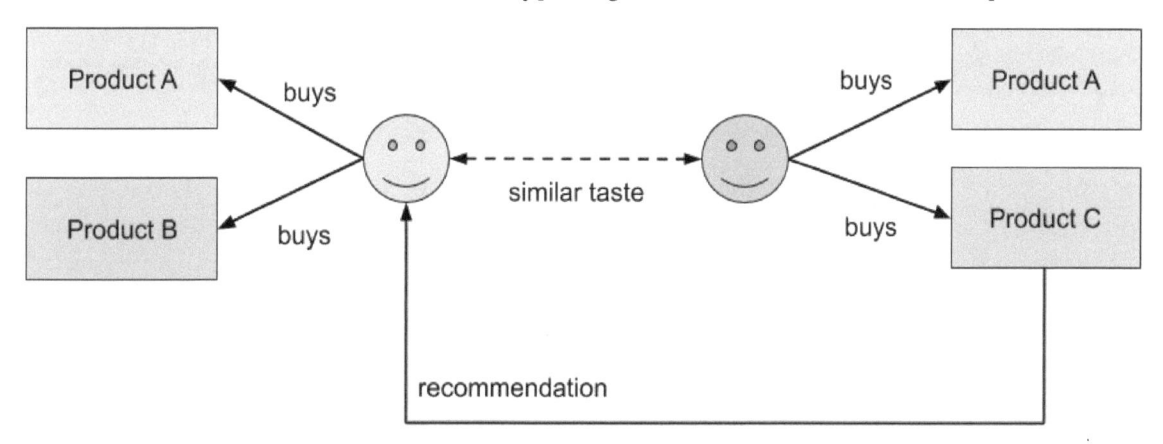

Figure 11.6: Collaborative filtering—rating-based recommendation

As the person on the left buys similar items to the person on the right, we can recommend a new item to the person on the right that the person on the left bought. In this case, the user-item interaction is a person buying a product. However, in recommender language, we speak about ratings as a term summarizing all possible interactions between a user and an item. Let's take a look at building such a rating function (also called a feedback function).

One great example for amazing rating-based recommendations are the personalized recommended playlists in Spotify, as shown in *Figure 11.7*. In contrast to the previous Spotify recommendation at the bottom of each playlist, these recommendations are personalized based on my interaction history and feedback:

Figure 11.7: An example of rating-based recommendation: Spotifys Made For You playlists

These playlists contain songs similar to the ones I listened to and that are also listened to by other people with my taste. Another nifty extension is that the song recommendations are categorized by genre into these six playlists.

What is a rating? Explicit feedback as opposed to implicit feedback

A feedback function (or rating) quantifies the interaction between a user and an item. We differentiate between two types of feedback: explicit ratings (or non-observable feedback) and implicit ratings (or directly observable feedback). An explicit rating would be leaving a 5-star review of a product on Amazon, whereas an implicit rating is buying said product.

While the former is a biased decision of the user, the latter can be objectively observed and evaluated.

The most obvious form of rating is to explicitly ask the user for feedback, for example, to rate a certain movie, song, article, or the helpfulness of a support document. This is the method most people think about when first implementing recommendations engines. In the case of an explicit rating, we cannot directly observe the user's sentiment but rely on the user's ability to quantify their sentiment with a rating, such as rating a movie on an ordinal scale from 1 to 5.

There are many problems with explicit ratings—especially on ordinal scales (for example, stars from 1 to 5)—that we should consider when building our feedback function. Most people will have a bias when rating items on an ordinal scale, for example, some users might rate a movie 3/5 if they are unsatisfied and 5/5 if they liked the movie, while other users might rate 1/5 for a bad movie, 3/5 for a good one and only very rarely 5/5 for an exceptional one.

Therefore, the ordinal scales either need to be normalized across users or you'll need to use a binary scale (such as thumbs up/thumbs down) to collect binary feedback. Binary feedback is usually much easier to handle as we can remove the user bias from the feedback function, simplify the error metric, and therefore provide better recommendations. Many popular streaming services nowadays collect binary (thumbs up/thumbs down, star/unstar, and so on) feedback.

Here is a little snippet to help normalize user ratings. It applies a normalization across each group of user ratings:

```python
import numpy as np


def normalize_ratings(df, rating_col="rating", user_col="user"):
    groups = df.groupby(user_col)[rating_col]

    # computes group-wise mean/std
    mean = groups.transform(np.mean)
    std = groups.transform(np.std)

    return (df[rating_col] - mean) / std
df["rating_normalized"] = normalize_ratings(df)
```

Another popular way to train recommender systems is to build an implicit feedback function based on the direct observation of an implicit user rating. This has the benefit that the user feedback is unbiased. Common implicit ratings include the user adding an item to the cart, the user buying the item, the user scrolling to the end of the article, the user watching the full video to the end, and so on.

One additional problem to consider is that the way a user interacts with items will change over time. This could be due to a user's habit due to consuming more and more items on the service or changing user preferences. Recommending a video to you that you once liked in your childhood might not be helpful to another adult. Similar to this user drift, the popularity of items will also change over time. Recommending the song *Somebody that I used to know* to a user today might not lead to the same effect as in 2011. Therefore, we also have to consider time and temporal drift in our item ratings and feedback function.

The time drift of explicit or implicit ratings can be modeled using an exponential time decay on the numeric rating. Depending on the business rules, we could, for example, use explicit ratings with a binary scale [1, -1] and exponentially decay these ratings with a half- life time of 1 year. Hence, after 1 year, a rating of 1 becomes 0.5, after 2 years, it becomes 0.25, and so on. Here is a snippet to exponentially decay your ratings:

```
import numpy as np


def cumsum_days(s, duration='D'):
    diff = s.diff().astype('timedelta64[%s]' % duration)
    return diff.fillna(0).cumsum().values
def decay_ratings(df, decay=1, rating_col="rating", time_col="t"):
    weight = np.exp(-cumsum_days(df[time_col]) * decay)
    return df[rating_col] * weighthalf_life_t = 1
half_life_t = 1
df["rating_decayed"] = decay_ratings(df, decay=np.log(2)/half_life_t)
```

We learned that the choice of a proper feedback function matters greatly and is as important for designing a rating-based recommendation engine as feature engineering is for content-based recommenders.

Predicting the missing ratings to make a recommendation

Everything we have until now is a sparse user-item-rating matrix that looks similar to the *Figure 11.8*. However, in order to make a recommendation, we first need to fill the unknown ratings displayed gray in the diagram. Collaborative filtering is about filling the blank rows or columns of the user-item-ratings matrix depending on the prediction use case.

To recommend the best movie for Alice, we only need to compute the first row of the rating matrix, whereas to compute the best candidates for Terminator, we only need to compute the last column of the matrix. It is important to know that we don't have to compute the whole matrix all the time, which helps to significantly improve the recommendation performance:

	Titanic	Matrix	...	Terminator
Alice	5		...	3
Bob		4	...	5
...	...	...	...	...
Chris	3		...	

Figure 11.8: A user item ratings matrix

You can also probably already guess that this matrix will get really, really large as the number of users and/or items grows. Therefore, we need an efficient parallelizable algorithm for computing the blank ratings in order to make a recommendation. The most popular method to solve this problem is to use of matrix factorization and, hence, decompose the matrix into a product of two lower dimensional matrices. These two matrices and their dimensions can be interpreted as user trait and item trait matrices; by way of analogy, the dimension refers to the number of different distinct traits—the so called latent representation.

Once the latent representation is known, we can fill the missing ratings by multiplying the correct rows and columns from the latent trait matrices. A recommendation can then be made by using the top n highest computed ratings. But that's enough of the theory – let's look at an example using the **Alternating Least Square (ALS)** method to perform the matrix factorization in PySpark. Apart from the method, everything else in the pipeline is exactly the same as in a standard ML pipeline.

Similar to all previous pipelines, we also compute a training and testing set for validating the model performance using a grouped selection algorithm (for example, LevePGroupsOut, and GroupShuffleSplit), perform training, optimize the hyperparameters, validate the model test performance, and eventually stack multiple models together. As in many other methods, most models are trained using gradient descent. We can also use a standard regression loss function, such as the **Root Mean Square Error (RMSE)**, to compute the fit of our recommendations on the test set. Let's dive into the example.

Scalable recommendations using ALS factorization

To train a large collaborative filtering model using matrix factorization, we need an algorithm that is easily distributable. The ALS algorithm of the Spark MLlib package is an excellent choice—however, many other algorithms for factorizing matrices are available, such as Bayesian personalized ranking, FastAI EmbeddingDotBias, or neural collaborative filtering.

> **Note**
>
> A summary of example applications using the preceding methods can be found on Microsoft's GitHub repository at https://github.com/Microsoft/Recommenders.

By using Spark, precisely PySpark—the Python bindings for Spark and its libraries—we can take advantage of the distribution framework of Spark. While it's possible to run Spark on a single-node, single-core process locally, it can be easily distributed to a cluster with hundreds and thousands of nodes. Hence, it is a good choice as your code automatically becomes scalable if your input data scales and exceeds the memory limits of a single node:

1. Let's first create and parametrize an ALS estimator in PySpark using MLlib, the standard ML library of Spark. We find ALS in the recommendation package of MLlib:

   ```
   from pyspark.ml.recommendation import ALS n_iter = 10
   rank = 10
   l2_reg = 1
   als = ALS().setMaxIter(n_iter).setRank(rank).setRegParam(l2_reg)
   ```

   In the preceding code, we initialize the ALS estimator and define the number of iterations for gradient descent optimization, the rank of the latent trait matrices, and the L2 regularization constant.

2. Next, we fit the model using this estimator:

   ```
   model = als.fit(train_data)
   ```

3. That's all we have to do. Once the model is successfully trained, we can now predict the ratings for the test set by calling the transform function on the trained model:

   ```
   y_test = model.transform(test_data)
   ```

4. To compute the performance of the recommendations, we use a regression evaluator and the rmse metric as a scoring function:

   ```
   from pyspark.ml.evaluation import RegressionEvaluator scoring_fn = RegressionEvaluator(
   metricName="rmse", labelCol="rating", predictionCol="prediction")
   ```

5. To compute the rmse score, we simply call the evaluate method on the scoring function:

   ```
   rmse = scoring_fn.evaluate(y_test)
   ```

Great—you successfully implemented a rating-based recommendation engine with a collaborative filtering approach by factorizing the user-item-ratings matrix. Have you realized that this approach is similar to finding the eigenvectors of a matrix and that these eigenvectors could be interpreted as user stereotypes (or user tastes, traits, and so on)?

While this approach is great for creating diverse recommendations, it requires the availability of (many) user-item ratings. Therefore, it would work great in a service with a lot of user interaction and poorly with completely new users (the cold-start problem).

Combining content and ratings in hybrid recommendation engines

Instead of seeing rating-based recommenders as a successor to content-based recommenders, you should consider them as a different recommender after having acquired enough user-item interaction data to provide rating-only recommendations. In most practical cases, a recommendation engine will exist for both approaches—either as two distinct algorithms or as a single hybrid model. In this section, we will look into training such a hybrid model.

Building a state-of-the-art recommender using the Matchbox Recommender

To build a state-of-the-art recommender using the Matchbox Recommender, we open Azure Machine Learning Designer, and add the building blocks for the Matchbox Recommender to the canvas as shown in *Figure 11.9*. As we can see, the recommender can now take ratings, and user and item features, as inputs to create a hybrid recommendation model:

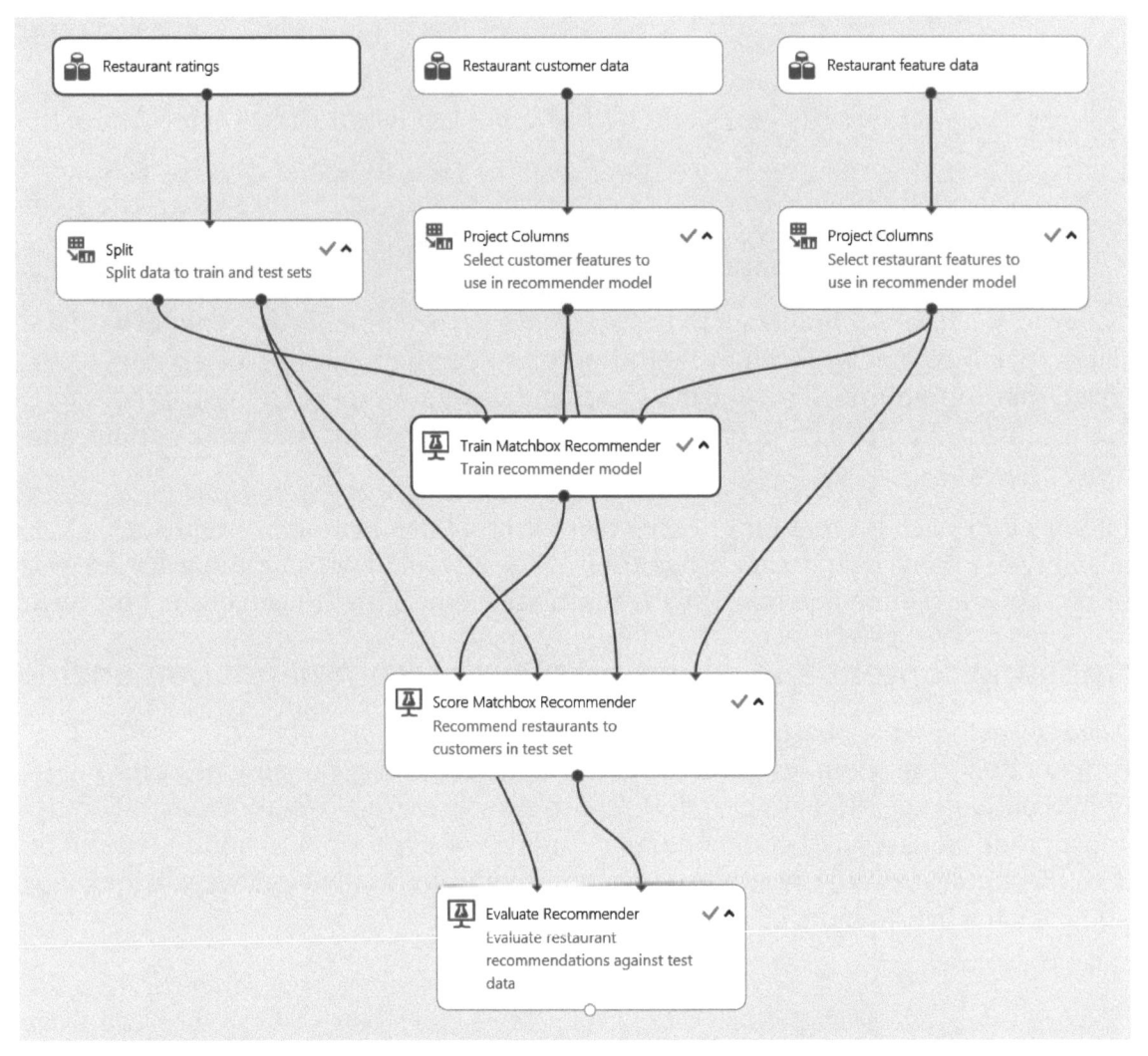

Figure 11.9: A hybrid recommendation model

In order to configure Matchbox Recommender, we need to configure the number of traits and, hence, the dimensions of the latent space matrices. We set this value to 10. Similar to the content-based recommender, instead of feeding raw unprocessed feature vectors into the recommender, we should pre-process the data and encode categorical variables using advanced NLP techniques.

Once you have built the recommendation engine in Azure Machine Learning designer, you simply press **Run** to train the model. You can also pull-request input and output blocks to the canvas to deploy this model as a web service.

Currently, Matchbox Recommender is only available through the graphical interface. However, you can use other hybrid models, such as Extreme Deep Factorization Machines and Wide and Deep, to train hybrid recommenders from Python.

Automatic optimization through reinforcement learning

You can improve your recommendations by providing online training techniques, which will retrain your recommender systems after every user-item interaction. By replacing the feedback function with a reward function and adding a reinforcement learning model, we can now make recommendations, take decisions, and optimize choices that optimize the reward function.

This is a fantastic new approach to training recommender models. The Azure Personalizer service offers exactly this functionality, to make and optimize decisions and choices by providing contextual features and a reward function to the user. Azure Personalizer uses contextual bandits, an approach to reinforcement learning that is framed around making decisions or choices between discrete actions in a given context.

> **Note**
>
> Under the hood, Azure Personalizer uses the Vowpal Wabbit (https://github.com/VowpalWabbit/vowpal_wabbit/wiki) learning system from Microsoft Research to provide high-throughput, low-latency optimization for the recommendation system.

From a developer's perspective, Azure Personalizer is quite easy to use. The basic recommender API consists of two main requests, the rank request and the reward request. During the rank request, we send the user features of the current user, plus all possible item features, to the API and return a ranking of those items and an event ID in the response.

Using this response, we can present the items to the user who will then interact with these items. Whenever the user creates implicit feedback (for example, they click on an item, or scroll to the end of the item), we make a second call to the service, this time to the reward API. In this request, we only send the event ID and the reward (a numeric value) to the service. This will trigger another training iteration using the new reward and the previously submitted user and item features. Hence, with each iteration and each service call, we optimize the performance of the recommendation engine.

An example using Azure Personalizer in Python

Azure Personalizer SDKs are available for many different languages and are mainly wrappers around the official REST API. In order to install the Python SDK, run the following command in your shell:

```
pip install azure-cognitiveservices-personalizer
```

Now, go to the Azure portal and deploy an instance of Azure Personalizer from your portal and configure the **Rewards** and **Exploration** settings as discussed in the following paragraphs.

First, you need to configure how long the algorithm should wait to collect rewards for a certain event, as shown in *Figure 11.10*. Up to this time, rewards are collected and aggregated by the reward aggregation function. You can also define the model update frequency, which allows you to train your model frequently when requiring recommendations for quick-changing user behaviors. It makes sense to set the reward time and model update frequency to the same value, for example, 10 minutes:

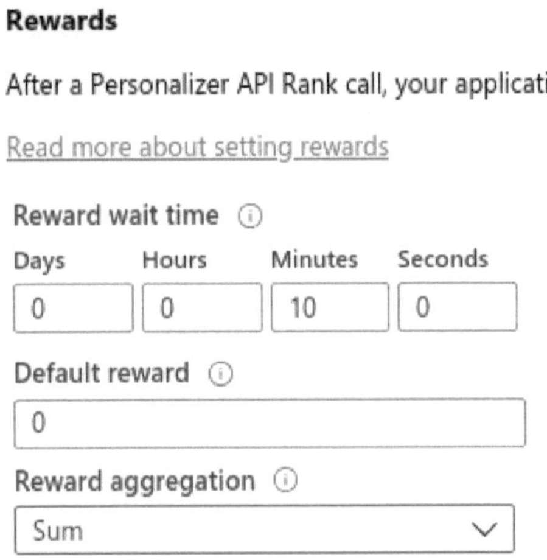

Rewards

After a Personalizer API Rank call, your application will call the Reward API with a score that is used to train the service.

Read more about setting rewards

Reward wait time

Days	Hours	Minutes	Seconds
0	0	10	0

Default reward

0

Reward aggregation

Sum

Figure 11.10: Computing the reward

In *Figure 11.10*, we can also select the aggregation function for rewards collected on the same event during the reward wait time. Possible options are **Earliest** and **Sum**—hence, using only the first reward or a sum over all rewards in the reward period.

The **Exploration** setting makes the algorithm explore alternative patterns over time, which is very helpful in discovering a diverse set of items through exploration. It can be set through the percentage of rank calls used for exploration, as shown in *Figure 11.11*:

Exploration

Personalizer uses exploration to discover new patterns and adapt to changes in user behavior.

Read more about choosing exploration proportion

% of Rank calls to use for exploration

20

Figure 11.11: Configuring exploration

Hence, in 20% of the calls, the model won't return the highest ranked item but will randomly explore new items and their rewards. It sounds reasonable that the value for exploration should be greater than 0 to let the reinforcement algorithm try variations of items over time—and to set it lower than 100% to avoid making the algorithm completely random:

> **Note**
>
> Read more about configuring Azure Personalizer in the official documentation at https://docs.microsoft.com/azure/cognitive-services/personalizer/how-to-settings.

1. Let's grab your resource key, open a Python environment, and start implementing the rank and reward calls. First, we define the API URLs for both calls:

   ```
   personalization_base_url =
   "https://<your-resource-name>.cognitiveservices.azure.com/" resource_key =
   "<your-resource-key>"
   rank_url = personalization_base_url + "personalizer/v1.0/rank" reward_url
   = personalization_base_url + "personalizer/v1.0/events/"
   ```

2. Next, we create a unique **eventid** function and an object containing the user features of the current user and the item features of all possible actions. Once the request is constructed, we can send it to the rank API:

   ```
   eventid = uuid.uuid4().hex
   data = {"eventid": eventid, "contextFeatures": user_features, "actions":
   item_features}
   response = requests.post(rank_url, headers=headers, json=data)
   ```

3. The response contains the ranking of the possible items/actions and a probability value, as well as the winning item under the **rewardActionId** property:

   ```
   {
     "result": {
       "ranking": [
         {
            "id": "ai-for-earth", "probability": 0.664000034
         }, ...
       ],
       "eventId": "482d82bc-2ff8-4721-8e92-607310a0a415",
       "rewardActionId": "ai-for-earth"
     }
   }
   ```

4. Let's parse **rewardActionId** from **response**—this contains the winning item and, hence, the recommended action for the user:

   ```
   prediction = json.dumps( response.json()["rewardActionId"]).
   replace('"','')
   ```

5. Using this ranking, we can return the winning item to the user based on **rewardActionId**. We now give the user some time to interact with the item. Finally, we use this ID to return the tracked implicit feedback as a reward value to the reward API:

   ```
   response = requests.post(reward_url + eventid + "/reward",
   headers=headers, json = {"value": reward})
   ```

That's all you need to embed a fully online self-training recommendation engine in your application using Python and Azure Personalizer. It's that simple. As previously mentioned, other SDKs that wrap the API calls are available for many other languages.

> **Note**
>
> A demo of Personalizer to test the reward function, as well as the request and response of the service, can be found at https://personalizationdemo.azurewebsites.net.
>
> Detailed up-to-date examples for other languages are provided on GitHub at https://github.com/Azure-Samples/cognitive-services-personalizer-samples.

Summary

In this chapter, we discussed the need for different types of recommendation engines, from non-personalized ones to rating- and content-based ones, as well as hybrid models.

We learned that content-based recommendation engines use feature vectors and cosine similarity to compute similar items and similar users based on content alone. This allows us to make recommendations via k-means clustering or tree-based regression models. One important consideration is the embedding of categorical data, which, if possible, should use semantic embedding to avoid confusing similarities based on one-hot or label encodings.

Rating-based recommendations or collaborative filtering methods rely on user-item interactions, so-called ratings or feedback. While explicit feedback is the most obvious possibility for collecting user ratings through ordinal or binary scales, we need to make sure that those ratings are properly normalized.

Another possibility is to directly observe the feedback through implicit ratings; for example, a user bought a product, a user clicked on an article, a user scrolled a page until the end, or a user watched the whole video until the end. However, these ratings will also be affected by user preference drift over time, as well as item popularity over time. To avoid this, you can use exponential time decay to decrease ratings over time.

Rating-based methods are great for providing diverse recommendations, but require a lot of existing ratings for a good performance. Hence they are often combined with content- based recommendations to fight this cold-start problem. Therefore, popular state-of-the-art recommendation models often combine both methods in a single hybrid model, of which Matchbox Recommender is one such example.

Finally, you learned about the possibility of using reinforcement learning to optimize the recommender's feedback function on the fly. Azure Personalizer is a service that can be used to create hybrid online recommenders.

In the next chapter, we will look into deploying our trained models as batch or real-time scoring systems directly from Azure Machine Learning.

Section 4: Optimization and Deployment of Machine Learning Models

After loading, preprocessing, and training models, in this section, the reader will now learn how to deploy models for batch and online scoring. The reader will automate the deployment to Azure Databricks and Azure Kubernetes Service using Azure Machine Learning.

This section comprises the following chapters:

- *Chapter 12, Deploying and operating machine learning models*
- *Chapter 13, MLOps–DevOps for machine learning*
- *Chapter 14, What's next?*

12
Deploying and operating machine learning models

In the previous chapter, we learned how to build efficient and scalable recommender engines through feature engineering, NLP, and distributed algorithms. **Collaborative filtering** is a popular approach for finding other users who rated similar products in a similar way, whereas content-based recommendations use a feature engineering and clustering approach. Therefore, you could combine all the methodologies that we have covered up until now to build even better hybrid recommenders.

In this chapter, we will tackle the next step after training a **recommender engine** or any **machine learning** (**ML**) model: we are going to register, deploy, and operate the model. Hence, we aim to jump from *here is my trained model, what now?* to packaging the model and execution runtime, registering both in a model registry, and deploying them to an execution environment.

First, we will take a look at an enterprise-grade model deployment of trained ML models. You will learn what you need to define to make your model executable (for example, as a web service in a Docker container) and under which circumstances this can happen automatically (for example, for a scikit-learn pipeline). The two most common deployment options—a real-time web service or a batch scoring pipeline—will define the compute target and VM considerations.

In the second section, we will dive deeper into optimization and profiling techniques and alternative deployment scenarios. One popular approach is to convert the ML model into a portable and executable format using an inference-optimized scoring framework or to embed the model into different environments and programming languages. **Open Neural Network eXchange (ONNX)** is one of the executable formats for acyclic computational graphs that can be ported to other languages and scored efficiently using the ONNX runtime scoring framework. However, we will also take a look at how to achieve even better performance by porting models to specific service runtimes, such as Azure IoT Edge or dedicated hardware, such as **Field Programmable Gate Arrays (FPGAs)**.

In the last section, we will focus on how to monitor and operate your ML scoring services at a scale. In order to optimize performance and cost, you need to keep track not only of system-level metrics, but also of telemetry data and scoring results in order to detect model or data drift. After this section, you will be able to confidently deploy, tune, and optimize your scoring infrastructure in Azure.

In this chapter, you will cover the following topics:

- Deploying ML models in Azure
- Building a real-time scoring service
- Implementing a batch scoring pipeline
- Inference optimizations and alternative deployment targets
- Monitoring Azure Machine Learning deployments

Deploying ML models in Azure

In previous chapters, we learned how to experiment, train, and optimize various ML models to perform classification, regression, anomaly detection, image recognition, text understanding, recommendations, and much more. This section continues on from successfully performing those steps and having a successfully trained a model. Hence, given a trained model, we want to now package and deploy these models with tools in Azure.

Broadly speaking, there are two common approaches to deploying ML models, namely deploying them as synchronous real-time web services and as asynchronous batch-scoring services. Please note that the same model could be deployed as two different services, serving different use cases. The deployment type depends heavily on the batch size and response time of the scoring pattern of the model. Small batch sizes with fast responses require a horizontally scalable real-time web service, whereas large batch sizes and slow response times require horizontally and vertically scalable batch services.

The deployment of a text understanding model (for example, an entity recognition model or sentiment analysis) could include a real-time web service that evaluates the model whenever a new comment is posted to an app, as well as a batch scorer in another ML pipeline to extract relevant features from training data. With the former, we want to serve each request as quickly as possible and so we will evaluate a small batch size synchronously. With the latter, we are evaluating large amounts of data and so we will evaluate a large batch size asynchronously. Our aim is that once the model is packaged and registered, we can reuse it for either a task or use case.

Independent of the use case, the deployment process looks very similar. First, the trained model needs to be registered in the model registry. Second, we need to specify the deployment assets; for example, the environment, libraries, assets, scoring file, compute target, and so on. These assets define exactly how the model is loaded, initialized, and executed, and will be stored as Docker files in your private image registry. Next, the specified compute target is created and the deployment image is deployed there. Finally, once the service is deployed and running, you can send requests to the service.

As you can imagine, the range of libraries, frameworks, and customized preprocessing in the scoring file is pretty large. However, if you stick to the standard functionality provided in scikit-learn or TensorFlow, you can also use no-code deployments. To do so, you have to add a few additional parameters during the model registration, such as the framework used, the version number, and the resource requirements.

Let's dive a bit deeper into these individual deployment steps.

Understanding the components of an ML model

When using Azure Machine Learning, there is a well-defined list of things you need to specify in order to deploy and run an ML model. Once we have gone through this list, it will be obvious that you need a runtime environment, a scoring file, and a compute target in order to deploy your ML model as a service. However, these things are often forgotten to be managed as integral parts of deployments.

First and most obviously, we need a model. A trained model—depending on the framework, libraries, and algorithm used—consists of one or multiple files storing the model parameters and structure. In scikit-learn, this could be a pickled estimator, in **Light Gradient Boosting Machine (LightGBM)** this could be a serialized list of decision trees, and in Keras, this could be a model definition and a binary blob storing the model weights. We call this the *model*, and we store and version it in blob storage. At the start-up time of your scoring service, the model will be loaded into the scoring runtime.

Hence, besides the model, we also need an execution runtime, which can be defined via InferenceConfig. In Azure Machine Learning deployments, the execution runtime will be stored as a single Docker file in your private Docker registry. The deployment process will automatically build the Docker image for you and load it into the registry. By default, the Azure Machine Learning workspace contains a private container registry, which will be used for this case.

The base for the execution environment builds the base Docker image. In Azure Machine Learning deployments, you can configure your own Docker base image. On top of the base image, you can define a list of Python dependencies (through a Conda environment) or pip dependencies. This should cover all the dependencies that your model needs for scoring. The environment, including all the packages, will automatically be set up on the Docker image and provided during runtime. On top of this, the environment can be registered and versioned by Azure Machine Learning. This makes it easy to track, reuse, and organize your deployment environments.

Next, we need a so-called **scoring file**. This file typically loads the model and provides a function to score the model when given some data as input. Depending on the type of deployment, you need to provide a scoring file for either a (real-time) synchronous scoring service or an asynchronous batch scoring service. The scoring files should be tracked in your version control system and will be mounted in the Docker image.

To complete `InferenceConfig`, we are missing one last but important step: the Python runtime used to run and execute your scoring file. Currently, Python and PySpark are the only supported runtimes.

Finally, we need an execution target that defines the compute infrastructure that the Docker image should be executed on. In Azure, this is called the **compute target** and is defined through the deployment config. The compute target can be a managed Kubernetes cluster, such as **Azure Kubernetes Service** (**AKS**), a container instance, such as **Azure Container Instances** (**ACI**), or one of the many other Azure compute services.

> **Note**
>
> Please note that this list of cloud services is used for automated deployments through Azure Machine Learning. Nothing stops you from running the Docker image on your on-premise environment.

With Azure IoT Edge as an alternative compute target, you can also deploy directly to edge devices in your own data center. We will take a closer look at this in the next section. So, you need a trained and registered model, an inference config (execution environment and scoring file), and a compute target to automatically deploy a model through an authoring environment.

As it can get quite complicated having all these customization options, you can also use a simplified approach to standard models and frameworks, such as scikit-learn, ONNX, or TensorFlow models. This approach is called **no-code deployment** and requires only the name and version of the used framework and a resource configuration; for example, the number of CPUs and the amount of RAM to execute. These options replace the inference configuration and the compute target and makes it very easy to deploy standard models.

Now that we know the basics about deployments in Azure Machine Learning, we can move on and look at an example of registering a model to prepare it for deployment.

Registering your models in a model registry

The first step in making your deployment pipeline should happen right after training during the training process, namely registering the best model from each run. Independent of whether your training script produces a single model, a model ensemble, or a model combined by multiple files, you should always register the best model from each run in your Azure Machine Learning workspace.

It literally takes you one additional line of code and less than a cent per month to store a model with around 200 MB of size. The blob storage and model registry is directly integrated with your Azure Machine Learning workspace. The added benefit is that you won't ever lose the best model of a run and you get a convenient interface to load the model from the Azure Machine Learning model registry:

1. Let's take a look at this one magic line:

   ```
   run = Run.get_context()

   # train your model
   clf = train_sklearn_mnist()

   # serialize the model and write it to disk from sklearn.externals import joblib
   joblib.dump(clf, 'outputs/sklearn_mnist_model.pkl')

   model = run.register_model(model_name='sklearn_mnist', model_path='outputs/sklearn_mnist_model.pkl')
   print(model.name, model.id, model.version, sep='\t')
   ```

   In the preceding code block, we first use the **dump()** function from **sklearn** to serialize and store a trained classifier to disk. We then call the **run.model_register()** function to upload a trained model to the model registry. This will automatically track and version the model by name and connect it to the current training run.

2. Once your model is stored in the model registry of your Azure Machine Learning workspace, you can not only use it for deployments but also retrieve it by name in any debugging, testing, or experimentation step. You can simply request the latest model by name; for example, by running the following snippet on your local machine:

   ```
   from sklearn.externals import joblib from azureml.core.model import Model
   model_path = Model.get_model_path('sklearn_mnist')
   model = joblib.load(model_path)
   ```

All we did in the preceding code is ran **Model.get_model_path()** to retrieve the latest version of a model by name. We can also specify a version number to load a specific model from the registry. This is one of the functionalities of the Azure Machine Learning workspace that gets you hooked and makes you never want to miss a model registry in the future. It gives you great flexibility and transparency when working with model artifacts on different environments and during different experiments.

> **Note**
>
> What if I told you that you could already deploy this model to a web service as a blue-green deployment using one additional line of code, namely **Model.deploy**? Well, I am pretty sure you would be surprised by how easy this is. Indeed, this is possible using the no-code deployment mentioned in the previous section.

3. By defining a model, framework, and compute resource configuration, you can deploy this model as a real-time web service in a single line of code. To do so, we need to add this additional information to the model by extending the **Model.register** arguments. Let's take a look at this in action:

   ```
   from azureml.core import Model
   from azureml.core.resource_configuration import ResourceConfiguration

   # register the model with no-code deployment configuration model = Model.
   register(workspace=ws,
            model_name='sklearn_mnist',
            model_path='./sklearn_mnist_model.pkl',
            model_framework=Model.Framework.SCIKITLEARN,
            model_framework_version='0.19.1',
   resource_configuration=ResourceConfiguration(
            cpu=1, memory_in_gb=0.5))
   service_name = 'my-sklearn-service'
   service = Model.deploy(ws, service_name, [model])
   ```

   In the preceding code, we added the framework and framework version to the model registry, as well as the resource configuration for this specific model. The model itself is stored in a standard format in one of the supported frameworks (scikit-learn, ONNX, or TensorFlow). This configuration gets added as metadata to the model in the model registry.

4. Finally, we can call the **Model.deploy()** function to start the deployment process, which will build the deployment runtime as a Docker image, register it in your container registry, and start the image as a managed container instance, including the scoring file, REST service abstraction, and telemetry collection. As you might have spotted in the code, you can also deploy multiple models at once by passing an array to the deployment function. To retrieve the URL of the scoring service once it is finished, we run the following code:

```
service.wait_for_deployment(True)
print(service.state)
print("Scoring URL: " + service.scoring_uri)
```

If you want more granular control over the execution environment, endpoint configuration, and compute target, you can use the advanced inference, deployment, and service configs in order to tune your deployment. Let's now take a look at customized deployments.

Customizing your deployment environment

In Azure Machine Learning, you use an execution environment to specify a base Docker image, Python runtime, and all the dependent packages required to score your model. Similar to models, environments can also be registered and versioned in Azure. So, both the Docker artifacts and the metadata are stored in your workspace. This makes it super simple to keep track of your environment changes, jump back and forth between multiple versions of an environment, and share an environment for multiple projects:

1. We can define an environment either with the CLI and Conda file or comfortably in an authoring environment using Python and the Azure Machine Learning SDK. Let's take a look at how to define the Python environment using Conda:

```
from azureml.core.environment import Environment
from azureml.core.conda_dependencies import CondaDependencies
# Create the environment myenv = Environment()
conda_dep = CondaDependencies()
# Define the packages needed by the model and scripts
conda_dep.add_conda_package("tensorflow") conda_dep.add_conda_package("numpy") conda_dep.add_conda_package("scikit-learn")
# You must list azureml-defaults as a pip dependency conda_dep.add_pip_package("azureml-defaults") conda_dep.add_pip_package("keras")
# Adds dependencies to PythonSection of myenv myenv.python.conda_dependencies=conda_dep
```

As you can see in the preceding code block, we first initialize an Environment instance and then add multiple packages to the **conda** dependency object. We assign the **conda** environment by overriding the **myenv.python.conda_dependencies** property with the **conda** dependency. Using the same approach, we can also override Docker, Spark, and any additional Python settings using **myenv.docker** and **myenv.spark**, respectively.

> **Note**
>
> The Azure Machine Learning SDK contains a detailed list of possible configuration options, which you can find at https://docs.microsoft.com/python/api/azureml-core/azureml.core.environment(class).

2. In the next step, you can now register the environment using a descriptive name. This will add a new version of the current environment configuration to your environment with the same name:

   ```
   myenv.register(workspace=ws, name="PythonEnv")
   ```

3. You can also retrieve the environment from the registry using the following code. This is also useful when you have registered a base environment, which can be reused and extended for multiple experiments:

   ```
   myenv = Environment.get(workspace=ws, name="PythonEnv")
   ```

4. As with the model registry, you can also load environments using a specified version as an additional argument. Once you have configured an execution environment, you can combine it with a scoring file to an **InferenceConfig** object. The scoring file implements all functionalities to load the model from the registry and evaluate it given some input data. The configuration can be defined as follows:

   ```
   from azureml.core.model import InferenceConfig inference_config =
   InferenceConfig(
   entry_script="score.py", environment=myenv)
   ```

   We can see, in the preceding example, that we simply specify a relative path to the scoring script in the local authoring environment. Therefore, you first have to create this scoring file—we will go through two examples of batch and real-time scoring in the following sections.

5. To build an environment, we can simply trigger a build of the Docker image:

   ```
   from azureml.core import Image build = myenv.build(workspace=ws)
   build.wait_for_completion(show_output=True)
   ```

6. The environment will be packaged and registered as a Docker image in your private container registry, containing the Docker base image and all specified libraries. If you want to package the model and the scoring file as well, you can package the model instead. This is done automatically when deploying the model or can be forced by using the `Model.package` function. Let's load the model from the previous section and package and register the image:

```
model_path = Model.get_model('sklearn_mnist')
package = Model.package(ws, [model], inference_config) package.wait_for_creation(show_output=True)
```

The preceding code will build and package your deployment as a Docker image. In the next section, we will find out how to choose the best compute target to execute your ML deployment.

Choosing a deployment target in Azure

One of the great advantages of Azure Machine Learning is that they are tightly integrated with many other Azure services. This is extremely helpful with deployments, where we want to run Docker images of the ML service on a manage d service within Azure. These compute targets can be configured and leveraged for automatic deployment through Azure Machine Learning.

It's possible that you might not be an expert in Kubernetes when your job is to productionize ML training and deployment pipelines. If that's the case, you might come to enjoy the tight integration of management of Azure compute services in the Azure Machine Learning SDK. Similar to creating execution environments, you can create whole GPU clusters, managed Kubernetes clusters, or simple container instances from within the authoring environment; for example, the Jupyter notebook orchestrating your workflow.

We can follow a general recommendation for choosing a specific service, similar to choosing a compute service for regular application deployments. So, we trade-off simplicity, cost, scalability, flexibility, and operational expense between the compute services that can easily start a web service from a Docker image.

Here is a recommendation of when to use which Azure compute service:

- For testing and experimentation, use ACI. It is super easy to set up and configure and it is made to run container images.

- For deployments of scalable real-time web services with GPU support, use AKS. This managed Kubernetes cluster is a lot more flexible and scalable but also a lot harder to operate.

- For batch deployments, use AML Compute, the same compute cluster environment we already used for training.

Depending on the type of deployment, you also need to modify your scoring file, which is a part of your deployment of **InferenceConfig**. For quick experiments, you can also deploy your service locally, using **LocalWebservice** as a deployment target. To do so, you would have to run the following snippet on your local machine:

```
from azureml.core.webservice import LocalWebservice, Webservice


deployment_config = LocalWebservice.deploy_configuration(port=8890) service = Model.deploy(ws, service_name, [model], inference_config,
deployment_config)


service.wait_for_deployment(show_output=True) print(service.state)
```

Building a real-time scoring service

For Azure Machine Learning, you can't really choose a specific deployment case to match your use case. To implement a real-time scoring service, you need to pick a highly scalable compute target (for example, AKS) and provide a scoring file that receives data with each request and returns the prediction of the model synchronously:

1. To do so, you need to provide the **init()** and **run()** functions in the scoring file. Let's take a look at a simple scoring file. In reality, this should be very simple, as we have seen most of the code already:

    ```
    import json
    import numpy as np
     import os
    from sklearn.externals import joblib
    def init():
        global model
        model_path = Model.get_model_path('sklearn_mnist')
        model= joblib.load(model_path)
    def run(data): try:
        result = model.predict(data)
        # You can return any JSON serializable data type return result.tolist()
    except Exception as e: error =
    (e) return error
    ```

In the preceding snippet, you can see that we have provided `init()` and `run()` functions. During the `init()` function, we load the model from the `model` registry in the same way that we would load it on a local machine. We then deserialize the model using the scikit-learn `joblib` library.

In the `run()` function, we are provided with a `data` object. The `data` object contains all the parameters of the request that are sent to the service as a JSON object with the `data` property. In the preceding case, we expect a client to send a request with a body that contains an array of data that we can feed into the `sklearn` classifier. Finally, we return a prediction, which will be automatically serialized into JSON and returned to the caller.

2. Let's deploy the service, for testing purposes, to an ACI compute target. To do so, we need to update the deployment configuration to contain the ACI resource configuration:

```
from azureml.core.webservice import AciWebservice, Webservice deployment_config = AciWebservice.deploy_configuration(
cpu_cores = 1, memory_gb = 1)
service = Model.deploy(ws, service_name, [model], inference_config, deployment_config)
service.wait_for_deployment(show_output=True) print(service.state)
```

As you might have already thought, it would be great to validate the user's request and provide the user with some information about how the service can be used. To solve this, Azure Machine Learning provides a way to auto-generate an OpenAPI specification that is available to the client through another endpoint. This specification was previously called **Swagger** and provides an automated standardized way to specify the service's data format.

> **Note**
>
> You can find more information about Azure Container Instance in the official documentation https://docs.microsoft.com/azure/container-instances/container-instances-overview.

3. You can enable automatic schema generation for pandas, NumPy, PySpark and standard Python objects in your service through annotations in Python. First, you need to include `azureml-defaults>=1.0.45` and `inference- schema[numpy-support]` as pip packages in your environment. Then, you can auto-generate the schema by providing sample input and output data for your endpoint:

```
from inference_schema.schema_decorators import input_schema, output_schema
from inference_schema.parameter_types.numpy_parameter_type import
NumpyParameterType

input_sample = np.array([[10, 9, 8, 7, 6, 5, 4, 3, 2, 1]]) output_sample =
np.array([3726.995])

@input_schema('data', NumpyParameterType(input_sample)) @output_
schema(NumpyParameterType(output_sample))
def run(data):
...
```

In the preceding example, we defined the schema through sample data and annotations in the **run()** method. This is everything that is required to auto-generate an API specification that your clients can use to validate endpoints and arguments or to auto-generate clients. Swagger Codegen can now be used to generate Java and C# clients for your new ML service.

4. Great, we now have input validation and can auto-generate clients to query the service. Let's now deploy this service to an AKS cluster so we can take advantage of the GPU acceleration and autoscaling:

```
from azureml.core.compute import AksCompute, ComputeTarget # Configure AKS
cluster with NVIDIA Tesla P40 GPU
prov_config = AksCompute.provisioning_configuration(
    vm_size="Standard_ND6s")
aks_name = 'aks-ml-prod' # Create the cluster
aks_target = ComputeTarget.create(workspace = ws,
    name = aks_name, provisioning_configuration = prov_config)
# Wait for the create process to complete aks_target.wait_for_
completion(show_output = True)
```

In the preceding code, we created an AKS configuration and a new AKS cluster as an Azure Machine Learning compute target from this configuration. All this happens from completely within your authoring environment. If you already have an AKS cluster up and running, you can simply use this cluster for Azure Machine Learning.

> **Note**
>
> You can find more information about Azure Kubernetes Services in the official documentation https://docs.microsoft.com/azure/aks/intro-kubernetes.

5. To do so, you have to pass the resource group and cluster name to the `AksCompute.attach_configuration()` method. Then, set the resource group that contains the AKS cluster and the cluster name:

```
resource_group = 'my-rg' cluster_name = 'aks-ml-prod'
attach_config = AksCompute.attach_configuration( resource_group = resource_
group, cluster_name=cluster_name)
aks_target = ComputeTarget.attach(ws, cluster_name, attach_config)
```

6. Once we have a reference to the cluster, we can now deploy the ML model to the cluster. This step is similar to the previous one:

```
deployment_config = AksWebservice.deploy_configuration( cpu_cores=1, memory_
gb=1)
service = Model.deploy(ws, service_name, [model], inference_config,
deployment_config, aks_target)
service.wait_for_deployment(show_output = True) print(service.state)
print(service.get_logs())
```

7. The cluster is up and running and the deployment is finished. Now, we can try a test request to the service to make sure everything is working properly. By default, Azure Machine Learning use key-based (primary and secondary) authentication. Let's retrieve **api_key** and send some test data to the deployed service:

```
X_test = load_test_data()
import json
input_data = json.dumps({'data': [X_test]})
api_key = aks_service.get_keys()[0]
headers = {'Content-Type': 'application/json', 'Authorization': ('Bearer '
+ api_key)}
resp = requests.post(aks_service.scoring_uri, input_data, headers=headers)
print("POST to url", aks_service.scoring_uri) print("label:", y_
test[random_index]) print("prediction:", resp.text)
```

Implementing a batch scoring pipeline

Operating batch scoring services is very similar to the previously discussed online-scoring approach—you provide an environment, compute target, and scoring file. However, in your scoring file, you would rather pass a path to a blob storage location with a new batch of data instead of the data itself. You can then use your scoring function to process the data asynchronously and output the predictions to a different storage location, back to the blob storage, or push the data asynchronously to the calling service.

It is up to you how you implement your scoring file as it is simply a Python script that you control. The only difference in the deployment process is that the batch-scoring script will be deployed as a pipeline on an Azure Machine Learning cluster, and triggered through a REST service. Therefore, it is important that your scoring script can be configured through command-line parameters. Remember that the difference with batch scoring is that we don't send the data to the scoring pipeline, but instead, we send a path to the data and a path to write the output asynchronously.

Instead of deploying a batch scoring script as a service using Azure Machine Learning deployments, we wrap the scoring script in a pipeline and trigger it from a REST service. The pipeline can now be defined to use an Azure Machine Learning compute cluster for execution:

1. Let's define a pipeline using a single step with a configurable batch size. In both the pipeline configuration and the scoring file, you can take advantage of parallelizing your work in the Azure Machine Learning cluster:

    ```python
    from azureml.core import Experiment
    from azureml.pipeline.core import Pipeline
    from azureml.pipeline.steps import PythonScriptStep

    from azureml.pipeline.core.graph import PipelineParameter batch_size_param = PipelineParameter(
        name="param_batch_size", default_value=20) inception_model_name = "inception_v3.ckpt"
    batch_score_step = PythonScriptStep( name="batch_scoring",
        script_name="batch_scoring.py", arguments=["--dataset_path", input_images,
            "--model_name",
            "inception", "--label_dir", label_dir,
            "--output_dir", output_dir,
            "--batch_size", batch_size_param],
        compute_target=compute_target, inputs=[input_images, label_dir], outputs=[output_dir],
        runconfig=amlcompute_run_config
    )
    pipeline = Pipeline(workspace=ws, steps=[batch_score_step]) pipeline_run = Experiment(ws, 'batch_scoring').submit(pipeline, pipeline_params={"param_batch_size": 20})
    ```

2. Using this pipeline configuration, we call our scoring script with the relevant parameters. The pipeline is submitted as an experiment in Azure Machine Learning, which gives us access to all the features in runs and experiments in Azure. One feature would be that we can simply download the output from the experiment when it has finished running:

   ```
   pipeline_run.wait_for_completion(show_output=True) step_run =
   list(pipeline_run.get_children())[0] step_run.download_file("./outputs/
   result-labels.txt")
   ```

3. If the batch scoring file produces a nice CSV output containing names and predictions, we can now display the results using the following pandas functionality:

   ```
   import pandas as pd
   df = pd.read_csv("result-labels.txt", delimiter=":", header=None)
   df.columns = ["Filename", "Prediction"]
   df.head()
   ```

4. Let's go ahead and publish the pipeline as a REST service:

   ```
   published_pipeline = pipeline_run.publish_pipeline( name="Inception_
   v3_scoring", description="Batch scoring using Inception v3 model",
   version="1.0")

   published_id = published_pipeline.id rest_endpoint = published_pipeline.
   endpoint
   ```

5. To run the published pipeline as a service through HTTP, we now need to use token-based authentication:

   ```
   from azureml.core.authentication import AzureCliAuthentication import
   requests
   cli_auth = AzureCliAuthentication()
   aad_token = cli_auth.get_authentication_header()
   ```

6. Having retrieved the authentication token, we can now run the published pipeline:

   ```
   # specify batch size when running the pipeline
   response = requests.post(rest_endpoint, headers=aad_token,
           json={"ExperimentName": "batch_scoring",
           "ParameterAssignments":
   {"param_batch_size": 50}}) run_id = response.json()["Id"]
   ```

Running a batch scoring pipeline on Azure Machine Learning is a bit different to running a synchronous scoring service. While the real-time scoring service uses Azure Machine Learning deployments and AKS or ACI as popular compute targets, batch scoring models are usually deployed as published pipelines on top of AML Compute. The benefit of a published pipeline is that it can be used as a REST service, which can trigger and parameterize the pipeline.

Inference optimizations and alternative deployment targets

Using Azure Machine Learning deployments, it's quite easy to get your first experimental service up and running. Through the versioning and abstracting of models and environments, it is painless to deploy the same model and environment to different compute targets. However, it's not that easy to know beforehand how many resources your model will consume and how you can optimize your model or deployment for a higher inferencing throughput.

Profiling models for optimal resource configuration

Azure Machine Learning provides a handy tool to help you evaluate the required resources for your ML model deployment through model profiling. This will help you estimate the number of CPUs and the amount of memory required to operate your scoring service at a specific throughput.

Let's take a look at the model profile of the model that we trained during the real-time scoring example:

1. First, you need to define **test_data** in the same format as the JSON request for your ML service—so, have **test_data** embedded in a JSON object under the **data** root property. Please note that if you defined a different format in your scoring file, then you need to use your own custom format:

   ```
   import json
   test_data = json.dumps({'data': [ [1,2,3,4,5,6,7,8,9,10] ]})
   ```

2. Then, you can use the **Model.profile()** method to profile a model and evaluate the CPU and memory consumption of the service. This will start up your model, fire requests with **test_data** provided to it, and measure the resource utilization at the same time:

   ```
   profile = Model.profile(ws, service_name, [model], inference_config, test_data)
   profile.wait_for_profiling(True) profiling_results = profile.get_results()
   print(profiling_results)
   ```

The output contains a list of resources, plus a recommended value for the profiled model:

```
{'cpu': 1.0, 'memoryInGB': 0.5}
```

It is good to run the model profiling tool before doing a production deployment, and this will help you set meaningful default values for your resource configuration.

To further optimize and decide whether you need to scale up or down, vertically or horizontally, you need to measure, track, and observe various other metrics. We will discuss more about monitoring and scaling in the last section of this chapter.

Portable scoring through the ONNX runtime

Some use cases require you to embed a trained ML model in an application that was written in a different language from Python. In most cases, you can still train your model with Python, export it to a common format, and then score it in a different language using the shared format. In some cases, if you use a specific runtime optimized for scoring, you can achieve a nice performance boost.

The ONNX format is a standard that originally exports neural network model structures and weights to an exchangeable format so that they can be loaded and inferred in other frameworks and languages. ONNX received a lot of traction and support from major companies (such as Microsoft, Facebook, AWS, ARM, Intel, and many more) and transitioned to a format for exchanging all kinds of ML models.

Most of today's ML frameworks, such as sklearn, TensorFlow, PyTorch, and so on, allow you to export trained models in an ONNX format. To run a model in an ONNX format, you can either choose an ML framework that can parse ONNX models or use an ONNX inferencing runtime. Microsoft developed the C++-based ONNX runtime, which takes advantage of many hardware acceleration features, such as GPUs, TensorRT, DNNL, nGraph, CUDA, MLAS, and so on, to provide great scoring performance. This advantage is especially significant when running inference in the cloud on Azure VMs, where we can't always control the underlying hardware features.

Luckily, Azure provides the ONNX runtime as an option in the Azure Machine Learning deployments and so provides us with optimized binaries for the underlying hardware. We often see performance gains using the ONNX runtime score engines in the range of two-times greater than for CPU-based models.

Let's see it in action:

1. The first step is to convert your current trained model to an ONNX model. Here's a snippet of how to export a TensorFlow frozen graph into an ONNX model:

   ```
   from onnx_tf.frontend import tensorflow_graph_to_onnx_model with tf.gfile.
   GFile("frozen_graph.pb", "rb") as f:
       graph_def = tf.GraphDef()
       graph_def.ParseFromString(f.read())
       onnx_model = tensorflow_graph_to_onnx_model(graph_def, "fc2/add",
   opset=6)
   file = open("mnist.onnx", "wb") file.write(onnx_model.SerializeToString())
   file.close()
   ```

2. Next, we need to register the ONNX model in the Azure Machine Learning model registry. This step is similar to the one used when registering sklearn or any other model, as models are simply stored as binary files in blob storage, with meta-information in the registry. We also add information about the framework so we can take advantage of no-code deployments:

   ```
   from azureml.core import Model
   from azureml.core.resource_configuration import ResourceConfiguration
   # register the model with no-code deployment configuration model = Model.
   register(workspace=ws,
       model_name='onnx_mnist',
       model_path='./mnist.onnx',
       model_framework=model_framework=Model.Framework.ONNX,
       model_framework_version='1.3',
       resource_configuration=ResourceConfiguration(cpu=1,
   memory_in_gb=0.5))
   ```

3. Once the model is registered, there is nothing left to do other than to kick off auto-deployment. Let's deploy the model and retrieve the scoring URL:

   ```
   service_name = 'my-onnx-service'
   service = Model.deploy(ws, service_name, [model])
   service.wait_for_deployment(True) print(service.state)
   print("Scoring URL: " + service.scoring_uri)
   ```

   In the preceding code, we took advantage of the no-code auto-deployment using the resource configuration and framework definition stored in the **model** registry. If you deploy the ONNX model using your own **InferenceConfig**, you need to also change the scoring file to use ONNX instead of the previous framework and include the **onnxruntime** Python package.

Fast inference using FPGAs in Azure

In the previous section, we exported a model to ONNX to take advantage of an inference- optimized and hardware-accelerated runtime to improve the scoring performance. In this section, we will take this approach one step further to deploy on even faster inferencing hardware—**FPGAs**. Azure offers FPGAs in the VMs of the PBS family, with pre-defined deep learning architectures to accelerate inference.

The general approach is very similar to ONNX—you take a trained model and convert it to a specific format that can be executed on the FPGAs. In this case, your model has to be either ResNet, DenseNet, VGG, or SSD-VGG and must be written in TensorFlow in order to be converted. In this case, we will use quantized 16-bit float model weights converted to ONNX models, which will be run on the FPGAs. For these models, FPGAs give you the best inference performance in the cloud.

Running models on FPGAs in Azure requires a few extra steps compared to the previous example. These are the steps:

1. Pick a supported model featurizer.
2. Train the supported model with a custom classifier.
3. Quantize the model featurizer's weights to 16-bit precision.
4. Convert the model to an ONNX format.
5. Register the model.
6. Create a compute target with PBS nodes.
7. Deploy the model.

> **Note**
>
> As the code is cluttered and hard to interpret, we will skip the code examples in this section. However, you can find detailed examples about FPGA model training, conversion, and deployments on Azure's GitHub repository at https://github.com/Azure/MachineLearningNotebooks/tree/master/how-to-use-azureml/deployment/accelerated-models.

In order to run a model on the FPGAs, you need to pick a supported model from the `azureml.accel.models` package. In the documentation, this part is referred to as a featurizer and only builds the feature extraction part of your model. You can attach any classification or regression head (or both) on top using TensorFlow or Keras. Only the feature extractor part of the model will later run on the FPGAs—similar to running only certain operations on GPUs.

In the next step, you can train the model, consisting of a pre-defined feature extractor and a custom classification head, using your own data and weights or by fine-tuning, for example, provided ImageNet weights. This should happen with 32-bit precision as convergence will be faster during training.

Once the training is finished, you need to quantize the feature extractor's weights into half-precision floats, using the quantized models provided in `azureml.accel.models`. This will make your model a lot smaller and optimized for FPGA-based inference.

Next, you convert the whole model into an ONNX model, using `AccelOnnxConverter` from the same Azure package. An `AccelContainerImage` class helps you define `InferenceConfig` for the FPGA-based compute targets.

Finally, you can register your model using the Azure Machine Learning model registry. In addition, you can create an AKS cluster using the `Standard_PB6s` nodes. Once the cluster is up and running, you use your `Model.deploy` command.

The workflow to deploy a model to accelerate FPGA-based compute targets is a bit different to simply deploying ONNX models, as you have to consider the limited supported selection of models right from the beginning. Another difference is that while you choose a pre-defined supported model for FPGA deployment, you only get the feature extractor part of the model. This means you have to attach an additional classification or regression head—a step that is not immediately obvious. Once you understand this, it will make more sense that you only quantize the feature extractor to half-precision floats after training.

While this process seems a bit difficult and customized, the performance gain, especially when dealing with predictions on image data, is huge (1.8ms). Therefore, you should take advantage of this optimization only if you are ready to modify your training process to build on the FPGA-supported models and quantized representation.

Alternative deployment targets

Relying on Azure Machine Learning either for experimentation, performing end-to-end training, or simply for registering your trained models and environments brings you a ton of value. Currently, we have mostly covered two common cloud deployment patterns; namely, a real-time scoring web service through automated deployments and batch scoring through a deployed pipeline. While these two use cases are quite different in requirement and deployment types, they show what is possible once you have a trained model and packaged environment stored in Azure Machine Learning. In this section, we will discuss some of the alternative deployment targets that you might not even think of immediately.

In many scenarios, abstracting your batch scoring pipeline from the actual data processing pipeline to separate concerns and responsibilities makes a lot of sense. However, sometimes your scoring should happen directly during the data processing or querying time and in the same system. Once your ML model is registered and versioned with Azure Machine Learning, you can pull out a specific version of the model anywhere using the Azure Machine Learning SDK, either in Python, C#, the command line, or any other language that can make a call to a REST service.

This makes it possible to pull trained and converted ONNX models from a desktop application, either during build or at runtime. You can load models while running Spark—for example, on Azure Databricks—when you don't want to move TBs of data to a separate scoring service. You can integrate this also with managed services supporting Python extensions, such as Azure Data Explorer.

Azure Data Explorer is an exciting managed service for storing and querying large amounts of telemetry data efficiently. It is used internally at Azure to power log analytics, app insights, and time-series insights. It has a powerful Python runtime, with many popular packages available at runtime, and so provides a perfect service for performing anomaly detection or time-series analysis, based on your custom models.

One of the most interesting integrations from an enterprise perspective is the Azure Machine Learning integration with Power BI. To enable your real-time scoring service for Power BI, your service must parse pandas DataFrames instead of NumPy arrays. By doing this and allowing the Power BI service to access your Azure Machine Learning workspace, you can now apply your ML model deployments on columns in Power BI in the query view. Think for a second how powerful this concept of rolling out ML models to be used by analysts in their BI tools is. The *Figure 12.1* shows the query view in the Power BI service, which allows you to use your trained models for predictions on your BI data:

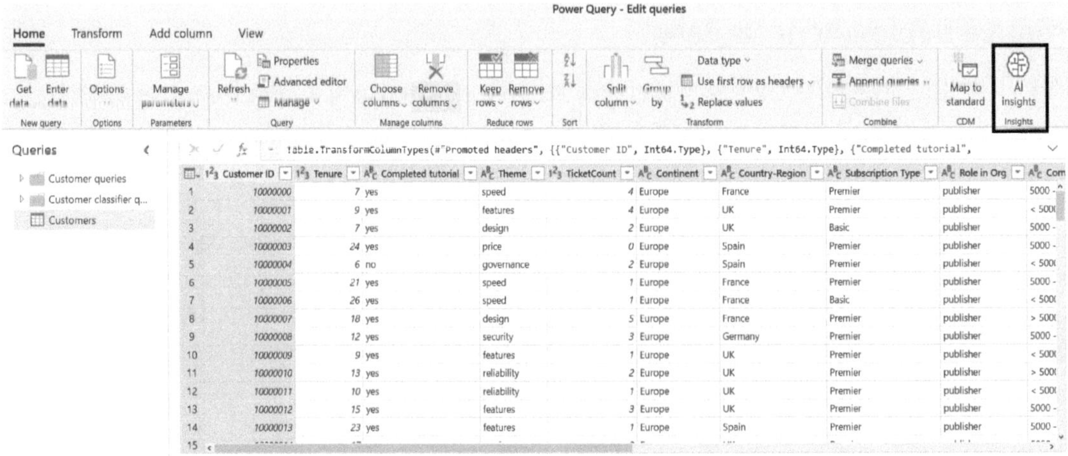

Figure 12.1: The query view in the Power BI

Another interesting deployment scenario is the integration of Azure Machine Learning with Azure IoT Edge. This integration will allow you to simply register a deployment service for IoT Edge, which will pull the service image and execute it on its local runtime. An interesting aspect of this scenario is that Azure IoT Edge devices are usually used in your own premises and so are not part of the cloud data center.

> **Note**
> Please note that you still get many benefits, such as managed environments and deployments, while the execution target sits in your own data center or data box.

We won't go into any more detail because many of these alternative deployment options are still in preview and could rapidly change or evolve from the current situation. However, it is worth noting that when using Azure Machine Learning for model deployments, you can take advantage of all the Azure ecosystem and expect to see integration with many of our favorite services.

Monitoring Azure Machine Learning deployments

You have successfully registered a trained model, an environment, a scoring file, and an inference configuration in the previous section. You have optimized your model for scoring and deployed it to a managed Kubernetes cluster. You auto-generated client SDKs for your ML services. So, can you finally lean back and enjoy the success of your hard work? Well, not yet! First, we need to make sure that we have all our monitoring in place so that you can observe and react to anything happening to your deployment.

First, the good things: with Azure Machine Learning deployments and managed compute targets, you will get many things included out of the box with either Azure, Azure Machine Learning, or your service used as a compute target. Tools such as the Azure dashboard, Azure Monitor, and Azure Log Analytics make it really easy to centralize log and debug information. Once your data is available through Log Analytics, it can be queried, analyzed, visualized, alerted, and/or used for automation using Azure Automation. A great deployment and operations process should utilize these tools integrated with Azure and the Azure services.

The first thing that should come to mind when operating any application is measuring software and hardware metrics. It's essential to know the memory consumption, CPU usage, I/O latency, and network bandwidth of your application. Particularly for an ML service, you should always have an eye on performance bottlenecks and resource utilization for cost optimization. For large GPU-accelerated deep neural networks, it is essential to know your system in order to scale efficiently. These metrics allow you to scale your infrastructure vertically, and so move to bigger or smaller nodes when needed.

Another monitoring target for general application deployments should be your users' telemetry data—how they are using your service, how often they use it, and which parts of the service they use. This will help you to scale horizontally and add more nodes or remove nodes when needed.

The last important portion to measure from your scoring service—if possible—is the user input over time and the scoring results. For optimal prediction performance, it is essential to understand what type of data users are sending to your service and how similar this data is to the training data. It's relatively certain that your model will require retraining at some point and monitoring the input data will help you to define a time that this is required; for example, through a data drift metric.

Let's take a look at how we can monitor the Azure Machine Learning deployments and keep track of all these metrics in Azure.

Collecting logs and infrastructure metrics

If you are new to cloud services, or Azure specifically, log and metric collection can be a bit overwhelming at first. Logs and metrics are generated in different layers in your application and can be either infrastructure- or application-based and collected automatically or manually. Then, there are diagnostic metrics that are automatic but sit behind a toggle and so must be activated actively. In this section, we briefly discuss how to collect this metric for the three main managed compute targets in Azure Machine Learning—ACI, AKS, and AML Compute.

By default, you will get access to infrastructure metrics and logs through Azure Monitor. It will automatically collect Azure resources and guest OS metrics and logs and provide metrics and query interfaces for logs based on Log Analytics. Azure Monitor should be used to track resource utilization—for example, CPU, RAM, disk space, disk I/O, network bandwidth, and so on—which then can be pinned to dashboards or alerted on. You can even set up automatic autoscaling based on these metrics.

Metrics are mostly collected as distributions over time and reported back at certain time intervals. So, instead of seeing thousands of values per second, you are asked to choose an aggregate for each metric; for example, the average of each interval. For most monitoring cases, I would recommend you either look at the 95% percentile (or maximum aggregation, for metrics where lower is better) to avoid smoothing any spikes during the aggregation process. In AKS, you are provided with four different views of your metrics through Azure Monitor—Cluster, Nodes, Controllers, and Containers.

More detailed resource, guest, and virtualization host logs of your Azure Machine Learning deployment can be accessed by enabling diagnostic settings and providing a separate Log Analytics instance. This will automatically load the log data into your Log Analytics workspace where you can efficiently query all your logs, analyze them, and create visualization and/or alerts.

I strongly recommend you take advantage of the diagnostic settings as they give you loads of insight into your Azure infrastructure. This is especially helpful when you need to debug problems in your ML service; for example, failing containers, non-starting services, crashes, application freezes, slow response times, and so on. Another great use case for Log Analytics is to collect, store, and analyze your application log. In AKS, you can send the Kubernetes master node logs, kubelet logs, API server logs, and much more, to Log Analytics.

One metric that is very important to track for ML training clusters and deployments, but is unfortunately not tracked automatically, is the GPU resource utilization. Due to this problem, GPU resource utilization has to be monitored and collected at the application level.

The most elegant way to solve this for AKS deployments is to run a GPU logger service as a sidecar with your application, which collects resource stats and sends them to **Application Insights (App Insights)**, a service that collects application metrics. Both App Insights and Log Analytics use the same data storage technology under the hood: Azure Data Explorer. However, default integrations for App Insights provide mainly application metrics, such as access logs, while Log Analytics provides system logs.

In AML Compute, need to start a separate monitoring thread from your application code to monitor GPU utilization. Then, for Nvidia GPUs, we use a wrapper around the **nvidia- smi** monitoring utility; for example, the **nvidia-ml-py3** Python package. To send data to App Insights, we simply use the Azure SDK for App Insights. Here is a tiny code example showing you how to achieve this:

```
import nvidia_smi
nvidia_smi.nvmlInit()
# get handle for card id 0
handle = nvidia_smi.nvmlDeviceGetHandleByIndex(0)
res = nvidia_smi.nvmlDeviceGetUtilizationRates(handle) from applicationinsights import TelemetryClient
tc = TelemetryClient("appinsights_key")
tc.track_metric("gpu", res.gpu) tc.track_metric("gpu-gpu-mem", res.memory)
```

In the preceding code, we first used the **nvidia-ml-py3** wrapper on top of **nvidia-smi** to return a handle to the current GPU. Please note that when you have multiple GPUs, you can also iterate over them and report multiple metrics. Then, we use the **TelemetryClient** API from App Insights to report these metrics back to a central place, where we can then visualize, analyze, and alert these values.

Tracking telemetry and application metrics

We briefly touched on Azure App Insights in the previous section. It is a really amazing service for automatically collecting application metrics from your services; for example, Azure Machine Learning deployments. It also provides an SDK to collect any user-defined application metric that you want to track.

To automatically track user metrics, we need to deploy the model using Azure Machine Learning deployments to AKS or ACI. This will not only collect the web service metadata but also the model's predictions. To do so, you need to enable App Insights' diagnostics, as well as data model collection, or enable App Insights via the Python API:

```
from azureml.core.webservice import Webservice aks_service= Webservice(ws, "aks-deployment") aks_service.update(enable_app_insights=True)
```

In the preceding snippet, we can activate App Insights' metrics directly from the Python authoring environment. While this is a simple argument in the service class, it gives you an incredible insight into the deployment.

Two important metrics to measure are data drift coefficients for both training data and model predictions. By automatically tracking the user input and the model predictions, you can compare a statistical correlation between the training data and the user input per feature dimension, as well as the training labels with the model prediction. This correlation should be tracked, monitored, and alerted daily to understand when your deployed model differs too much from the training data and so needs to be retrained.

Summary

In this chapter, you learned how to take a trained model and deploy it as a managed service in Azure through a few simple lines of code. To do so, we learned that Azure Machine Learning deployments are structured in multiple components: a binary model registered, versioned, and stored in blob storage; a deployment environment based on Docker and Conda registered, versioned, and stored in a container registry; a scoring file, which defines the inference config and a compute target and resources defining the deployment config.

While this gives you great flexibility to configure every detail of your environment and deployment targets, you can also use no-code deployments for specific frameworks (such as scikit-learn, TensorFlow, and ONNX). This will take your model and deploy it using an out-of-the-box default environment and deployment target. When specifying a custom compute target, you need to trade off scalability, flexibility, cost, and operational expense for each supported service. It's recommended you deploy prediction service experiments to ACI and production deployments to AKS. When you need to score hundreds of data points at once, you could also deploy an ML pipeline on AML Compute.

To improve the scoring performance, you can deploy your model to dedicated inferencing hardware on top of FPGAs. You need to deploy your nodes from the PBS family of Azure VMs and choose one of a few models that are currently supported (ResNet, DenseNet, VGG, and SSD-VGG based on TensorFlow). This will result in a 2x performance boost in scoring ML models compared to GPUs.

We also learned about another optimization technique that helps you port your models to other languages at the same time. The ONNX format provides a unified format to store ML pipelines that can be changed over multiple runtimes—for example, ONNX models can be run in PyTorch, TensorFlow, or MXNet. Microsoft provides its own standalone ONNX runtime that is written in C and optimized for scoring.

In the last section, we learned about monitoring and operating your models using Azure Machine Learning deployments. While it is fairly obvious to monitor metrics and telemetry, we also saw how to measure data drift of your service by collecting user input and model output over time. Detecting data drift is an important metric that allows you to know when a model needs to be retrained.

In the next chapter, we will automate the complete end-to-end ML process—everything that we learned so far—using Azure DevOps. This methodology, also referred to as MLOps and AIOps, will help you combine relevant ideas from DevOps and modern software development with ML and data engineering. The output will be a fully automated pipeline with automatic, auto-scaling blue-green deployments and automatic retraining.

13
MLOps—DevOps for machine learning

In the previous chapter, we covered **machine learning** (**ML**) deployments in Azure using automated Azure Machine Learning deployments for real-time scoring services, Azure Pipelines for batch prediction services, and ONNX, FPGAs, and Azure IoT Edge for alternative deployment targets. If you have read all of the chapters preceding this one, you will have seen and implemented a complete end-to-end ML pipeline with data cleansing, preprocessing, labeling, experimentation, model development, training, optimization, and deployment.

Congratulations on making it this far! You now possess all the skills needed to connect the bits and pieces together for MLOps and to create DevOps pipelines for your ML models.

Throughout this book, we have emphasized how every step of the ML training and deployment process can be scripted through Bash, PowerShell, the Python SDK, or any other library wrapping the Azure Machine Learning REST service. This is true for creating environments, starting and scaling clusters, submitting experiments, performing parameter optimization, and deploying fully fledged scoring services on Kubernetes. In this chapter, we will reuse all of these concepts to build a version-controlled, reproducible, automated ML training and deployment process as a **continuous integration/continuous deployment (CI/CD)** pipeline in Azure.

First, we will take a look at how to ensure reproducible builds, environments, and deployments with Azure DevOps. We will look at this from a code and artifact perspective and decide what to do with both to ensure that the same model is trained each time a build is started. We will take this very approach and map it to register and version data. This will allow you to audit your training and know what data was used to train a specific model at all times.

Next, we will take a look at validating your code, and code quality, automatically. You are probably already familiar with some testing techniques for application development.

However, we will take these techniques to the next level to test the quality of datasets and the responses of ML deployments.

In this chapter, we will cover the following topics:

- Ensuring reproducible builds and deployments
- Validating your code, data, and models

We'll begin by exploring a number of methods to ensure the reproducibility of your builds and deployments.

Ensuring reproducible builds and deployments

DevOps has many different meanings, but it is usually oriented toward enabling rapid and high-quality deployments when source code changes. One way of achieving high-quality operational code is to guarantee reproducible and predictable builds, which is also crucial for creating reproducible ML pipelines. While it seems obvious for application development that the compiled binary will look and behave in a similar manner, with only a few minor configuration changes, the same is not true for the development of ML pipelines.

There are four main problems that ML engineers and data scientists face that make building reproducible deployments very difficult:

- The development process is often performed in notebooks, so it is not always linear.
- There are mismatching library versions and drivers.
- Source data can be changed or modified.
- Non-deterministic optimization techniques can lead to completely different outputs.

We have discussed these issues in the first few chapters of this book, and you have probably seen them in a lot of places when implementing ML models and data pipelines, particularly in interactive notebooks such as Jupyter, JupyterLab, Databricks, Zeppelin, and Azure notebooks. While interactive notebooks have the great advantage of executing cells to validate blocks of models iteratively, they also often encourage a user to run cells in a non-linear order. The very benefit of using a notebook environment becomes a pain when trying to productionize or automate a pipeline.

The second issue that is quite common in ML is ensuring that the correct drivers, libraries, and runtimes are installed. While it is easy to run a linear regression model based on scikit-learn in either Python 2 or 3, it makes a huge difference if those CUDA, cuDNN, libgpu, OpenMPI, Horovod, and PyTorch versions match and work in deployment as they did during development. Using Docker helps a lot in providing reproducible environments, but it's not straightforward when using it throughout the experimentation, training, optimization, and deployment processes.

Another big problem faced by many data scientists is that often, data changes over time. Either a new batch of data is added during development, or data is cleaned, written back to the disk, and reused as input for a new experiment. Data, due to its variability in format, scale, and quality, can be one of the biggest issues when producing reproducible models. Thinking about data versions and checkpoints similarly to how you would think about version-controlling source code is absolutely essential, not only for reproducible builds but also for auditing purposes.

The last problem that makes ML deployments very difficult is that they often contain an optimization step, as discussed in *Chapter 9, Hyperparameter tuning and Automated Machine Learning*. While this optimization, either for model selection, training, hyperparameter tuning, or stacking, is essential to the ML life cycle, it adds a layer of uncertainty to your automatic deployment if non-deterministic processes are used. Let's find out how we can fight these problems step by step.

Azure DevOps gives you a great set of functionalities to automate everything in your CI/CD process. In general, it lets you run pieces of functionality, called tasks, grouped together in pipelines on a compute infrastructure that you define. You can either run pipelines that are triggered automatically through a new commit in your version control system or manually trigger them through a button; for example, for semi-automated deployments. **Build pipelines** run statelessly and don't output anything, whereas **release pipelines** are stateful pipelines that are supposed to generate artifacts and use them for releases and deployments. The reproducibility of your ML pipelines ensures that all the stages that you go through for training your model, such as data prep, hyperparameter tuning, and model evaluation, can, and do, flow into each other without you having to reinvent the wheel.

Version-controlling your code

This is not optional; using version control for your source code, data transformations, experiments, training scripts, and so on is essential. While many people and organizations might not be OK with storing code in private GitHub, GitLab, or Bitbucket repositories, you can also create your private repository in Azure DevOps. Creating a new project in Azure DevOps automatically creates a new Git repository for you.

Using version control for your code at all is more important than which version control system you use. Git works well, but so does Mercurial, and some people work with **Subversion** (**SVN**). However, making yourself familiar with the basic workflows of the version control system that you choose is essential. In Git, you should be able to create branches and commits, submit **pull requests** (**PRs**), comment on and review requests, and merge and squash changes.

This is also where the power lies: documenting changes. Changing your code should trigger an automatic pipeline that validates and tests your changes and, when successful and merged, trains your model and rolls it out to production. Your commit and PR history will not only become a great source of documenting changes, but is also useful when it comes to triggering, running, and documenting whether these changes are ready for production.

In order to work effectively with version control, it is essential that you try to move business logic out of your interactive notebooks as soon as possible. I would recommend using a hybrid approach, where you first test your code experiments in a notebook and gradually move the code to a module that is imported at the beginning of each file. Using auto-reload plugins, you can make sure that these modules get automatically reloaded whenever you change them, without needing to restart your kernel.

Moving code from notebooks to modules will not only make your code more reusable in your own experiments—there will be no need to copy utility functions from notebook to notebook—but it will also make your commit log much more readable. When multiple people change a few lines of code in a massive JSON file (that's how your notebook environment stores the code and output of every cell), then the changes made to the file will be almost impossible to review and merge. However, if those changes are made in a module—a separate file containing only executable code—then these changes will be a lot easier to read, review, reason about, and merge.

Figure 13.1 shows the Azure DevOps repository view, which is a good starting point for all subsequent MLOps tasks. Please note that your source code doesn't have to be stored in Azure DevOps Git repositories; you can use many other popular code hosting services, such as GitHub, Bitbucket, or SVN, or you can even use your own custom Git server:

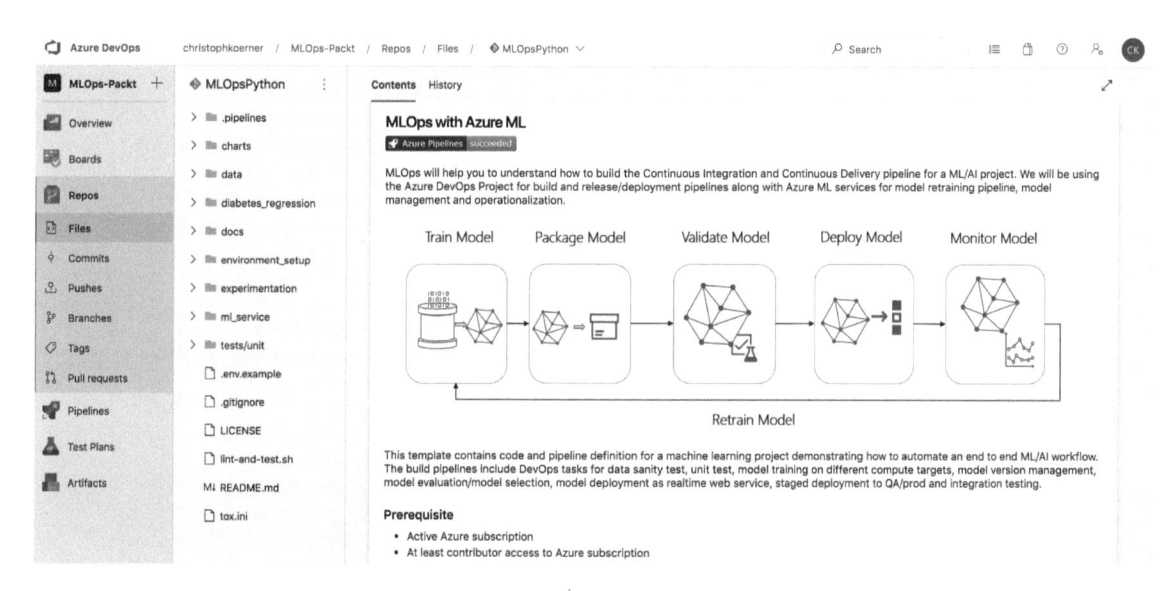

Figure 13.1: The Azure DevOps repository view

So, if you haven't already, brush up on your Git skills, create a (private) repository, and get started with version control; we will need it in the following sections.

Registering snapshots of your data

Building a versioning process around your training data is probably the hardest step that we will cover in this section. It is fairly obvious to check any data files that are small and readable (non-binary and non-compressed) in the version control system. However, together with your source code, it is usually the case for most data sources to be binary, compressed, or not small enough to store in Git. This is what makes this step so complicated and is the reason why many ML engineers prefer to skip it rather than do it properly from the beginning.

So then, how is it done properly? You can think of it like this: whenever you execute the same code, it should always pull and use the same data predictably—regardless of whether you execute the script today or in a year from now. A second constraint is that when you change your data or the input source of the training data, then you want to make sure the change is reflected in the version control system. Sounds simple, right?

In general, we need to differentiate operational data (transactional, stateful, or mutable) from historical data (analytical, partitioned, or immutable). When working with operational data—for example, an operational database storing customer data—we need to always create snapshots before pulling in the data for training. When using efficient data formats, such as Parquet or Arrow, and scalable storage systems, such as Azure Blob storage, this should never be an issue—even if you have multiple TBs of data. Snapshots could, and should, be incremental, such that only new data is added in new partitions.

The other obvious example is that your data might change when you change sensors, or you could see the effects of seasons on your data, which will showcase **data drift** on the datasets. Suddenly, your model does not perform as expected, and performance degrades. Therefore, once you have set up the pipelines as mentioned in this chapter, there is the possibility to retrain the model without having to change all the steps involved. This is because, as a result of using pipelines, data preprocessing should become a process that is automated and reproducible.

When dealing with historical, immutable data, we usually don't need to create extra snapshots if the data is partitioned—that is, organized in directories. This will make it easier to modify your input data source to point to a specific range of partitions instead of pointing to a set of files directly.

Once you have the data in place, it is strongly recommended that you use Azure Machine Learning to create snapshots of your datasets before you get started. This will create and track a reference to the original data, and provide you with a pandas or PySpark interface to read the data. This data will define the input of your pipeline.

Whenever you process data, it is helpful to parameterize your pipeline using a predictable placeholder. Looking up the current date in your program to determine which folder to write to is not very useful, as you will most likely have to execute the pipeline with the same parameters on multiple days when you run into errors. You should always parameterize pipelines from the calling script, such that you can always rerun failed pipelines and it will create the same outputs every time.

When using Azure DevOps pipelines to wrap your data preprocessing, cleaning, and feature engineering steps, your pipelines should always create—and eventually overwrite—the same output folder when called with the same arguments. This ensures that your pipeline stays reproducible, even when executed multiple days in a row for the same input data.

So, make sure that your input data is registered and versioned and that your output data is registered and parameterized. This takes a bit of configuring to set up properly, but it is worth it for the whole project life cycle.

Tracking your model metadata and artifacts

Moving your code to modules, checking it into version control, and versioning your data will help to create reproducible models. If you are building an ML model for an enterprise, or you are building a model for your start-up, knowing which model and which version is deployed and used in your service is essential. This is relevant for auditing, debugging, or resolving customer inquiries regarding service predictions.

We have covered this in previous chapters, and hopefully you are convinced by now that it's not only beneficial but absolutely essential to track and version your models in a model registry. The model consists of artifacts, files that are generated while training (for example, the model architecture and model weights), and metadata (for example, the dataset snapshot and version used for training, validation, and testing, the commit hash to know which code has produced the model, and the experiment and run IDs to know which other parameter configurations were tested before the model was selected).

Another important consideration is to specify and version-control the seed for your random number generators. During most training and optimization steps, algorithms will use pseudo-random numbers based on a random seed to shuffle data and choices. So, in order to produce the same model after running your code multiple times, you need to ensure that you set a fixed random number seed for every operation that is built on randomized behaviors.

The good thing about tracking your model artifacts in a model registry—for example, in Azure Machine Learning—is that you automatically trigger release pipelines in Azure DevOps when the artifacts change. *Figure 13.2* shows an Azure DevOps release pipeline, where you can select one or more ML models as artifacts for the pipeline, so updating a model in the registry can now trigger a release or deployment pipeline:

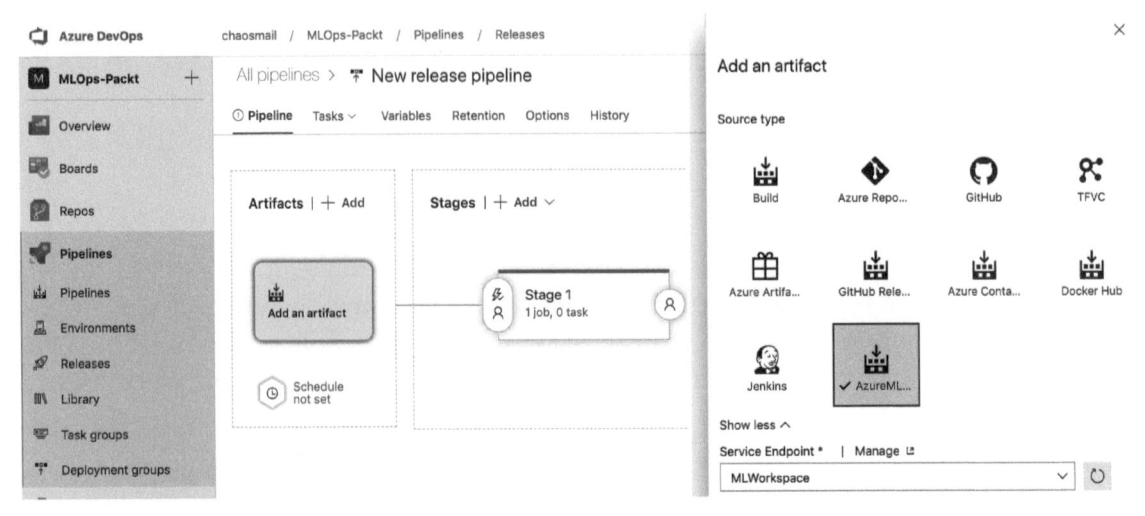

Figure 13.2: The Azure DevOps release pipeline

Once you understand the benefits of source code version control to your application code, you will understand that it makes a lot of sense for your trained models as well. However, instead of readable code, you now store the model artifacts—binaries that contain the model weights and architecture—and metadata for each model.

The ability to enable MLflow Tracking with your Azure Machine Learning workspace is another option in terms of tracking and logging experiment metrics and artifacts. The integration of MLflow with Azure Machine Learning enables you to explore a number of options. For example, when you're using MLflow Tracking for an experiment, and you've set up MLflow experiments, you can store the training metrics and models on a central environment within the Azure Machine Learning workspace. If you have read through this book from the beginning, you will recall that we have previously talked about the capabilities and functionalities across the different aspects of Azure Machine Learning. Therefore, if you deploy an MLflow experiment to your Azure Machine Learning—which is possible by deploying the experiment as a web service—you can still use all the functionalities with Azure Machine Learning, such as monitoring capabilities and the ability to detect data drift from your models.

Scripting your environments and deployments

Automating everything that you do more than once will ultimately save you a lot of time during development, testing, and deployment. The good thing with cloud infrastructure and services such as Azure Machine Learning and Azure DevOps is that the services provide you with all the necessary tools to automate every step easily. Sometimes, you will get an SDK, and sometimes, a specific automation will be built into the SDK directly—we have seen this for ML deployments where we could simply spin up an AKS cluster using Azure Machine Learning.

First of all, if you haven't done so already, you should start organizing your Python environments into requirements, **pyenv**, or **conda** files, and always start your projects with a clean standard environment. Whenever you add a package, add it to your requirements file and re-initialize your environment from the requirements file. This way, you'll ensure that you always have the libraries from your requirements file installed and nothing else.

Azure DevOps can help you with this by running integration tests on clean images, where all of your used tools need to be installed automatically during the test. This is usually one of the first tasks to implement on an Azure DevOps pipeline. Then, whenever you check in new code and tests to your version control system, the Azure DevOps pipeline is executed and also tests the installation of your environment automatically. Therefore, it's good practice to add integration tests to all of your used modules, such that you can never miss a package definition in your environment.

Figure 13.3 shows you how to add a simple Python task to a release pipeline:

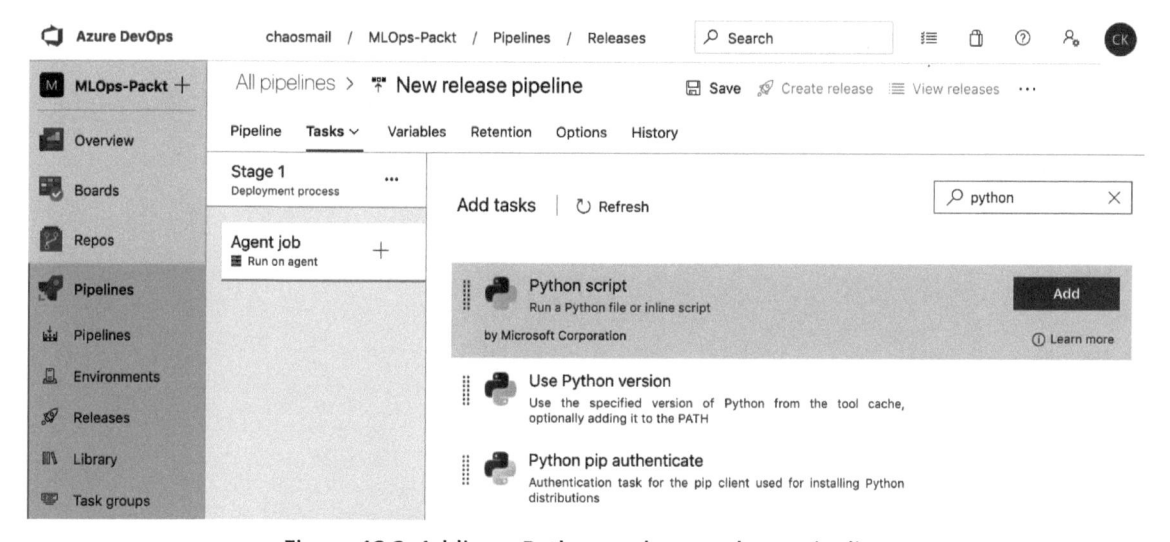

Figure 13.3: Adding a Python task to a release pipeline

If you have followed the previous chapters in this book, you might have figured out by now why we did all the infrastructure automation and deployments through an authoring environment in Python. If you have scripted these things, you can simply run and parameterize these scripts in the Azure DevOps pipelines.

The next step, which is usually a bit more difficult to achieve, is to script, configure, and automate the infrastructure. If you run a release pipeline that generates a model, you most likely want to spin up a fresh Azure Machine Learning cluster for this job so you don't interfere with other release or build pipelines or experimentation. While this level of automation is very hard to achieve on on-premises infrastructures, you can do this easily in the cloud. Many services, such as ARM templates in Azure or Terraform from HashiCorp, provide full control over your infrastructure and configuration.

The last part is to always automate deployments, especially with Azure Machine Learning. Deployments can be done through the UI and we know it's easy to click and configure the right model, compute target, and scoring file from there. However, doing so using code doesn't take much longer and gives you the benefit of a repeatable and reproducible deployment. If you have ever wondered whether you could simply deploy a new scoring endpoint to an AKS cluster—or even, simply, to no-code deployments—whenever you change the model definition, then let me tell you that this is exactly what you are supposed to do.

You will often be confronted to do the same thing in many different ways; for example, deploying an ML model from Azure Machine Learning via the CLI, Python, the UI, or a plugin in Azure DevOps. *Figure 13.4* shows the package for deploying ML models directly through a task in Azure DevOps:

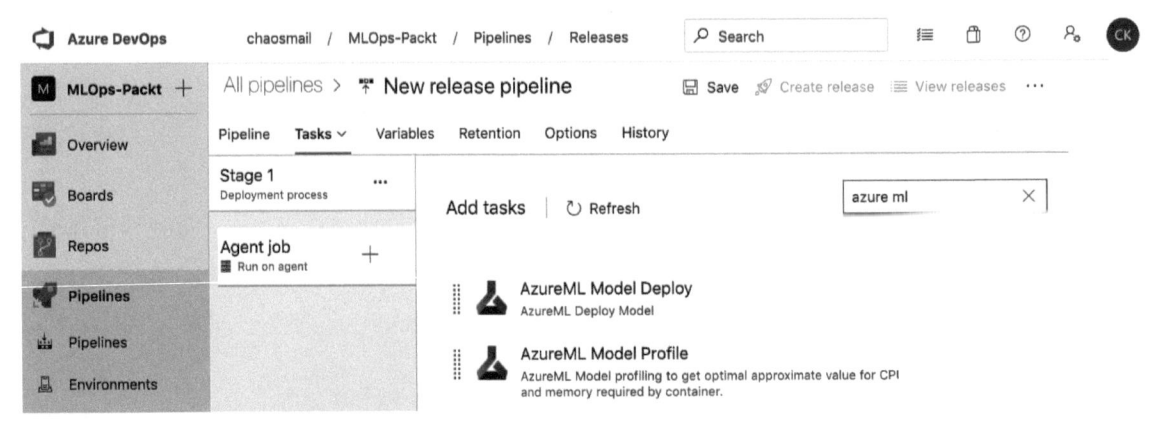

Figure 13.4: Deploying ML models in Azure DevOps

However, I recommend you stick to one way of doing things and then do all the automation and deployments in the same way. Having said this, using Python as the scripting language for deployments and checking your deployment code in version control is a good approach to take.

Reproducible builds and release pipelines are key and they have to begin at the infrastructure and environment level. Within the cloud, especially in Azure, this should be very easy, as most tools and services can be automated through the SDK.

> **Note**
>
> You can find an up-to-date example of an Azure Machine LearningOps pipeline in the Microsoft GitHub repository: https://github.com/microsoft/MLOps.

The Azure Machine Learning team put a lot of work into the SDK so that you can automate each piece, from ingestion to deployment, from within Python. Therefore, I strongly recommend you use this functionality.

Validating your code, data, and models

When implementing a CI/CD pipeline, you need to make sure you have all the necessary tests in place to deploy your newly created code with ease and confidence. Once you are running a CI or a CI/CD pipeline, the power of automated tests will become immediately evident. It not only protects certain pieces of code from failing while you are developing them, but it also protects your entire process—including the environment, data requirements, model initialization, optimization, resource requirements, and deployment—for the future.

When implementing a validation pipeline for our ML process, we align ourselves with the classical application development principles:

- Unit testing
- Integration testing
- End-to-end testing

We can translate these testing techniques directly to input data, models, and the application code of the scoring service.

Rethinking unit testing for data quality

Unit tests are essential to writing good-quality code. A unit test aims to test the smallest unit of code—a function—independently of all other code. Each test should only test one thing at a time and should run and finish quickly. Many application developers run unit tests either every time they change the code, or at least every time they submit a new commit to version control.

Here is a simple example of a unit test written in Python using the **unittest** module provided by the standard library in Python 3:

```
import unittest

class TestStringMethods(unittest.TestCase):
    def test_upper(self):
        self.assertEqual('foo'.upper(), 'FOO')
```

As you can see, we run a single function and test whether the outcome matches a predefined variable.

In Python, and many other languages, we differentiate between frameworks and libraries that help us to write and organize tests, and libraries to execute tests and create reports. **pytest** is a great library to execute tests, and so is **tox**. **unittest** and **mock** help you to set up and organize your tests in classes and mock out dependencies on other functions.

When you write code for your ML model, you will also find units of code that can, and should, be unit tested and should be tested on every commit. However, ML engineers, data engineers, and data scientists now deal with another source of errors in their development cycle: data. Therefore, it is a good idea to rethink what unit tests could mean in terms of data processing.

Once you get the hang of it, many doors open. Suddenly, you can see your input data feature dimensions as a single unit of something that you need to test in order to ensure that it is fulfilling requirements. This is especially important as we are always thinking of collecting new data and retraining the model at one point—if not even retraining it continuously as new training data is collected. Therefore, we always want to make sure that the data is clean.

So, when dealing with changing data over time and implementing CI/CD pipelines, you should always test your data to match the expected criteria. Good things to test in relation to each dimension include the following:

- Unique/distinct values
- Correlation
- Skewness
- Minimum/maximum values
- The most common value
- Values containing zero

Your unit test could look like the following example, and you can test all the individual requirements in separate tests:

```python
import unittest import pandas as pd
class TestDataFrameStats(unittest.TestCase):
    def setUp(self):
        # initialize and load df
        self.df = pd.DataFrame(data={'data': [0,1,2,3]}) def
    test_min(self):
        self.assertEqual(self.df.min().values[0], 0)
```

In the preceding code, we used **unittest** to organize the unit test in multiple functions within the same class. Each class could correspond to a specific data source, where we have wrappers testing each feature dimension. Once set up, we can install **pytest** and simply execute **pytest** from the command line to run the test.

In Azure DevOps, we can set up **pytest** or **tox** as a simple step in our build pipeline. For a build pipeline step, we can simply add the following block to the **azure-pipelines.yml** file:

```yaml
- script: |
    pip install pytest
    pip install pytest-cov
    pytest tests --doctest-modules
  displayName: 'Test with pytest'
```

In the preceding code, we first installed **pytest** and **pytest-cov** to create a **pytest** coverage report. In the next line, we executed **test**, which will now use the dataset and compute all the statistical requirements. If the requirements are not met according to the tests, the tests will fail and we will see these errors in the UI for this build. This adds great protection to your ML pipeline, as you can now ensure that no unforeseen problems with the training data make it into the release without you noticing.

Unit testing is essential, and so is unit testing for data. As with testing in general, it will take some initial effort to be implemented, the value of which isn't immediately obvious. However, you will soon see that having these tests in place will give you some peace of mind when deploying new models faster, as it will catch errors with the training data at build time and not when the model is already deployed.

Integration testing for ML

In application development, integration testing tests the combinations of multiple smaller units as individual components. You normally use a test driver to run the test suite and mock or stub other components in your tests that you don't want to test. In graphical applications, you could test a simple visual component while mocking the modules the component is interacting with. In the back-end code, you test your business logic module while mocking all dependent persistence, configuration, and UI components.

Integration tests, therefore, help you to detect critical errors when combining multiple units together, without the expense of scaffolding the entire application infrastructure. They sit between unit testing and end-to-end testing and are typically run per commit, branch, or PR on the CI runtime.

In ML, we can use the concept of integration testing to test the training process of an ML pipeline. This can help your training run find potential bugs and errors during the build phase. Integration testing allows you to test whether your model, pretrained weights, a piece of test data, and optimizer can yield a successful output. However, different algorithms require different integration tests to test whether something is wrong in the training process.

When training a deep neural network model, you can test a lot of interesting aspects with integration tests. Here is a non-exhaustive list:

- Verify correct weight initialization
- Verify default loss
- Verify zero input
- Verify single-batch fitting
- Verify activations
- Verify gradients

Using a similar list, you can easily catch cases where all activations are capped at the maximum value (for example, 1) in a forward pass, or when all gradients are 0 during a backward pass. Any experiment, test, or check you would perform manually before working with a fresh dataset and your model can, in theory, be run continuously in your CI runtime. So, any time your model gets retrained or fine-tuned, these checks run automatically in the background.

A more general assumption is that when training a regression model, the default mean should be close to the mean prediction value. When training a classifier, you could test the distribution of the output classes. In both cases, you can detect issues due to modeling, data, or initialization error sooner rather than later, and before embarking on the costly training and optimization process.

In terms of the runner and framework, you can choose the same libraries as used for unit testing because, in this case, integration testing differs only in the components that are tested and the way they are combined. Therefore, `unittest`, `mock`, and `pytest` are popular choices for scaffolding your integration testing pipeline.

Integration testing is essential for application development and for running end-to-end ML pipelines. It will save you a lot of worry, trouble, and expense if you can detect and avoid these problems automatically.

End-to-end testing using Azure Machine Learning

In end-to-end testing, we want to make a request to a deployed service in a staging environment and check the result of the service. To do so, we need to deploy the complete service altogether. End-to-end testing is critical for catching errors that are created when connecting all the components together and running the service in a staging or testing environment without mocking any of the other components.

In ML deployments, there are multiple steps where a lot of things can go wrong if not tested properly. Let's discard the more straightforward ones, where we need to make sure that the environment is correctly installed and configured. A more critical aspect of the deployment in Azure Machine Learning is the code for the application logic itself: the scoring file. There is no easy way to test the scoring file, the format of the request, and the output together, without a proper end-to-end test.

As you might imagine, end-to-end tests are usually quite expensive to build and to operate. First, you need to write code and deploy applications simply to test the code, which requires extra work, effort, and costs. However, this is the only way to truly test the scoring endpoint in a production-like environment from end to end.

The good thing is that by using Azure Machine Learning deployments, end-to-end testing becomes so easy that it should be part of everyone's pipeline. If the model allows it, we could even do a no-code deployment where we don't specify the deployment target. If this is not possible, we can specify an **Azure Container Instances (ACI)** as a compute target and deploy the model independently. This means taking the code from the previous chapter, wrapping it in a Python script, and including it as a step in the build process.

End-to-end testing is usually complicated and expensive. However, with Azure Machine Learning and automated deployments, a model deployment and sample request could just be part of the build pipeline.

Continuous profiling of your model

Model profiling is an important step during your experimentation and training phase. This will give you a good understanding of the amount of resources your model will require when used as a scoring service. This is critical information for designing and choosing a properly sized inference environment.

Whenever your training and optimization processes run continuously, your model requirements and profile might evolve. If you use optimization for model stacking or automated ML, your resulting models could grow bigger to fit the new data. So, it is good to keep an eye on your model requirements to account for deviations from your initial resource choices.

Luckily, Azure Machine Learning provides a model profiling interface, which you can feed with a model, scoring function, and test data. It will instantiate an inferencing environment for you, start the scoring service, run the test data through the service, and track resource utilization.

Summary

In this chapter, we introduced MLOps, a DevOps-like workflow for developing, deploying, and operating ML services. DevOps aims to provide a quick and high-quality way of making changes to code and deploying these changes to production.

We first learned that Azure DevOps gives us all the features to run powerful CI/CD pipelines. We can run either build pipelines, where steps are coded in YAML, or release pipelines, which are configured in the UI. Release pipelines can have manual or multiple automatic triggers—for example, a commit in the version control repository or if the artifact of a model registry was updated—and creates an output artifact for release or deployment.

Version-controlling your code is necessary, but it's not enough to run proper CI/CD pipelines. In order to create reproducible builds, we need to make sure that the dataset is also versioned and that pseudo-random generators are seeded with a specified parameter.

Environments and infrastructure should also be automated and deployments can be done from the authoring environment.

In order to keep the code quality high, you need to add tests to the ML pipeline. In application development, we differentiate between unit, integration, and end-to-end tests, where they test different parts of the code, either independently or together with other services. For data pipelines with changing or increasing data, unit tests should test the data quality as well as units of code in the application. Integration tests are great for loading a model or performing a forward or backward pass through a model independently from other components. With Azure Machine Learning, writing end-to-end tests becomes a real joy, as they can be completely automated with very little effort and expense.

Now you have learned how to set up continuous pipelines that can retrain and optimize your models and then automatically build and redeploy the models to production. In the final chapter, we will look at what's next for you, your company, and your ML services in Azure.

14
What's next?

Congratulations, you made it—what an incredible journey you've been on! By now, you should have learned how to preprocess data in the cloud, experiment with ML models, train deep learning models and recommendation engines on auto-scaling clusters, and optimize models and deploy them as web services to Kubernetes. Also, in the previous chapter, we learned how to automate this process as an MLOps pipeline, while ensuring high-quality builds and deployments.

In this last chapter, we will look at the most important points during this journey and help you to make the right decisions when implementing your ML project on Azure. It's easy to get lost or overwhelmed by technological and algorithmic choices; you could dive deep into modeling, infrastructure, or monitoring without getting any closer to having a good predictive model.

First, we will again remind you that ML really is mostly about data. AI should probably be called data cleansing and labeling, but of course, this doesn't sound as good as AI. You will come to understand that your data is key to great performance and hence the only thing you should care about at first. Your data is all that matters!

Once that's been covered, we will take a little look at the future, where ML will be mostly automated—or branded as MLaaS. It's always great to understand where the future is heading, and in case of AI, it is meta-learning and ML models that already know which models you should use and stack to achieve good predictive performance. And what is left when ML is fully automated? Exactly—your data!

We will then talk about the constant change and evolution of cloud services, especially focusing on PaaS offerings. We will take a look at why PaaS solutions are built and what their foundation is. This will help you know how to best prepare for change and why you are still betting on the right foundation despite the ever-coming change.

We will be covering multiple sections about ML without even talking about ML, but only about the importance of data. I know you must feel betrayed, disappointed, or confused. Where are the deep neural networks? Where are the 100 million parameters that we need to train? Where are all the cool new frameworks that we should try? Where are the TPUs and FPGAs that are supposed to run these models?

In the section following that, we will take a look at some important infrastructure and monitoring best practices when training and deploying ML models in Azure.

Lastly, we will talk about systematic measurements and rollouts of ML models. You will find out that in this field where we can track, measure, and tune everything, we won't rely on personal feelings, taste, or intuition. We measure the performance of ML models using hard metrics, we A/B test them for comparison, and we roll out the best version for our users.

The following topics will be covered in this chapter:

- Understanding the importance of data
- The future of ML is automated
- Change is the only constant—preparing for change
- Focusing first on infrastructure and monitoring
- Controlled rollouts and A/B testing

Understanding the importance of data

Many algorithmic problems for predictions and model fitting are hard to model, compute, and optimize using classic optimization algorithms or complex heuristics. Supervised machine learning provides a powerful new way to solve the most complex problems using optimization and a ton of labeled training data. The more data there is, the better the model.

One important thing to remember when working with ML algorithms is that models are powered by the training data you provide them and the training labels. Good data is the key to good performance. By data, we usually mean training data and using label annotations, one of the most notorious but also most important tasks in an ML project.

In most ML projects, you'll spend over 75% of the time with data analysis, preprocessing, and feature engineering. Understanding your data inside and out is critical to developing a successful predictive model. Think about it this way—the only thing that makes you stand out from your competition is your data. Most likely, your competitors have access to a similar set of algorithms, optimizations, and compute infrastructure as you; the only thing they don't have is your data (hopefully). Hence, this is where your secret to success lies: in understanding, interpreting, modeling, and preparing your data for high-quality predictions.

It's also important to keep in mind that the biggest opportunity you have to increase the predictive baseline performance of any of your models is to improve your data, for example, through better feature engineering or the addition of more or new data. Don't get lost trying, tuning, and stacking models—rather, spend most of your time and resources on data preprocessing and feature engineering.

Feature engineering is where you can shine and win the prediction game. Are you dealing with dates? Pull in other data sources, such as local and global holidays, and nearby events; add relative dates, for example, days before a holiday, days before a weekend; and so on.

Are you dealing with locations, cities, or countries? Pull in demographic data, pull in political data, pull in geographic data. You get the point: the better your data gets, the better your model will be.

There is only so much that your model can do. Yes, you can stack multiple models, tune and optimize them, optimize for different metrics, and so on. However, your biggest leverage is your data. A good plan for any ML model is to start with a very simple baseline model. Working with categorical data? Choose a gradient-boosted tree ensemble and stick with the default parameters. Predicting continuous values? Choose a logistic regression model. Start small and make sure you get your data right before starting to fiddle with your model.

Always start with a baseline model. Use this model to build all your automation, infrastructure, and metrics around, then deploy the baseline model. It's worth noting that the baseline model should perform better than a random approach. Once the pipeline is finished, you can now dive into the data, add new data, perform better feature engineering, deploy again, test, and re-iterate. Reducing your model to a primitive baseline model is a difficult step, but it will help you to succeed in managing your priorities during the first phase of the project.

Why is the baseline model approach so important? Because it sets your mindset for an iterative project, where you constantly measure, add data, retrain, and improve your model. Your model will require retraining and you need to measure when this is the case. In order to retrain, you need new training data.

In a perfect setup, you would install a continuous data collection pipeline that collects new training data and training labels directly from your current product. Does your model predict search relevance? Collect search queries and the clicked results. Does your model predict fraud? Collect new data and the results of manually verified fraud cases. Does your model predict hashtags? Track predictions and let your users change them if they're not accurate.

In all these examples, we continuously track relevant training data, which we can use for constant retraining and fine-tuning. Having this constant stream of training data could be the competitive advantage for your business that sets you up for success. Hence, when you are in charge of an ML project, think about how you are going to retrain the model in the future.

Last but not least, you need to get C-level buy-in for a data strategy. Data is your fuel— you need loads of it to implement and improve ML models. This often requires a mental shift in most companies, as data is now directly used for predictions. Hence, data quality matters, data lineage is important so that you can understand where it came from, timeliness is important, and correctness is absolutely essential. So, make sure that data is a first-class citizen in your company that gets the support, love, and care it deserves.

The future of ML is automated

Training an ML model is a complex iterative process that includes data preparation, feature engineering, model selection, optimization, and deployment. Above all, an enterprise-grade end-to-end ML pipeline needs to be reproducible, interpretable, secure, and automated, which poses an additional challenge for most companies in terms of know-how, costs, and infrastructure requirements.

In previous chapters, we learned the ins and outs of this process, and hence we can confirm that there is nothing simple or easy about it. Tuning a feature engineering approach will affect model training; the missing value strategy during data cleansing will influence the optimization process.

On top of all this, the information captured by your model is rarely constant and therefore most ML models require frequent retraining and deployments. This leads to a whole new requirement for MLOps: a DevOps pipeline for ML to ensure continuous integration and continuous deployment of your data, pipelines, and models. We covered this in a previous chapter.

Automated Machine Learning helps to simplify this complex iterative process by automating many of the challenges in AI. Instead of manually tuning the input data, then selecting, optimizing, and deploying an ML model, an Automated Machine Learning service just requires the input data as well as a few business-related configurations, such as the type of prediction to train and perform.

The Azure Automated Machine Learning service currently allows the user to choose between classification, regression, or time-series forecasting tasks. By automating all manual steps, the service can optimize the complete ML pipeline and even stack multiple models to improve prediction performance. The outcome is a single model. The biggest benefit of this is that the user can now focus on the most important part of the ML process: understanding, acquiring, and cleaning data.

In many cases, Automated Machine Learning services will outperform manually trained models while requiring significantly less in the way of training and operation costs. The reason for this is that many tasks, such as choosing the correct categorical embedding, handling imbalanced data, selecting the best model, finding the best parameters, and combining multiple models to improve performance, can be systematically optimized as opposed to being chosen manually.

Every major cloud provider offers mature services to perform Automated Machine Learning in the cloud and functionalities to deploy these models conveniently. Automated Machine Learning is a great way to save time and costs while providing your existing employees with the tools needed for training complex end-to-end ML pipelines. This helps your company to focus on understanding your data and business requirements rather than tinkering with ML models and tools. This makes Automated Machine Learning a real service—MLaaS.

Change is the only constant – preparing for change

When working with any of the big cloud providers, you should differentiate their offerings broadly into three types of service:

- **Infrastructure as a Service (IaaS)**
- **Platform as a Service (PaaS)**
- **Software as a Service (SaaS)**

IaaS services are all-infrastructure abstractions such as virtual machines (compute), disks (storage), and networking; PaaS services are platforms built on top of these components with additional functionality that exposes the underlying services. SaaS services, in contrast, are just exposed through a UI and don't give you any access to the underlying data.

Azure Machine Learning is a great example of a PaaS offering, as it combines different infrastructure services, UIs, and SDKs to give you great new features and full access to the underlying services, such as blob storage, training clusters, and container registries. You will also see on your monthly Azure bill that you will spend most of your money on infrastructure services when using a PaaS solution.

While IaaS solutions build the foundation for all other cloud services, they are not very likely to change drastically over the next few years. New improvements will make their way to the market, such as ultra SSDs and new compute instance types, but the existing APIs and offerings are not likely to be discontinued.

The same is not true for PaaS services, as they are usually built as managed services for when a lot of customers all have a similar problem to solve. PaaS solutions are built to help customers use other infrastructure services without implementing tons of boilerplate over and over again. How many times have you seen a feature of Azure Machine Learning and thought, "*Hey, I could easily implement this on my own*"? Trust me, you are not alone. And that's why PaaS exists in the first place.

However, the downside with customer-driven needs is that those needs and usage patterns are constantly evolving. New use cases are coming up (such as MLOps) that ask for new services or extensions to existing services to be supported. Hence, you should always expect that PaaS will change over time, and in this section, I will help you prepare for this change.

When reading through this book, you might have found a small discrepancy between features or APIs that we describe and the current APIs and features in Azure. If you were understandably confused and asked yourself how this book could possibly already be out of date, I want to assure you that what we presented is the right technology to bet on. PaaS offerings in general and MLaaS offerings specifically undergo massive changes and improvements all the time. Expect change!

Expect names to change—this is probably the most common change. Companies are notoriously bad at naming products, and Azure and all other cloud providers are no exception. This might look like a big change or inconvenience, but in fact it is nothing more than changing the name of a service or component or hiding it somewhere else in the UI. In the past year, we went from ML Studio Azure Machine Learning to Azure Machine Learning, and compute instances were called Azure Batch, BatchAI, AML Compute, and training clusters. Don't let this distract you—expect some new interesting names popping up for the functionality that you know and love.

Expect UIs to change—this is the most visible and quite a common pattern in Azure lately. Many services get revamped UIs, some integrated into the Azure UI and some in a separate application. Expect some functionality to be exposed only in one UI and not another. Most often, however, a new UI means just the same or similar functionality being accessible through a new interface. This is one of the reasons why we work so much with the Python API instead of the graphical interface—and so should you.

Expect classes to change and packages to move around in the SDK. Most APIs of most cloud providers for ML solutions are constantly evolving (Automated Machine Learning and MLOps are currently in preview and undergo loads of changes). Azure has invested a lot of money in its ML service, so change is inevitable. A good way to prepare for this change is to abstract code into specific implementations that can be swapped out easily with new functionality. Another good practice is to be cautious with library updates, but also don't stay behind the most recent version for too long.

Do you agree that change is the only constant, given all these circumstances? And also, don't forget that all PaaS solutions ultimately build on an IaaS solution, which provides a rock-solid foundation for your compute, storage, and networking infrastructure—a foundation using auto-scale multi-GPU training clusters and real-time scoring deployments on Kubernetes.

Despite constant change, you are building on the right foundation!

Focusing first on infrastructure and monitoring

Successfully applied ML projects depend on an iterative approach to tackle data collection, data cleansing, feature engineering, and modeling. After a successful deployment and rollout, you should go back to the beginning, keep an eye on your metrics, and collect more data. By now, it should be clear that you will definitely repeat some of your development and deployment steps during your project.

Getting the infrastructure around your ML project right will save you a lot of trouble. The key to successful infrastructure is automation and versioning, as we discussed in the previous chapter. So, I recommend that you take a few extra days to set up your infrastructure automation and register your datasets, models, and environments—all within Azure Machine Learning.

The same is true for monitoring. In order to make educated decisions about whether your model is working as intended, whether the training data is still accurate, or whether the resource utilization is high enough, you need accurate metrics. Adding metrics to a project after deployment is quite tricky, and so you should really be aware of what you measure, what you monitor, and what you alert on. Take some extra time at the beginning of your project to think about the metrics that you are going to track.

Prioritizing infrastructure while working on the data and models is hard. If you can afford the luxury to split these into separate teams for ML infrastructure, modeling, and data, then this might not be the case for you. However, this is often not feasible. In order to avoid this prioritization issue, I always recommend starting with a simple baseline model and start building your infrastructure automation using the simple baseline model.

Pick the simplest model with default parameters for your use case, a small set of training data, and the most important engineered features. In the next step, you build this into a pipeline that builds your model automatically and deploys it into a staging environment. The great thing about this approach is that you automatically prioritize infrastructure and always output a deployed scoring service. This will set you up for success.

As a next step, dive into the data. Make sure you understand the data and its quality, how to fill missing values, and how to preprocess features. You can add additional data and work on feature engineering to turn your raw input data into interpretable data. If you pick a good baseline model, this work should greatly improve the performance of the baseline and give your colleagues a scoring service API to use with the new service.

Once you are confident that you have built a solid data pipeline, you can tackle modeling, including model selection, training, validation, optimization, and stacking. Again, you should be able to see incremental improvements that can be measured and continuously deployed to any QA environment. Once your performance is good enough, roll out the service to your customers and start collecting metrics and more training data.

When you develop using compute infrastructure in the cloud, it is easy to quickly spend a few thousand dollars for a couple of unused or under-utilized virtual machines. So, I would also recommend that you regularly check the number of machines and their utilization. If something is not used anymore, shut it down or scale it to only a few instances. Remember that the cloud's number-one benefit is scalable infrastructure. So, please take advantage of it. Shut down your authoring notebook machines when you don't use them anymore.

Controlled rollouts and A/B testing

Deployments of ML models can be considered similar to that of features and changes in application development. Consider a retrained and reoptimized model to be similar to a small UI change in the application when rolling a model out to your users. This might not be obvious at first, but put yourself into a user's shoes in a scenario where suddenly a recommendation algorithm changes from its previous behavior.

Rollouts should never be uncontrolled or based on personal feelings or preferences— they should be based solely on hard metrics. The best and most systematic way to roll out new features and updates to your users is to define a key metric, roll out your new model to one section of the users (group B) and serve the old model to the remaining section of the users (group A). Once the metrics for the users in group B exceed the metrics from group A over a defined period of time, you can confidently roll out the feature to all your users.

This concept is called A/B testing and is used in many tech companies to roll out new services and features. As you can see in the *Figure 14.1*, you split your traffic into a control group and a challenger group, where only the latter is served the new model:

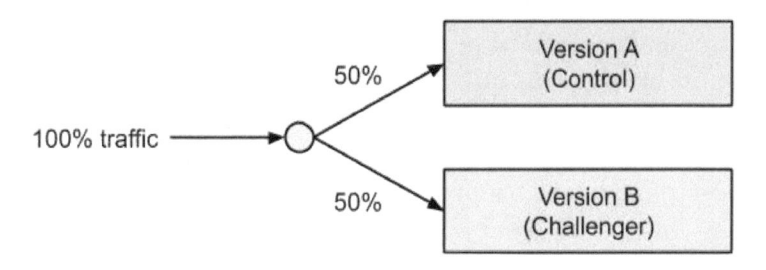

Figure 14.1: Splitting traffic into control and challenger groups

Another best practice for deploying code changes was covered in a previous chapter: blue-green deployments. In this deployment method, you deploy a separate service with each code change. Each service connects to your database but each service contains a different version of your code. First, you serve all traffic from the old service. Once the new service is up and running and the health checks have finished successfully, the router will send all requests to the new service. Finally, if there are no active requests left on the old service, you can shut it down.

This process is a very safe way to update stateless application services with zero or minimal downtime. It also helps you to fall back to the old service if the new one doesn't deploy successfully. The *Figure 14.2* shows the blue-green strategy, where blue and green represent completely separate versions of your application service or ML model. We can see that both stateless services connect to the same database, and we switch from one service to the second fully-functional service:

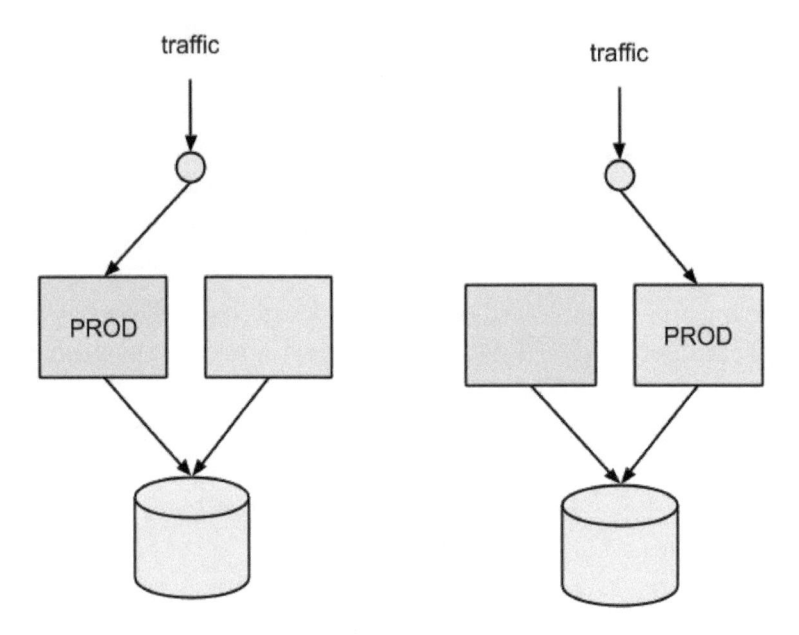

Figure 14.2: The blue-green strategy

A/B testing and blue-green deployments work very well together as they are really similar. Both require the deployment of a fully functional service that is accessible to a subset of your users through routing policies. If you use Azure Machine Learning for your deployment and rollout strategy, you are very well covered. First, all deployments through Azure Machine Learning to ACI or AKS are blue-green deployments, which makes it easy for you to fall back to a previous version of your model.

Azure Machine Learning deployments on AKS support up to six model versions behind the same endpoint to implement either blue-green deployments or A/B testing strategies. You can then define policies to split the traffic between these endpoints; for example, you can split traffic by percentage. Here is a small code example of how to create another version on an AKS endpoint that should serve another version of your model to 10% of the users:

```
from azureml.core.webservice import AksEndpoint
endpoint.create_version(version_name = "version-2",
        inference_config=inference_config,
        models=[model],
        tags = {'modelVersion':'2'},
        description = "my second version", traffic_percentile = 10)
```

In the preceding code, we show the preview feature of controlled rollouts for Azure Machine Learning and AKS. We use a different combination of model and inference configuration to deploy a separate service under the same endpoint. The traffic splitting now happens automatically through routing in Kubernetes. However, in order to align with a previous section of this chapter, expect this functionality to improve in the future, as it gets used by many customers when rolling out ML models.

Summary

In this chapter, we took a look at a few things from a high level—data, automation, change, infrastructure, monitoring, and rollouts. I hope that our coverage of these topics made sense to you after reading through experimentation, feature engineering, training, optimization, and deployment in the earlier chapters.

It's important to understand that your data will control and influence everything, and hence making data a first-class citizen in your company is a first great step. Hiring a *VP of Data* and defining standards on data quality, lineage, and discoverability are just a few of the measures you can take.

Automated Machine Learning will run the world in a couple of years. The idea is quite simple: a trained meta-model will always be better at proposing, training, optimizing, and stacking models for higher predictive performance than humans. This makes total sense; it's just another parameter optimization step that also includes the model architecture. Another interesting thought is that Automated Machine Learning will offer true MLaaS to users who aren't ML-savvy. Maybe a prediction column will be provided in Excel, or an ML transformation step in Power BI, meaning regular office users can suddenly harness the power of ML through spreadsheet applications.

We mentioned in this chapter that change is inevitable when working with PaaS in the cloud. This is because PaaS solutions are designed to implement typical customer solutions and drive you toward consuming more infrastructure services. As customer needs evolve, so do these PaaS offerings. Hence, a good takeaway is to not get too attached to product names, UIs, or SDK packages, but rather to understand whether the underlying infrastructure is the right thing for you. If so, then you can easily abstract the implementation details from your code to be prepared for change.

In the final section, we covered the idea of controlled rollouts through A/B testing and blue-green deployments. These are best practices for ML deployments, as blue-green deployments help you to implement zero-downtime deployments while A/B testing enables you to verify and compare the performance of a new model against a control group.

We hope you enjoyed this book and learned how to master Azure Machine Learning. Reach out to us on social media and tell us what you learned, what you liked, and also what could be improved in this book. We would love to hear your feedback.

Until then, happy machine learning!

Index

About

All major keywords used in this book are captured alphabetically in this section. Each one is accompanied by the page number of where they appear.

A

accelerate: 18, 368-369
active: 18, 117, 158, 333, 404
acyclic: 129, 151, 350
adaboost: 222
adadelta: 316
adapters: 140
aggregate: 86, 372
algorithm: 4, 16, 22, 27-28, 30-31, 38-39, 53-54, 101, 105, 107, 176-177, 190-191, 195-199, 203, 220-225, 253, 258, 286, 309-310, 326, 337-338, 342-343, 352, 403
amazon: 324-325, 327-328, 334
analysis: 15, 24, 26, 32, 44, 49, 53, 72, 97, 104-105, 109, 139, 147, 186, 197, 205-206, 274, 351, 370, 397
apache: 302, 306, 311, 314-315, 321
append: 163
argument: 119, 127, 130-132, 134, 139-140, 154-155, 157, 159-161, 163, 168, 198, 231, 233, 259, 264, 266, 276, 293, 319, 357, 374
arrays: 127-128, 254, 258, 350, 370
artifacts: 61, 71, 73, 75, 82, 85, 88, 90, 96, 109, 146, 236, 355-356, 380, 383-384

assets: 351
attribute: 114, 201, 277
auditing: 119, 145, 379, 383
augmented: 245, 253, 258-259, 268
automated: 29
authoring: 41-42, 44, 58, 61, 67, 71-72, 76-77, 89, 93, 96, 114, 119, 147, 156, 169, 225, 230, 236-237, 253-254, 260, 281, 314, 353, 356-358, 361, 374, 386, 393, 403
automation: 25, 67, 73, 371, 385-386, 398, 402, 405
automl: 295-296
automlstep: 148
automobile: 55
auto-scale: 152, 401
azure-cli: 76
azureml: 42, 56, 63, 74-75, 77-78, 84, 88-89, 91-95, 114, 126-128, 131, 135, 139, 149-152, 157-160, 162-167, 226-227, 229-232, 237, 260, 264, 275-278, 280-284, 287, 296, 304, 319, 354-357, 359-361, 363-364, 367-369, 374, 405

B

bag-of-words: 22, 100, 176, 186, 187, 189, 190, 193, 194, 195, 198, 199, 208,
bandit: 281, 283-284
barrier: 309, 317, 320
baseline: 12-13, 23-26, 57, 274, 397-398, 402
bayesian: 27, 271-272, 274, 276, 281, 285-290, 298, 309, 320, 326, 338
bearer: 362
binary: 5, 9, 20, 43, 126, 128, 141, 224-226, 234, 244-245, 247, 332, 335-336, 345, 352, 367, 374, 378, 381
bindings: 165, 173, 338
blocks: 54-56, 143, 146-148, 151, 154, 165, 168-169, 171, 302, 308, 326, 340-341, 3
boolean: 131, 138
boosting: 25, 213-214, 218, 221-225, 233-234, 236, 240, 332, 352
bootstrap: 219, 240
boundary: 215, 217, 247-248
boxplots: 8-9
branch: 26, 130, 390
builders: 133, 135

C

callback: 81, 87-88, 234-235, 257, 259, 264-265, 316
categories: 17, 20, 24, 37, 45-47, 49, 177-178, 180, 183, 185, 200, 216
characters: 130, 195-196, 223, 245
classes: 15-16, 43, 101-102, 104, 108, 221, 266, 388, 391, 401
client: 360, 371
cluster: 6, 26, 31, 40-42, 44, 52, 61, 67, 71-72, 89, 91-94, 96, 101-104, 107, 109, 114-115, 147, 149, 153, 157, 163, 214, 222, 229-232, 236-237, 239, 253, 260-261, 263-264, 267-268, 272, 277-278, 295-296, 301-302, 306-307, 314, 317-319, 321, 338, 353, 358, 361-363, 369, 371-372, 385-386
code-first: 40, 53, 169, 171
codegen: 361
cognitive: 36-37, 39, 44-46, 49-53, 67, 203, 205-207, 258
complexity: 27-29, 38, 101, 253
component: 15, 72, 197, 390, 401
compose: 146
compressed: 6, 381
compute: 6, 11-12, 21, 27, 32, 35-38, 40-42, 44, 54, 60-61, 71-72, 74-78, 89, 91-97, 105, 109, 112, 114-116, 119, 129, 135, 143-149, 152-153, 156-157, 161, 163-164, 167, 176, 185-186, 193, 195, 198-200, 202, 208, 214, 219, 221-222, 225-226, 229-232, 235, 239, 251, 253-254, 257-258, 260-262, 264, 268, 274, 277-278, 281, 283, 286, 288, 296-298, 302, 304, 310, 314, 317-321, 327, 330, 337, 339, 345, 350-353, 355-356, 358-363, 365, 368-369, 371-374, 380, 386, 389, 391, 397, 400-401, 403
concurrent: 277-278, 287, 304-305
configure: 57, 63, 66-67, 73, 92-94, 96, 144, 146, 149-151, 154, 159, 162-163, 166, 170, 172-173, 198, 226, 229-230, 232, 235-236, 259-260, 273, 281, 283, 315, 340, 342, 352, 358, 361, 374, 386
constraint: 26, 382
construct: 138, 223, 231, 255-256, 267, 282
consumers: 116, 118, 121, 139
containers: 37, 61, 372-373
continuous: 5, 8, 10-11, 20, 25, 27, 41, 45, 105, 146, 148, 159-160, 178, 201-202, 215, 218, 223-224, 274, 279-281, 286-287, 297, 331, 378, 392-393, 398-399
contrast: 92, 202, 217, 233, 244, 268, 334, 400
controls: 282
conversion: 127, 132, 191, 203, 368
cosine: 21, 193, 324, 329-331, 345
covariance: 100
cpu-based: 277, 304, 312, 366
custom: 3, 32, 35-37, 39-40, 44-45, 49-53, 55, 59, 61, 63, 66-67, 71, 131, 134, 138, 152, 159-160, 164, 166, 203, 207, 231, 234, 255, 258, 265, 267, 314-315, 317, 333, 365, 368-370, 374, 381
cyclic: 21

D

database: 6, 32, 112-113, 125, 152, 192, 246, 290, 382, 404
databricks: 37, 40, 44, 66, 92, 148, 302, 314, 317-318, 370, 379
dataflow: 126-131, 134-135, 137-140

dataframe: 56, 112, 115, 118, 120, 123-124, 155, 227, 229, 232, 295, 330, 389
dataset: 4-5, 7-12, 14-18, 20-21, 25, 37, 56-57, 60-61, 72, 97-103, 105-106, 108, 112-130, 133-134, 137, 139-141, 143, 146-147, 151-157, 164-165, 168, 173, 176-181, 184, 195-196, 198-199, 201, 214, 219, 222-223, 225-229, 232-233, 244, 254, 258-259, 262, 265-266, 289, 293, 295-297, 302-303, 305, 330, 332, 363, 383, 389-390, 392
datastore: 74, 114, 143, 146, 151-154, 156, 160-161, 163-166, 168, 227, 237, 263-264
debugging: 255, 317, 354, 383
decimal: 24, 131-132
decoder: 203
decouple: 119, 148, 154
delimited: 139, 152, 155, 227
dependency: 12-14, 21, 26, 32, 162, 356-357
deployment: 29, 32, 35, 37, 41, 44, 52, 56, 62, 66, 75, 146, 148, 163, 168, 331, 350-356, 358-360, 362-363, 365-369, 371-372, 374, 377-379, 384-387, 391-392, 399, 402, 404-405
derived: 4, 47, 133, 141, 180, 218

detection: 9, 18, 23, 31-32, 37-39, 44-45, 47, 49-50, 53, 67, 147, 159, 206, 214, 244, 265, 351, 370
deviations: 392
devops: 144, 159, 168, 171-173, 375, 377-378, 380-381, 383-386, 389, 392, 399
diagnostic: 372-373
dimension: 7, 10, 20-22, 98, 100, 105, 107, 178, 197, 201, 217, 220, 246, 275, 279, 337, 374, 388-389
distribute: 112, 307, 310, 317, 319-320
diverse: 279, 333, 339, 343, 345
docker: 29, 40, 60, 66, 94-96, 147, 230-231, 237, 264, 278, 350-353, 356-358, 374, 379
domain: 8, 18, 21, 29, 36, 38-39, 45, 49, 53, 244, 249-250, 265-266, 285, 288, 293, 306
downstream: 18

E

eigenvalue: 100
embedded: 6, 29, 91, 140, 204, 239, 365
enable: 161, 165-166, 231, 295, 306, 315, 319, 360, 370, 374, 384
encode: 21-22, 32, 98, 135-136, 178, 200, 223, 228, 340

endpoint: 36, 46, 51, 67, 143, 146, 158-159, 168, 173, 206, 356, 360, 364, 386, 391, 405
end-to-end: 3, 26-27, 32, 35-36, 39-40, 45, 56, 61, 65-67, 116, 140, 144, 146, 148, 168, 176, 203-205, 208, 251, 262, 268, 272, 288-291, 331, 369, 375, 377, 387, 390-393, 399-400
enforcing: 162
engine: 30, 53, 59, 126-127, 165-166, 314, 317-318, 323-326, 329, 331-333, 336, 339, 341, 344, 349
ensemble: 14, 23, 25-26, 28, 105, 213-214, 217-224, 240, 243-244, 250, 274, 289, 302, 305-307, 354, 398
entity: 44, 50, 203, 206, 351
entropy: 14, 224
epochs: 43, 63, 81, 85, 88, 253, 257, 259, 264-265, 271, 276, 282, 302, 316
explode: 195
extract: 17, 20, 22, 46, 111, 113, 125-127, 129-130, 140, 143, 152, 173, 175-176, 185, 188, 191, 200, 206, 213, 232, 252, 306, 351

F

feature: 3-8, 10, 12-18, 20-24, 26-29, 32, 42, 53-54, 59, 66, 79, 86, 97-98, 100-101, 104-105, 107, 109, 111-112, 125-126, 129, 136-137, 145-147, 151, 157, 171, 175-180, 184-185, 187, 193-194, 196-197, 199, 203, 205-206, 208, 217, 220, 223, 226-227, 233-235, 239, 244-245, 250-253, 256, 265-268, 272, 274, 288, 290, 293, 295, 298, 301, 321, 324, 326-327, 329-332, 336, 340, 345, 349, 364, 368-369, 374, 383, 388-389, 397-400, 402-403, 405
fields: 19, 118
fine-tune: 18, 36, 39, 201, 253, 265, 267
frequency: 119, 143, 156, 159-160, 173, 176, 186, 194, 199, 342
function: 20, 26, 51, 56, 79, 84, 87-88, 93, 99, 119, 122-124, 132, 134-135, 137-140, 172, 176, 188, 199, 202, 205-206, 208, 215, 217-218, 222, 224-225, 227, 230-231, 234-235, 246-249, 254, 256, 258-259, 276, 279, 283, 285-286, 297, 307, 317-318, 324, 326, 329, 333-337, 339, 341-345, 353-354, 356, 358, 360, 362, 387-388, 392

G

gaussian: 286, 298
general: 26, 29, 38, 44-45, 73, 107, 124, 128, 134, 140, 216, 236, 243, 260-261, 266, 272, 281, 291, 312, 314, 331, 358, 368, 372, 380, 382, 389, 391, 401
generative: 205
github: 100, 150, 326, 338, 341, 344, 368, 380-381, 387
gradient: 26, 178, 203, 213, 217-218, 222, 224, 234, 236, 239-240, 247, 308, 310-313, 316-318, 320, 332, 337-338, 352

H

histogram: 228, 245
horovod: 302, 310-311, 314-321, 379
hybrid: 37, 252, 324, 326, 339-341, 345, 349, 380
hyperdrive: 28, 100, 148, 154, 271, 275-278, 280-284, 287, 297, 301-302, 304

I

image-: 265
implicit: 205, 244, 324, 326, 334-336, 341, 344-345
inactivity: 96
inception: 249, 363-364
inference: 218, 307, 320, 350, 353, 356-362, 365-366, 368-369, 371, 374, 392, 405
insights: 3, 5, 17-18, 23, 27, 29, 32, 58-59, 62, 96-97, 100, 107, 217, 370, 373-374
iterator: 258-259

J

jupyter: 60-61, 71, 76, 122, 225, 232, 235-237, 253-254, 260-261, 268, 358, 379

K

kubelet: 373
kubernetes: 37, 40-41, 44, 52, 61, 66-67, 272, 314, 318, 353, 358, 361, 371, 373, 378, 395, 401, 405

L

labels: 17-18, 20, 42, 49, 97, 100, 102-103, 105, 112, 200, 204, 227, 232, 252, 255, 258, 313, 374, 397-398
latent: 197, 200, 204, 251, 337-338, 340
lemmas: 191
leverage: 29, 44, 203, 317, 398

linear: 10, 12-13, 15,
  19-20, 25, 54, 72, 97,
  100-101, 103-105, 109,
  147, 177, 197, 202, 217,
  244-246, 248, 250, 252,
  272, 293, 313, 379
logistic: 13, 19, 23, 26, 217,
  244, 250, 272, 398

M

machine: 3-4, 6, 19, 24-26,
  28-30, 32, 35-42, 44,
  53-67, 71-79, 81-83,
  85-92, 94-100, 109,
  111-112, 114-117, 119-123,
  125-126, 128-129,
  140-141, 143-152,
  156-157, 159-173, 175,
  178, 203, 206, 208,
  213-214, 218, 222-223,
  225-229, 231-232,
  234-240, 243-244,
  253-255, 257-258, 260,
  263-265, 268, 271-272,
  274-275, 277, 280-281,
  284-286, 288-298,
  301-305, 310-314,
  317-321, 323-324, 326,
  340-341, 345, 349-350,
  352-367, 369-372,
  374-375, 377-379, 382,
  384-387, 391-393, 397,
  399-402, 404-406
median: 5, 8, 10, 12,
  125, 281-282, 284
memory: 20, 26, 32, 92,
  123, 125, 203, 223, 232,
  240, 254, 261-262, 298,
  304-305, 307, 312, 320,
  338, 355, 360, 362,
  365, 367, 371, 373

metadata: 46, 355-356,
  374, 383-384
metrics: 8, 21, 24, 30,
  32, 43, 50-51, 53, 58,
  61-65, 67, 71-73, 75, 78,
  84-85, 88, 90, 96-97,
  100, 109, 204, 214, 225,
  234-235, 238-239, 253,
  257, 265, 291, 297, 316,
  331, 350, 366, 371-375,
  384, 396, 398, 402-403
modeling: 15, 26, 29, 37,
  109, 145, 186, 203, 208,
  391, 395, 397, 402-403
monitoring: 30, 32, 67, 78,
  350, 366, 371-373, 375,
  384, 395-396, 402, 405
mutable: 382

N

namespace: 223, 225
nested: 126-128,
  138, 215-218, 244,
  248-249, 288
network: 23, 43, 203, 205,
  244, 248-251, 255, 263,
  265-267, 273-274, 282,
  288, 303, 310, 312, 350,
  366, 371-372, 390
neural: 19-20, 23, 26, 43,
  92, 100, 176-177, 203,
  205, 218, 243-244, 246,
  248, 250, 255, 271-274,
  282, 298, 302-303, 338,
  350, 366, 371, 390, 396
neuron: 248-249
normalize: 8, 19, 42, 187,
  190-191, 193, 335

numeric: 7, 17, 23, 86, 132,
  135-137, 139, 176-180,
  182, 185-186, 193, 197,
  200-202, 207-208,
  228, 232, 276, 293, 326,
  329-331, 336, 341
nutshell: 223
nvidia: 262, 361, 373

O

openai: 205, 208
openapi: 360
openmpi: 379
operate: 176, 349-350,
  358, 365, 391
optimizing: 27, 40-41, 201,
  221, 249, 268, 271, 281,
  285, 288-289, 399, 405
orthogonal: 20, 100, 136,
  178, 184-185, 197, 330
outliers: 5, 7-8, 111
override: 357

P

package: 59, 129, 162,
  188, 236, 275, 280, 315,
  338, 351, 356, 358,
  367-369, 373, 385-386
pandas: 6, 56, 94, 112, 115,
  118, 120, 123-124, 126,
  133, 155, 183, 226-227,
  229, 232-233, 295, 360,
  364, 370, 382, 389
parallel: 26, 61, 111, 119,
  140, 144, 147-148,
  161-164, 167, 169,
  173, 229, 248-249,
  260, 263, 274-276,
  279-280, 284, 301-305,
  307, 312, 318, 320

parameter: 24-25, 27-29,
    51, 85, 88, 117, 124, 127,
    139-140, 157, 159-161,
    163, 166, 194, 196,
    201, 217, 224-225,
    228, 234, 263, 271,
    273-289, 297-298,
    301-302, 304-305,
    309-311, 317-319, 361,
    378, 383, 392, 405
parser: 141, 154-155,
    157, 233, 264, 276
payload: 46, 51, 206
perceptron: 191, 246-248
pipeline: 3, 18, 29, 32,
    35-39, 41, 45, 53-56,
    61, 64, 66-67, 74,
    78, 112, 119, 124, 129,
    139-140, 143-173, 176,
    185-189, 193-195, 200,
    203-204, 206, 208,
    217-218, 226, 250, 259,
    272, 288-291, 297-298,
    307, 314, 337, 350-351,
    354, 362-365, 369-370,
    374-375, 377-380,
    382-387, 389-393, 395,
    398-399, 402-403
pixels: 251
postgresql: 112, 126
powershell: 378
predict: 4, 17-18, 25,
    221-222, 226, 235, 252,
    273, 287, 289, 297, 309,
    331-332, 339, 359, 398
premises: 371
publish: 146, 157-158,
    165-166, 364
pycharm: 71
pyplot: 235

pyspark: 44, 66, 115,
    118-120, 123-124,
    307, 318, 337-339,
    353, 360, 382
pytest: 388-389, 391
pytest-cov: 389
python: 23, 40-42, 46, 51,
    53, 55-56, 58, 60-63,
    65-67, 71-73, 75-79,
    85, 89, 92, 94, 96, 112,
    114-115, 119, 122-123,
    125, 139, 147-149, 155,
    159, 162, 165-166, 168,
    171-173, 183, 188-189,
    201, 203, 214, 223,
    229-232, 236, 254-255,
    260, 264, 307, 313,
    317, 324, 338, 341-344,
    352-353, 356-357,
    360, 363, 366-367,
    370, 373-374, 378-379,
    385-388, 391, 401
pytorch: 169, 205, 255,
    264, 302, 310-311,
    313, 315, 317, 321,
    366, 375, 379

Q

quantile: 19, 137, 224-225
queues: 96, 171

R

rastrigin: 286
reactive: 143, 146,
    159-161, 173
real-time: 4, 29, 31, 62,
    170, 237, 345, 350-351,
    353, 355, 357-359, 365,
    369-370, 377, 401

real-world: 20-21, 29, 37,
    100, 104, 177, 197, 200,
    213-214, 216, 302, 320
recurrence: 160
redeploy: 393
redundant: 113, 197
register: 64, 73, 78, 82,
    84-85, 91, 97, 109,
    111-115, 117, 141, 156,
    222, 225-227, 231, 236,
    297, 325, 349, 354-358,
    367-369, 371, 378, 402
regression: 5, 10, 12-14,
    19-20, 23-26, 53-54,
    57, 59, 100, 168-169,
    177, 213-217, 219,
    224-225, 240, 244,
    246, 250-252, 272, 291,
    293, 331-332, 337, 339,
    345, 351, 368-369,
    379, 391, 398-399
reiterate: 253
release: 105, 380,
    384-387, 389, 392
repository: 100, 150,
    326, 338, 368,
    380-381, 387, 392
requests: 30, 46, 51, 159,
    206, 341, 343-344, 351,
    362, 364-365, 380, 404
resnet: 244, 266-267,
    368, 375
response: 30-31, 46,
    52, 159, 207, 341,
    343-344, 351, 364, 373
retrieve: 92, 114, 123-124,
    153-155, 158-159, 172,
    227, 229-230, 253, 297,
    307, 354-357, 362, 367

runtime: 41, 44, 61, 66-67, 107, 139, 271, 279-282, 317, 349-350, 352-353, 356, 366, 368, 370-371, 375, 390

S

sampling: 25, 27, 123-125, 224, 271, 274-281, 284-289, 297-298, 304
scalable: 28, 32, 49, 72, 82, 89, 116, 141, 239, 253, 326, 338, 349, 351, 358-359, 382, 403
scaling: 19, 137, 239, 253, 258, 278, 295, 301-302, 314, 317, 320, 366, 378
scatter: 12, 98, 101, 284, 308
scenario: 97, 225, 263, 310, 371, 403
scheduling: 88-89, 96, 143, 145-146, 156, 159-160, 162, 164, 167, 173, 225, 236, 284
schema: 126, 140, 360-361
seaborn: 94, 97-98, 229
semantic: 20, 22, 173, 175-177, 185, 189, 194, 197, 200-205, 208, 223, 293, 331, 345
sensor: 39
sequences: 204-205
server: 112, 126, 246, 253, 302, 310-311, 317, 373, 381

sklearn: 66, 180-181, 184, 194, 196, 198-199, 225, 232, 235-236, 252, 295, 297, 307, 354-355, 358-360, 366-367
softmax: 43, 204-205, 255-256, 267, 306
spectrum: 266
staging: 65-66, 72, 391, 402
statistics: 8, 119, 202, 258
status: 10, 63, 77, 80, 84, 86, 119, 260
stemming: 22, 176, 188, 190-191, 193-194, 200, 203, 208
streaming: 30, 214, 324-325, 335
subversion: 380
supervised: 18, 23, 28, 72, 97, 103, 109, 193, 214-215, 265, 397
swagger: 360-361
symmetric: 197
systematic: 396, 403

T

tabular: 6, 125, 152, 155, 227
tagging: 67, 147, 191, 194, 214
telemetry: 32, 66-67, 75, 128, 350, 356, 370, 372, 374-375

tensorflow: 42, 52, 129, 149, 162, 169, 205, 252, 255, 257-258, 264, 268, 277, 302, 310-312, 315, 317, 319, 321, 352-353, 355-356, 366-368, 374-375
terraform: 73, 386
terram: 192
threshold: 32, 51, 136, 220, 246, 281
tokenize: 188
transform: 17, 21-22, 32, 58-59, 111, 129, 131, 134, 137, 141, 143, 152, 177, 179-181, 184, 186, 190, 193-194, 196-199, 206, 208, 226, 245, 293, 335, 339
trigger: 32, 41, 49, 66, 143-144, 146-148, 156-161, 168, 170-173, 341, 357, 363, 365, 380, 384
tuning: 4, 24-25, 27-29, 92, 103, 145, 222, 237, 263, 268, 271-275, 279-280, 282, 284-286, 288-290, 297-298, 301, 304, 320, 379-380, 397, 399

U

upsampling: 265

V

validate: 150, 154-155, 253, 274, 295, 337, 360-361, 379
values: 3, 5-9, 11-12, 19-23, 25, 32, 52, 64, 85-87, 91, 97, 111, 123, 125, 128-129, 131-132, 134-136, 138-139, 141, 163, 175-176, 178-180, 182, 184-186, 199-200, 206, 216, 227, 232, 254, 273-274, 279, 281, 287, 291, 297, 331, 336, 366, 372-373, 388-389, 398, 402
variable: 4-5, 7-8, 10, 12-14, 20-21, 24, 57, 113-114, 201, 203, 217, 232, 234, 245, 280, 388
variance: 19, 100-101, 103, 105-106, 109, 197-198, 219
vector: 19-20, 177, 184, 186-187, 193-194, 197, 201-202, 205, 208, 246-247, 250, 252, 272, 293, 326
velocity: 17
veracity: 17
verbose: 64, 84, 257, 265, 316
virtual: 6, 36, 75, 173, 314, 400, 403
vision: 26, 36-37, 39, 44-46, 49-52, 67, 203, 206, 244-245, 250, 253, 258, 266
visualize: 12, 72, 85, 96-98, 101, 105, 109, 248, 373
vowpal: 341

W

wabbit: 341
waveforms: 245
webhook: 147, 156, 158-159
webservice: 359-360, 374, 405
westus: 74, 206
widget: 90, 235, 237
workflow: 6, 42, 63, 73, 116, 121, 144-148, 151, 157, 165, 173, 263, 358, 369, 392
workspace: 36, 40, 54-56, 60-63, 67, 71-79, 81-82, 85-86, 88-96, 99, 109, 112-115, 117, 122, 146-147, 149-152, 156, 158-160, 162, 164, 166-172, 225-230, 232, 234, 238-239, 254, 260, 263-265, 278, 281, 287, 304, 352, 354-357, 361, 363, 367, 370, 372, 384
wrapper: 233, 317, 321, 373

X

xgboost: 213, 222, 240, 289, 306-307

Y

yandex: 217
yields: 84, 222, 246, 259, 283, 285-286, 288, 330

Printed in Poland
by Amazon Fulfillment
Poland Sp. z o.o., Wrocław